A Division of EMC Publishing

A Guide to Web Development Using Adobe® Dreamweaver® CS5

with Fireworks® CS5 and Flash® CS5

Jan Marrelli

The data files used in this text can be downloaded from
www.emcschool.net/DreamweaverCS5 (hardcover)
www.paradigmcollege.net/DreamweaverCS5 (softcover)

Care has been taken to verify the accuracy of information presented in this book. However, the authors, editors, and publisher cannot accept responsibility for Web, e-mail, newsgroup, or chat room subject matter or content, or for consequences from application of the information in this book, and make no warranty, expressed or implied, with respect to its content.

Trademarks: Some of the product names and company names included in this book have been used for identification purposes only and may be trademarks or registered trade names of their respective manufacturers and sellers. The authors, editors, and publisher disclaim any affiliation, association, or connection with, or sponsorship or endorsement by, such owners.

We have made every effort to trace the ownership of all copyrighted material and to secure permission from copyright holders. In the event of any question arising as to the use of any material, we will be pleased to make the necessary corrections in future printings. Thanks are due to the aforementioned authors, publishers, and agents for permission to use the materials indicated.

ISBN 978-0-82196-208-4 (Hardcover)
ISBN 978-0-82196-209-1 (Softcover)

© 2012 by EMC Publishing, LLC
875 Montreal Way
St. Paul, MN 55102
E-mail: educate@emcp.com
Web site: www.emcp.com

All rights reserved. No part of this publication may be adapted, reproduced, stored in a retrieval system, or transmitted in any form or by any means, electronic, mechanical, photocopying, recording, or otherwise, without prior written permission from the publisher.

Printed in the United States of America

20 19 18 17 16 15 14 13 12 11   1 2 3 4 5 6 7 8 9 10

Preface

We believe the best way to introduce students to web development is with a course that meets two primary expectations. First, students need to understand general design concepts and the process of developing a website from sketches to publishing. Second, students need to transfer this knowledge to web development projects, which requires considerable "hands on" computer experience using web development tools such as Adobe Dreamweaver CS5, Fireworks CS5, and Flash CS5. Prior to starting web development, students need a foundation of knowledge that includes an understanding of networks, the Internet and intranets, and copyright issues. A basic understanding of HTML and familiarity with World Wide Web terminology is also required. Students can achieve these expectations with this text. The text is designed to strengthen problem-solving skills, and is written to be used either in a one or two term course.

A Guide to Web Development Using Adobe Dreamweaver CS5 presents material for Dreamweaver CS5, Fireworks CS5, Flash CS5, Internet Explorer, and Notepad. The text is written to be appropriate for students at a variety of levels. Chapters introduce all aspects of website development, including web page layout, typography, color, editing, and graphics. Other chapters introduce the Internet and the World Wide Web, publishing a website, and cascading style sheets.

Design and Features

Hands-on Practices Concepts are presented, discussed, and then followed by a "hands-on" practice that requires the student to test newly learned skills using the computer.

Sidebars and Tips Additional topics and tips that complement the text are in the margin.

Chapter Summaries Concepts covered in the chapter are reviewed.

Vocabulary Sections At the end of each chapter is a list of new terms and definitions and a list of commands and buttons covered in the chapter.

Review Questions Numerous review questions provide immediate reinforcement of new concepts.

Exercises Numerous exercises of varying difficulty are appropriate for students with a wide range of abilities.

Networks and the Internet Before learning to use Dreamweaver, Chapter 1 introduces students to the Internet, networks, and effective search techniques. Also covered is the vocabulary needed to understand concepts presented in later chapters.

HTML and CSS An introduction to HTML is presented before students are introduced to CSS to facilitate understanding.

Copyright Concerns The issues related to copyright, copyright protection, copyright infringement, and the use of copyrighted materials are discussed throughout the text.

Web-Related Careers It is hoped that many students will become interested in IT and web-related careers based upon their experience in this course. Chapter 1 includes information on different careers related to IT and the educational requirements needed to pursue them.

Appendices Appendix A discusses banner ads and ActionScript. Appendix B discusses digital camera files. Appendix C discusses website collaboration using templates. Appendix D lists HTML tags and attributes. Appendix E contains several final projects.

Online Resources Students can download all the files needed to complete the practices and exercises from www.emcschool.net/DreamweaverCS5 (hardcover) and www.paradigmcollege.net/DreamweaverCS5 (softcover).

Software The browser screen captures in this text were taken using Internet Explorer 9 and the Dreamweaver captures were taken using the Designer workspace.

Instructor Resources

Our Instructor Resources correlate directly to the textbook and provide all the additional materials required to offer students an excellent web design course. The Instructor Resources include:

- **Lesson Plans** Lessons in PDF format keyed to the chapters in the text. Each lesson includes assignments, teaching notes, worksheets, and additional topics.
- **Visual Aids** PowerPoint presentations to support each chapter.
- **Vocabulary** Word files of the vocabulary presented in the text.
- **Rubrics** Rubrics keyed to exercises in the text for assessment.
- **Worksheets** Problems that supplement the exercises in the text provide additional reinforcement of concepts.
- **Critical Thinking Worksheets** Thought-provoking written-response questions keyed to concepts practiced in the text.
- **Review Question Answers** Answers to the text review questions that are presented in the text.
- **Data Files** All files that the student needs to complete the practices and exercises in the text, as well as the files needed to complete the worksheets, quizzes, and tests in the resource materials.
- **ExamView® Assessment Suite** Question banks keyed to the text and the popular **ExamView®** software are included to create tests, quizzes, and additional assessment materials.
- **Answer Files** Answers to the practices, exercises, worksheets, and tests.

Using This Text

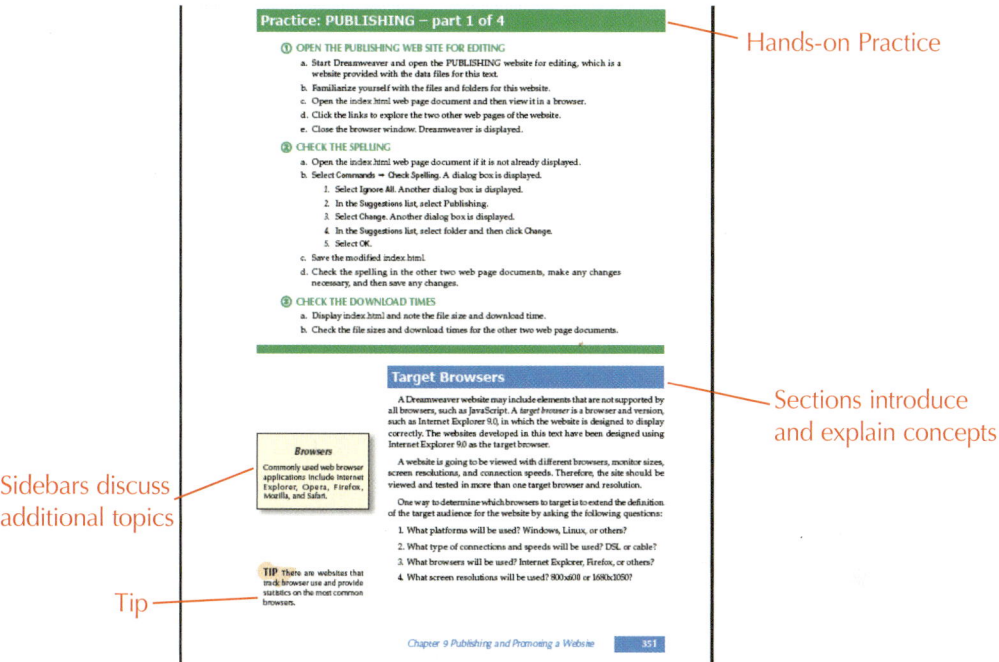

Within each chapter, you will find:

>   **Alternatives** – Other ways to perform actions.
>
>   **TIPs** – Additional information that complements the text.
>
>   **Sidebars** – Additional topics that complement the text.
>
>   **Text in the margin** –Indicates new terminology and subtopics.
>
>   **Practices** – Concepts are presented, discussed, and then followed by a "hands-on" step-by-step practice that allows you to try out newly learned web development and design skills and knowledge. Some practices stand alone, while others build on work completed in previous practices. Therefore, it is recommended that the practices are completed in the order in which they are presented.

The end of each chapter contains:

>   **Chapter Summaries** – Concepts covered in the chapter are reviewed.
>
>   **Review Questions** – Critical thinking questions that will let you review and deepen your understanding of the concepts covered in the chapter.
>
>   **Vocabulary and Dreamweaver/Flash/Fireworks Commands and Button Sections** – A list of new terms and definitions and a list of the application commands and buttons covered in the chapter.
>
>   **Exercises**– A variety of exercises where you can apply your web development and design skills and knowledge.

Chapter Expectations

Chapter 1 – Networks and the Internet

After completing this chapter, students will be able to:

1. Discuss current computing technologies.
2. Explain what a network is and describe the benefits of using a network.
3. Identify the differences in network topologies.
4. Distinguish between different types of transmission media.
5. Understand network protocols.
6. Apply netiquette rules when using a network.
7. Organize files and folders.
8. Distinguish between an intranet and extranet.
9. Summarize how the Internet works and explain different ways to access the Internet.
10. Identify various Internet services.
11. Describe several categories of websites and the purpose of each.
12. Demonstrate the basic features and functions of Internet Explorer.
13. Use the History list and Favorites list in Internet Explorer.
14. Locate information using search engines and subject trees.
15. Evaluate and cite web pages.
16. Analyze Internet privacy issues.
17. Understand the need for an Internet Use Agreement.
18. Discuss social and ethical implications associated with computer use.
19. Describe how copyright applies to material on the Internet.
20. Discuss ethical responsibilities of the web developer.
21. Describe IT careers.

Chapter 2 – HTML

After completing this chapter, students will be able to:

1. Define terminology associated with the World Wide Web.
2. Describe the structure of an HTML document.
3. Create an HTML document using Notepad.
4. View HTML documents in a web browser.
5. Distinguish between the break tag and the paragraph tag.
6. Create headings and horizontal rules.
7. Use attributes to modify HTML elements.
8. Create lists and tables.
9. Create hyperlinks to different HTML documents.
10. Add images to HTML documents.
11. Use comments to clarify HTML for a reader.
12. Apply embedded and linked style sheets to an HTML document.
13. Change the background and text color of an HTML document.
14. Embed scripts and applets in an HTML document.

Chapter 3 – Introducing Dreamweaver

After completing this chapter, students will be able to:

1. Define a website.
2. Create a home page and change the page title.
3. Display a web page in different document views.
4. Change headings and insert text.
5. Insert an image on a web page.
6. Edit the content of web page documents and check spelling.
7. Print and close a web page document.
8. Quit Dreamweaver.
9. Edit a website.
10. Create and open web page documents.
11. Create text and external hyperlinks.
12. Display a linked web page in a new window.
13. Display the Dreamweaver site map.
14. Use Dreamweaver help.

Chapter 4 – Website Development

After completing this chapter, students will be able to:

1. Outline the steps involved in developing a website.
2. Define the purpose and target audience of a website.
3. Determine the web pages and navigation structure of a website.
4. Determine the content of a website.
5. Distinguish between different types of navigation bars.
6. Implement usability standards for web page layout.
7. Apply design concepts to a web page.
8. Organize website files and folders.
9. Use the Assets panel.
10. Create and edit library items.
11. Insert a time stamp.
12. Create e-mail hyperlinks.
13. Describe how copyright applies to websites.
14. Edit HTML in Dreamweaver.

Chapter 5 – Images in Dreamweaver and Fireworks

After completing this chapter, students will be able to:

1. Differentiate between GIF, JPG, and PNG file formats.
2. Explain why alternative text should be added to an image.
3. Create a graphic hyperlink.
4. Create an image map.
5. Align, resize, and resample images.
6. Demonstrate the basic features and functions of Fireworks.
7. Draw objects and add text in Fireworks.
8. Optimize and export a Fireworks document.
9. Create and modify a button symbol in Fireworks.
10. Distinguish between the four states of a button symbol and change the behavior of a state.
11. Export HTML and images from Fireworks.
12. Use an exported HTML document in Dreamweaver.
13. Crop images in Fireworks and in Dreamweaver.
14. Swap images and edit an image in Fireworks from Dreamweaver.
15. Create a Web photo album.

Chapter 6 – Typography, Style Sheets, and Color

After completing this chapter, students will be able to:

1. Define typography and explain how it affects the navigation and usability of a website.
2. Explain what a style sheet is using appropriate terminology.
3. Link and create a CSS style sheet document.
4. Create and apply a rule, class, and selector styles.
5. Check the existing HTML tags of a web page document for inconsistencies.
6. Edit, duplicate, delete, and remove styles.
7. Tag indented text and redefine the blockquote tag.
8. Create and format numbered and bulleted lists.
9. Determine appropriate colors for a web page document.
10. Change the background and text color of web page document with a style sheet.
11. Create a hyperlink to a named anchor.
12. Create selector styles to change link colors.
13. Use content from external sources in a website.
14. Control images with CSS.
15. Use CSS to create a page layout.
16. Modify CSS starter layouts.

Chapter 7 – Introducing Flash

After completing this chapter, students will be able to:

1. Understand the potential of Flash.
2. Use the Assets panel to access Flash movie files.
3. Explain animation.
4. Demonstrate the basic features and functions of Flash.
5. Outline the process of creating a Flash movie.
6. Create a frame-by-frame animation.
7. Export Flash documents.
8. Organize and use Flash movie files in Dreamweaver.
9. Create an animation using shape tweening.
10. Optimize a Flash movie by creating symbols.
11. Create an animation using motion tweening.
12. Use layers in a Flash document.
13. Animate text.
14. Import and export sound files and video.

Chapter 8 – Website Content, Forms and Dynamic Web Pages

After completing this chapter, students will be able to:

1. Discuss advantages of an electronic portfolio over a traditional portfolio.
2. Design an electronic portfolio.
3. Explain the purpose and content of an informational website.
4. Explain the purpose and content of a commercial website.
5. Distinguish between a corporate presence website and an e-commerce website.
6. Create a FAQ page.
7. Import tabular data.
8. Create a site map web page.
9. Create a jump menu.
10. Include a form on a web page.
11. Validate the contents of a form field.
12. Understand how a form allows a user to interacts with a web server.
13. Distinguish between static and dynamic web pages.
14. Add Spry Widgets to a web page.

Chapter 9 – Publishing and Promoting a Website

After completing this chapter, students will be able to:

1. Outline the process of publishing a website.
2. Check the spelling and grammar on each web page of a website.
3. Assess the download time of a web page document.
4. Define target browser and determine which target browser should be used to test a site.
5. Use Adobe BrowserLab and Device Central to view preview a website in a variety of target browser.
6. Test the HTML associated with a web page for target browser compatibility.
7. Test a website for broken and missing links.
8. Check a website for HTML problems.
9. Explain what a web host is and distinguish between virtual and non-virtual hosting.
10. Publish a website to a web server and to a local/network server.
11. Update a published site.
12. Use collaboration features in Dreamweaver.
13. Promote a published website.
14. Add meta tags.
15. Describe ways to measure the success of a website.
16. Discuss issues associated with website security.

Table of Contents

Chapter 1 – Networks and the Internet

Desktop and Mobile Computing 1
Computer Hardware 2
Operating Systems and Environment 3
Networks 4
Files and Folders 7
Storage Devices 8
Intranets, Extranets, and the Internet 9
Telecommunications 9
Internet Services 10
Using Internet Explorer 12
   Practice: Using Internet Explorer 13
Searching the Web 17
   Practice: Searching the Web 18
Evaluating and Citing Web Pages 19
   Practice: Citing a Website 19
E-mail Etiquette 20
Internet Privacy Issues 20
Internet Acceptable Use Policy 21
The Social and Ethical Implications of
Computer Use 22
Protecting Computer Software and Data 23
The Ethical Responsibilities of the
Web Developer 24
Careers 24
IT Departments and Companies 25
Pursuing an IT Career 26
   Chapter Summary 26
   Vocabulary 28
   Internet Explorer 9 Commands and Buttons .. 31
   Review Questions 32
   Exercises 34

Chapter 2 – HTML

The World Wide Web 39
HTML 40
Using Notepad 42
Creating an HTML Document 43
Viewing HTML Documents in a Web
Browser 44
   Practice: first_document.html 44
Creating Paragraphs and Line Breaks 46
Headings 46
Adding Horizontal Rules 47
   Practice: Computer Viruses – part 1 47
Creating Lists 49
   Practice: Computer Viruses – part 2 49
Tables 51
Hyperlinks 51
   Practice: Computer Viruses – part 3 52
Adding Images 54
Using Comments 54
Style Sheets 55
Adding Color 55
Changing Alignment 56
   Practice: Computer Viruses – part 4 56
JavaScript 58
   Practice: Computer Viruses – part 5 58
Java Applets 59
   Practice: Java Applet 60
   Chapter Summary 62
   Vocabulary 63
   Notepad Commands 64
   Internet Explorer Commands and Buttons 64
   HTML Tags 64
   Review Questions 65
   Exercises 66

Chapter 3 – Introducing Dreamweaver

Dreamweaver 71
Defining a Website in Dreamweaver 72
    Practice: Computer Ergonomics – part 1 72
The Welcome Screen 74
Creating a Web Page Document 75
Saving a Web Page 76
The Page Title 76
Viewing a Web Page Document 77
    Practice: Computer Ergonomics – part 2 77
Changing Headings and Inserting Text 79
Checking Spelling 80
    Practice: Computer Ergonomics – part 3 81
Inserting Images 82
    Practice: Computer Ergonomics – part 4 84
Printing a Web Page Document 84
Closing a Web Page Document and
Quitting Dreamweaver 84
Opening a Website for Editing 85
    Practice: Computer Ergonomics – part 5 85
Opening and Displaying Web Page
Documents 86
    Practice: Computer Ergonomics – part 6 87
Creating Internal Hyperlinks 88
External Hyperlinks 90
Displaying a Linked Web Page
in a New Window 90
    Practice: Computer Ergonomics – part 7 91
Using Help 92
    Practice: Computer Ergonomics – part 8 92
Reflection 94
    Chapter Summary 95
    Vocabulary 96
    Dreamweaver Commands and Buttons 97
    Review Questions 98
    Exercises 99

Chapter 4 – Website Development

Website Development 109
Defining the Purpose and Target
Audience 110
    Practice: Pasta Restaurant – part 1 111
Determining the Web Pages
and Navigation Structure 111
Determining the Content 112
    Practice: Pasta Restaurant – part 2 112
Defining Navigation Bars 113
The Web Page Layout 114
    Practice: Pasta Restaurant – part 3 115
Concepts of Design 116
Design Concepts: Appropriateness 116
Design Concepts: Placement 117
Design Concepts: Consistency 118
Design Concepts: Usability 118
    Practice: Pasta Restaurant – part 4 119
Organizing Files and Folders 120
    Practice: Pasta Restaurant – part 5 121
Maintaining Consistency in a Website 122
    Practice: Pasta Restaurant – part 6 123
Creating and Editing Library Items 124
Inserting a Date 126
E-mail Hyperlinks 126
Copyright Information 127
    Practice: Pasta Restaurant – part 7 127
Modifying HTML in Dreamweaver 129
    Practice: Computer Ergonomics 130
    Chapter Summary 131
    Vocabulary 132
    Dreamweaver Commands and Buttons 133
    Review Questions 134
    Exercises 136

Chapter 5 – Images in Dreamweaver and Fireworks

Graphic File Formats for Web Pages 147
Alternative Text 149
Graphic Hyperlinks 149
    Practice: SCUBA – part 1 149
Creating an Image Map 151
    Practice: SCUBA – part 2 152
Aligning an Image 155
Resizing and Resampling an Image 155
    Practice: SCUBA – part 3 155
Introducing Fireworks 156
Drawing Objects in Fireworks 158
Adding Text in Fireworks 159
Aligning Objects in Fireworks 160
Modifying the Canvas 161
Optimizing and Exporting a Fireworks
Document 161
    Practice: SCUBA – part 4 164
Creating a Button Symbol in Fireworks 167
Button Symbol Rollover Behavior 168
    Practice: SCUBA – part 5 169
Exporting HTML and Images from
Fireworks 173
Using an Exported HTML Document
in Dreamweaver 174
Changing Behaviors in Dreamweaver 175
    Practice: SCUBA – part 6 176

Cropping an Image in Fireworks and
in Dreamweaver 177
Editing an Image in Fireworks
from Dreamweaver 178
Swap Images 179
    Practice: SCUBA – part 7 180
Creating a Web Photo Album 182
    Practice: Web Photo Album 183
    Chapter Summary 185
    Vocabulary 187
    Dreamweaver Commands and Buttons 188
    Fireworks Commands and Buttons 188
    Review Questions 189
    Exercises 191

Chapter 6 – Typography, Style Sheets, and Color

Typography 199
Design Considerations: Choosing Font 199
Design Considerations: Font Size 200
Design Considerations: Line Height 201
Design Considerations: Type Styles 201
Design Considerations: Alignment 202
Style Sheets 202
Creating and Applying a CSS Rule 204
Creating and Applying a CSS Class 205
Editing HTML Code 206
    Practice: COFFEE – part 1 207
Working with CSS Styles 210
Formatting Headings 211
    Practice: COFFEE – part 2 212
Indenting with Blockquotes 214
Lists 214
    Practice: COFFEE – part 3 215
Using Color in a Website 217
Changing Background and Text Color 219
    Practice: COFFEE – part 4 220
Hyperlinks to Named Anchors 221
    Practice: COFFEE – part 5 222
Changing Hyperlink Colors 223
Using Content from Other Sources 224
    Practice: COFFEE – part 6 224
Controlling Images with CSS 227
CSS Layouts 228
    Practice: Time Management 229
Editing CSS Starter Layouts 232
    Practice: Etiquette/Layout 232
    Chapter Summary 238
    Vocabulary 240
    Dreamweaver Commands and Buttons 241
    Exercises 243

Chapter 7 – Introducing Flash

Flash 245
What is Animation? 246
Introducing Flash 246
The Flash Tools Panel 247
Creating a Flash Movie 248
Frame-by-Frame Animation 250
Editing Techniques 251
    Practice: SAMPLER – part 1 252
Exporting a Flash Document 254
Flash Movie Files 254
Organizing and Using Flash Movie Files
in Dreamweaver 255
    Practice: SAMPLER – part 2 256
Shape Tweening 257
    Practice: SAMPLER – part 3 257
Creating Symbols to Optimize a
Flash Movie 259
Motion Tweening 260
    Practice: SAMPLER – part 4 261
Using Layers 264
Animating Text 265
    Practice: SAMPLER – part 5 267
Importing Sound Files 268
    Practice: SAMPLER – part 6 269
Importing Video 270
    Practice: SAMPLER – part 7 272
    Chapter Summary 273
    Vocabulary 274
    Dreamweaver Commands and Buttons 274
    Flash Commands and Buttons 275
    Review Questions 276
    Exercises 277

Chapter 8 – Website Content, Forms, and Dynamic Web Pages

Electronic Portfolios 281
Website Categories 282
Creating a FAQ Page 284
    Practice: BELLUR – part 1 285
Importing Tabular Data 285
    Practice: BELLUR – part 2 288
Creating a Site Map 288
    Practice: BELLUR – part 3 289
Adding Jump Menus 290
    Practice: BELLUR – part 4 291
Creating a Form 292
Check Boxes and Radio Buttons 295
Scrolling Lists and Drop-Down Menus 296
The Validate Form Action 298

Pop-up Messages 299
    Practice: BELLUR – part 5.............................. 299
Interactive Forms 304
Dynamic Web Pages 305
Adding Spry Widgets 306
    Practice: BELLUR – part 6 308
    Dreamweaver Commands and Buttons 310
    Vocabulary 311
    Review Questions 312
    Exercises.. 313

Chapter 9 – Publishing and Promoting a Website

Publishing a Website 317
Checking Spelling and Grammar....................... 318
Checking the Download Time 318
    Practice: PUBLISHING – part 1 319
Target Browsers 319
Previewing in a Target Browser......................... 320
    Practice: PUBLISHING – part 2 321
Testing the HTML for Target Browser
Compatibility... 322
Testing for Broken Links and Missing Links.... 323
Checking for HTML Problems........................... 324
    Practice: PUBLISHING – part 3 324
What is a Web Host?... 326
Publishing to a Web Server 326
Publishing to a Local/Network Server.............. 328
Maintaining a Website 329
Collaboration 330
Promoting a Website... 332
    Practice: PUBLISHING – part 4 333
Measuring Success 335
Website Security Issues 335
    Chapter Summary 336
    Vocabulary 337
    Dreamweaver Commands and Buttons 338
    Review Questions 339
    Exercises.. 340

Appendix A – Banner Ads and ActionScript

Banner Ads... 343
Creating a Banner Ad Using an Ad Template
in Flash 343
Adding Banner Ad Content............................... 344
Adding ActionScript 346
Completing and Testing the Banner Ad 346
Other Types of Web Ads 346
More on ActionScript 348

Appendix B – Digital Camera Files

Digital Camera File Formats.............................. 349
Maintaining Image Quality in JPG Files 349
Digital Camera Image Resolution..................... 350
Changing Image Size and Resolution
in Fireworks 350

Appendix C – Templates

Templates... 353
Creating a Child Page... 355

Appendix D – HTML Tags and Attributes

HTML Tags and Attributes 357

Appendix E – Final Projects

Final Projects... 359

Index

Index 363

Chapter 1
Networks and the Internet

This chapter discusses current computing technologies, networks, the Internet, and the World Wide Web. Issues related to computers, including privacy, viruses, and copyright are also discussed.

Desktop and Mobile Computing

Computers come in many shapes, sizes, and with a variety of features. A *desktop computer* and its components are designed to fit on or under a desk:

TIP PC (personal computer) is often used to refer to a desktop computer that is Windows-compatible and to differentiate from Mac (Apple) computers.

Desktop computers are single-user systems designed with microprocessor technology where an entire CPU (Central Processing Unit) is contained on a single computer chip.

Mobile computing devices, such as laptops, netbooks, tablet PCs, and smartphones contain long-lasting batteries and wireless technology that allow them to be portable:

Wearable computers are designed to be worn. Wearable computers are used in many occupations. For example, auto mechanics can examine a car while wearing a head-mounted wearable computer which displays computer drawings of the car for comparison purposes. They are also used to monitor health problems, such as heart rate and respiration flow.

Computer Hardware

The physical components of the computer, such as the monitor and *base unit*, are referred to as *hardware*:

Software

Windows, Linux, Unix, and Mac OS X are examples of operating system software. Dreamweaver, Fireworks, Flash, and Microsoft Word are examples of applications software. Applications software is sometimes bundled together in a suite, such as Adobe Creative Suite 5.

- *Input devices*, such as a keyboard, mouse, scanner, microphone, digital camera, and DVD drive are used to enter data and instructions into the computer.

- *Peripheral devices*, such as printers, webcams, and microphones, are added to make a computer more versatile. A peripheral device either has a wireless connection or is attached to a *port* on the computer. There are different types of ports, such as serial, parallel, FireWire, USB, and Bluetooth ports.

- Computers process data into meaningful, useful information. Processed data is conveyed using *output devices*. Monitors and printers display data, DVD+RWs, disk drives, and memory keys store data, and speakers communicate audio output.

Printers

A laser printer uses a laser and toner to generate characters and graphics on paper. An ink-jet printer uses an ink cartridge to place very small dots of ink onto paper to create characters and graphics.

The base unit also contains the *motherboard*, which is the main circuit board. The motherboard contains several components:

- *Expansion boards* are circuit boards that connect to the motherboard to add functionality to the computer. Examples include sound cards and video adapters.

- The *CPU (Central Processing Unit)* processes data and controls the flow of data between the computer's other units. Within the CPU is the *ALU (Arithmetic Logic Unit)*, which can perform arithmetic and logic operations. It can also make comparisons, which is the basis of the computer's decision-making power. The ALU is so fast that the time needed to carry out a single addition is measured in nanoseconds (billionths of a second). The speed at which a CPU can execute instructions is determined by the computer's *clock rate*. The clock rate is measured in *megahertz* (*MHz*, million of cycles per second) or *gigahertz* (*GHz*, billion of cycles per second).

TIP Intel and AMD are two processor manufacturers.

- A *bus* is a set of circuits that connect the CPU to other components. The data bus transfers data between the CPU, memory, and other hardware devices on the motherboard. The *address bus* carries memory addresses that indicate where the data is located and where the data should go. A *control bus* carries control signals. All data flows through the CPU:

Real-time Clock

A battery chip called a real-time clock keeps track of the date and time in a computer even when the computer is off.

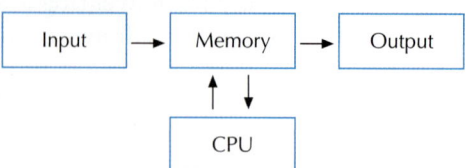

Chapter 1 Networks and the Internet

> **Integrated Circuits**
>
> Integrated circuits, also called chips, are created from silicon wafers which are etched with intricate circuits and coated with a metallic oxide that allows the circuits to conduct electricity. The silicon wafers are housed in special plastic cases that have metal pins. The pins allow the integrated circuits to be plugged into circuit boards.

- Memory in the form of *integrated circuits (ICs)* stores data electronically. *ROM (Read Only Memory)* contains the most basic operating instructions for the computer. The data in ROM is a permanent part of the computer and cannot be changed. *RAM (Random Access Memory)*, also called *primary* or *main memory*, is memory where data and instructions are stored temporarily. Data stored in RAM can be written to *secondary memory*, which includes any type of storage media, such as a hard disk, memory key, or DVD+RW. Secondary memory must be copied into primary memory before it is processed by the CPU. SRAM (Static Random Access Memory) is high-speed memory referred to as *cache* (pronounced "cash"). This memory is used to store frequently used data so that it can be quickly retrieved by an application.

Operating Systems and Environment

Computers also contain programs, or software. *Operating system* (OS) software is run automatically when the computer is turned on and is used to control processing and peripherals, run application software, and control input and output, among other tasks. Desktop operating system software includes Windows, Mac OS X, Unix, and Linux. Each of these operating systems have different features and functions. *Applications software* is written by programmers to perform a specific task, such as a word processor.

> **TIP** *Cloud computing* refers to accessing software from an online provider's website as opposed to having it installed on the local computer.

Environment refers to a computer's hardware and software configuration. For example, a Windows 7 environment means that the computer is running a version of the Windows 7 OS software and hardware includes a 1GHz processor or better, 1GB of RAM or more, and at least 16 GB of hard disk space available. The hardware requirements are based on what will be needed to allow the OS software to properly manage the computer's tasks. The term platform is sometimes synonymous with environment. Most environments run an OS with a graphical user interface (GUI). For example:

Windows 7 operating system

Chapter 1 Networks and the Internet

utility program

device driver

memory-resident

OS functions are implemented through *utility programs* which have one clearly defined task. Utility programs manage input and output, read and write to memory, manage the processor, maintain system security, and manage files and disks. A *device driver* is one type of utility program. Device drivers are needed for printing, viewing graphics, using a CD/DVD drive, and using peripherals in general. Some utility programs load when the computer starts and are called *memory-resident* because they are always in memory. Features are added to an OS by incorporating utility programs to perform tasks that are in addition to the tasks required to run the computer. For example, an OS intended for a desktop or notebook environment will often include utilities for backing up the computer, restoring files, and other tools for improving performance:

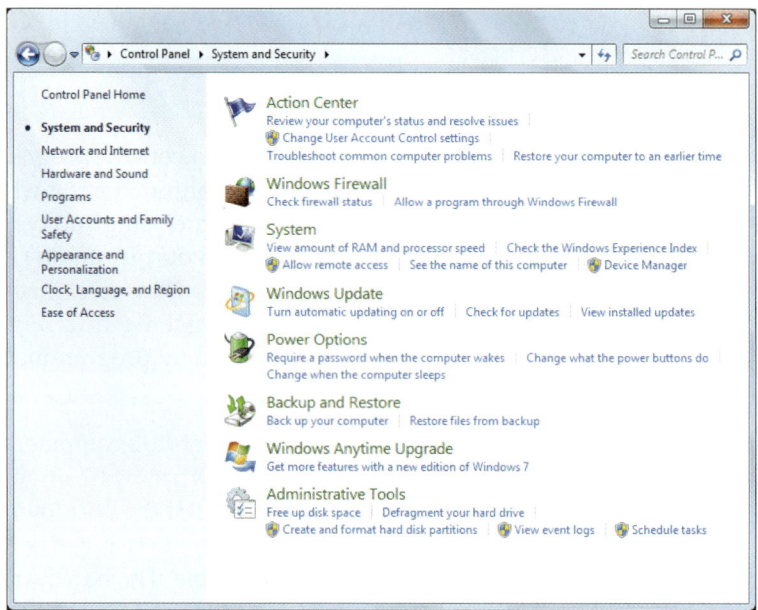

Windows 7 utilities

cross-platform connectivity

Cr*oss-platform connectivity* is the ability of one type of computer to link to and share data with a different type of computer. A conversion program may be required if the computers use a different OS and/or generate different file formats.

> **Sync**
> Software utilities are available that allow for the transfer of data from to a computer to a mobile device, such as a smartphone.

Networks

A *network* is a combination of hardware and software that allows computers to exchange data and share software and devices, such as printers. Networks are widely used by businesses, universities, and other organizations because a network:

- allows users to reliably share and exchange data.
- can reduce costs by sharing devices such as printers.
- offers security options including password protection to restrict access to certain files.
- simplifies file management through centralized software updates and file backups.

Chapter 1 Networks and the Internet

Networks are classified by their size, architecture, and topology. A common size classifications is *LAN (Local-Area Network)*, which is a network used to connect devices within a small area such as a building or a campus. A *WAN (Wide-Area Network)* is used to connect devices over large geographical distances. A WAN can be one widespread network or it can be a number of LANs linked together.

The computers and other devices in a LAN each contain an expansion card called a *network interface card*:

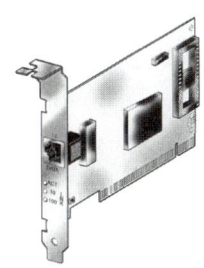

Network interface card

A cable plugs into the adapter card to connect one device to another to form a LAN. Cables are not required for network cards that have wireless capabilities. Network interface cards are available for desktop and mobile computers and take various other forms including an adapter card, a PC card, or a Flash memory card.

Along with the physical, or hardware, aspects of setting up a network, there is also the software aspect. A *network operating system* is software that allow users and devices to communicate over the network. The operating system installed must be capable of supporting networking functions, such as security access features and support for multiple users. Operating systems capable of network functions are available for Linux, Windows, Unix, and Mac. The network architecture, discussed next, must also be considered when choosing a network OS.

Network architecture includes the type of computers on the network and determines how network resources are handled. Two common models are peer-to-peer and client/server. In a *peer-to-peer network*, each computer on the network is considered equal in terms of responsibilities and resource sharing. A *client/server network* consists of a group of computers, called *clients*, connected to a server. A *server* is a computer with more RAM, a larger hard disk, and sometimes multiple CPUs that is used to manage network functions.

Physical *topology* refers to the arrangement of the nodes on a network. A *node* is a location on the network with a device capable of processing information, such as a computer or a printer. There are three common physical topologies:

- The *bus topology* is a physical LAN topology that uses a single central cable, called the bus or backbone to attach each node directly:

Transmission Media

Computers must be connected in order to transmit data between the nodes. Cable transmission media includes twisted-pair wiring, coaxial cable, and fiber optic cable.

Wireless transmission media includes infrared signals, broadcast radio, cellular radio, microwaves, and communications satellites.

The amount of data and the speed at which data can travel over a media is called bandwidth, which is measured in bits per second (bps). Each transmission medium has a specific length or range restriction, data transmission rate, and cost.

---

peer-to-peer network

client/server network

Chapter 1 Networks and the Internet

Ethernet

The Ethernet LAN protocol was developed by Bob Metcalfe in 1976. Ethernet uses a bus or star topology with twisted-pair wiring, coaxial cable, or fiber optic cable transmission media. Newer protocols include 40 Gigabit Ethernet and 100 Gigabit Ethernet.

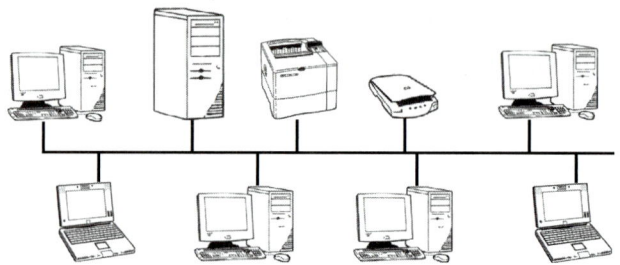

LAN using a bus topology

- In a *star topology*, each node is attached to a *hub*, which is a device that joins communication lines at a central location on the network:

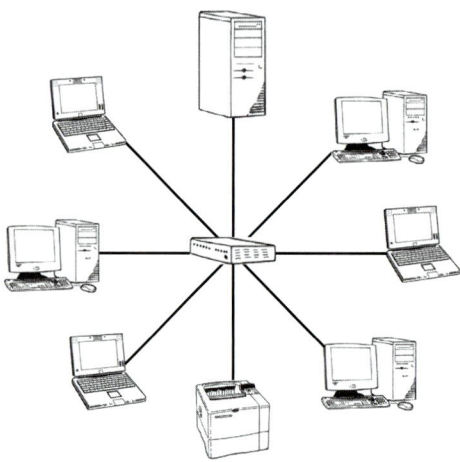

LAN using a star topology

Baseband and Broadband Technology

Most LANs use baseband technology which means the transmission media carries one signal at a time. Broadband technology allows for data transmission of more than one signal at a time and is found in cable television transmission.

- In a *ring topology*, each node is connected to form a closed loop. A LAN with a ring topology can usually cover a greater distance than a bus or star topology:

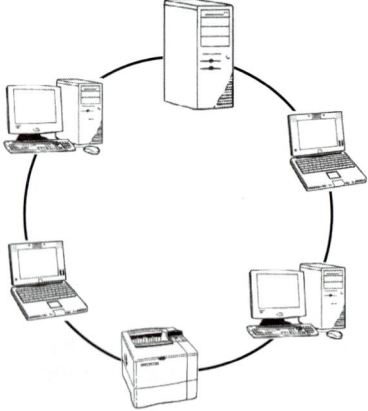

LAN using a ring topology

Bluetooth

Bluetooth is a wireless technology used to link phones, computers, and headsets.

- *Wireless networks* use high frequency radio waves or infrared signals instead of cables to transmit data. A router/wireless access point device is used to allow nodes to transfer data wirelessly.

logical topology

Another type of topology is *logical topology*, which refers to the way data is passed between the nodes on a network. A LAN's logical topology is not always the same as its physical topology.

Network users are given a user name and password to log on to a network through a computer connected to the network. Users are also assigned a level of access to maintain security. Network users should follow a certain etiquette referred to as *netiquette*:

netiquette

- Do not attempt to access the account of another user without authorization.
- Do not share your password, and change it periodically.
- Use appropriate subject matter and language, and be considerate of other people's beliefs and opinions.

Files and Folders

A collection of related data stored on a lasting medium, such as a hard disk, is called a *file*. A file can be an application (program) or the product of an application. For example, a word processor application is used to create document files. As another example, a digital camera is used to create image files. A file is stored on a persistent media so that it is retained even after the computer or computerized device is turned off.

Each file is identified by a unique *file name*. When a new document is created, a temporary generic file name, such as Untitled-1 is assigned to the file until it is saved. Applications automatically add an extension to the file name when saved. An extension indicates the file type. For example, Dreamweaver automatically adds the .html extension to basic HTML documents and .css to cascading style sheets. Extensions are also an indicator of what application the file was created in. For example, Microsoft Word files have a .docx extension.

TIP The original form the file is saved in is referred to as the native format.

Folders are used to organize commonly related files. Like files, folders are also identified by a unique name. Folders are an organizational tool and a folder can contain other folders. For example, the Cats folder shown below is used to store all the folders and files associated with a website about cats:

File Size Limitations

File size can be decreased or compressed using a compression program. This technique is often used to accommodate storage device and e-mail account limitations.

Chapter 1 Networks and the Internet

Storage Devices

Storage devices use a persistent media to maintain files. These devices, which are also referred to as drives, mass storage, and auxiliary storage, can be categorized in three ways:

- internal, such as a hard disk, or external, such as a memory key
- removable or permanent media
- magnetic, optical, or solid state technology

Storage device technologies determine the media, size, and portability of a device. Magnetic technology uses a mechanical drive with tiny electromagnetic heads for reading and writing data to media. The media required with magnetic technology is a disk, usually made of aluminum or Mylar®, coated with iron oxide. The disk is either encased in hard plastic or several disks, called platters, are sealed in a case (hard disk). A data signal sent through the heads in the drive magnetize a bit of the media in one direction to store a 1 and in the other direction to store a 0.

Optical technology uses a drive with a laser and an optoelectronic sensor. The media required with optical technology is a compact or DVD disc made of polycarbonate plastic.

Solid state technology allows for the smallest, most portable storage devices because the technology requires no moving parts. The media is Flash memory, which consists of a grid with two tiny transistors at each cell. Each cell corresponds to a bit. Applying a charge to a cell stores a 0, while applying a stronger charge stores a 1. The grid of transistors is encased in hard plastic and is very small. Some devices can store 2MB or more within a package thinner and smaller than a quarter. Slightly larger media can store gigabytes of data. Encased media is often directly attached to a USB plug for use with a computer, or simply has conductive material imprinted so the media can slide into a digital camera slot.

Magnetic technology allows for storage devices that range in capacity up to many gigabytes (hard disk drives with many platters). Optical technology includes DVDs that can store at least 4GB of data. Solid-state devices store from 64KB of data to many gigabytes.

On a Windows computer, storage media is accessed using a drive letter, such as *C* or *E*. On a Macintosh computer, storage media is accessed through a drive name, such as *Macintosh HD*. On a home computer, files are typically saved to the hard disk which is an internal storage device. It is always a good idea to back-up any files saved to the hard drive. Storage media can be very sensitive. Care should be taken to avoid damaging files:

- Keep magnetic media away from magnets.
- Handle CD/DVDs by the center hole or by the edges.
- Store CD/DVDs in a jewel case or sleeve to prevent scratches.
- Keep media away from moisture and extreme temperatures.

Storage Media

The capacity of storage media varies. For example, a CD has a storage capacity of 650 MB, and a DVD has a storage capacity of over 4GB.

Tera, Peta, Exa

As more and more data is stored electronically, file sizes become very large and require storage devices with very large capacities. A terabtye (TB) is 2^{40} bytes or 1 trillion bytes, petabyte (PB) is 2^{50} bytes or 1,024 terabytes, and EB (exabyte) is 2^{60} bytes or 1,024 petabytes. Devices with TB storage capacities are gradually coming into use, especially for database files.

Blu-ray Disc

Blu-ray Disc is an optical disc storage media format that has the same dimensions as a CD or DVD. A dual layer Blu-ray Disc can store 50GB.

Intranets, Extranets, and the Internet

An *intranet* is a network that is used by a single organization, such as a corporation or school, and is only accessible by authorized users. The purpose of an intranet is to share information. However, a firewall is also used to lock out unauthorized users. A *firewall* is a network security system that prevents unauthorized network access.

firewall

An *extranet* extends an intranet by providing various levels of accessibility to authorized members of the public. For example, a corporation may extend their intranet to provide access to specific information, such as their ordering system, to registered customers.

The largest and most widely accessed network is the *Internet*, a worldwide network of computers that is not controlled by any one organization. The Internet has had an undeniable impact on modern society because it allows users worldwide to communicate in a matter of seconds.

> **History of the Internet**
>
> The Internet evolved from ARPANET, a network created in the late 1960s by the Department of Defense's Advanced Research Projects Agency (ARPA), and the theory of open architecture networking.

The Internet is actually numerous networks all linked together through routers. A *router* is a device that can connect different network technologies together. Networks connected to routers use *TCP/IP (Transmission Control Protocol/Internet Protocol)* software to communicate.

Computers on the Internet are either servers or clients. The client is sent information from a server. The client/server structure of the Internet is called *interactive* because the information accessed is a result of selections made by the user. For example, a computer with just minimal software for accessing the Internet is a client. The client user selecting options from the Internet is receiving the information from a server, a computer with additional software and files that is also connected to the Internet. A server that has web server software installed is called a *web server* and is designed to deliver web pages to the client.

Telecommunications

Telecommunications is the transmitting and receiving of data. Data can be in various forms including voice and video. Telecommunications requires a modem or adapter and a line or cable. The speed of data transmission (sending) and receipt (receiving) is measured in *Kbps* (thousands of bits per second) or *Mbps* (millions of bits per second). Numerous telecommunications options are available, which vary in speed and cost:

> **PLC**
>
> Power line communications (PLC) uses existing power grid networks to send broadband data communications. Internet connections are established by plugging a computer device into a power outlet.

- A **conventional modem** uses standard telephone lines to convert analog signals to digital data. A conventional modem is a 56 Kbps modem, which transmits data at 28.8 Kbps and 36.6 Kbps, and receives data at 56 Kbps. Today, most home and business users select options other than conventional modems if they are available in their area, due to the slow access time associated with conventional modems.

- A **DSL (Digital Subscriber Line) modem** uses standard telephone lines with data transmission up to 640 Kbps. Data receipt is from 1.5 Mbps to 9 Mbps. A DSL (Asymmetric DSL) is the most common form used.

Chapter 1 Networks and the Internet

- A **cable modem** transmits data through a coaxial cable television network. Data transmission is from 2 Mbps to 10 Mbps and data receipt is from 10 Mbps to 36 Mbps.
- **Leased/Dedicated lines** are used by many businesses and schools for Internet access. They allow for a permanent connection to the Internet that is always active. The cost of a leased line is usually a fixed monthly fee. A T-1 carrier is a type of leased line that transmits data at 1.544 Mbps.
- **ISDN (Integrated Services Digital Network)** is a digital telephone network provided by a local phone company. ISDN is capable of transmitting and receiving data at up to 64 Kbps. ISDN requires the use of an ISDN terminal adapter instead of a modem.

Internet Services

Internet services include the World Wide Web, e-mail, instant messaging, and mailing lists. The *World Wide Web* (WWW), also called the *Web* is the most widely used Internet service. The Web can be used to search and access information available on the Internet. A *web browser* application, such as Microsoft Internet Explorer, provides a graphical interface to present information in the form of a *website*:

Blog

Blog is short for weblog and is a type of website where users can post entries in a journal format.

Feeds

Feeds, also known as RSS feeds, XML feeds, syndicated content, or web feeds, contain frequently updated content published by a website. They are typically used for news and blog websites. Feeds can also be used to deliver audio content, typically in MP3 format. This is referred to as podcasting.

A web page that is part of the EMC Publishing website

The Web offers access to a multitude of information, and most websites are considered to be in one of the following categories: social media, commercial, informational, media, and portal:

- **Social media websites,** such as Facebook, Twitter, and YouTube allow for the creation and exchange of user-generated content. They are used for social interaction and interactive dialogue.
- **Commercial websites** include *corporate presence websites*, which are created by companies and organizations for the purpose of displaying information about their products or services. It also

includes *e-commerce websites*, which are created by businesses for the purpose of selling their products or services online.

- **Informational websites** are created for the purpose of displaying factual information about a particular topic and are often created by educational institutions, governments, and organizations.
- **Media websites** are online newspapers and periodicals that are created by companies for the purpose of informing readers about current events and issues.
- **Portal websites** are created by businesses for the purpose of creating a starting point for people to enter the Web. Portals contain hyperlinks to a wide range of topics, such as sport scores and top news stories, and most portals include access to a search engine.

While the Internet and Web were originally developed to help the academic and scientific communities, the Web is being used more and more for advertising and e-commerce. It is common to find advertisements, such as *banner ads*, on websites:

A banner ad is designed to entice a user to click it, which in turn displays the advertiser's page. Most websites host banner ads for a fee.

Every web page has a URL (Uniform Resource Locator) associated with it. A *URL* is an address that is interpreted by a web browser to identify the location of a page on the web. For example, consider the URL for the Earth Day Network:

http://www.earthday.net

- **http** is the web *protocol* used to handle requests and for the transmission of pages between a web server and a web browser.
- **//** separates the protocol from the domain name.
- **www.earthday.net** is the domain name. A *domain name* identifies a particular web page and is made up of a sequence of parts, or subnames, separated by a period. The *subnames* are called labels and may represent a server or organization. The suffix of a domain name is called the *top-level domain* and identifies the type of website. In this case .net indicates the site is a network organization.

Another widely used Internet service is *e-mail* or *electronic mail*, which is the sending and receiving of messages and computer files over a communications network, such as a LAN (Local Area Network) or the Internet. E-mail can be received in a matter of seconds, even if the recipient is located half way around the world.

An e-mail address is required in order to send and receive e-mail messages. A typical e-mail address is similar to:

christina@emcschool.net

user name — host or domain name — top-level domain

Web Advertising

The Interactive Advertising Bureau (IAB) sets standards and guidelines for Internet advertising, including guidelines for the size of banner, button, rectangle, interstitial, pop-up, skyscraper, and webmercial ads.

Top-level Domains

Top-level domains include:
.gov - government agency
.edu - educational institution
.org - non profit organization
.com - commercial business

Each country also as a 2 character top-level domain, such as .uk for the United Kingdom.

E-mail Protocols

POP3 is an e-mail protocol that connects to an e-mail server to download messages to a local computer.

IMAP is an e-mail protocol that connects to an e-mail server to read message headers and then the user selects which e-mail messages to download to a local computer.

HTTP is used as an e-mail protocol when a web page is used to access an e-mail account.

TIP HTTPS (Hypertext Transfer Protocol Secure) protocol is often used for payment transactions on the Web.

E-mail software is also required for sending and receiving e-mail messages. An example of e-mail software is Outlook. Browser-based e-mail only requires a web browser and is available through sites such as Yahoo!, Google, and Hotmail.

Instant messaging (IM) is a communication tool that allows for *real time*, or immediate text-based communication. Instant messaging allows for private on-line chat sessions and is useful for brief communication that is faster than e-mail.

Voice over Internet Protocol (VoIP) is a transmission technology used to make phone calls over the Internet using a service such as Skype. VoIP is also used for Web conferences.

A *mailing list server* is a server that manages mailing lists for groups of users. Two mailing list servers are Listserv and Majordomo. Often users subscribe to mailing lists for discussion purposes. When a subscriber posts a message to a mailing list server, every subscriber receives a copy of the message. Subscribers are identified by a single name or e-mail address.

Internet protocols include *HTTP (Hypertext Transfer Protocol)*, which is used for handling the transmission of pages between a web server and a web browser and *FTP (File Transfer Protocol)*, which is used to rapidly transfer (upload and download) files from one computer to another over the Internet. FTP is also discussed in Chapter 9.

Using Internet Explorer

A web browser is needed to view web pages:

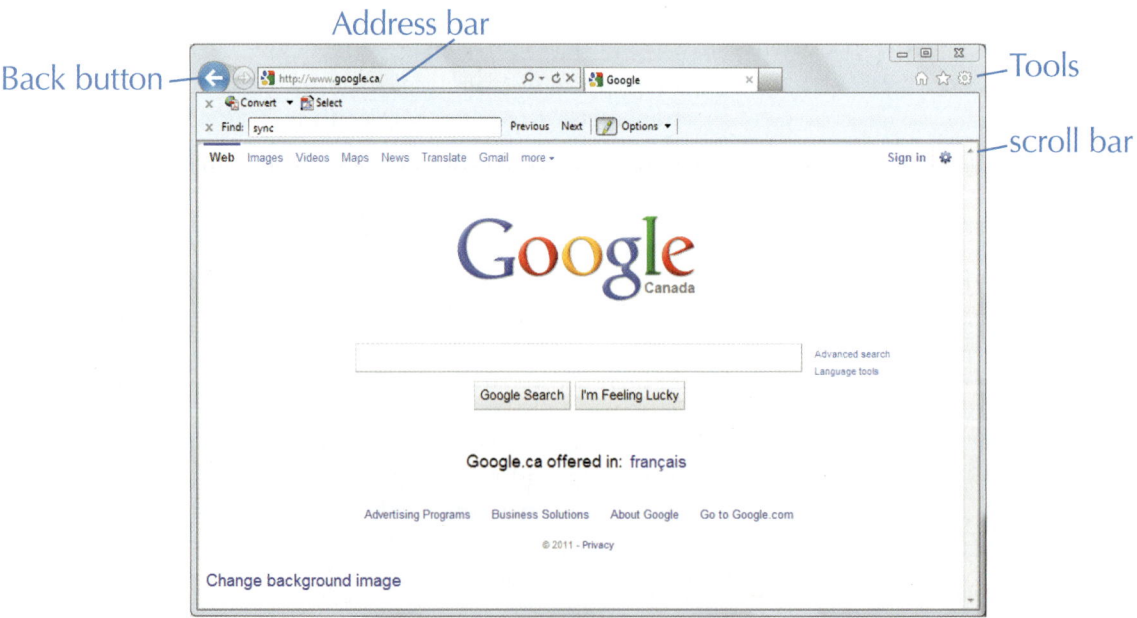

Internet Explorer 9 window

- Click the **Back button** to display the previously displayed web page.

- ↪ Click the **Forward button** to display the next web page from the previously selected pages.
- ✕ Click the **Stop button** to stop the transmission of a web page.
- ↻ Click the **Refresh button** to update the displayed web page.
- 🏠 Click the **Home button** to display a preselected web page, which is the web page displayed when Internet Explorer is started.
- ⭐ Click the **View favorites, feeds, and history button** to display the *Favorites list*, which is used to maintain a list of web pages.
- Type a URL in the **Address bar** and then press Enter to open a web page. Press Alt+Enter to open the web page in a new tab. A previously typed URL can also be selected from the Address bar list.
- Drag the **scroll bar** to bring unseen parts of the document into view.

> **TIP** Tabbed browsing is a feature that allows multiple websites to be open in a single browser window. Press Ctrl+T to open a new tab.

Web pages do not always print on a single sheet of paper. Therefore, it is important to preview a web page before printing to avoid printing unwanted pages. Select ⚙ → Print → Print preview to display the Print Preview window, which indicates the number of pages that will be printed. Click ⚙ on the Print Preview window toolbar to add a header and footer to the web page printout. Click 🖨 to display the Print dialog box. Options in the Print dialog box can then be used to specify which pages should be printed.

Practice: Using Internet Explorer

This practice requires Internet access.

① START INTERNET EXPLORER

a. Ask your instructor for the appropriate steps to start Internet Explorer. The preselected home page is displayed.
b. What is the URL of the home page?

② GO TO THE MSNBC HOME PAGE

a. In the Address bar, replace the existing URL with www.msnbc.com, the URL for the MSNBC home page.
b. Press Enter. The web page is opened.
c. Use the scroll bar to scroll through the home page.

③ VIEW MSNBC STORIES

a. Click a hyperlink that interests you.
b. Continue to surf MSNBC web pages. Realize that a hyperlink may display a web page at a site other than MSNBC. To return to the MSNBC site, click ↩.
c. Which website category would the MSNBC website be in?

④ GO TO THE CNN HOME PAGE

a. In the Address bar, replace the existing URL with www.cnn.com, the URL for the CNN home page.
b. Press Enter. The web page is opened. Use the scroll bar to scroll through the CNN home page.

Chapter 1 Networks and the Internet

c. Which website category would the CNN website be in?

⑤ GO TO THE FLORIDA ATLANTIC UNIVERSITY HOME PAGE
a. In the Address bar, type www.fau.edu, the URL for the Florida Atlantic University home page, and then press Alt+Enter. The web page opens in a new tab.
b. Which website category would this website be in?
c. Press Ctrl+T. A new tab is opened.
d. Click the CNN icon. The CNN web page is the active website.
e. Click × to close the CNN tab.

⑥ GO TO THE AMAZON HOME PAGE
a. In the Address bar, replace the existing URL with www.amazon.com, the URL for the Amazon home page.
b. Press Enter. The web page is opened. Use the scroll bar if necessary to scroll through Amazon's home page.

⑦ ADD A WEB PAGE TO THE FAVORITES LIST
a. On the toolbar, click ★. The Favorites pane is displayed. The Favorites pane contains the *Favorites list*, which is used to maintain a list of web pages. Selecting any of the web pages in the list will access that page and display it in the pane in the right side of the window.
b. What pages are displayed in your Favorites list? Click anywhere on the web page to close the Favorites list.
c. A Favorites list can be organized using folders. Click ★ → Add to favorites. The Add a Favorite dialog box is displayed. Change the Name box text to Amazon:

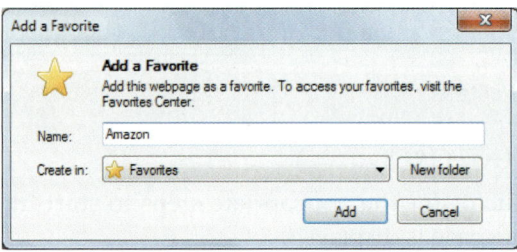

1. Click New folder. The Create a Folder dialog box is displayed.
2. In the Folder name box, type: Shopping Sites.

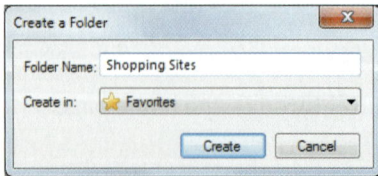

3. Click Create. The dialog box is removed and a folder is added to the Favorites list.
4. Click Add. The dialog box is removed and the current page is added to the Shopping Sites folder in the Favorites list.

⑧ GO TO ANOTHER WEB PAGE

    a. In the Address bar, replace the existing URL with www.roots.com, the URL for the Roots home page.

    b. Press Enter. The web page is opened.

⑨ RETURN TO A FAVORITE WEB PAGE

    a. On the toolbar, click ⭐. The Favorites pane is displayed. In the Favorites pane, click the Shopping Sites folder to display the page that was added:

    b. Click the link for Amazon. The selected page is displayed in the right pane.

⑩ USE THE HISTORY LIST TO ACCESS WEB PAGES

    a. On the toolbar, click ⭐. The Favorites pane is displayed.

    b. Click `History`. The History pane is displayed. The *History list* displays URLs and websites that have been visited previously.

    c. Click `View By Date`. Options for displaying the History pane are displayed. Select View By Order Visited Today:

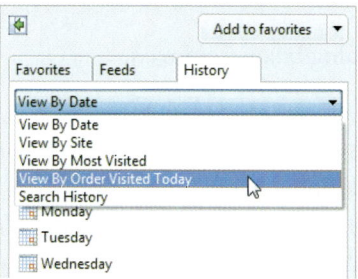

    d. Click CNN.com. The CNN home page is displayed.

    e. Click ⭐ → `History` → View By Date.

    f. Click the Today folder `Today`. In the Today folder, note that a folder is displayed for each of the sites visited today.

    g. Click the fau folder:

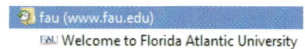

The title of the home page is displayed as a hyperlink to the home page. Click the link to display the Florida Atlantic University home page.

⑪ DELETE A FOLDER FROM THE FAVORITES LIST

The Organize favorites option in the **Add to favorites** drop-down list is used to display a dialog box where folders can be created and renamed, moved, or deleted. The URLs can also be renamed, moved, or deleted.

    a. Click ⭐ → **Add to Favorites** → **Organize favorites**. The Organize Favorites dialog box is displayed.

    b. Click the Shopping Sites folder to select it:

Chapter 1 Networks and the Internet   **15**

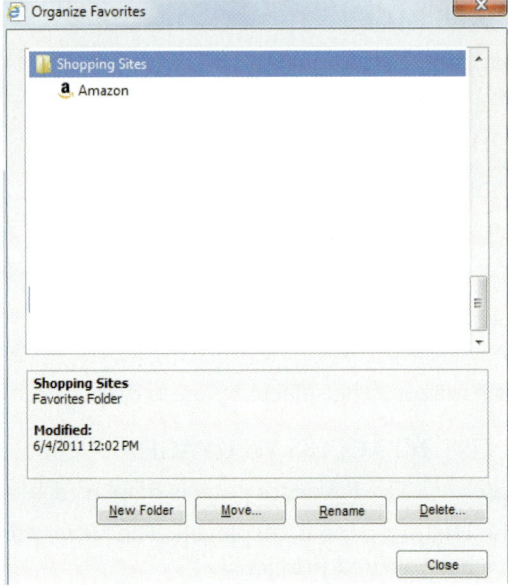

c. Select [Delete...]. A warning is displayed. Select Yes to delete the folder and its contents.

d. Select [Close]. The dialog box is removed.

⑫ PRINT A WEB PAGE

a. In the Address bar, replace the existing URL with www.earthday.net, the URL for the Earth Day Network home page. Press Enter.

b. Select ✱ → Print → Print preview. The Print Preview window is displayed:

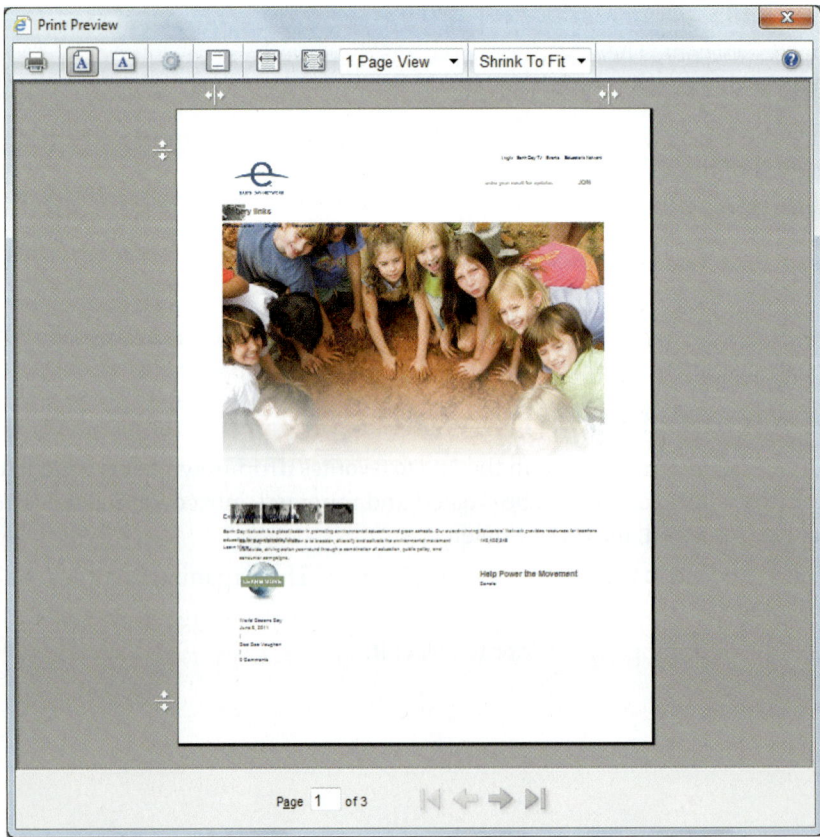

Chapter 1 Networks and the Internet

1. How many pages will be printed?
2. Select the Page Setup button . A dialog box is displayed.
3. Create a Custom header with your name. and then click OK.
4. In the Print Preview window, click . A dialog box is displayed.
5. Select Print. The web page is printed.

Searching the Web

A *search engine* is a program that searches a database of web pages for keywords and then lists hyperlinks to pages that contain those keywords. Commonly used search engines include:

Yahoo! (www.yahoo.com)
Google (www.google.com)
MSN (www.msn.com)
AOL (www.aol.com)
Bing (www.bing.com)
Ask Jeeves (www.ask.com)
Lycos (www.lycos.com)
WebCrawler (www.webcrawler.com)
About.com (www.about.com)

A search engine can be queried to display specific web pages. *Search criteria* can include single words or phrases that are then used by the engine to determine a match. A *match* is a web page that contains the search criteria. Surrounding phrases with quotation marks finds web pages that contain the entire phrase. The more specific the search criteria, the better the chance the information will be found.

Most searches yield far too many matches to be useful. Limiting the number of matches to a reasonable number can usually be accomplished by using Boolean logic in the search criteria:

- The + (*plus sign*) is used in search criteria to limit a search to only web pages that contain all of the specified words. For example, a search for florida +hotel or florida hotel returns only links to pages containing both words. AND can be used in place of + in most search engines.

- OR can be used in most search engines to find web pages that contain any one of the words in the criteria. For example, the criteria florida OR hotel returns links to pages containing either of the words.

- The – (*minus sign*) is used to exclude web pages. For example, a search for shakespeare –play returns links to pages containing the word shakespeare, but eliminates pages that also contain the word play. NOT can be used in place of – in most search engines.

Some search engines provide categories, such as *Images* and *Videos* to help narrow a search. For example, Google has a web directory in the top left corner:

Search Engines

A search engine usually works by sending out an agent, such as spider. A spider is an application that gathers a list of available web page documents and stores this list in a database that users can search by keywords.

When displaying information, search engines often show "Sponsored Sites Results" first. These are sites that contain the information being searched for but have paid the search engine to list their sites at the top of the list.

Boolean Logic

Boolean logic uses three logical operators that evaluate to True or False:

AND locates pages that include both words

OR locates pages that include one word or the other or both

NOT locates pages that include the first word, but not the second word.

Chapter 1 Networks and the Internet

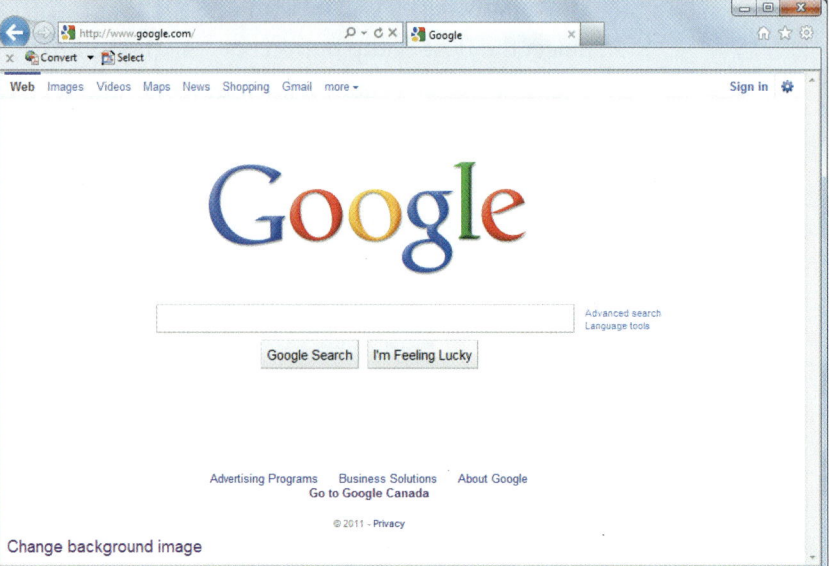

TIP Click the Advanced search link to display additional search options.

Practice: Searching the Web

① GO TO THE YAHOO! SEARCH ENGINE

In the Address bar, replace the existing URL with www.yahoo.com.

② TYPE SEARCH CRITERIA

a. In the **Search** box, type: shakespeare.

b. Click **Web Search** to start the search. How many results matches are there?

c. Scroll down to display the results of the search, then click one of the hyperlinks that interests you. A new page is opened.

③ SELECT OTHER WEB PAGES LOCATED IN THE SEARCH

a. On the toolbar, click ⬅. The website hyperlinks are again displayed. Click a different web page hyperlink.

b. Continue this process to access additional pages.

④ DEFINE CRITERIA USING BOOLEAN OPERATORS

a. Refine the search criteria to: shakespeare OR "Globe Theatre" and see how many web page matches there are.

b. Refine the search criteria to: shakespeare +"Globe Theatre" and see how many web page matches there are. Note that there is no space after the + sign.

c. Further refine the criteria to: shakespeare +"Globe Theatre" +reconstruction –usa and see how many web page matches there are.

d. Click a few of the hyperlinks to determine if their web pages include the information that is being searched for.

⑤ GO TO THE GOOGLE HOME PAGE

⑥ USE A CATEGORY TO FIND INFORMATION

a. On the Google home page, click the **Images**.

b. In the search box, type flowers and then click **Search Images**.

Evaluating and Citing Web Pages

Information found at a website, regardless of the category, should be evaluated for accuracy. Anyone can post a website on the Web. There are no rules as to the accuracy or reliability of the information. This means that you must discriminate, read carefully, and check sources. A few topics to think about and questions to answer when evaluating a source are:

- **Up-to-date**. On what date was the web page last updated? Is the information current?
- **Bias**. Is the information incorrect or incomplete in order to give a particular or slanted view of a topic?
- **Validity**. Is the information truthful and trustworthy? What is the primary source of the information? Information posted by NASA or Yale University is more likely to be valid than information posted by an anonymous person who does not cite sources.
- **Author**. Does the author present his or her credentials?

If information from a website is to be referenced or quoted in a report, essay, or other document, a citation must be used to give credit to the original author and allow the reader to locate the cited information. A widely accepted form for citation is published by the *Modern Language Association (MLA)* in its publication *MLA Handbook for Writers of Research Papers, Seventh Edition*.

TIP MLA no longer requires the use of URLs in MLA citations because Web sites are not static and typically documents can be located by searching the title in a search engine. If an instructor still requires the use of URLs, they are placed in angle brackets after the date of access.

> Author's Last Name, First Name. "Article Title." Site Title. Publisher Name, Last-updated date. Web. Access date. <URL>.

If no publisher name is available, n.p. should be used and if no publication date is listed, n.d. is used. A citation of a page on a website:

> Marrelli, J. "How to use Internet Explorer". *Lawrenceville Press - Download Data Files.* Lawrenceville Press, 23 Dec. 2010. Web. 15 May 2012.

Practice: Citing a Website

Internet Explorer should already be started.

① SEARCH FOR INFORMATION

Use one of the search engines listed in the "Searching the Web" section to search for web pages about the Egyptian Step Pyramid of Djoser.

② EVALUATE WEBSITES

Browse the links to find a web page that contains reliable information. Refer to the "Evaluating and Citing Web" section for a few topics to think about and questions to answer when evaluating a source to be reliable.

③ CITE THE WEB PAGE

Use the information on the web page to write a citation on paper.

Chapter 1 Networks and the Internet

E-mail Etiquette

Rules to follow when composing e-mail messages include:

- Use manners. Include "please" and "thank you" and appropriately address individuals as Mr., Ms., Mrs., Dr., and so on.
- Be concise. Write in short, complete sentences.
- Be professional, which includes using the proper spelling and grammar. E-mail software usually has a built-in spelling checker.
- Re-read a message before it is sent. Always fill in the To box last to avoid sending a message before it is complete.

E-mail messages are not private. An e-mail message goes through several mail servers before it reaches the recipient, making it easily accessible for others to read. Therefore, a certain etiquette needs to be followed:

- Send messages through your account only.
- Use appropriate subject matter and language.
- Be considerate of other people's beliefs and opinions.

When sending e-mail at work or school, it is important to remember that employers and school administrators have the right to read any e-mail messages sent over the corporate or school network, as well as the right to track online activity.

Internet Privacy Issues

The growth of the Internet has caused additional concerns about personal privacy. Searching for information on the Internet is not as anonymous as it might seem.

The collection of data about consumers visiting a website is a marketing technique known as *online profiling*. When a commercial website is visited, information about the user may be collected using various methods such as cookies or web beacons.

A *cookie* is a text file created by the server computer when a user enters information into a website. The cookie file is then stored on the user's computer and accessed each time the user visits that website. Cookies are often created when online purchases are made. Although cookies can only store information that the user has selected or entered, their use has raised concerns over privacy issues.

Web beacons, also called web bugs or pixel tags, are tiny, transparent graphics located on web pages or in e-mail messages that are used in combination with cookies to collect data about web page users or e-mail senders. Usually the monitoring is done by an outside advertising company. The information a web beacon collects includes the IP address of the computer, the URL being visited, the time the web page was viewed, the type of browser being used, and the cookie file.

Spyware

Spyware is software that uses the Internet to gather personal information from an unsuspecting user. Spyware is unknowingly downloaded and installed with another file, such as freeware or shareware programs.

TIP A website's privacy policy is typically found as a link at the bottom of the site's home page.

Before providing a company with personal information through a website, check the site's privacy policy. A *privacy policy* is a legally binding document that explains how any personal information will be used.

Information on a website is sometimes in the form of a downloadable file. *Downloading* is the process of copying a file from a website to the user's computer. For example, virus definitions can be downloaded from a antivirus software company's website and software updates can be downloaded from the software company's website. When a file is downloaded, the user specifies where the file should be saved on the local computer. Files should only be downloaded from known, authentic websites since downloadable files are often associated with viruses.

The Internet has opened up access to many files that were previously inaccessible. To protect both the privacy of an individual and the accuracy of data stored about individuals, several laws have been passed:

- The **Electronic Communications Privacy Act of 1986 (ECPA)** makes it a crime to access electronic data without authorization. It also prohibits unauthorized release of such data.

- The **Electronic Freedom of Information Act of 1996 (E-FOIA)** requires federal government agencies to make certain agency information available for public inspection and is designed to improve public access to agency records by making more information available online.

- The **Children's Online Privacy Protection Act of 1998 (COPPA)** requires commercial websites that collect personal information from children under the age of 13 to obtain parental consent.

- The **Safety and Freedom through Encryption Act of 1999 (SAFE)** gives Americans the freedom to use any type of encryption to protect their confidential information.

Other laws have been passed that may invade the privacy of some to protect the safety of others. For example, the **Provide Appropriate Tools Required to Intercept and Obstruct Terrorism (PATRIOT) Act of 2001** gives law enforcement the ability to monitor individual's e-mail and web activity.

Passwords
Many Internet sites require a login and password. Strong passwords are ones that include a combination of upper and lowercase letters, numbers, and punctuation.

Encryption
Encryption is the process of translating data into a code that is not readable without the key to the code. Encryption prevents unauthorized access to the data. Data that is encrypted is referred to as cipher text.

Internet Acceptable Use Policy

Internet content, unproductive use, and copyright have prompted many schools and businesses to develop an Acceptable Use Policy or Internet Use Agreement. Acceptable Use Policies typically contain rules similar to:

- Use appropriate language.
- Do not reveal personal address or phone numbers.
- Do not access, upload, download, or distribute inappropriate materials.
- Do not access another user's account.
- Use of the network for private business is prohibited.
- Only administrator installed software may be used.

Internet Filtering Software
Many schools and organizations install Internet filtering software to block offensive material.

The Social and Ethical Implications of Computer Use

The society in which we live has been so profoundly affected by computers that historians refer to the present time as the *information age*. This is due to the our ability to store and manipulate large amounts of information (data) using computers. As an information society, we must consider both the social and ethical implications of our use of computers. By ethical questions we mean asking what are the morally right and wrong ways to use computers.

ergonomics

Ergonomics is the science that studies safe work environments. Many health-related issues, such as carpal tunnel syndrome and computer vision syndrome (CVS) are related to prolonged computer use.

Power and paper waste are environmental concerns associated with computer use. Suggestions for eliminating these concerns include recycling paper and printer toner cartridges and turning off monitors and printers when not in use.

Employee monitoring is an issue associated with computers in the workplace. It is legal for employers to install software programs that monitor employee computer use. As well, e-mail messages can be read without employee notification.

As discussed in a previous section in the chapter, the invasion of privacy is a serious problem associated with computers. Because computers can store vast amounts of data we must decide what information is proper to store, what is improper, and who should have access to the information. Every time you use a credit card, make a phone call, withdraw money, reserve a flight, or register at school, a computer records the transaction. These records can be used to learn a great deal about you—where you have been, when you were there, and how much money was spent. Should this information be available to everyone?

Computers are also used to store information about your credit rating, which determines your ability to borrow money. If you want to buy a car and finance it at a bank, the bank first checks your credit records on a computer to determine if you have a good credit rating. If you purchase the car and then apply for automobile insurance, another computer will check to determine if you have traffic violations. How do you know if the information being used is accurate? The laws listed below have been passed to help ensure that the right to privacy is not infringed by the improper use of data stored in computer files:

- The **Fair Credit Reporting Act of 1970** gives individuals the right to see information collected about them for use by credit, insurance, and employment agencies. If a person is denied credit they are allowed to see the files used to make the credit determination. If any of the information is incorrect, the person has the right to have it changed. The act also restricts who may access credit files to only those with a court order or the written permission of the individual whose credit is being checked.

Identity Theft

Identity theft is a growing crime where personal information is stolen electronically in order to make fraudulent purchases or loans.

- The **Privacy Act of 1974** restricts the way in which personal data can be used by federal agencies. Individuals must be permitted access to information stored about them and may correct any information that is incorrect. Agencies must insure both the security and confidentiality of any sensitive information. Although this law applies only to federal agencies, many states have adopted similar laws.

- The **Financial Privacy Act of 1978** requires that a government authority have a subpoena, summons, or search warrant to access an individual's financial records. When such records are released, the financial institution must notify the individual of who has had access to them.

Protecting Computer Software and Data

copyright

As society becomes more and more reliant on digital information, copyright and exposure to malicious code have become two important issues among computer users. *Copyright* is protection of digital information. Copyright infringement is the illegal use or reproduction of data (text, pictures, music, video, and so on). Laws, such as the NET Act (No Electronic Theft Act) of 1997, protect against copyright infringement. There have been several well-known cases of high penalties for individuals guilty of copyright infringement.

piracy

Copyright infringement includes duplication of computer software when copies are being used by individuals who have not paid for the software. This practice is called *piracy* when illegal copies are distributed. Developing, testing, marketing, and supporting software is an expensive process. If the software developer is then denied rightful compensation, the future development of all software is jeopardized. Therefore, it is important to use only legally acquired copies of software, and to not make illegal copies for others.

Malicious code comes in many forms and is delivered in many ways. A virus, a Trojan horse, and an Internet worm are three forms of malicious code. They can appear on a system through executable programs, scripts, macros, e-mails, and some Internet connections. One devastating effect of malicious code is the destruction of data.

virus

A *virus* is a program or series of instructions that can replicate without the user's knowledge. Often a virus is triggered to run when given a certain signal. For example, a virus might check the computer's clock and then destroy data when a certain time is reached. A virus is easily duplicated when the file is copied, which spreads it to other computers.

Trojan horse

A *Trojan horse* program appears as something else, usually a program that looks trustworthy. Running the program runs the malicious code and damages files on the computer. A *worm* is a program that is able to reproduce itself over a network. *Worms* are a threat because of the way they replicate and use system resources, sometimes causing the system to shut down.

antivirus programs Malicious code has become so widespread that software called *antivirus programs* must be installed on computers and networks to detect and remove the code before it can replicate or damage data. Precautions can also be taken to prevent damage from malicious code:

- Update antivirus software. An antivirus program can only detect the viruses, Trojan horses, and worms it is aware of. Antivirus programs have a web link for updating the virus definitions on the computer containing the antivirus program.

- Do not open e-mail attachments without scanning for malicious code. One estimate states that 80% of virus infection is through e-mail.

crackers, hackers Newspapers have carried numerous reports of *crackers*, or *hackers*, gaining access to large computer systems to perform acts of vandalism. This malicious act is illegal and can cause expensive damage. The Electronic Communications Privacy Act of 1986 specifically makes it a federal offense to access electronic data without authorization. Networks usually include a firewall, which is helps prevent unauthorized access.

The willful destruction of computer data is no different than any other vandalizing of property. Since the damage is done electronically the result is often not as obvious as destroying physical property, but the consequences are much the same. It is estimated that computer crimes cost billions of dollars each year.

phishing *Phishing* is the act of sending an e-mail to a user falsely claiming to be a legitimate business in an attempt to trick the user into revealing personal information that could be used for crimes such as identity theft.

The Ethical Responsibilities of the Web Developer

dynamic pages Websites often contain *dynamic pages* that link to databases to provide the user real-time information. It is extremely difficult, if not impossible, for a web developer to guarantee that data is always valid. A cause for concern is the increased reliance by computer users on the data presented. This places a strong ethical burden on the web developers to ensure, as best they can, the reliability of the data.

Careers

The growth of the Web has created many new job opportunities in the
IT IT *(information technology)* field. IT encompasses all aspects of computer-related technology.

Education requirements for IT careers vary. However, a formal education, such as an undergraduate degree in computer science, engineering, or business, is often required. A graduate degree may also be required in highly specialized fields. Some careers require a specialized certification course in an area such as networking. Other skills that are required in this industry are teamwork, problem-solving skills, oral and written communication, technical knowledge, and computer experience.

web developer   *Web developers* design, build, and program websites. They determine the website strategy, which includes the hardware to be used and the design and navigation of the site. They also design tools, such as reports and databases, to measure the success of the website.

Web developers require programming and technical skills. Often the development is divided into back-end development and front-end development. Back-end development involves designing the hardware and database infrastructure, such as where orders are fulfilled. Front-end development involves the navigation and design of the website.

web designer   *Web designers* create the web page layouts and graphics for websites. The work a web designer does usually determines whether users will stay at a website. Their job involves presenting web pages so they are interesting and accessible.

A web designer requires knowledge of HTML, web implementation software such as Dreamweaver and Flash, and graphic editing software such as Fireworks, Photoshop, or Illustrator. Since technology changes rapidly, web designers must keep up-to-date on new technologies, techniques, and design standards.

webmaster   *Webmaster* responsibilities can include designing and creating web pages and maintaining the site. A webmaster is also responsible for answering e-mail about the website. A webmaster possesses extensive Internet knowledge, programming skills, and design experience.

web author   *Web authors* create textual content for web pages. A web author has good writing skills and carefully considers the text as it will be presented on the Web.

IT Departments and Companies

Most large companies have an IT department. Careers in these departments include the Web careers discussed in the previous section as well as:

intranet analysts
- *Intranet analysts* set up and maintain an intranet for a company or organization. This involves managing company intranet projects, technical support, and creating reports. This job requires technical knowledge of networks, network security features, computers, and software as well as personal communication skills.

network administrator
- A *network administrator* is responsible for a company's network. Duties could include installing the network hardware and software, as well as maintaining the network so it runs properly. LAN manager is another term for network administrator.

There are also many small to large companies that strictly provide IT services. These companies include:

ISP
- *ISPs (Internet Service Providers)* provide access to the Internet. Employees have a wide range of technical knowledge about networks, computers, and software since clients will have a variety of equipment. Personal communication skills are also necessary for sales and technical support.

web host
- *Web hosts* provide space on a server where users can post their web pages. Employees have technical knowledge of networks, computers, and the World Wide Web. Personal communication skills are also necessary for sales and technical support.

Pursuing an IT Career

The growth of the Web has resulted in colleges and universities changing their program offerings to better prepare students for careers in IT. Some degree options that are offered at a variety of schools include:

- Media, Information, and Technoculture
- Computer Arts
- Computer Engineering
- Computer Animation
- Information Technologies Support Services
- International Telecommunications Systems and Service
- Internet Commerce and Technology
- Electronic Media, Arts, and Communication

Many colleges, universities, and employers are requiring the submission of an electronic portfolio as part of the admissions or interview process. An example electronic portfolio is created in Chapter 8.

It is a good idea to keep an updated list of any acquired computer skills and knowledge in order to update a portfolio, create a resume, or complete a job application. Working through this text will help develop valuable computer skills that could help with a future job including:

- data entry skills
- knowledge of HTML
- website design and development using Dreamweaver, Flash, and Fireworks

Chapter Summary

A desktop computer and its components are designed to fit on or under a desk. Mobile computers include notebooks, tablets, smart phones, and wearables.

The physical components of the computer are referred to as hardware. Computers also contain programs, or software.

A network is a combination of hardware and software that allows computers to exchange data and share software and devices, such as printers. Networks are classified by their size, architecture, topology, and protocol. Network users should use netiquette.

A collection of related data stored on a lasting medium, such as a hard disk, is called a file. A file can be an application (program) or the product of an application. Folders are used to organize commonly related files.

An intranet is a network that is used by a single organization and is only accessible by authorized users. A firewall is a network security system that prevents unauthorized network access. An extranet extends an intranet by providing various levels of accessibility to authorized members of the public. The largest and most widely accessed network is the Internet.

Telecommunications is the transmitting and receiving of data. Telecommunication options include a conventional modem, a DSL modem, a cable modem, leased/dedicated lines, and ISDN.

The most widely used Internet service is the World Wide Web, also called the Web. Another widely used Internet service is e-mail. E-mail etiquette should be used when sending e-mail messages.

A web browser, such as Internet Explorer, is needed to view web pages. In Internet Explorer, the History list is a list of the pages that have been visited in the last 20 days and the Favorites list is used to maintain a list of web pages.

A search engine is a program that searches a database of web pages for keywords and then lists hyperlinks to pages that contain those keywords. Information found at a website, regardless of the category, should be evaluated for accuracy.

The growth of the Internet has caused concerns about personal privacy. Online profiling, cookies, and web bugs are all areas of concern. Before providing personal information through a website, check the site's privacy policy. To protect an individual's privacy, several laws have been passed. Concerns about Internet content, unproductive use, and copyright have prompted many schools and businesses to develop an Internet Use Agreement.

Historians refer to our present time as the information age. The potential for the use of computers to invade our right to privacy has prompted legislation to protect individuals. Piracy is the illegal act of duplicating software without permission. A virus is a computer file that erases data and can cause considerable damage.

Web developers should ensure, as best they can, the reliability of the data they provide in dynamic web pages.

The growth of the World Wide Web has created many new job opportunities in the IT field. IT stands for information technology and encompasses all aspects of computer-related technology. Web careers include web developer, web designer, webmaster, and web author. The growth of the Web has resulted in colleges and universities changing their program offerings to better prepare students for careers in web authoring or IT.

Vocabulary

Address bus Carries memory addresses that indicate data storage locations.

ALU (Arithmetic Logic Unit) The part of the CPU that handles arithmetic and logic operations.

Antivirus program Software installed on computers and networks to detect and remove viruses.

Applications software Program written to perform a specific task.

Banner ad One type of advertisement on websites.

Base unit Housing that contains the motherboard, CD-RW/DVD drive, disk drive, and hard disk drive.

Bus A central network cable. Also a set of circuits that connect the CPU to other components.

Bus topology A physical LAN topology that uses a single central cable to attach each node directly.

Cable modem A modem that transmits data through a coaxial cable television network.

Cache High-speed memory used to store frequently used data so that it can be quickly retrieved by an application.

Client A computer that is sent information from a server computer.

Client/server network A type of network that consists of a group of computers, called clients connected to a server computer.

Clock rate The speed at which a CPU can execute instructions, measured in megahertz or gigahertz.

Commercial website A business-related website such as corporate presence or e-commerce.

Control bus Carries control signals.

Conventional modem A modem that uses standard telephone lines to convert analog signals to digital data.

Cookie Text file created by the server computer when a user enters information into a website.

Copyright Protects a piece of work from reproduction without permission from the work's author.

Corporate presence website A website created by companies and organizations for the purpose of displaying information about their products or services.

CPU (Central Processing Unit) Processes data and controls the flow of data between the computer's other units. Also contains the ALU. Located on the motherboard.

Cracker Person who accesses a computer system without authorization.

Cross-platform connectivity The ability of one type of PC to link to and share data with a different type of PC.

Dedicated line *See* Leased line.

Desktop computer A computer designed to fit on or under a desk.

Device driver One type of utility program.

Domain name Part of the URL that identifies a particular web page and is made up of a sequence of parts, or subnames, separated by a period.

Downloading The process of copying a file from a website to the user's computer.

DSL (Digital Subscriber Line) modem A modem that uses standard telephone phone lines. ADSL is the most common form used.

Dynamic pages Web pages that link to databases to provide the user real-time information.

E-commerce website A website created by businesses for the purposes of selling their products or services to consumers online.

E-mail (electronic mail) The sending and receiving of messages and electronic files over a communications network such as a LAN or the Internet.

Environment A computer's hardware and software configuration. Also referred to as platform. Environment types include desktop, multiuser, network, handheld, distributed, multiprocessing, and multitasking.

Ergonomics The science that studies safe work environments.

Expansion boards Circuit boards that connect to the motherboard to add functionality to the computer.

Extranet An extended intranet that provides various levels of access to authorized members of the public.

Favorites list A list of web pages that have been added to the Internet Explorer Favorites list.

File A collection of related data stored on a lasting medium.

File name A unique name used to identify a file.

Firewall A network security system that prevents unauthorized network access.

Folder Used to organize commonly related files.

FTP (File Transfer Protocol) Used to rapidly upload and download files from one computer to another over the Internet.

Gigahertz (GHz) Billion of cycles per second.

Hacker *See* Cracker.

Handheld computer A mobile computing device.

Hardware The physical components of the computer, such as the monitor and system unit.

History list A list of URLs and websites that have been visited in the previous days and weeks.

HTTP (Hypertext Transfer Protocol) Handles the transmission of pages between a web server and a web browser.

Hub A communication device that joins communication lines at a central location on the network.

Information age Present time characterized by increasing dependence on the computer's ability to store and manipulate large amounts of information.

Informational website A website created by educational institutions, governments, and organizations for the purpose of displaying information about a particular topic.

Input device Device used to enter data and instructions into the computer.

Instant messaging (IM) A communication tool that allows for real time, or immediate text-based communication.

Integrated circuits (ICs) Memory that stores data electronically.

Interactive Information accessed as a result of selections made by the user.

Internet The largest and most widely accessed network.

Intranet A network used by a single organization and only accessible by authorized users.

Intranet analyst Sets up and maintains intranets for companies or organizations.

ISDN (Integrated Services Digital Network) A digital telephone network provided by a local telephone company.

ISP (Internet Service Provider) A company that provides access to the Internet.

IT (Information Technology) A term that encompasses all aspects of computer-related technology.

Kbps Thousands of bits per second.

LAN (Local Area Network) A network used to connect devices within a small area.

Leased line A telecommunication option used for a permanent connection to the Internet that is always active.

Logical topology Refers to the way in which data is passed between the nodes on a network.

Mailing list server A server that manages mailing lists for groups of users.

Main memory *See* Random Access Memory.

Match A web page that contains the search criteria.

Mbps Millions of bits per second.

Media website Online newspaper and periodicals that are created by companies for the purpose of informing readers about current events and issues.

Megahertz (MHz) Million of cycles per second.

Memory-resident Programs that are always in the computer's memory.

Minus sign (–) Used in search criteria to exclude unwanted Web pages.

Modern Language Association (MLA) Organization that publishes standards used for citations.

Motherboard The main circuit board inside the base unit.

Netiquette The etiquette that should be followed when using a network.

Network A combination of software and hardware that allows computers to exchange data and to share software and devices, such as printers.

Network administrator Responsible for a company's network. Also called LAN Manager.

Network architecture The structure of a network.

Network interface card A circuit board that goes into a computer or other device in a LAN.

Network operating system Software that allows users and devices to communicate over a network.

Node A location on the network capable of processing information, such as a computer or a printer.

Notebook A portable, lightweight computer.

Online profiling A marketing technique that collects online data about consumers.

Operating system Software that allows the user to communicate with the computer.

Output device A device used to convey processed data.

Overwrite Update an original file with changes.

Peer-to-peer network A type of network that does not have a server.

Peripheral device A device attached to a PC.

Phishing The act of sending an e-mail to a user falsely claiming to be a legitimate business in an attempt to trick the user into revealing personal information that could be used for crimes such as identity theft.

Piracy Illegally copying or distributing software.

Plus sign (+) Used in search criteria to limit a search to only those web pages containing two or more specified words.

Port Used to attach a peripheral device to a computer.

Portal website A website created by businesses for the purpose of creating a starting point for people to enter the Web.

Primary memory *See* RAM.

Privacy policy A legally binding document that explains how personal information will be used.

Protocol A standard.

RAM (Random Access Memory) Memory that temporarily stores data and instructions.

Real time Occurs immediately.

Ring topology A physical LAN topology where each node is connected to form a closed loop.

ROM (Read Only Memory) Memory that stores data and is a permanent part of the computer.

Router A device that connects different network technologies.

Search criteria A single word or phrase that is used by the search engine to match web pages.

Search engine A program that searches a database of web pages for keywords and then lists hyperlinks to pages that contain those keywords.

Secondary memory Any type of storage media, such as a hard disk, memory key, or CD-RW.

Server A computer used to manage network functions such as communication and data sharing.

Smartphone Cellular phone that is able to send and receive e-mail messages and access the Internet.

Social media website A website that allows for the creation and exchange of user-generated content.

Star topology A physical LAN topology where each node is attached to a hub.

Subject tree A list of sites separated into categories.

Subname Part of the URL that represents a server or organization. Also called a label.

Tablet PC A computer designed similar to a pad of paper.

TCP/IP (Transmission Control Protocol/Internet Protocol) Software used by networks connected to routers to communicate.

Telecommunications The transmitting and receiving of data.

Top-level domain Part of the URL that identifies the type of website.

Topology The physical or logical arrangement of the nodes on a network.

Transmission media The media that joins the nodes on a network to enable communication.

Trojan horse Malicious code in the form of a program that appears as something else, usually a program that looks trustworthy.

URL An address that is interpreted by a web browser to identify the location of a page on the Web.

Utility program Program run by the operating system to manage input and output, read and write to memory, manage the processor, maintain system security, and manage files and disks.

Virus A program that is designed to reproduce itself by copying itself into other programs stored on a computer without the user's knowledge.

WAN (Wide Area Network) A network used to connect computers over large geographical distances.

Wearable computer A mobile computing device that is incorporated into clothing, eyewear, wristwear, and other wearables.

Web *See* World Wide Web.

Web author Writes content for web pages.

Web beacon A tiny, transparent graphic located on a web page used to collect data about the web page user. Also called a web bug or pixel tag.

Web browser Interprets an HTML document to display a Web page.

Web designer Creates the web page layouts and graphics for websites.

Web developer Designs, builds, and programs websites.

Web directory *See* Subject tree.

Web host A company that provides a web server where web authors can post their websites.

Web server A server that has web server software installed and is designed to deliver web pages to clients.

Webmaster Designs and creates web pages, creates graphics for the site, and maintains the site.

Website A series of related web pages.

Wireless network A type of network that does not require the use of cables.

World Wide Web The most widely used Internet service. Used to search and access information available on the Internet.

Internet Explorer 9 Commands and Buttons

Back button Displays the previously selected web page.

View favorites, feeds, and history button Displays the Favorites list, which is used to maintain a list of web pages

Forward button Displays the next web page from the previously selected pages.

History tab Displays a pane with the URLs of websites that have been visited in the previous days and weeks. Found in the Favorites pane.

Home button Displays a preselected web page. Found on the toolbar.

Refresh button Updates the displayed web page. Found on the toolbar.

Stop button Stops the transmission of a web page. Found on the toolbar.

Tools button Displays a menu drop-down menu containing Print and Zoom options

Review Questions

1. a) List four types of mobile computing devices.
   b) Describe one type of wearable computer.

2. a) What is hardware?
   b) What are input and output devices used for?
   c) What is a peripheral device?

3. List and describe five components found on the motherboard.

4. Describe the flow of data between the components of a computer, starting with input.

5. Describe one difference between operating system software and applications software.

6. List four benefits of using a network.

7. a) What are the two common size classifications for networks?
   b) What size classification is used to connect devices over large geographical distances?

8. What is a network operating system?

9. a) What does network architecture refer to?
   b) List two common network architecture models.

10. a) What does physical topology refer to?
    b) What is a node?
    c) Which topology uses a hub?
    d) Which topology connects each node to form a closed loop?
    e) What is the difference between physical and logical topology?

11. List three netiquette rules.

12. a) Why is it important to give files and folders descriptive names?
    b) Why would organizing files into folders be considered a good practice?

13. List three examples of storage media.

14. What is the difference between an intranet and an extranet?

15. a) What is the Internet?
    b) Who controls the Internet?

16. List three telecommunications options.

17. a) If a business needed constant access to the Internet, what type of connection line would be a good choice? Why?
    b) What does a cable modem use instead of analog phone lines?

18. What is the most widely used Internet service?

Answer question 19 using Internet search skills or by discussing the answers with a partner.

19. a) E-commerce websites are often an extension of a traditional or "brick-and-mortar" business. List one traditional business that uses an e-commerce website as a method of extending their business.
    b) Amazon.com is an example of a business that only does transactions on-line. List an example of another business that only conducts business through their website.
    c) Compare shopping at an e-commerce website with traditional shopping. List two advantages and two disadvantages of shopping at an e-commerce website.
    d) List an example of a media website.
    e) Yahoo! is an example of a portal website. List another example of a portal website.

20. a) What is a URL?
    b) Label and describe each part of the URL http://www.emcp.com.

21. a) What is e-mail?
    b) List one benefit of e-mail over standard mail.
    c). Write your e-mail address and label the parts of the address.
    d) What are the two requirements for sending and receiving e-mail messages?

22. a) What is instant messaging?
    b) What is VoIP?

23. a) What is the History list?
    b) What is the Favorites list used for?

24. a) What is a search engine?
    b) List three commonly used search engines.
    c) Which search engine do you prefer to use, and why?
    d) What is search criteria?
    e) What is a match?

25. Write search criteria to locate web pages that contain the following information:
    a) restaurants in Los Angeles
    b) art museums in Boston
    c) auto repair jobs in Montreal, Canada
    d) mosquitoes and bees, but not ants
    e) the English author Jane Austen
    f) the phrase *to each his own*
    g) George Washington and John Adams, but not Thomas Jefferson
    h) travel to Ireland, but not Dublin

26. What is the purpose of a subject tree?

27. a) List four questions to answer when evaluating a website source.
    b) Why is it necessary to cite sources?
    c) On August 2, 2012 you accessed a posting on the Clewiston Kite Surfing discussion list at http://www.emcp.com/kitesurf/color.txt. The posting was made by Tara Perez on the topic of kite colors. Write a citation for a research paper that quotes Tara's posting.

28. a) Explain why sending an e-mail message should be thought of the same as sending a postcard.
    b) List three examples of e-mail etiquette.

29. What is online profiling?

30. What is a cookie?

31. a) What is a web beacon?
    b) Who usually monitors the information collected by web beacons?

32. What is a privacy policy?

33. Name and briefly describe one law that helps protect the privacy of an individual.

34. a) List three reasons why many schools have developed an Acceptable Use Policy.
    b) List an example of a rule that typically appears on an Acceptable Use Policy.

35. What can you do if you are turned down for credit at a bank and believe that the data used to deny credit is inaccurate?

36. a) What is necessary for a federal government authority to access an individual's financial records?
    b) What must a financial institution do after releasing an individual's records?

37. a) What is copyright infringement?
    b) What is computer piracy?
    c) What is a computer virus?
    d) What is a firewall used for?

38. What ethical responsibilities does a web developer have?

39. Describe four IT careers.

40. a) What do ISPs provide?
    b) Which career includes setting up and maintaining an intranet for a company or organization?
    c) What duties are typical of a network administrator?

True/False

41. Determine if each of the following are true or false. If false, explain why.
    a) FireWire and USB are types of ports.
    b) A peer-to-peer network has a server.
    c) A LAN's logical topology is always the same as its physical topology.
    d) The most widely accessed network is the Internet.
    e) A conventional modem transmits data faster than a cable modem.
    f) .com is a top-level domain.
    g) E-mail allows for real-time communication.
    h) E-mail messages are private.
    i) Web pages always print on a single sheet of paper.
    j) Information found at a website is always accurate.
    k) The present time is referred to as the industrial age.
    l) A virus is a harmless computer game.

Exercises

Exercise 1

In this exercise you will research your classroom computer network by answering a series of questions:

a) Is your computer network a LAN or a WAN?

b) List one device that is shared on the network.

c) Locate the cable that plugs into the network interface card on your workstation.

d) What type of physical topology is used?

e) What type of transmission media is used?

f) What network protocol is used?

g) What operating system is used?

h) What telecommunication option is used?

i) Does the school have an intranet?

j) List four rules on the school's Internet Use Agreement.

Exercise 2

In this exercise you will assess the input and output devices you have access to.

a) List the input devices accessible on the classroom network. Which of these devices will be helpful in the development of a website?

b) Describe one additional input device that is not available but would be helpful when developing a website.

c) List the output devices accessible on the classroom network. List advantages and disadvantages associated with each accessible output device.

Exercise 3

Become familiar with different categories of websites by completing the following steps:

a) Use the Internet to locate an example of a social media website. List the URL and briefly describe the content at the site.

b) Use the Internet to locate an example of an e-commerce website. List the URL and briefly describe the products that can be purchased at this site.

c) Use the Internet to locate an example of an informational website. List the URL and briefly describe the information available at the site.

d) Use the Internet to locate an example of a media website. Print the home page of the media website and note how up-to-date the content is.

e) Use the Internet to locate an example of a portal website. Print the home page of the portal website and circle four hyperlinks available on the portal home page.

Exercise 4

Examine and evaluate website content by completing the following steps:

   a) Go to the www.cnn.com web page.

   b) Read the content on the home page.

   c) On what date was the web page last updated?

   d) Is the information incorrect or incomplete in order to give a particular or slanted view of a topic? Explain your answer.

   e) Is the information truthful and trustworthy? Explain your answer.

   f) Describe an advertisement displayed on this site.

   g) Go to the www.earthday.net web page.

   h) Repeat steps (b) through (g) for the Earth Day Network website.

Exercise 5

YouTube.com is a popular social media site where users can post videos that they have created. Discuss the pros and cons of a site like YouTube with a classmate. Prepare a presentation on the pros and cons of YouTube or post your thoughts on the course wiki site.

Exercise 6

Your English instructor has assigned a report on the American authors Kurt Vonnegut, Jr. and Ernest Hemingway. Keep in mind that knowledge of information like the titles of their books might help in your search. Because people maintain web pages as homages to their favorite authors, but are not obligated to check their facts for accuracy, it is a good idea to double check the information you find with more than one web page.

   a) Conduct a search on the Internet using at least two search engines to find biographical data on each author.

   b) Create a folder named American Authors in the Favorites list and add three relevant web pages to this folder.

   c) Write a paragraph of biographical information for each author.

   d) Write a citation for each source.

Exercise 7

In this exercise you will organize your existing files.

a) Examine the files you currently have saved on your computer. Use the appropriate operating system command to rename any files that do not have descriptive names.

b) Use the appropriate operating system commands to organize your existing files into appropriate folders.

Exercise 8

A good friend has been diagnosed with Carpal Tunnel Syndrome and would like you to find out as much as you can about the injury and possible treatments.

a) Conduct a search on the Internet using at least two search engines to find three web pages that have information about Carpal Tunnel Syndrome.

b) Create a folder named: Carpal Tunnel Syndrome in the Favorites list and add relevant web pages to this folder.

c) Write a brief description of the injury.

d) In a second paragraph, write about possible treatments for the injury.

e) Write a citation for each source.

Exercise 9

Expand on the information presented in this chapter by researching one of the following topics:

- Green Computing
- Operating Systems
- Mobile Computing Devices

a) Use the Internet, magazines, and books to find at least three sources of information.

b) Write a two page report or prepare a posting to the course wiki site that summarizes your research.

c) Write a citation for each source.

Exercise 10

In this exercise you will research and compare the advantages and cost of obtaining Internet access through three different telecommunication options.

a) Use the Internet and newspapers to find information about ISPs.

b) Compare the costs and the advantages of at least three different telecommunication options.

c) Prepare a presentation that summarizes your research.

Exercise 11

In this exercise you will further research emerging technologies and find real-life examples of how these technologies have impacted individuals and businesses.

a) Use the Internet, magazines, and books to learn more about at least three emerging technologies. Look specifically for information on how these emerging technologies impact individuals and businesses. For example, speech recognition technology greatly impacts those individuals who must rely on voice input rather than keyboard input for a PC.

b) Write a two-page report that summarizes the impact of and lists several functions of the emerging technologies you have researched. Alternatively, post your summary to the course wiki site.

c) Write a citation for each source.

Exercise 12

Many computer viruses have been associated with e-mail attachments.

a) Conduct a search on the Internet to find information about a virus associated with an e-mail attachments.

b) Write a one-paragraph description of the virus. Include details, such as the damage caused by the virus and steps necessary to remove the virus.

c) Write a citation for each source.

Exercise 13

You have decided to research *search engine optimization* to figure out how a web site can score high in a Web search.

a) Use the Internet to do your research.

b) Create a list of tips or prepare a posting to the course wiki site that summarizes your research.

Exercise 14

In this exercise you will investigate mailing lists.

a) Join an appropriate mailing list.

b) Participate on the mailing list as a learner.

c) Contribute to the mailing list content.

d) Research the process of starting a mailing list. Present your research in a written report, citing all sources.

Chapter 2
HTML

This chapter introduces HTML, which is the primary language of the Web. In order to maximize the potential of Dreamweaver, you must first have a good understanding of HTML.

The World Wide Web

The most widely used Internet service is the World Wide Web (WWW), also called the Web. The *Web* is used to search and access information available on the Internet. A *web browser application*, such as Internet Explorer, provides a graphic interface to present information from a website. A *website* consists of a series of related web pages. For example, a web page that is part of the National Park Service website:

web browser application

website

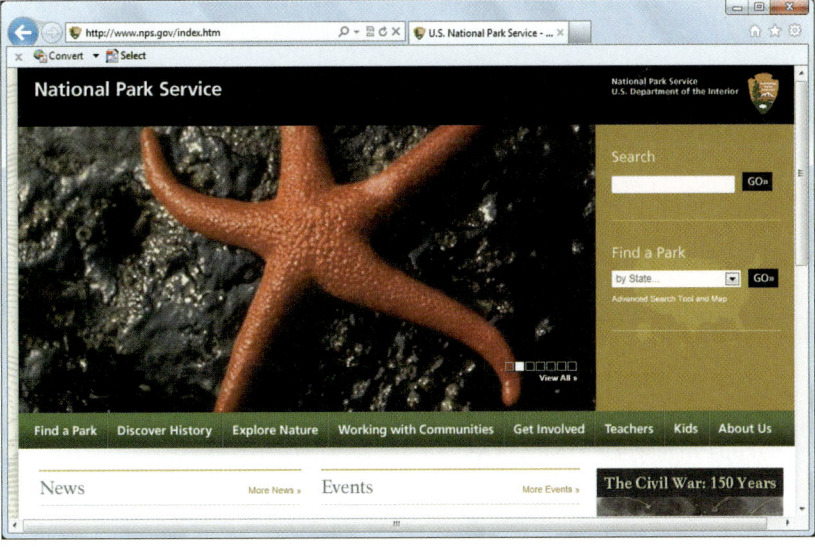

A web page displayed in a web browser

Browsers

Commonly used web browser applications include Internet Explorer, Opera, Firefox, and Safari.

Most web pages are created using *HTML (HyperText Markup Language)* and other code. HTML is a markup language that is well suited for the Web because it supports hypertext and multimedia. *Hypertext* is a database system where objects, such as text and images, can be linked. *Multimedia* includes images, video, audio, and Java applets, which can be embedded in an HTML document.

**Tim Berners-Lee
(b. 1955)**
Tim Berners-Lee is credited with creating the World Wide Web. Berners-Lee now heads a non-profit group, the W3C (World Wide Web Consortium), which sets technical standards for the Web.

TIP HTML is not case sensitive, so tags may be uppercase or lowercase. This text uses lowercase tags.

XHTML

XHTML (Extensible Hypertext Markup Language) is a markup language that is similar to HTML but also conforms to XML syntax. XHTML is actually a reformulation of HTML that is supported by all newer browsers.

Millions of people all over the world are able to view and author Web content because the World Wide Web Consortium (W3C) continuously develops standards for the Web. These standards include HTML standards to ensure that HTML documents display similarly in different browsers and across different platforms. They have also developed Web accessibility standards for those with disabilities.

HTML

HTML uses a set of codes, called *tags*, to "mark up" plain text so that a browser application, such as Internet Explorer, knows how to interpret the text. A tag is comprised of an *element* inside angle brackets (<>). For example, <title> is called the title tag, where title is the element. Tags affect the text they surround, and are usually paired to indicate the start and end of an instruction. A slash (/) before the element indicates the end of an instruction, such as </title>.

A web page with one line of text will be displayed when the HTML document below is opened in a browser.

```
<html>

<head>
<title>An example HTML document</title>
</head>

<body>
<p>Hello world!</p>
</body>

</html>
```

Text marked up with <title> and </title> will be the text displayed when the page is added to a Favorites or Bookmark list. This text is also displayed in the browser's title bar or website tab. The text Hello world! is marked to be displayed as a paragraph (<p> and </p>) in the body of the browser window (<body> and </body>). When viewed in Internet Explorer 9, the document appears similar to:

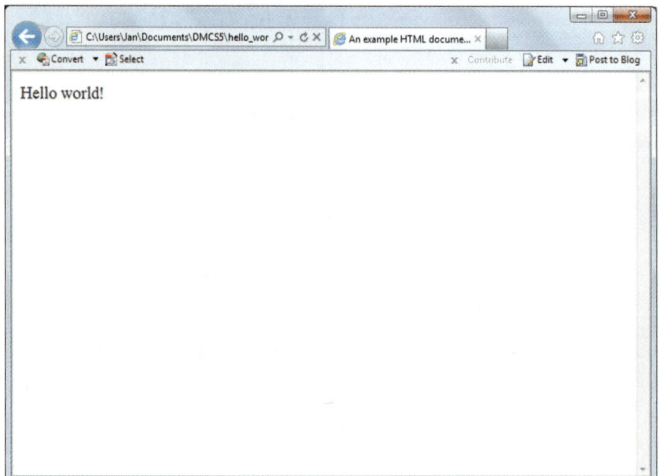

Chapter 2 HTML

If you were to create the same web page document in Dreamweaver, the interface would look similar to:

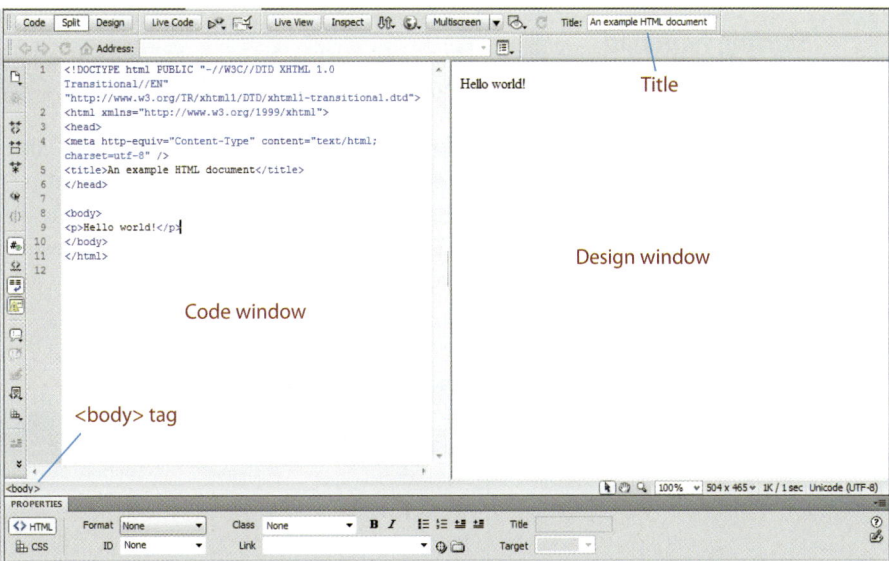

Dreamweaver interface in Split View

The interface above is displayed in Split view. In this view you are able to see the web page in both Design view and Code view. Working in Design view is similar to working within a word processor interface. The document you see in Design view is similar to the way it will be displayed in a browser. As the web page is created in Design view, Dreamweaver automatically generates the HTML you see in the Code window. All the user had to do was type the title in the Title box and type Hello world!! in the Design window.

So why learn HTML?

As you work through the text, you will see why it is important to have a basic understanding of HTML in order to work efficiently in Dreamweaver. For example, it is very difficult to understand CSS which is used for page layout and formatting if you do not have a basic understanding of HTML. It is also much easier to edit web pages and trouble-shoot issues if you are able to understand the code behind the web page.

This chapter will quickly teach you the basics of HTML and then you will be able to start mastering Dreamweaver in Chapter 3.

Using Notepad

Starting Notepad

To start Notepad, select Start → All Programs → Accessories → Notepad.

Notepad is a text editor that comes with the Windows operating system and is well suited for creating and editing plain text files, such as HTML documents. When Notepad is started, a new, blank document is displayed in the Notepad window. An HTML document can then be typed.

To save an HTML document, select File → Save. The Save As dialog box is displayed the first time a document is saved. Navigate to the location where the file is to be saved, select the Text Documents (*.txt) option in the Save as type list and then type a descriptive file name in the File name box:

Word Wrap

To make long paragraphs of text easier to read in Notepad, select Format → Word Wrap.

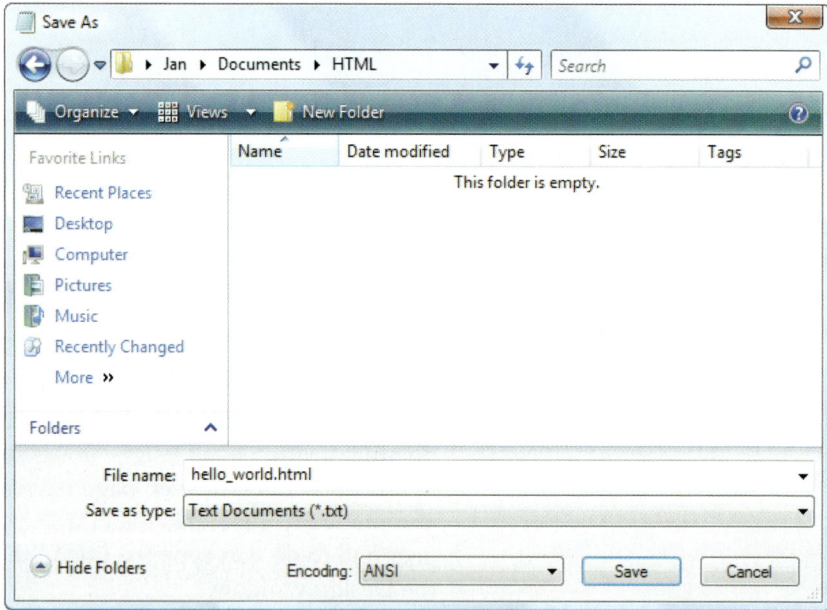

TIP If using a word processor, be sure to save the document as a TXT file.

The descriptive file name should be lowercase and should not contain any spaces. The underscore character is used to separate words. The .htm or .html extension needs to be added to the file name so that a browser recognizes the file as an HTML document.

File Names

File names can contain letters, the underscore character (_), and numbers. File names cannot contain colons (:), asterisks (*), question marks (?), or some other special characters. File names for HTML documents should not contain spaces.

To print a document, select File → Print. Notepad automatically prints a centered header containing the file name and a centered footer containing the page number.

To create a new document, select File → New. To open an existing document, select File → Open, which displays a dialog box. Change the Files of type to All Files to display the HTML document file name in the contents box. Click the appropriate file name and then select Open.

To quit Notepad, select File → Exit. A warning dialog box is displayed if the document has been modified since it was last saved.

42 Chapter 2 HTML

Creating an HTML Document

HTML documents are plain text files and can be created using any text editor such as Notepad or by using a word processor. In general, the structure of an HTML document should be similar to:

```
<html>

    <head>
    <title>document title</title>
    </head>

    <body>
    content
    </body>

</html>
```

An HTML document contains pairs of tags

TIP To help make an HTML document easier to understand, place document tags on separate lines, except the title tags, and use blank lines to separate sections of HTML.

The html, head, title, and body tags are called *document tags*:

- The <html> tag tells the browser that the file contains HyperText Markup Language.

- The <head> tag defines the section that contains information about the document, including its title. This section will not be displayed as part of the document content.

- The <title> tag marks the document title. The title section must be within the head section. The document title should be descriptive and meaningful because it is displayed in the browser's title bar or tab and is also used when the user adds the document to the Favorites list.

- The <body> tag defines the body section, which contains the document's content. All content must be enclosed in the appropriate tags. For example, on the previous page, the content is marked as a paragraph. Paragraph tags are discussed later in this chapter.

HTML documents are *free-form*, which means that spaces and blank lines generally have no effect on how the document is interpreted. Therefore, the document:

```
<html><head><title>An example HTML document</title>
</head>
<body>  <p>Hello world!</p></body></html>
```

Poorly structured HTML document

TIP A tag should not have any spaces between the opening bracket and the element or slash.

displays exactly the same as the HTML document on the previous page. However, editing a poorly structured document can be time-consuming and error-prone.

Chapter 2 HTML 43

Viewing HTML Documents in a Web Browser

TIP In Internet Explorer, press Alt to display the View menu.

A web browser is used to access and view HTML documents that have been published to a web server. The web browser first interprets the URL to identify the location of the of the page on the Web and then interprets the HTML document to display a web page in the browser window. In Internet Explorer, select View → Source to view the HTML associated with a displayed web page.

HTML documents saved on a local computer can also be viewed in a browser. In Internet Explorer, select File → Open to display the Open dialog box. Select Browse to display a dialog box, which is used to navigate to the location where the HTML document is saved.

HTML documents that are posted to the Internet are the designer's intellectual property and are protected by copyright. This applies even if a copyright notation (©) is not included on the page.

When developing an HTML document, frequent viewing in a browser is usually necessary. This is easily done by having both Notepad and a web browser open at the same time and using the Windows taskbar to switch between the applications. In Internet Explorer, the Refresh button ↻ or the F5 key is used to check the HTML file for changes and then update the document in the browser window. Any changes made to the HTML document in Notepad must be saved before refreshing the browser.

Multitasking

Multitasking is an operating system feature that allows more than one application to run at a time.

Practice: first_document.html

This practice assumes that you have Notepad and Internet Explorer.

① **START NOTEPAD**

Ask your instructor for the appropriate steps to start Notepad.

② **CREATE AN HTML DOCUMENT**

Type the following HTML document exactly as shown. Be sure to include a blank line between sections, as indicated, and replace Name with your name:

```
<html>

<head>
<title>First HTML Document</title>
</head>

<body>
<p>My name is Name. Hello world!</p>
</body>

</html>
```

③ **SAVE THE HTML DOCUMENT**

a. Select File → Save. The Save As dialog box is displayed.

b. Use the Save in list and the contents box below it to select the appropriate location for the file to be saved.

c. In the Save as type list, select Text Documents (*.txt) if it is not already selected.
  d. In the File name box, replace the existing text with: first_document.html.
  e. Select Save. The document is saved with the name first_document.html.

④ **START INTERNET EXPLORER**

⑤ **OPEN FIRST_DOCUMENT.HTML IN INTERNET EXPLORER**
  a. Press the Alt key and then select File → Open. A dialog box is displayed:

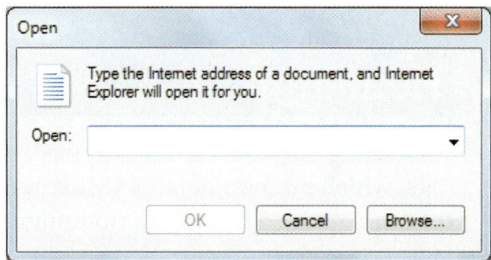

  b. Select Browse. A dialog box is displayed.
  c. Use the Look in list and the contents box below it to locate the file name first_document.html.
  d. In the contents box, click: first_document.html.
  e. Select Open.
  f. Select OK. The tags are interpreted and the HTML document appears in the browser:

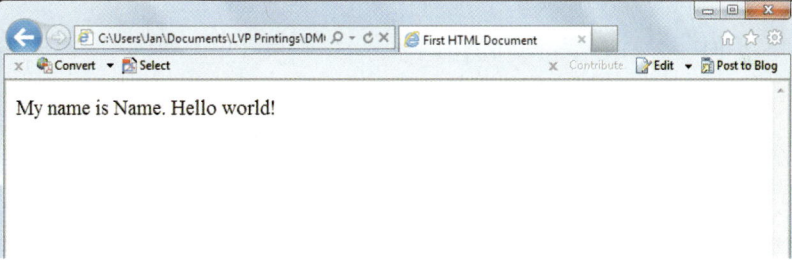

⑥ **SWITCH TO NOTEPAD AND MODIFY FIRST_DOCUMENT.HTML**
  a. On the taskbar, click the Notepad button. The first_document.html document is displayed.
  b. Place the insertion point to the right of the ! in world! and type a space followed by: This is my first HTML document.
  c. Save the modified file.
  d. Select File → Print and then select Print in the dialog box. A copy of the HTML document is printed.

⑦ **SWITCH TO INTERNET EXPLORER AND REFRESH THE VIEW**
  a. On the taskbar, click the Internet Explorer button. The first_document.html document is displayed without the additional content.
  b. Press the F5 key. Internet Explorer updates the displayed document.

Chapter 2 HTML

Creating Paragraphs and Line Breaks

<p>

TIP Tags that do not need to be paired are called empty tags.

The body section of an HTML document includes the content and tags that format the content. Text enclosed by <p> and </p> is a paragraph. Lines of paragraph text are automatically wrapped by the browser, and blank space is added after each paragraph.

To move a line of text within a paragraph to the next line, a break tag <br> is used. A break tag does not need to be paired.

Headings

<h1> through <h6>

Heading tags are used to emphasize text. There are six levels of headings, which are numbered 1 through 6 and represented with tags <h1> through <h6>. The HTML document below includes all six heading tags:

```
<html>

<head>
<title>Heading Formats</title>
</head>

<body>
<h1>Heading 1</h1>
<h2>Heading 2</h2>
<h3>Heading 3</h3>
<h4>Heading 4</h4>
<h5>Heading 5</h5>
<h6>Heading 6</h6>
</body>

</html>
```

Each heading level has specific formatting associated with it, which includes font size, bold text, and space above and below the heading. Heading 1 has the largest font size and is used to represent the most important information. Heading 6 has the smallest font size. For example, the above HTML document viewed in a browser will look similar to:

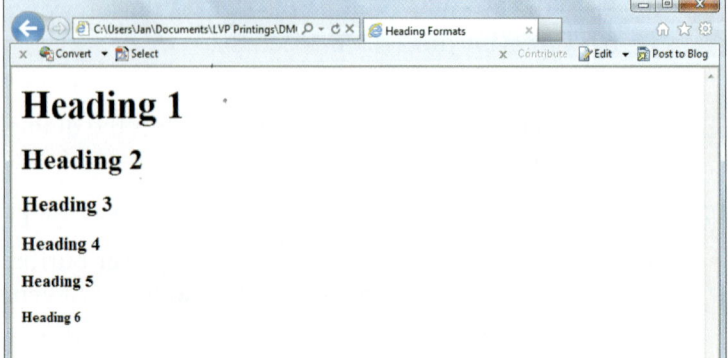

Browser Preferences

The formatting associated with heading tags varies between browsers and is dependent on the preferences set by the user.

Adding Horizontal Rules

The <hr> tag places a horizontal rule (line) across the width of the browser window. This feature is used to divide the text in the browser window into sections for easier reading. The horizontal rule tag does not need to be paired.

attribute Tags may also contain attributes. An *attribute* is placed in the start tag and set to a value that modifies the element. For example, the horizontal rule width attribute specifies the width of the line in the browser window as a percentage:

<hr width="50%">

Other attributes of the <hr> tag include:

- size="*value*" specifies the thickness of the rule in pixels
- align="*value*" specifies the rule alignment. The default alignment is center

Practice: Computer Viruses – part 1 of 5

Internet Explorer and Notepad should already be started.

① **SWITCH TO NOTEPAD**

② **CREATE A NEW HTML DOCUMENT**
   a. Select File → New.
   b. Type the following HTML document exactly as shown, replacing Name with your name:

   <html>

   <head>
   <title>Computer Viruses</title>
   </head>

   <body>
   <h1>Computer Viruses</h1>
   <hr>
   <p>A computer virus is a program that is loaded onto the computer without the user's knowledge. Computer viruses have varying effects, such as:
   displaying annoying messages
   causing programs to run incorrectly
   erasing the contents of the hard drive</p>
   <p>In order to protect against viruses:
   install an antivirus program
   update antivirus definitions on a regular basis</p>
   <h4>Report by Name</h4>
   </body>

   </html>

③ SAVE THE HTML DOCUMENT

Save the document in the same folder as first_document.html and name it: computer_viruses.html.

④ OPEN COMPUTER_VIRUSES.HTML IN INTERNET EXPLORER

a. Switch to Internet Explorer.

b. Select File → Open. A dialog box is displayed.

c. Select Browse. A dialog box is displayed.

d. Use the Look in list and the contents box below it to locate the file name computer_viruses.html.

e. In the contents box, click: computer_viruses.html.

f. Select Open. The dialog box is removed and the location and file name are placed in the Open box.

g. Select OK. The tags are interpreted and the HTML document appears in the browser:

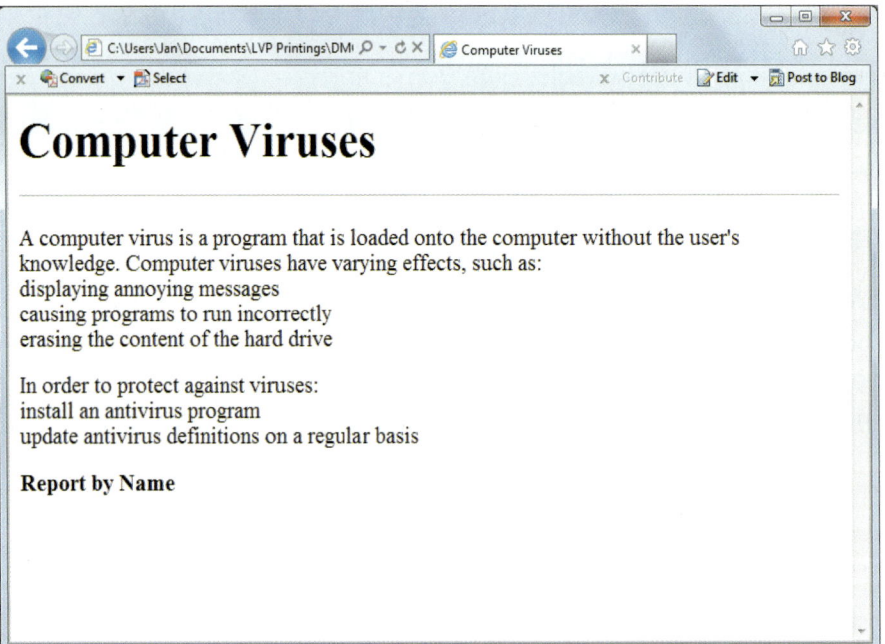

⑤ PRINT THE HTML DOCUMENT

a. Switch to Notepad.

b. If necessary, make corrections to the HTML document.

c. From Notepad, print a copy of the computer_viruses.html document.

Creating Lists

bulleted list

Lists are used to organize information. Bulleted and numbered are two types of lists that can be created in an HTML document. A *bulleted list*, also called an *unordered list*, is used when each item is equally important:

Bulleted list tags include:

- <ul> </ul> defines the start and end of a bulleted list
- <li> </li> defines the start and end of an item

numbered list

A *numbered list*, also called an *ordered list*, is used to show priority of importance, for example as steps in a recipe:

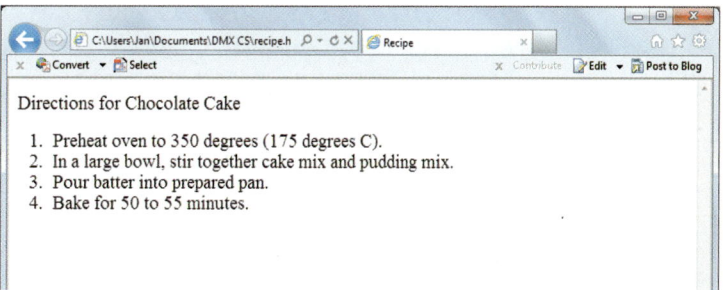

Numbered list tags include:

- <ol> </ol> defines the start and end of a numbered list
- <li> </li> defines the start and end of a list item

Practice: Computer Viruses – part 2 of 5

Internet Explorer and Notepad should already be started with computer_viruses.html displayed in Notepad.

① MODIFY COMPUTER_VIRUSES.HTML TO INCLUDE LISTS

Modify the BODY section of computer_viruses.html to include a bulleted and numbered list by removing the existing <br> tags and adding the list tags as shown:

```
<body>
<h1>Computer Viruses</h1>
<hr>
<p>A computer virus is a program that is loaded onto the computer
without the user's knowledge. Computer viruses have varying
effects, such as:</p>
<ul>
<li>displaying annoying messages</li>
```

```
<li>causing programs to run incorrectly</li>
<li>erasing the contents of the hard drive</li>
</ul>
<p>In order to protect against viruses:</p>
<ol>
<li>install an antivirus program</li>
<li>update antivirus definitions on a regular basis</li>
</ol>
<h4>Report by Name</h4>

</body>
```

② **SAVE THE MODIFIED COMPUTER_VIRUSES.HTML**

③ **SWITCH TO INTERNET EXPLORER AND REFRESH THE VIEW**
   a. On the taskbar, click the Internet Explorer button. The computer_viruses.html document is displayed without the modified content.
   b. On the toolbar, press the F5 key. The document is updated:

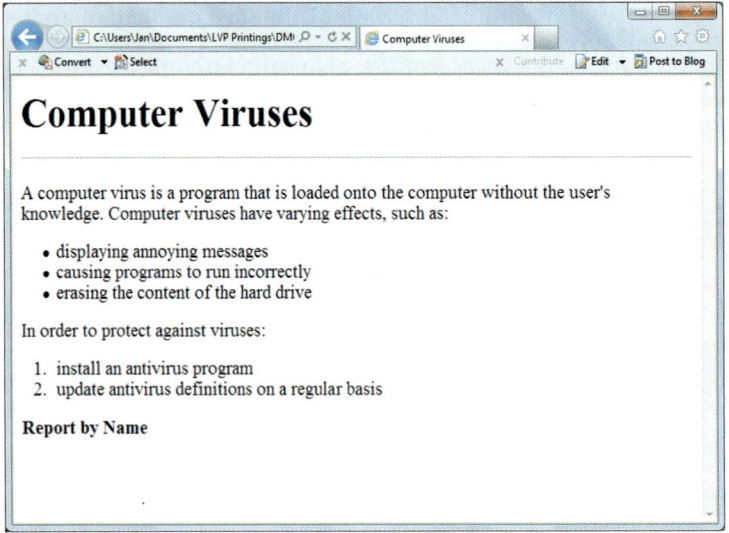

④ **PRINT THE HTML DOCUMENT**
   a. Switch to Notepad.
   b. If necessary, make corrections to the HTML document.
   c. From Notepad, print a copy of the computer_viruses.html document.

Tables

Tables are used to arrange data in an HTML document:

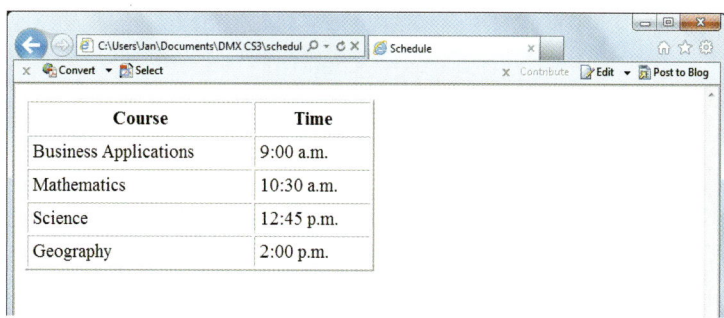

Table tags include:

- <table> </table> creates a table
- <th> </th> creates a table header, which is a cell with bold, centered text in the first row of the table
- <tr> </tr> defines the start and end of a table row
- <td> </td> defines the start and end of a table data cell

The table tag may also contain attributes. For example, the border attribute is used to change the thickness of a table border:

<table border="2">

Table attributes include:

- border=*"value"* specifies the thickness of the cell border where value is in pixels
- cellpadding=*"value"* sets the amount of space between table cells where value is a number
- width=*"value"* specifies the width of a table where value is a number in pixels or as a percentage of the document's width

Pixels

A pixel (picture element) is a single point in a graphic. A graphic is made up of thousands of pixels.

Hyperlinks

A *hyperlink*, also called a *link*, is text displayed in a browser window that can be clicked to display a different HTML document in the browser window. Hyperlinks are what make a hypertext system, such as the Web work. Countless documents can all be linked, allowing the user to go from topic to topic, or browse HTML documents. By default, hyperlinks are displayed as blue underlined text in the browser window. Links that have been clicked are referred to as *visited hyperlinks* and display in purple underlined text.

visited hyperlink

Chapter 2 HTML   51

The anchor tag (<a>) is used in an HTML document to mark text that is a link. The href attribute is set in the tag to the name of the linked document:

```
<html>

<head>
<title>Images</title>
</head>

<body>
<p>Images can come from a variety of sources
including <a href="digicam.html">digital cameras</a>.</p>
</body>

</html>
```

When viewed in a browser, the HTML document above will look similar to:

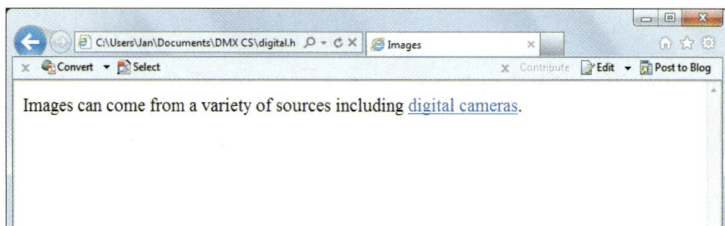

The text digital cameras is called the hyperlink label. Click digital cameras to display the digicam.html document.

Practice: Computer Viruses – part 3 of 5

Internet Explorer and Notepad should already be started.

① **CREATE A NEW HTML DOCUMENT**
   a. In Notepad, select File → New.
   b. Type the following HTML document exactly as shown, replacing Name with your name:

```
<html>

<head>
<title>Antivirus Program</title>
</head>

<body>
<h2>Checking for Viruses</h2>
<p>A computer can be checked for viruses using an antivirus program. An antivirus program is a utility that scans a hard disk for viruses. If a virus is located, it will be removed by the antivirus program.</p>
<h2>Example Virus Threats</h2>
<table border="2" width="300" cellpadding="5">
<th>Virus</th>
<th>Threat</th>
<tr><td>BackDoor-AWQ.e</td>
<td>Low</td></tr>
```

```
<tr><td>MultiDropper-RV</td>
<td>Low</td></tr>
<tr><td>Spy-Agent.cm</td>
<td>Medium</td></tr>
</table>
<h5>Report by: Name</h5>
</body>

</html>
```

② SAVE THE DOCUMENT

a. Save the document in the same folder as computer_viruses.html and name it: antivirus.html

b. In Internet Explorer, open antivirus.html in a browser. The tags are interpreted and the HTML document appears in the browser:

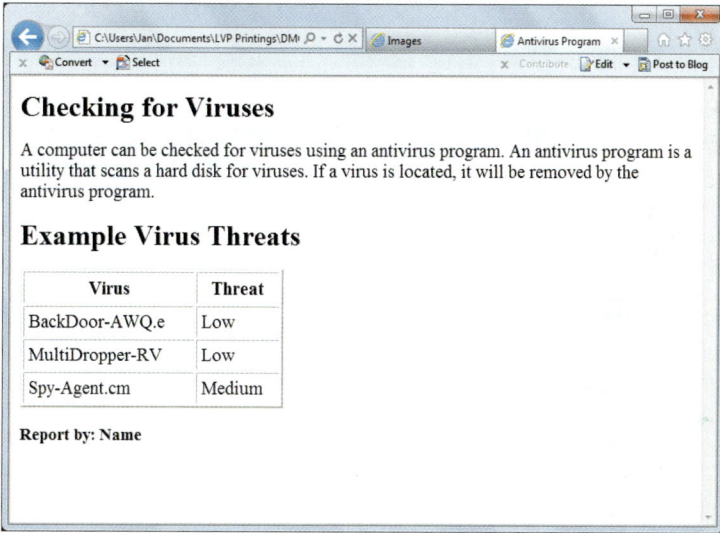

c. If necessary, make corrections to the HTML document.
d. From Notepad, print a copy of the antivirus.html document.

③ OPEN COMPUTER_VIRUSES.HTML IN NOTEPAD

a. Select File → Open. A dialog box is displayed.
b. Click [Text Documents (*.txt)] and select All Files.
c. Navigate to computer_viruses.html and click: computer_viruses.html.
d. Select Open. The dialog box is removed and the computer_viruses.html document is displayed in the Notepad window.

④ ADD A HYPERLINK

a. Near the bottom of the body contents, place the insertion point right after the space after the text install an.
b. Type the tag:

    `<a href="antivirus.html">`

c. Place the insertion point to the right of the text "antivirus program" and to the left of </li> and then add the tag </a>

   Check — The line should look like:
   install an <a href="antivirus.html">antivirus program</a></li>

d. Save the modified computer_viruses.html document.

⑤ TEST THE HYPERLINK
a. In Internet Explorer, open computer_viruses.html.
b. Click <u>antivirus program</u>. The antivirus.html document is displayed in the browser.

⑥ PRINT THE HTML DOCUMENT
a. Switch back to Notepad.
b. If necessary, make corrections to the HTML document.
c. From Notepad, print a copy of the computer_viruses.html document.

Adding Images

Images can be used to enhance the display of an HTML document. The <img src="file name"> tag inserts an image where file name is the file name of the graphic. Image files added to an HTML document should be GIF, JPG, or PNG format. The image tag does not need to be paired.

Attributes of the <img> tag include:

- border=*"value"* specifies the size of the border around the image where value is a number in pixels
- alt=*"value"* specifies alternate text for the graphic where value is the alternative text
- height=*"value"* specifies the height of the image in pixels
- width=*"value"* specifies the width of the image in pixels

> **GIF, JPG, PNG**
>
> GIF (Graphics Interchange Format) format is limited to 256 colors and best used for clip art or logos. JPG (Joint Photographic Experts Group) format supports millions of colors and is best used for photographs. PNG (Portable Network Graphic) format is a newer format only supported by recent browser versions. Graphic file formats are discussed in Chapter 5.

Using Comments

Comments are text used to explain and clarify HTML to the reader of an HTML document. They do not appear in a browser window. Comments start with an angle bracket, followed by an exclamation mark and two hyphens. At the end of the comment are two more hyphens and an ending bracket. For example:

<!--draws a centered horizontal line across 75% of the screen-->
<hr width="75%">

> **Accessibility**
>
> In response to the Americans with Disabilities Act (ADA), enacted in 1990, the W3C has developed guidelines called the Web Accessibility Initiative (WAI). These guidelines call for alternative text to be provided for any content on a web page that is not text.

Style Sheets

A *style sheet* is used to define the type, paragraph, and page formats for an HTML document. Style sheets give HTML documents a consistent appearance because they override the browser settings that interpret how tags are displayed.

embedded style sheet

A style sheet can be embedded or linked. An *embedded style sheet* is defined within <style type="text/css"> and </style> tags in the head section of the HTML document. A linked style sheet is a separate file that contains style rules only. *Linked style sheets* are saved with a .css extension and applied using a <link rel="stylesheet" href"style.css" type="text/css"> tag, where style.css is the name of the style sheet.

linked style sheet

rule
selector
declarations

Style sheets can include rules and classes. A *rule* modifies an HTML element and is comprised of a selector and declarations. The *selector* is the HTML element being redefined and the *declarations* are the formats to be applied. Rules are defined using the HTML element name. For example:

> p {font-family: Georgia, "Times New Roman", Times, serif;
> font-size: 14px;}

Style Sheet Rule

The rule above will automatically display paragraphs in 14 px Georgia. The font-family property can also be specified as generic font, such as serif, sans serif, or monospace and the font-size may be defined in points, pixels, inches, or centimeters (pt, px, in, cm).

> **Font-Family Declarations**
>
> Font-family declarations indicate the first font that a browser should display, and then alternate fonts if the first is not installed on the user's computer.

A *class* is a set of declarations that can be applied to different tags. Class names begin with a dot (.). For example:

> .para_with_space {
> font-family: Georgia, "Times New Roman", Times, serif;
> font-size: 14 px;
> line-height: 28 px;
> }

Style Sheet Class

TIP Classes override rules.

The class above can be applied to individual paragraphs to format the paragraph in 14 px Georgia with a line-height of 28 px. For example:

> <p class="para_with_space">Spyware is software that collects information without the user's knowledge. The information is usually for advertising purposes.</p>

Adding Color

hexadecimal

Text and background colors are specified using hexadecimal numbers. *Hexadecimal* is a base-16 numbering system that consists of the numbers 0 through 9 and the letters A through F. Color constants and corresponding hexadecimal values include:

Black	(#000000)	Silver	(#C0C0C0)
Gray	(#808080)	White	(#FFFFFF)
Maroon	(#800000)	Red	(#FF0000)

Purple	(#800080)	Fuchsia	(#FF00FF)
Green	(#008000)	Lime	(#00FF00)
Olive	(#808000)	Yellow	(#FFFF00)
Navy	(#000080)	Blue	(#0000FF)
Teal	(#008080)	Aqua	(#00FFFF)

To change the background and text color of an HTML document, the HTML body element is modified in a style sheet rule:

body {background-color : #000000; color : #FFFFFF}

To change the text color of a selected tag, the appropriate HTML element is modified in a style sheet rule. For example:

h1 {color : #0000FF}

Changing Alignment

HTML content is left aligned by default. To change the *alignment* of an entire HTML document, the HTML body element is modified in a style sheet rule:

body {text-align : center}

To change the alignment of certain parts of a document, modify the appropriate HTML element. For example, the Heading 1 tag is modified in a style sheet rule to be right aligned:

h1 {text-align : right}

Practice: Computer Viruses – part 4 of 5

Internet Explorer and Notepad should already be started with computer_viruses.html displayed in Notepad.

① MODIFY COMPUTER_VIRUSES.HTML TO INCLUDE AN EMBEDDED STYLE SHEET

Modify the head section of computer_viruses.html as shown:

```
<html>

<head>
<title>Computer Viruses</title>
<!--apply style sheet rules to the document-->
<style type="text/css">
h1 {color: #FF0000; text-align: center}
p {font-family: Georgia, "Times New Roman", Times, serif;
font-size: 16 px; line-height: 18 px}
ul {font-family: Georgia, "Times New Roman", Times, serif;
font-size: 14 px; line-height: 18 px}
ol {font-family: Georgia, "Times New Roman", Times, serif;
font-size: 14 px; line-height: 18 px}
h4 {text-align:right}
</style>
</head>
```

② ADD AN IMAGE

a. Add the COMPUTER.gif image, which is a data file for this text, to the web page by modifying the line of text before the numbered list as shown:

   `<p><img src="COMPUTER.gif" height="150", width="100">In order to protect against viruses:</p>`

b. Save the modified computer_viruses.html.

③ APPLY THE EMBEDDED STYLE SHEET

In Internet Explorer, open computer_viruses.html. The style sheet rules are applied:

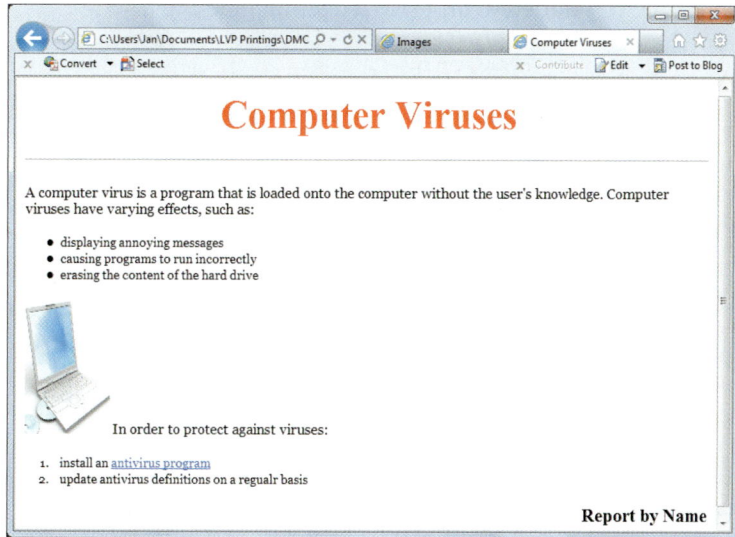

④ CREATE A LINKED STYLE SHEET

a. Switch to Notepad and select File → New.

b. Type the style sheet rules as shown:

   h2 {color: #FF0000}
   h5 {text-align: right}

c. Select File → Save. A dialog box is displayed:

d. Use the Save in list and the contents box below it to select the same folder location as the antivirus.html document.

e. In the Save as type list, select Text Documents (*.txt) if it is not already selected.

f. In the File name box, replace the existing text with: antivirus.css.

g. Select Save.

⑤ LINK THE EXTERNAL STYLE SHEET AND ADD AN IMAGE

a. In Notepad, open antivirus.html.

b. In the line after the <title> tag in the head section, add the following tag:

   `<link rel="stylesheet" href="antivirus.css" type="text/css">`

c. Save the modified document.

d. Switch to Internet Explorer and click the antivirus program link. The style sheet rules are applied.

Chapter 2 HTML   57

JavaScript

Scripts are used to add dynamic content to an HTML document and consist of a list of commands that execute without user interaction. Scripts are written in a scripting language, such as JavaScript. *JavaScript* is an open scripting language that is interpreted by a browser's built-in JavaScript engine.

The code for a JavaScript is written in an HTML document between <script> and </script> tags or as a separate JavaScript file. Displaying a message in an alert dialog box is one form of dynamic content that can be added to an HTML document using a script:

```
<head>
<title>JavaScript Greeting</title>
<script type="text/javascript">
// Display a greeting
alert("Hello World!");
</script>
</head>
```

> **Java vs. JavaScript**
> JavaScript is similar to the Java programming language, but it is a separate language.

> **TIP** JavaScript is case sensitive.

- The type attribute in the script tag specifies which **scripting language** is used to define the script.
- // is used to add a single line **comment** that explains the script.
- The **alert function** displays an alert dialog box. The text to be displayed in the dialog box is enclosed in quotation marks.
- A **semicolon** is used to end each JavaScript statement.

> **Blocked Content**
> When you open a web page that contains JavaScript, you may be prompted to Allow blocked content.

The script above is interpreted when the HTML document is loaded:

Practice: Computer Viruses – part 5 of 5

Internet Explorer and Notepad should already be started.

① ADD JAVASCRIPT

a. In Notepad, open computer_viruses.html.

b. Modify the head section of computer_viruses.html to include a script that displays a message in the status bar and an alert dialog box:

```
<html>

<head>
<title>Computer Viruses</title>
<script type="text/javascript">
// Display a greeting
```

```
alert("Welcome!");
</script>
<!--apply style sheet rules to the document-->
<style type="text/css">
…
</head>
```

   c. Save the modified computer_viruses.html.

② TEST THE MODIFIED DOCUMENT

In Internet Explorer, open computer_viruses.html. The document is interpreted sequentially. Therefore, the alert dialog box is displayed with the greeting first. Click OK. The rest of the HTML document is then interpreted and displayed in the browser window.

Java Applets

A *Java applet* is a small Java application that is embedded in an HTML document and run in a browser window. When a browser interprets a document that contains a Java applet, the program files are downloaded onto the user's machine and then the browser's Java interpreter runs the applet. Java applets are well suited for the Web because they are able to run on different hardware and across different platforms. Applets are secure because they do not have the ability to read or write to files on a user's computer.

Numerous applets can be downloaded from the Web and embedded in an HTML document to add dynamic content. Applets take various forms, such as animated banners, stock ticker tapes, photo cubes, and animated video clips. Original applets can also be created.

A Java applet is embedded in an HTML document within the <applet> and </applet> tags. The tags can surround a text message that will be displayed if the applet cannot run in the browser:

```
<html>

<head>
<title>Embedding an Applet</title>
</head>

<body>
<applet code = "FirstApplet.class" width = "300" height = "60">
<param name="image" value="scenery.gif">
You are unable to view the applet.
</applet>
</body>
```

> **<object> Tag**
>
> The <object> tag allows for multimedia resources, such as video and audio, to be embedded in an HTML document. When interpreting an <object> tag, the browser determines if another application, such as the Windows Media Player, is needed to display the object.
>
> The <object> tag can also be used to embed a media player console in an HTML document using Microsoft ActiveX controls.

The <applet> tag has three required attributes:

- code=*"value"* specifies the name of the applets class to run
- width=*"value"* specifies the width for the applet display in pixels
- height=*"value"* specifies the height for the applet display in pixels

Applets may also require parameters. *Parameters* allow users to specify custom values to use in a Java applet. For example, the <param> tag above specifies a specific image file, scenery.gif, to use in the applet.

Practice: Java Applet

Internet Explorer and Notepad should already be started.

① CREATE A NEW HTML DOCUMENT

a. In Notepad, select File → New.

b. Type the following HTML document as shown:

```
<html>

<head>
<title>Java Applet Example</title>
</head>

<body>
</body>

</html>
```

c. An applet available at the Sun Microsystems website, http://java.sun.com, is an analog clock. Modify the body section of the HTML document as follows, which embeds the JavaClock.class applet data file:

```
<applet code="JavaClock.class" width="150" height="150">
<param name="bgcolor" value="FFFFFF">
<param name="border" value="5">
<param name="ccolor" value="DDDDDD">
<param name="cfont" value="TimesRoman|BOLD|18">
<param name="delay" value="100">
<param name="hhcolor" value="0000FF">
<param name="link" value="http://java.sun.com/">
<param name="mhcolor" value="00FF00">
<param name="ncolor" value="000000">
<param name="nradius" value="80">
<param name="shcolor" value="FF0000">
You are unable to view the applet.
</applet>
```

② SAVE THE HTML DOCUMENT

a. Save the document naming it clock.html in the classes folder in the CLOCK website included in the data files for this text.

b. Print a copy of the clock.html document.

c. Quit Notepad.

③ **VIEW THE APPLET**

a. In Internet Explorer, open clock.html. If displayed, click the **Allow Blocked Content** button. The Java applet is displayed:

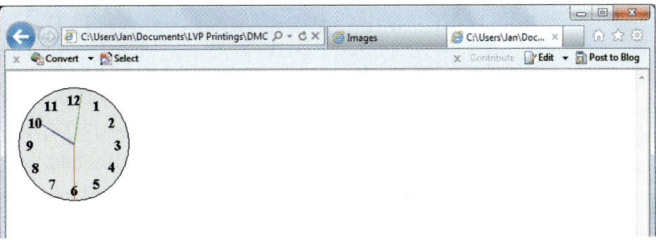

b. Close the browser window.
c. Quit Internet Explorer.

Chapter Summary

Having a basic understanding of HTML is helpful prior to learning Dreamweaver. Most web pages are created using HTML (HyperText Markup Language) and other code. HTML is a markup language that is well suited for the Web because it supports hypertext and multimedia. HTML (HyperText Markup Language) is a set of special codes, called tags, that are used to "mark up" plain text so that a browser application, such as Internet Explorer, knows how to display the text in a browser window. Text that has been marked up with HTML is called an HTML document.

A tag is comprised of an element inside angle brackets (<>). Tags affect the text they surround, and are usually paired to indicate the start and end of an instruction. A slash (/) before the element indicates the end of an instruction, such as </body>. The html, head, title, and body tags are called document tags. Other tags introduced in this chapter include:

- the paragraph tag, <p>
- the break tag,
- the heading tags, <h1> through <h6>
- the horizontal rule tag, <hr>
- the unordered list tag, <ul>
- the ordered list tag, <ol>
- the table tag, <table>
- the image tag, <img>
- the anchor tag, <a>
- the comment tag, <!--comment-->
- the style sheet tag, <style>

TIP Refer to Appendix D for a list of HTML tags and attributes.

Tags may also contain attributes. An attribute is placed in the start tag and set to a value that modifies the element.

HTML documents are plain text files and can be created using any text editor such as Notepad or a word processor. Both Notepad and Internet Explorer can be running at the same time when developing an HTML document, and the Windows taskbar is used to switch between the applications. The HTML associated with the document in a browser window can be viewed in Internet Explorer. HTML documents that are posted to the Internet are the designer's intellectual property and are protected by copyright. This applies even if a copyright notation (©) is not included on the page.

Scripts are used to add dynamic content to an HTML document. Scripts are written in a scripting language, such as JavaScript. A Java applet is a small Java application that is embedded in an HTML document and run in a browser window.

Vocabulary

Alignment Position of text in a paragraph relative to the sides of the page: left, right, centered, and justified.

Attribute Used to modify an element in an HTML tag.

Bulleted list A list that is used when each item is equally important.

Class A set of declarations that can be applied to different tags.

Comment Text used to explain and clarify HTML for a reader.

Declarations The formats to be applied in a style sheet rule.

Document tags The html, head, title, and body tags.

Element The part of an HTML tag placed inside angle brackets (<>). For example, <title> is called the title tag, where title is the element.

Embedded style sheet A style sheet defined with <style> and </style> tags in the head section of an HTML document.

Free-form Spaces and blank lines generally have no effect on how the document is interpreted. The format of an HTML document.

Hexadecimal A base-16 numbering system that consists of the numbers 0 through 9 and the letters A through F.

HTML (HyperText Markup Language) A set of tags used to "mark up" plain text so that a browser application knows how to display the text.

Hyperlink Text that can be clicked to display another HTML document. Also called a link.

Hypertext A database system where objects, such as text and images, can be linked.

Java applet A small Java application that is embedded in an HTML document and run in a browser window.

JavaScript An open scripting language that is interpreted by a browser's built-in JavaScript engine.

Link *See* Hyperlink.

Linked style sheet A style sheet saved as a separate file with a .css extension and applied using a <link> tag.

Multimedia Images, video, audio, and Java applets embedded in an HTML document.

Numbered list A list that is used to show a priority of importance.

Ordered list *See* Numbered list.

Parameter Specifies custom values to use in a Java applet.

Rule A line in a browser window for dividing content.

Scripts Used to add dynamic content to an HTML document. Scripts are written in a scripting language, such as JavaScript.

Selector The HTML element being redefined in a style sheet rule.

Style sheet Used to define the type, paragraph, and page formats for an HTML document.

Table Arranges data in an HTML document.

Tag Comprised of an element inside angle brackets that is used to "mark up" plain text so that a browser application knows how to display the text.

Unordered list *See* Bulleted list.

Visited hyperlink A link that has been clicked. Visited hyperlinks are displayed in purple underlined text.

Web Tool used to search and access information available on the Internet.

Web browser application Provides a graphic interface to present information in the form of a website.

Website A series of related web pages.

HTML Tags

`<a>` The anchor tag. Links text to another HTML document. Attributes include href.

`<applet>` The applet tag. Embeds an applet in an HTML document. Attributes include code, width, and height.

`<body>` The body tag. Defines the body section, which contains the document's content.

`<br>` The break tag. Moves a line of text within a paragraph to the next line.

`<!--comment-->` A comment tag. Explains and clarifies HTML to the reader.

`<h1>` through `<h6>` The heading tags. Emphasizes text.

`<head>` The head tag. Defines the section that indicates information about the document, including its title.

`<hr>` The horizontal rule tag. Displays a line in the browser window. Attributes include width, align, and size.

`<html>` The HTML tag. Indicates that the file contains HTML.

`<img>` The image tag. Inserts an image. Attributes include border, alt, height, and width.

`<li>` The list item tag. Defines the start and end of an item.

`<link>` The link tag. Links a style sheet.

`<ol>` The ordered list tag. Defines the start and end of a numbered list.

`<p>` The paragraph tag. Formats the content.

`<script>` The script tag. Defines a script.

`<style>` The style sheet tag. Embeds a style sheet.

`<table>` The table tag. Creates a table. Attributes include border, cellpadding, and width.

`<title>` The title tag. Displays the document title in the title bar of the browser window. Must be in the head section of an HTML document.

`<ul>` The unordered list tag. Defines the start and end of a bulleted list.

Notepad Commands

Exit command Quits Notepad. Found in the File menu.

New command Creates a new document. Found in the File menu.

Print command Prints a copy of the document. Found in the File menu.

Save command Displays a dialog box that is used to copy the document to a file. Found in the File menu.

Internet Explorer Commands and Buttons

Open command Displays a dialog box that is used to open an HTML document. Found in the File menu.

Refresh button Checks the HTML file for changes and then updates the page.

Source command Displays the HTML of the current document. Found in the View menu.

Review Questions

1. a) What is the most widely used Internet service?
   b) List two examples of web browsers.

2. a) What is used to create most web pages?
   b) Why is HTML well suited for the Web?
   c) Why is it important for the W3C to develop Web standards?

3. a) What is the element in the tag <html>?
   b) What does a slash (/) before the element indicate?

4. a) List the four document tags.
   b) Why is it important to properly structure an HTML document when HTML is a free-form language?

5. a) What is Notepad?
   b) List three guidelines for the file name of an HTML document.
   c) What does Notepad automatically add to a printed document?

6. List the steps required to open and view an HTML document in a web browser.

7. The HTML document below has five errors. What are they?

   ```
   <html>
   <head>
   <title>Operating Systems</title>
   </body>

   <body>
   <!--adds a horizontal rule>>
   <hr width is "50%">
   <p>Every computer must have an operating system. Types of operating systems include:
   </p>
   <ul>
   <li>Windows<li>
   <li>UNIX</li>
   <li>Linux</li>
   <li>OS/2</li>
   </ul>
   </head>
   </html>
   ```

8. What happens to any multiple spaces in the text between paragraph tags when a document is viewed in a browser?

9. a) What does a style sheet define?
   b) Why are style sheets used?
   c) What is the difference between an embedded and a linked style sheet?

10. What element is modified to change the background color or alignment of a web page?

11. a) Where are scripts placed in an HTML document?
    b) Write a script to display "Good-bye" in an alert dialog box.

12. a) What is a Java applet?
    b) How is a Java applet interpreted by a web browser?
    c) List two reasons why Java applets are well suited for the Web.

True/False

13. Determine if each of the following are true or false. If false, explain why.
    a) A website consists of a series of web pages.
    b) Hypertext is a database system.
    c) An HTML document must be published to a web server in order to be viewed in a web browser.
    d) The <p> tag moves a line of text within a paragraph to the next line.
    e) The <h1> tag is used to represent the most important information.
    f) A horizontal rule must have a width of 100%.
    g) Comments are displayed on a web page.
    h) Hyperlinks link the pages of a website.
    i) The anchor tag creates a hyperlink.
    j) A rule modifies an HTML element.
    k) Scripts must be placed in the head section of an HTML document.
    l) Java applets are interpreted on web servers.

Exercises

Exercise 1 — tourist_attractions.html

Research tourist attractions in a particular city by using the Internet, magazines, and books and then create an HTML document named tourist_attractions.html that lists tourist attractions for a particular city. The HTML document should include:

- a comment with your name
- an appropriate title
- the city name in Heading 1 format
- the text Tourist Attractions in Heading 2 format
- a horizontal rule
- at least five tourist attractions, each displayed in a bulleted list
- a style sheet with at least three rules
- a script

Exercise 2 — sports_report.html

Create an HTML document named sports_report.html that documents recent sports related news. The HTML document should include:

- a comment with your name
- appropriate titles formatted with heading tags
- a horizontal rule
- at least three news stories
- an image
- a style sheet with at least three rules
- a script

Exercise 3 — html_reference.html, html_links.html

Extend your HTML learning and share your knowledge by completing the following steps:

a) Create an "HTML Reference" document named html_reference.html that lists HTML tags, describes each tag, and provides corresponding examples. Research and include at least three HTML tags not covered in this chapter. The www.w3.org website has information about HTML tags. You can also refer to Appendix D at the end of the text.

b) Create a link to another HTML document named html_links.html that contains links to HTML reference websites. If necessary, include navigation instructions for the user to locate the appropriate HTML information.

Exercise 4 ───────────────────── passwords.html

Create an HTML document named passwords.html that discusses password protocol.

a) The passwords.html document should include:

- the title Computer Passwords by Name replacing Name with your name
- at least one horizontal rule
- the text About Computer Passwords in Heading 2 format
- your name in Heading 4 format
- the following text in the BODY of the document:

  It is important to keep your password a secret so that other individuals cannot gain unauthorized access to your computer. Do not share your password with anyone and if you receive an e-mail requesting your password, even if it looks like it is from a legitimate source, do not provide the requested information. When selecting a password, do not select a password that is easy to guess. Passwords should be changed frequently.

b) Find two websites that present guidelines for creating secure passwords. Add the information to the passwords.html document, and then include citations for the two sources.

Exercise 5 ───────────────── movie.html, characters.html, director.html, favorite_part.html

Create four HTML documents that detail a movie you have recently seen. Name the HTML documents movie.html, characters.html, director.html, and favorite_part.html and complete the following steps:

a) The movie.html document should include:

- the title Movie Report
- an appropriate background and text color
- the title of the movie in Heading 3 format
- at least one paragraph of at least 30 words summarizing the movie
- a list of hyperlinks below the summary paragraph that link to characters.html, director.html, and favorite_part.html
- your name in Heading 4 format

b) The characters.html document should include:

- the title Characters
- an appropriate background and text color
- the title of the movie in Heading 3 format
- the text Characters in Heading 2 format
- one paragraph for each important character in the movie—there should be at least 40 words total on this page
- a hyperlink with the label Home that links to movie.html
- your name in Heading 4 format

c) The director.html document should include:
- the title Director
- an appropriate background and text color
- the title of the movie in Heading 3 format
- the text Director in Heading 2 format
- one paragraph of at least 12 words that describe the director, including the date of birth, education, and other biographical information
- a hyperlink with the label Home that links to movie.html
- your name in Heading 4 format

d) The favorite_part.html document should include:
- the title Favorite Part
- an appropriate background and text color
- the title of the movie in Heading 3 format
- the text Favorite Part in Heading 2 format
- one paragraph of at least 20 words describing your favorite part of the movie
- a hyperlink with the label Home that links to movie.html
- your name in Heading 4 format

Exercise 6

Research the history of computers by using the Internet, magazines, and books and then create four linked HTML documents that outline key events in computer history by decade. Describe at least five key events for the 1970s, 1980s, 1990s, and 2000s. Use a style sheet to format the HTML documents.

Exercise 7

Research copyright laws and issues as they pertain to digital information. Present your research in the form of at least two linked HTML documents. Include a third linked HTML document that contains citations, one for each source. Use an established method to cite the sources, such as MLA or APA style.

Exercise 8 ———————————————————technology_report.html

Research a recently released software application or hardware device. Create an HTML document named technology_report.html that lists the product specifications and target market for the product. Include your opinion on whether you think the product will be successful or useful.

Exercise 9

Interview a local web developer or designer about the importance of mastering HTML before learning a web development software applications, such as Dreamweaver. Ask which other tools or knowledge they feel are important when designing websites. Document your interview. In small groups, share your interview documentation.

Exercise 10

Collaborate in small groups to create HTML documents that outline the History of the Internet. As a group, present your research to the class by having them view the documents while discussing the research in an oral presentation.

Exercise 11 — xhtml_reference.html

Extend your knowledge of web page languages by completing the following:

> Research XHTML and then create an "XHTML Reference" document named xhtml_reference.html that explains differences between XHTML and HTML. The document should also list XHTML tags, describe each tag, and provide corresponding examples.

Chapter 3
Introducing Dreamweaver

This chapter introduces Dreamweaver and discusses how to create a website and web page documents.

Dreamweaver

Dreamweaver is the web development application that is part of the Adobe Creative Suite 5 Web Premium. Dreamweaver is used to create websites. The Adobe Creative Suite 5 Web Premium also includes Fireworks and Flash, two applications that are introduced later in the text.

The windows, toolbars, and panel groups that are displayed when Dreamweaver is running are collectively called the *workspace*. In the Dreamweaver workspace below, an empty web page document is displayed and the Files panel displays the folder for the active website:

Starting Dreamweaver

To start Dreamweaver select Start → All Programs → Adobe Web Premium CS5 → Adobe Dreamweaver CS5, or double-click the Dreamweaver icon on the Desktop:

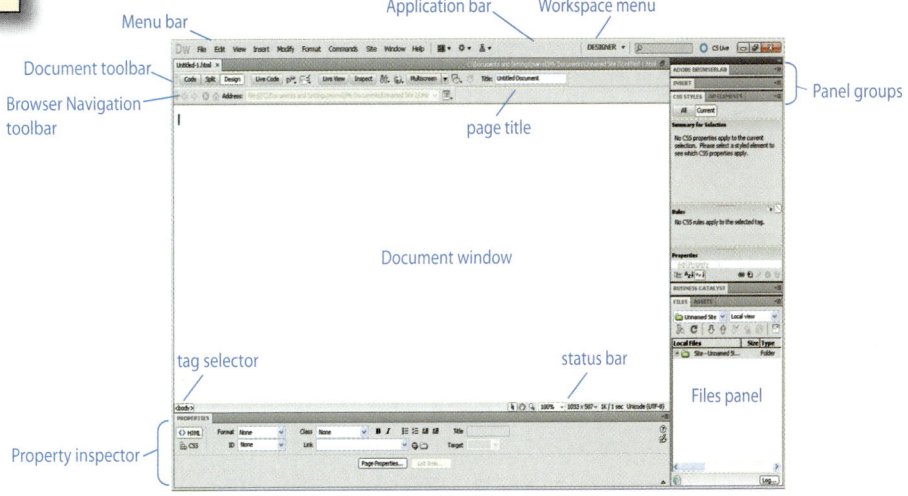

- The **Application bar** contains a workspace menu, menu bar, and other application controls.
- Change views and perform some common actions using the **Document toolbar**.
- Navigate pages using the **Browser Navigation toolbar**.
- The **page title** is the text that will be displayed in the title bar or tab of the browser window when a user views the web page.

- Click the Minimize button to reduce the Document window to a button in the Dreamweaver window.
- Click the Maximize button to expand the Document window in the Dreamweaver window.
- Click a Close button to remove the Document window or the Dreamweaver window.
- Click the **Workspace menu** to select a different workspace. The *Designer* workspace is the default.
- Files and folders associated with the active website are displayed in the **Files panel**.
- The **panel groups** contain tools which can be used in developing a website. The Window menu is used to open specific panels.
- The web page document is displayed in the **Document window**.
- Select a tag and its contents using the **tag selector**.
- Change properties of the selected text or object using the **Property inspector**.

TIP Press F4 to close panels and increase the work area.

Using Panel Groups

Click a panel group tab to expand the group:

Click in the right corner of a panel group title bar to display a menu of commands.

Defining a Website in Dreamweaver

In Dreamweaver, a website needs to be defined or set up before any web page documents are created. This process is called *site definition* or defining a site. Select Site → New Site to display the Site Setup dialog box. The process of defining a site includes specifying a folder name where the files will be stored. A Dreamweaver website typically has a local folder where the website files are stored. Within that folder, another folder should be created to store website images. When you are ready to post the files to the Web, you will also need to define a remote folder on a web server. This process will be discussed in Chapter 9.

When the site is defined, a folder is created with the specified name and the folder is displayed in the Files panel. Refer to the Practice below for the steps to define a site.

Practice: Computer Ergonomics – part 1 of 8

① START DREAMWEAVER

Ask your instructor for the appropriate steps to start Dreamweaver.

② DEFINE A NEW SITE

a. Select Site → New Site. The Site Setup dialog box is displayed.

b. Select Site if those options are not already displayed. The Site category of the Site Setup dialog box is the only one you need to fill out to begin working on your Dreamweaver site. This category lets you specify the local folder where you'll store all of your site files. The local folder can be on your local computer or on a network server.

c. In the **Site Name** box type: Computer Ergonomics:

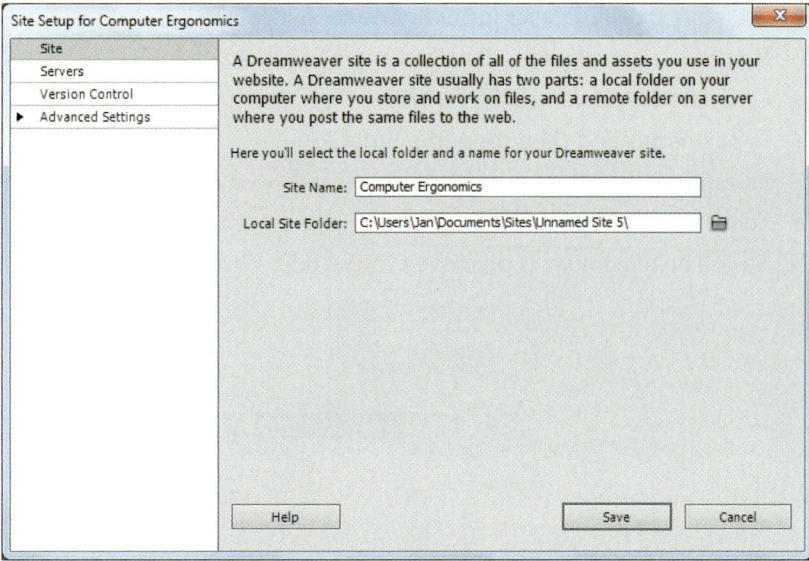

d. Click the **Local Site Folder** icon. A dialog box is displayed for browsing the local disk.

   1. Navigate to the appropriate location where a folder can be created to store the website files.
   2. Click the **Create New Folder** button:

   3. A new folder is created. Type Computer Ergonomics to replace the New Folder name and press Enter.
   4. Select **Open**. The Computer Ergonomics folder appears in the **Select** list.
   5. Select **Select** to choose the new folder as the website folder.

e. Click **Advanced Settings**:

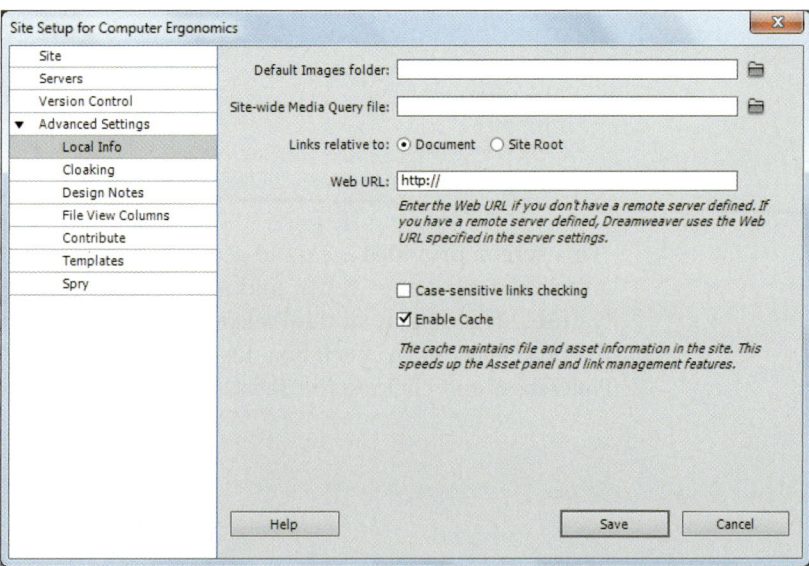

Chapter 3 Introducing Dreamweaver 73

1. Click the Default Images folder Browse for folder icon.
2. If necessary, navigate to the Computer Ergonomics folder.
3. Click the **Create New Folder** button.
4. Type images and then press the Enter key.
5. Select **Open**.
6. Select **Select** to choose the new folder as the website folder.

f. Select **Save**. The Site folder is displayed in the Files panel:

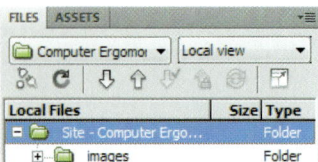

The Welcome Screen

The Dreamweaver Welcome screen is displayed when Dreamweaver is started or when no other documents are open:

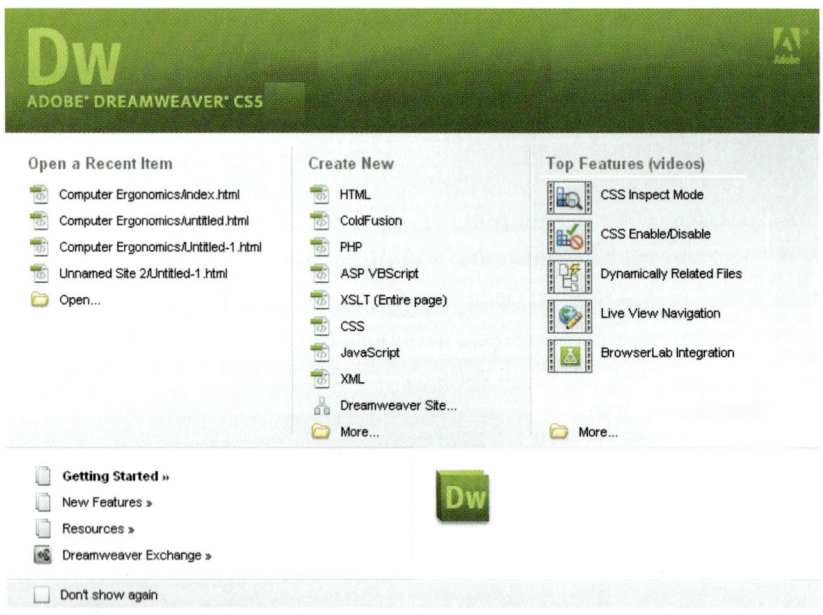

This screen provides access to recent pages, allows for easy creation of a variety of new page types, and a direct connection to help and tutorial features. The display of the Welcome Screen can be disabled by clicking the **Don't show again** check box. Re-enable the display by selecting **Edit → Preferences** and clicking the **Show Welcome Screen** check box.

Chapter 3 Introducing Dreamweaver

Creating a Web Page Document

A newly defined website does not contain any web page documents. To add a web page document to a website, a document is created and then saved to the website folder that was created during site definition. Select File → New to display a dialog box:

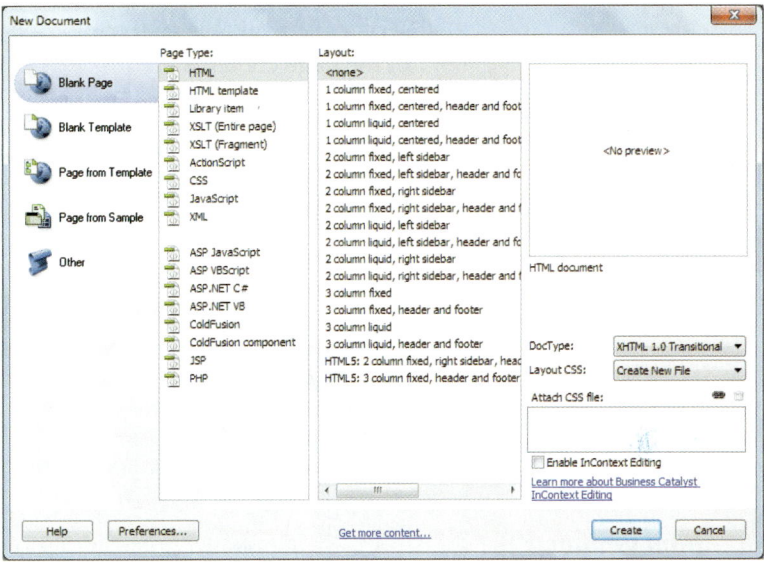

TIP HTML is used to create the web page structure, but was never intended to be used as a design medium. CSS avoids problems associated with HTML formatting and saves time. CSS is discussed in more detail in Chapter 6.

Dreamweaver provides several options for creating a new web page document. In this section, you will use one of the predesigned HTML page layouts to quickly create a web page. The predesigned HTML layouts use a Cascading Style Sheet (CSS) to format the page. A *cascading style sheet* defines the type, paragraph, and page formats for a web page document. A single style sheet can be applied to all the pages in a website to achieve a consistent look. The CSS predesigned or starter layouts are designed to comply with Web standards and to display similarly cross-platform in all major browsers. The predesigned CSS starter layouts provide two types of columns:

- *Fixed Column* width is specified in pixels. The column does not resize based on the size of the browser or the site visitor's text settings.

- *Liquid Column* width is specified as a percentage of the site visitor's browser width. The design adapts if the site visitor makes the browser wider or narrower, but does not change based on the site visitor's text settings.

After a **Page Type** and **Layout** are selected, click **Create** to display a new web page document in the Document window. You will also be prompted to save the CSS style sheet file in the website folder.

Chapter 3 Introducing Dreamweaver 75

Saving a Web Page

When a web page document is saved, it must be given a name. File names for web page documents can contain lowercase letters, numbers, and underscores (_). Do not use spaces or uppercase letters, and it is best to not start the file name with a number. These file name guidelines will ensure that the website can be viewed by most users once it is posted to a server and available on the Internet. A file name should also be descriptive of the page contents.

To save a web page document, select File → Save. The Save As dialog box is displayed the first time a web page document is saved:

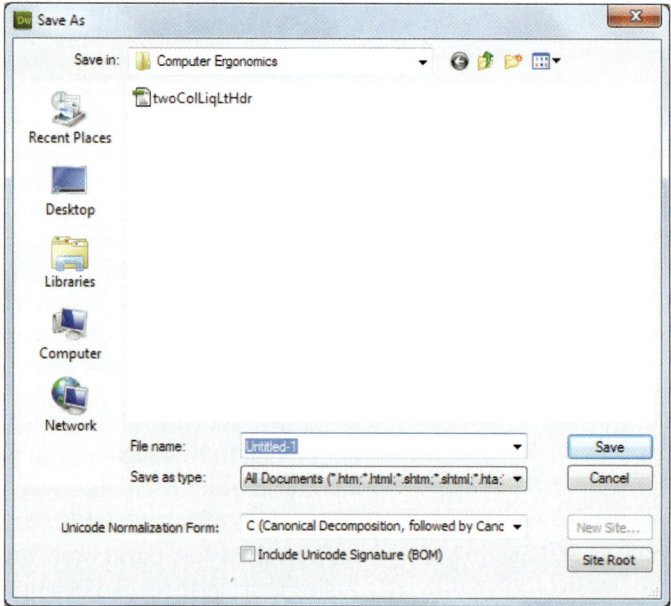

.html vs .htm

In Dreamweaver CS5, the default extension for new documents is .html. To change the default to .htm, click **Edit → Preferences** and then select **New Document**.

The Save in list and the contents box below it are used to navigate to the location where the file is to be saved. A web page document should be saved in the appropriate website folder. Type a descriptive file name in the File name box and select Save to save the document. The extension .html is automatically added to the file name.

home page

The *home page* of a website is the main page or starting point of the website. A web page document that is saved with the file name index.html is automatically designated by Dreamweaver as the website's home page. Most web servers recognize index.html as the home page as well.

The Page Title

The *page title* of a web page is the text displayed when the user adds the page to their Favorites list. It is also displayed in the browser window's title bar or tab when a user views the web page. To change the page title of a web page document, select Modify → Page Properties and then select Title/Encoding in the Category list of the dialog box. Type a title in the Title box and select OK.

TIP Unlike previous versions, Internet Explorer 9 does not display the page title in the title bar of the browser window. Instead it is displayed in the website tab.

An easier way to change the page title is to type the new title in the Title box in the Document toolbar and press Enter:

Title box

Viewing a Web Page Document

Design view

Code view

Split view

In Dreamweaver, web page documents are displayed in *Design view* by default, which displays the document similar to how it will appear in a browser window. Changing to *Code view* displays the code generated for the web page, which is useful for studying the HTML and for editing tags and code. A document can be displayed in *Split view*, which is a combination of Code and Design view. Use the buttons in the Document toolbar to change the view:

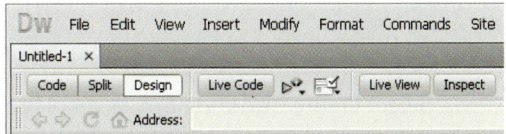

Multiple Browsers

Websites should be previewed in different browsers to detect display differences. Select File → Preview in Browser → Edit Browser List to add an installed browser to the Preview in Browser submenu.

As a web page document is developed, it should be previewed in a browser to see what it will look like to the user. In Dreamweaver, press the F12 key or select File → Preview in Browser and then select a browser from the submenu to preview the active web page document in a browser. A web page document cannot be modified in the browser window. Changes are made by switching back to Dreamweaver and modifying the document in the Document window. Press F12 in Dreamweaver to again view the document in a browser or click the browser's Refresh button.

Alternatively, click the *Live View* [Live View] button to see what your page looks like "live" without having to leave the Dreamweaver workspace. In Live view you will not be able to edit the web page in Design view but you can edit the code and then refresh the Live view.

Practice: Computer Ergonomics – part 2 of 8

① CREATE A NEW WEB PAGE DOCUMENT

Select File → New. A dialog box is displayed.

1. Select **Blank page**.

Chapter 3 Introducing Dreamweaver

2. In the Page Type list, select HTML and select 2 column fixed, left sidebar, header and footer in the Layout list:

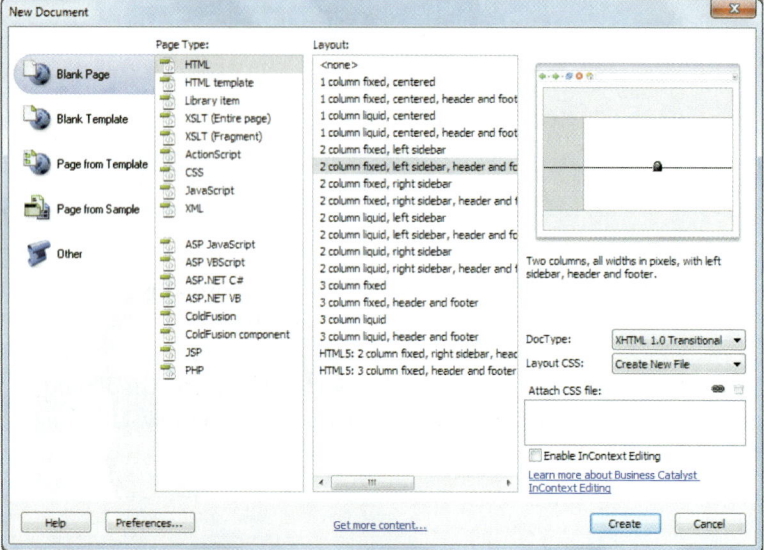

3. Select Create. A dialog box is displayed.
4. Select Save. The CSS file is saved in the website folder and the web page document is displayed.

② SAVE THE DOCUMENT AND DESIGNATE IT AS THE SITE'S HOME PAGE

Select File → Save. A dialog box is displayed.

1. Navigate to the Computer Ergonomics folder if it is not already displayed.
2. In the File name box, replace the existing text with: index.html.
3. Select Save. The file is saved in the Computer Ergonomics folder with the file name index.html. The web page document is listed in the Files panel. The CSS file is also displayed in the Fles panel:

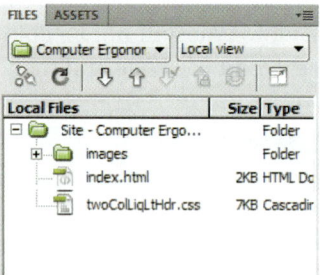

③ CHANGE THE PAGE TITLE AND PREVIEW THE DOCUMENT IN A BROWSER

a. In the Document toolbar, in the Title box, replace the existing text with: Computer Ergonomics and then press Enter:

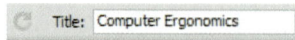

b. Press F12. A dialog box is displayed with the message "Save changes to index.html?"
c. Select Yes. The document is displayed in a browser window.
d. Click the Close button [x] to close the browser window.

④ **CHANGE VIEWS**

a. In the Document toolbar, click [Code]. The code for the web page document is displayed in the Document window. Scroll to the top of the code and locate the title tags and the page title:

    `<title>Computer Ergonomics</title>`

b. In the Document toolbar, click [Split]. The Document window displays both Code and Design view.

c. In the Document toolbar, click [Design]. The web page document is again displayed in Design view.

Changing Headings and Inserting Text

Dreamweaver's CSS layouts contain sample headings and body text. The placeholder headings and text will help you visualize the layout as you customize the web page. To change a heading, double-click the placeholder text to select it and then type replacement text:

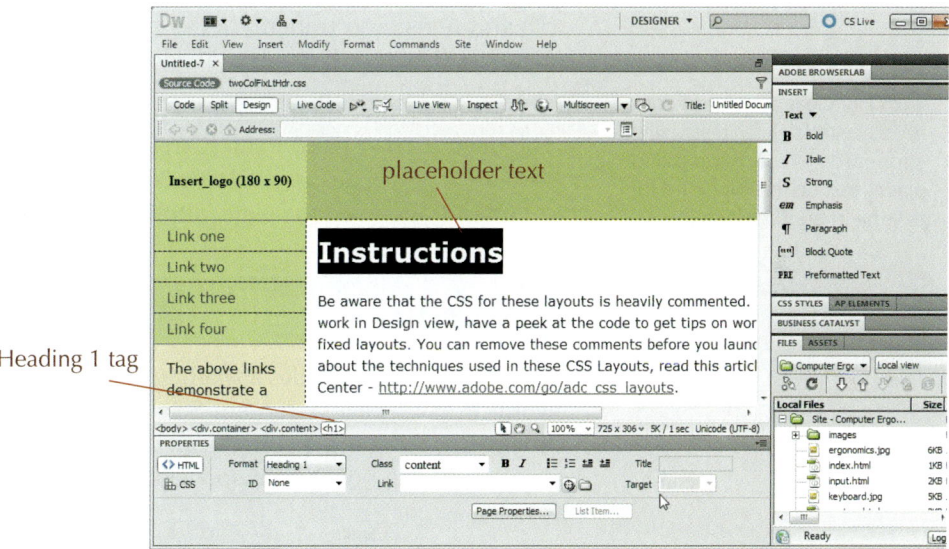

Notice that when the heading placeholder text is selected, the Heading 1 tag `<h1>` is also selected indicating that the Heading 1 format has been applied to the selected text.

Paragraph text is changed the same way as heading text. Select the placeholder text and then type replacement text. Alternatively, text can be copied (Ctrl+C) and pasted (Ctrl+V) from another document.

Paragraphs automatically have extra space below the paragraph. To have lines of text without extra space between them, insert a line break `<br>` by pressing Shift+Enter instead of pressing Enter. Another method of inserting a line break is to select **Line Break** from the Characters button menu in the **Text** category in the Insert panel:

Chapter 3 Introducing Dreamweaver 79

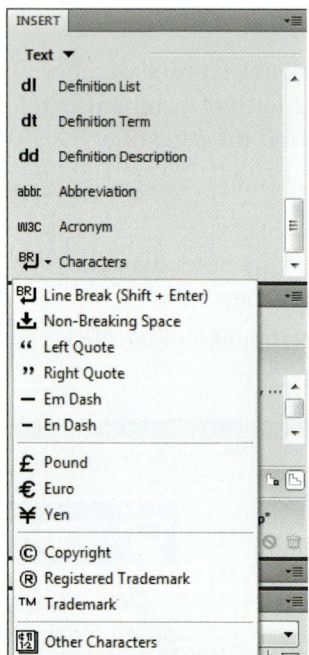

The Characters button menu includes other characters such as proper quotation marks, the em dash (—), currency symbols, and the copyright (©) and registered trademark (®) symbols. Click Other Characters in the menu to display a dialog box of additional special characters.

TIP The Clear command does not place the deleted text on the clipboard. The Cut command places text on the clipboard for pasting in another location.

The Edit menu contains commands that are helpful when editing text. The Undo (Ctrl+Z) and Redo (Ctrl+Y) commands are used to cancel or redo an action. The Cut (Ctrl+X), Copy (Ctrl+C), Paste (Ctrl+V), and Clear commands are used to delete, duplicate, and move content.

Checking Spelling

Dreamweaver includes a spelling checker that can help find misspelled words in a web page document. Select Commands → Check Spelling (Shift+F7) to start checking the spelling from the insertion point. A misspelled word causes a dialog box to be displayed:

The Importance of Error-Free Content

A web page may be the first impression a user has of a person or a business. Errors such as misspellings make that person or business seem unprofessional and less credible.

Chapter 3 Introducing Dreamweaver

TIP To check the spelling of just some of the text in a document, select the text and then start the spell check. Only the selected text will be checked.

Select the correct spelling in the Suggestions list and then select Change to change the word and continue checking the spelling. Select Ignore to leave the word unchanged, which is useful for proper names that are not in Dreamweaver's dictionary. Select Ignore All to skip over all occurrences of the word.

Practice: Computer Ergonomics – part 3 of 8

The index.html web page document in the Computer Ergonomics website should be displayed.

① **ADD CONTENT**
   a. Double-click the placeholder heading Instructions. Note the `<h1>` tag is selected.
   b. Type: Ergonomics.
   c. Triple-click to select the paragraph of text below the Ergonomics heading.
   d. Type the following text, but do NOT press the Enter key to end lines of text; allow the text to wrap:

   Ergonomics, also known as human engineering, is the science of designing working environments to be safe and efficient during interaction. The term "ergonomics" is derived from two Greek words: "ergon," meaning work, and "nomoi," meaning natural laws.

   e. Triple-click the placeholder heading Clearing Method.
   f. Type The Workplace.
   g. Triple-click to select the paragraph of text below the The Workplace heading.
   h. Type: Ergonomics is a key factor in an organization's health and safety program. Studies show that improper ergonomics can lead to repetitive stress injuries such as carpal tunnel syndrome.

② **EDIT CONTENT**
   a. Select the "The Workplace" heading by dragging or triple-clicking in the text.
   b. Select Edit → Cut. The text no longer appears in the document.
   c. Select Edit → Undo. The last action is cancelled and the heading is redisplayed.

③ **REMOVE CONTENT PLACEHOLDERS**
   a. Select the remaining placeholder text from *Logo replacement* to *...from the column*.
   b. Press the Delete key. The document should appear similar to:

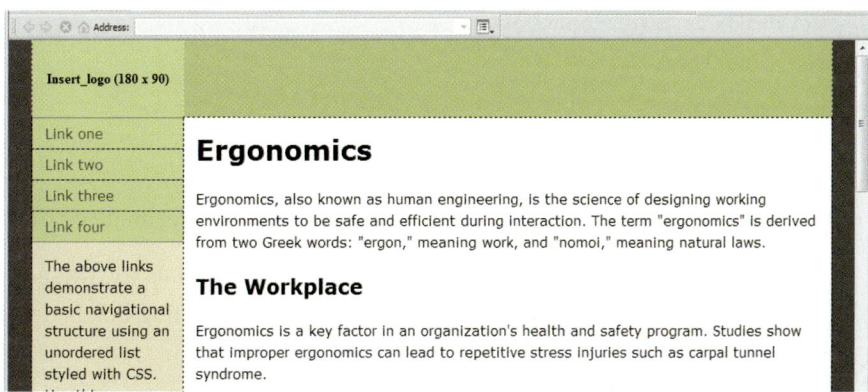

④ CHECK THE SPELLING

a. Place the insertion point to the left of the Ergonomics heading.
b. Select Commands ➔ Check Spelling. A dialog box is displayed. Dreamweaver finds that the word "ergon" is not in its dictionary.
   1. Since the word is correctly spelled as is, select Ignore.
   2. Correct any other spelling errors that are displayed.
   3. Select No when the message "Do you want to continue checking from the start of the document?" is displayed.

⑤ SAVE THE CHANGES AND VIEW THE DOCUMENT IN A BROWSER

a. Select File ➔ Save. The changes are saved.
b. Press F12. The web page is displayed in a browser.
c. Close the browser window.

Inserting Images

Many of the CSS starter layouts include an image placeholder. Select an image placeholder to display the image properties in the Property inspector:

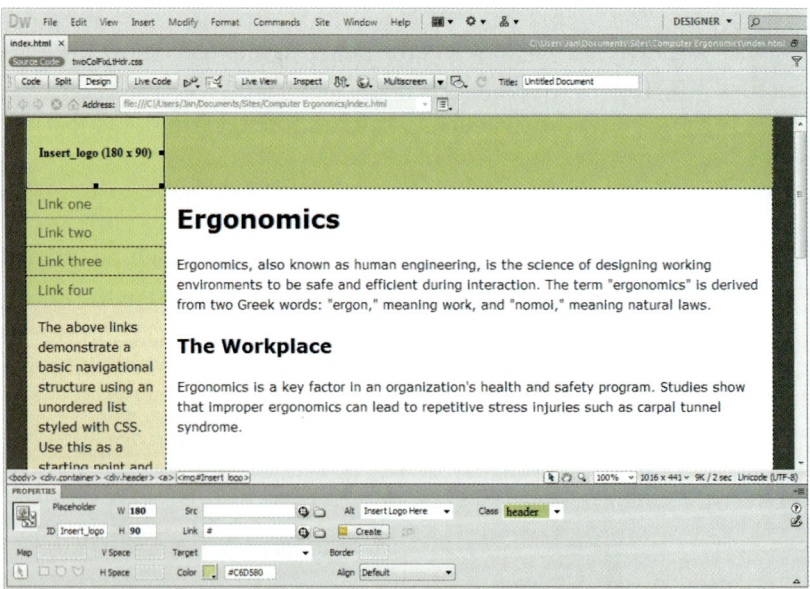

TIP If the Property inspector is not displayed, select Window ➔ Properties.

- W is the width of the image either in a percentage of the page width or in a number of pixels.
- H is the height of the image in a percentage or in pixels.

To replace the image placeholder with an image, double-click the placeholder. The Select Image Source dialog box is displayed:

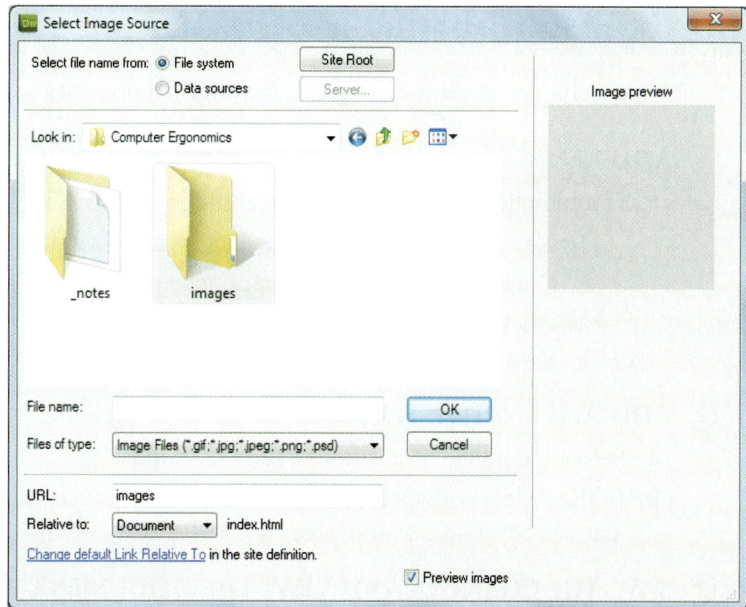

Navigate to the image and select it in the File list. The image size and the estimated download time is displayed below the image preview:

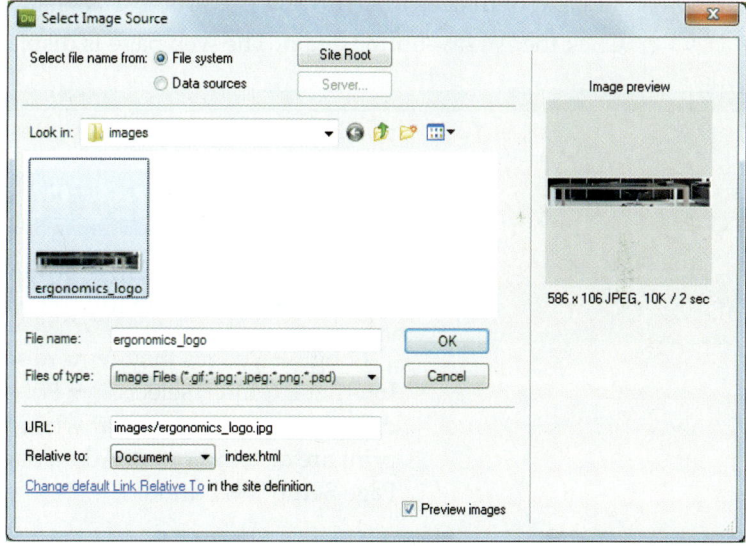

If the placeholder image is a different size that the inserted image, Dreamweaver will use the actual size of the image not the placeholder dimensions. Once an image is inserted, its properties can be adjusted using the Property inspector at the bottom of the Dreamweaver window.

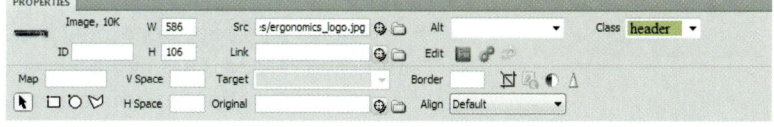

TIP Images and alternative text are discussed further in Chapter 5.

All images should include a brief description in the Alt (alternative text) box. This description is displayed if the image is not visible for users of certain mobile devices or screen readers.

Chapter 3 Introducing Dreamweaver 83

Practice: Computer Ergonomics – part 4 of 8

The index.html web page document in the Computer Ergonomics website should be displayed.

① ADD AN IMAGE

a. Double-click the Insert_logo placeholder. A dialog box is displayed.
   1. Navigate to ergonomics_logo.jpg, which is a data file for this text.
   2. Click to select the ergonomics_logo.jpg file and then select OK.
   3. Click Yes to copy the image file to the website's root folder and then click Save.

② ADD ALTERNATIVE TEXT

a. Select the image, if it is not already selected.
b. In the Property inspector, in the Alt box, select the text *Insert logo here* and then type ergonomics banner. and press the Enter key.

③ SAVE THE CHANGES AND VIEW THE DOCUMENT IN LIVE VIEW

a. Select File → Save. The changes are saved.
b. On the Document toolbar, click the [Live View] button. The web page is displayed in a simulated live view without having to switch to a browser. Note that you can't add text or images in Live View.
c. Click the [Live View] button again. The web page is displayed in Design view.

Printing a Web Page Document

A web page document is printed from a browser. In Internet Explorer, select ✱ → Print → Print to print one copy of a web page.

Long web pages may require several sheets of paper for a printout. In Internet Explorer, select ✱ → Print → Print preview to display the web page document as it will appear when printed. The number of pages that will print are also indicated. Add a page header and/or footer by clicking the Page Setup ✱ button.

The code for a web page document can be printed in Dreamweaver by selecting File → Print Code.

Closing a Web Page Document and Quitting Dreamweaver

When a web page document is not being worked on, it should be saved and then closed. *Closing a web page document* means that its window is removed from the Dreamweaver workspace and the file is no longer in the computer's memory. Select File → Close or click the Close button in the Document window to close a web page document.

Chapter 3 Introducing Dreamweaver

An indication that a web page has been modified but not saved, is an asterisk (*) in the file name tab:

index.html* ×

Attempting to close a web page that has been edited but not saved displays a reminder dialog box with the message "Save changes to file name?" Select Yes to save the changes in a file and remove the Document window. Select No to remove the Document window without saving changes. Select Cancel to leave the web page document open without saving changes.

When Dreamweaver is no longer needed, it should be quit properly. *Quitting Dreamweaver* means that its window is removed from the Desktop and the program is no longer in the computer's memory. Select File → Exit to quit Dreamweaver, or click the Close button in the upper-right corner of the Dreamweaver window to close the application window. Closing an application window quits the application.

Opening a Website for Editing

In the Files panel, Dreamweaver maintains a list of existing websites:

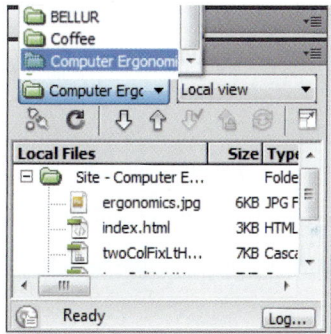

A website selected from this list will become the active website.

If a website is not listed, select → View → Refresh. If the site is still not displayed, select Site → Manage Sites and then click the New button. Type a site name in the Site Name box, then click the Local Site Folder and navigate to the location of the website folder. Click Select and then click Save. The Manage Sites dialog box is again displayed. Click Done to add the website name to the Site list in the Files panel.

Practice: Computer Ergonomics – part 5 of 8

The index.html web page document in the Computer Ergonomics website should be displayed.

① **PRINT THE CODE FOR THE INDEX.HTML WEB PAGE**
   a. Select File → Print Code. A dialog box is displayed.
   b. Select OK. The dialog box is removed and the code is printed.

Chapter 3 Introducing Dreamweaver   85

② PRINT THE WEB PAGE DOCUMENT FROM A BROWSER

a. Press F12. The document is displayed in a browser window.
b. Select ✽ → Print → Print → Print. The web page document is printed.
c. Close the browser window.

③ CLOSE THE WEB PAGE DOCUMENT AND QUIT DREAMWEAVER

a. Select File → Close. The Document window is removed.
b. Select File → Exit. The Dreamweaver application window is removed.

④ OPEN A SITE FOR EDITING

Start Dreamweaver. The Files panel may already show Computer Ergonomics as the working website. If not, in the Files panel click the arrow next to the Site list and select **Computer Ergonomics**. If Computer Ergonomics is not the active website nor in the Site list, the site needs to be opened for editing. Select ▦ → View → Refresh.

If the site is still not displayed, complete the following steps:

a. Select **Site** → **Manage Sites**. A dialog box is displayed.
   1. Click **New**. A Site Setup dialog box is displayed.
   2. In the **Site Name** box, type: Computer Ergonomics.
   3. Next to the **Local Site Folder** box, click the folder icon 📁. A dialog box is displayed.
      i. Navigate to the Computer Ergonomics website folder.
      ii. Click **Select**.
   4. Select **Save**. The Manage Sites dialog box is displayed with the Computer Ergonomics site selected.
   5. Select **Done**. The Computer Ergonomics website is the active website.

Opening and Displaying Web Page Documents

Opening a file transfers a copy of the file contents to the computer's memory and displays the file contents in an appropriate window. Double-click the file name in the Files panel to open a web page document:

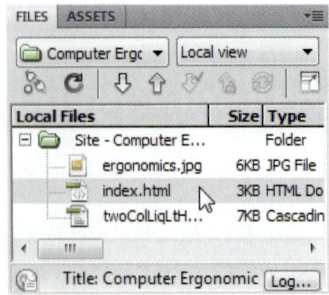

Web page documents may also be opened by selecting **File** → **Open**, which displays the Open dialog box. Navigating to the file, clicking the file name, and then selecting **Open** transfers a copy of the file to a Document window in Dreamweaver.

Several web page documents can be open at the same time, which makes it easy to cut and paste between documents or quickly view different documents. To view an open document that is not displayed, click the document's file name tab at the top of the Document window:

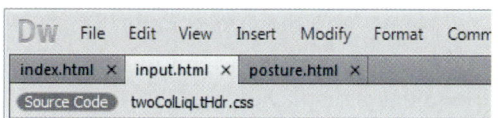

The file names of open documents

An open document can also be displayed by selecting the file name from the Window menu.

Practice: Computer Ergonomics – part 6 of 8

Dreamweaver should be started and the Computer Ergonomics website should be the working site.

① OPEN THE INDEX.HTML WEB PAGE DOCUMENT

In the Files panel, double-click the index.html file name. The index.html web page document is opened in a Document window.

② CREATE AND SAVE A NEW WEB PAGE DOCUMENT

a. Select File → New. A dialog box is displayed.

  1. Select Blank page.
  2. In the Page Type list, select HTML and select 2 column fixed, left sidebar, header and footer in the Layout list.
  3. Select Create.
  4. Select Save and then select Yes. A web page document is displayed in a Document window.

b. Select File → Save. A dialog box is displayed.

  1. Use the Save in list to navigate to the Computer Ergonomics folder if it is not already displayed.
  2. In the File name box, replace the existing text with: input.html
  3. Select Save. The file is saved and is now listed in the Files panel.

③ CREATE AND SAVE ANOTHER NEW WEB PAGE DOCUMENT

a. Select File → New. A dialog box is displayed.

  1. Select Blank page.
  2. In the Page Type list, select HTML and select 2 column fixed, left sidebar, header and footer in the Layout list.
  3. Select Create.
  4. Select Save and then select Yes.

b. Select File → Save. A dialog box is displayed.

  1. Use the Save in list to navigate to the Computer Ergonomics folder if it is not already displayed.
  2. In the File name box, replace the existing text with: posture.html
  3. Select Save. The file is saved and is now listed in the Files panel.

④ CHANGE THE PAGE TITLES AND DISPLAY DIFFERENT DOCUMENTS

a. At the top of the Document window, click the input.html tab. The web page document is displayed.
b. In the Document toolbar, in the Title box, replace the existing text with Input Device Ergonomics and then press Enter.
c. At the top of the Document window, click the posture.html tab The web page document is displayed.
d. Change the page title to Posture Ergonomics.

⑤ ADD CONTENT

a. In the posture.html page, double-click the placeholder heading Instructions.
b. Type: Your Posture.
c. Triple-click to select the paragraph of text below the Your Posture heading.
d. Type the following text, but do NOT press the Enter key to end lines of text; allow the text to wrap:

   When working at a computer workstation, your feet should be flat on the floor and your back should be straight. The keyboard should be at a height that allows for neutral hand and wrist positions.

e. Select the remaining content text from *Clearing Method... to ...from the column*.
f. Press the Delete key.
g. Save the modified posture.html.
h. Display the input.html web page document.
i. Double-click the placeholder heading Instructions.
j. Type: Workstation Input Devices.
k. Triple-click to select the paragraph of text below the Workstation Input Devices heading and type the following text, but do NOT press the Enter key to end lines of text; allow the text to wrap:

   A keyboard and a mouse are the two most frequently used input devices. Ergonomic aspects related to a keyboard include height, tilt, and keystroke pressure. Ergonomic aspects related to a mouse include shape, button activation pressure, and ease of movement.

l. Select the remaining content text from *Clearing Method... to ...from the column*.
m. Press the Delete key.
n. Save the modified input.html.

Creating Internal Hyperlinks

Websites are typically made up of more than one web page. Hyperlinks are used to link the pages of a web site. A hyperlink that displays a different web page document from the same website or folder is called an *internal hyperlink*.

To create an internal hyperlink, select the text for the hyperlink and then drag the Point to File icon ⊕ from the Property inspector to a web page document's file name in the Files panel:

TIP If multiple documents are open, select File → Close All to close all of the documents.

Chapter 3 Introducing Dreamweaver

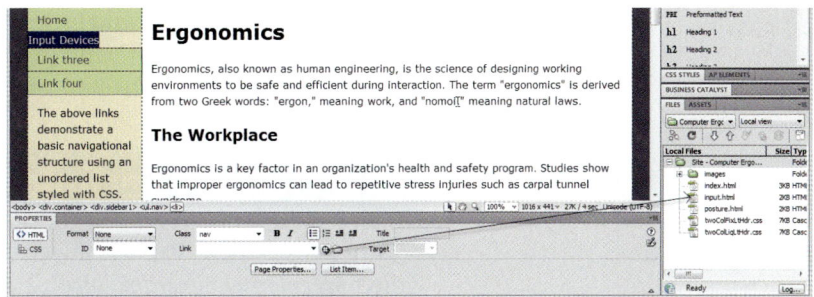

An internal hyperlink can also be created by selecting text and then clicking the Browse for File icon 📁 in the Property inspector:

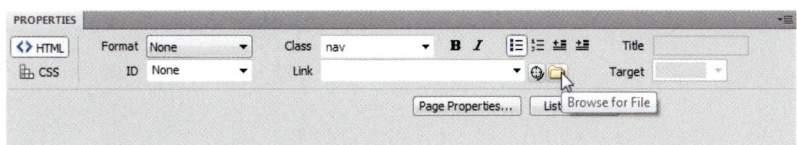

The Select File dialog box is displayed with the current website and its web page documents:

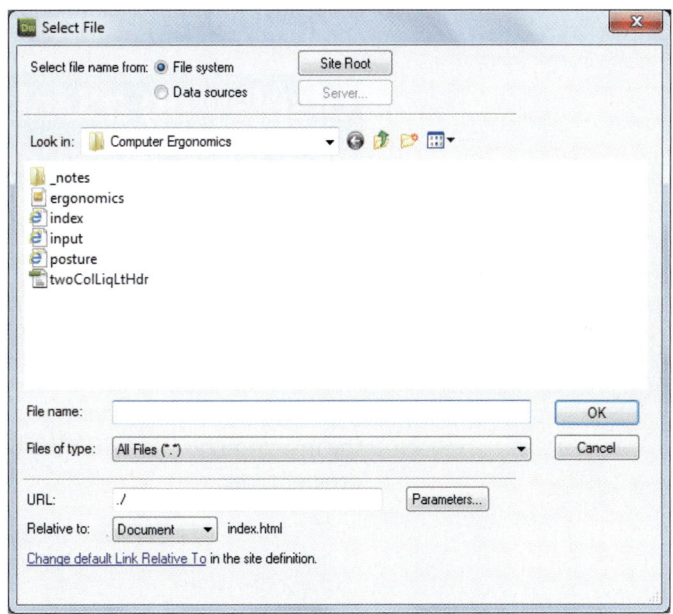

Click a file name and then OK to link the selected text to that web page document.

The Link list in the Property inspector displays the file name of the linked web page document when the insertion point is in a hyperlink:

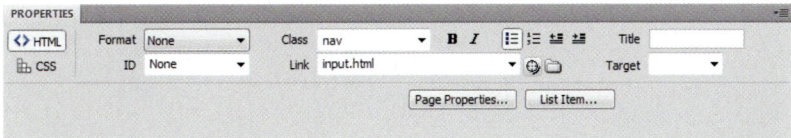

Internal hyperlinks should be tested in a browser window. If necessary, select the linked text in Dreamweaver and then select Modify → Change Link or Modify → Remove Link to change or remove a link.

External Hyperlinks

A hyperlink that displays a web page document in another website is called an *external hyperlink*, also called an *absolute hyperlink*. To create an external hyperlink, select the text for the link and then type the entire URL of the web page to be displayed in the Link box in the Property inspector. Be sure to include the protocol in the URL, such as http://. For example:

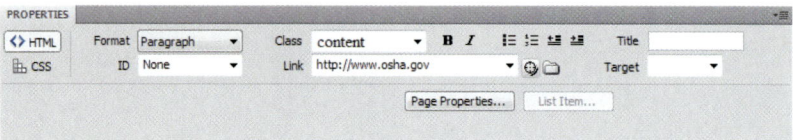

External hyperlinks should be tested in a browser window. If necessary, select the linked text in Dreamweaver and then select Modify → Change Link or Modify → Remove Link to change or remove a link.

Displaying a Linked Web Page in a New Window

External hyperlinks take the user away from the current website. In cases where the user should be able to easily get back to the original site, a new browser window should open when the link is clicked. Displaying a new window allows the user to browse the other website and then close the window to again display the original website.

To specify how the web page should be displayed in a browser, place the insertion point within the hyperlink text and click the Target list drop-down arrow:

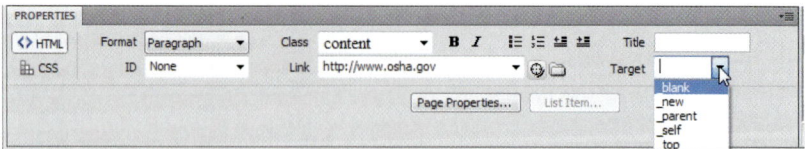

- Select _blank to create a link that displays a web page in a new browser window

- Select _self to change a link back to displaying the web page in the current browser window

Practice: Computer Ergonomics – part 7 of 8

Dreamweaver should be started and the Computer Ergonomics website should be the working site.

① ADD HYPERLINKS TO THE INDEX PAGE

   a. Display the index.html web page document.
   b. In the navigation bar, replace the text *Link one* with Home.
   c. In the navigation bar, replace the text *Link two* with Input Devices.
   d. Select the text Input Devices.
   e. In the Property inspector, next to the Link box, click the Browse for File icon 📁. A dialog box is displayed.
      1. Click the input.html file name.
      2. Select OK. The dialog box is removed.
   f. In the navigation bar, replace the text *Link three* with Posture.
   g. Select the text Posture.
   h. In the Property inspector, drag the Point to File icon to the posture.html file name in the Files panel.
   i. Click in the Input Devices hyperlink to place the insertion point. The Link box in the Property inspector displays input.html.
   j. Save the modified web page document.

② CREATE AN EXTERNAL HYPERLINK

   a. Display the index.html web page document.
   b. In the paragraph under The Workplace heading, select the word safety.
   c. In the Property inspector, in the Link box type http://www.osha.gov and press Enter. This is the URL for the United States Department of Labor website.
   d. In the Property inspector, in the Target box select _blank.
   e. Click anywhere to deselect the text. The linked text is now underlined to indicate it is a hyperlink.
   f. Save the modified web page document.

③ TEST THE HYPERLINKS

   a. Press F12. The index.html document is displayed in a browser window.
   b. Click the Input Devices hyperlink. The Input Device Ergonomics web page is displayed.
   c. Click ⬅. The index.html web page is again displayed.
   d. Click Posture. The Posture web page is displayed.
   e. Click ⬅. The index.html web page is again displayed.
   f. Click the safety hyperlink. A new browser window is opened and the United States Department of Labor web page is displayed in the new browser window.
   g. Close the browser window. The index.html web page is again displayed.

Using Help

Questions about Dreamweaver can be answered through Dreamweaver Help. Press the F1 key or select Help → Dreamweaver Help to display the Adobe Community Help window:

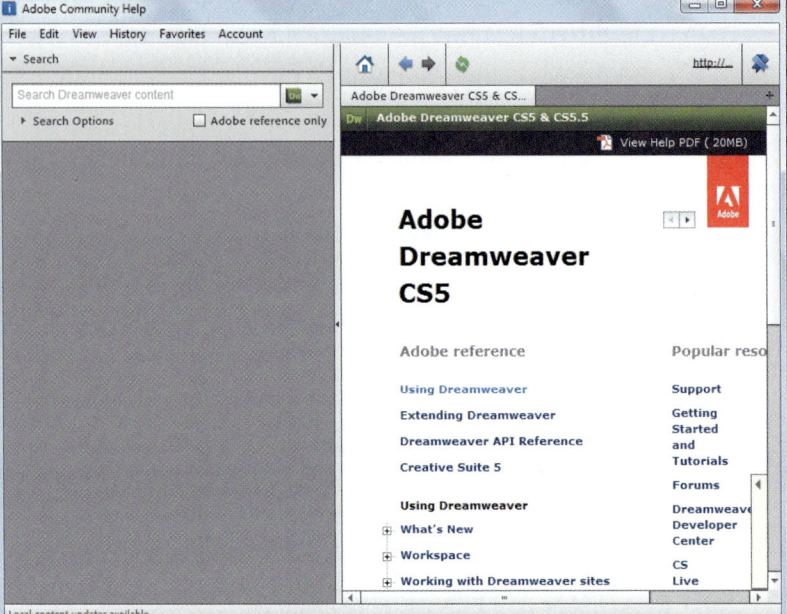

TIP Click the ? icon to access context-sensitive help which is available in dialog boxes, panels, and in the Property inspector.

The Adobe Community Help window includes:

- A search feature
- Adobe reference links
- Links to popular Adobe Dreamweaver resources including tutorials

Use the Home, Go Back, Go Forward, and Refresh toolbar buttons to navigate the Help window:

Practice: Computer Ergonomics – part 8 of 8

In this practice, you will complete the website.

① COMPLETE THE INDEX.HTML PAGE

a. Select the text *Link four* and then press the Delete key.

b. Triple click to select the footer placeholder text and then press the Delete key.

c. Delete any placeholder text in the sidebar area.

d. Save the modified web page document.

Check—the page should look similar to:

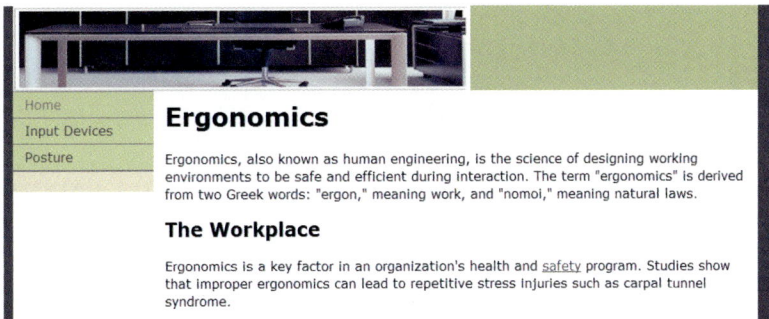

② COMPLETE THE INPUT.HTML PAGE

    a. Replace the *Link one* placeholder text with the text Home.
    b. Link the text *Home* to index.html.
    c. Replace the *Link two* placeholder text with the text Input Devices.
    d. Replace the *Link three* placeholder text with the text Posture.
    e. Link the text *Posture* to posture.html.
    f. Select the text *Link four* and then press the Delete key.
    g. Triple click to select the footer placeholder text and then press the Delete key.
    h. Delete any placeholder text in the sidebar area.
    i. In the image placeholder, insert the ergonomics_banner.jpg image.
    j. Save the modified web page document.

Check—the page should look similar to:

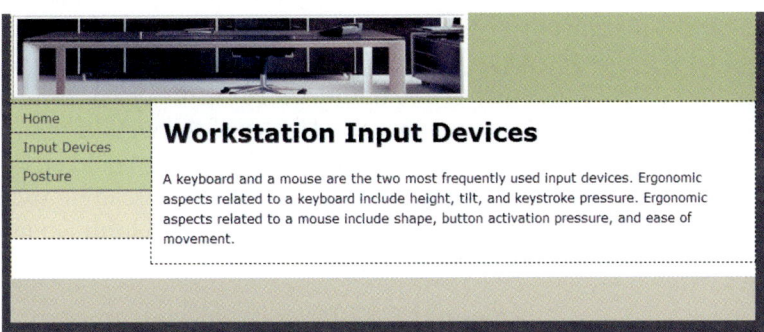

③ COMPLETE THE POSTURE.HTML PAGE

    a. Replace the *Link one* placeholder text with the text Home.
    b. Link the text *Home* to index.html.
    c. Replace the *Link two* placeholder text with the text Input Devices.
    d. Link the text *Input Devices* to input.html.
    e. Replace the *Link three* placeholder text with the text Posture.
    f. Select the text *Link four* and then press the Delete key.
    g. Triple click to select the footer placeholder text and then press the Delete key.
    h. Delete any placeholder text in the sidebar area.
    i. In the image placeholder, insert the ergonomics_banner.jpg image.
    j. Save the modified web page document.

Check—the page should look similar to:

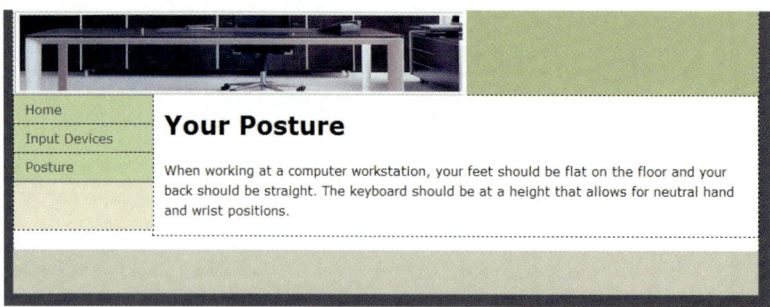

④ **PREVIEW THE SITE AND TEST THE HYPERLINKS**
   a. Display the index.html document and then press F12.
   b. Test the hyperlinks on all three pages.
   c. Print all three pages.
   d. Close the browser.

⑤ **QUIT DREAMWEAVER**
   Select File ➝ Exit.

Reflection

In this chapter, you learned to define a website and create web pages using a CSS starter layout. The CSS starter layout let you easily create web pages that contained a navigation bar, text, and an image. This was a quick way of illustrating the structure of a website and explaining how to link the pages in a site. However, the website you created in this chapter would need some design work before it could be published. As you work through the text, you will understand cascading style sheets and learn how to modify CSS styles, which will be helpful when using the CSS starter layouts to design websites.

When using a CSS starter layout, you can save time by adding elements common to all pages, such as the navigation structure, page banner, and footer text. This page can then be copied and used to develop the other pages in the site.

To copy a web page, right-click the filename in the Files panel and select **Edit** ➝ **Copy**. *Next, right-click the site root folder and select* **Edit** ➝ **Paste**. *Finally, rename the page by right-clicking the pasted file and selecting* **Edit** ➝ **Rename**.

Alternatively, you may want to refer to *Appendix C - Templates* to learn how to create a template and then use the template to quickly create the other pages in the website.

Chapter Summary

The Adobe Creative Suite CS5 Web Premium suite includes several applications including Dreamweaver CS5, Fireworks CS5, and Flash CS5. The Dreamweaver workspace contains features used in the development of web page documents.

In Dreamweaver, a website needs to be defined before creating any web page documents. Predesigned HTML pages with CSS layouts can be used to quickly create a web page document. A web page document named index.html is designated as the home page of the website.

In Dreamweaver, web page documents are displayed in Design view by default, and can also be displayed in Code view, Split view, or Live view. The code of a web page document can be printed from Dreamweaver. A browser is used to preview and print web page documents.

Dreamweaver's CSS starter layouts contain sample headings and body text. The placeholder headings and text will help you visualize the layout as you customize the web page.

A website selected from the Site list in the Files panel becomes the active website. If a website is not listed, the Manage Sites command in the Site menu is used to redefine the site.

Selected text can be designated an internal hyperlink, linking to another page in the site. External hyperlinks that link to a specific URL are created by typing the URL in the Link box in the Property inspector. Commands in the Modify menu are used to edit or remove the hyperlink.

Questions about Dreamweaver can be answered through Dreamweaver Help.

Vocabulary

Absolute hyperlink *See* external hyperlink.

Application bar The Dreamweaver application interface, which contains a workspace menu, menu bar, and other application controls.

Closing a web page document Removing a web page's Document window from the Dreamweaver workspace, which also removes the file from the computer's memory.

Code view Displays the code generated for the web page.

Content The information presented to the user in a web page.

Design view Displays the web page document similar to how it will appear in a browser window.

Document toolbar Area at the top of the Document window that contains buttons and menus for changing views and performing common actions.

Document window Area of the Dreamweaver workspace that contains the web page document.

Dreamweaver An application used to develop websites.

External hyperlink A hyperlink that displays a web page document from another website.

File name The name of the file that stores the web page document.

Files panel Area of the Dreamweaver workspace that displays files and folders associated with the active website.

Fixed width A width that is specified in pixels. A fixed width table will not change when a user resizes the browser window.

Home page The main page or starting point of the website.

Insert panel Area below the menu bar that contains buttons for adding objects to a web page document.

Internal hyperlink Text that can be clicked to display a different web page document in the browser window from the same website.

Menu bar Area at the top of the Dreamweaver workspace that displays the names of menus.

Opening a file The process of transferring a copy of the file contents to the computer's memory, which displays the file in an appropriate window.

Page title The text displayed when the user adds the page to their Favorites list. It is also displayed in the title bar or tab of some browser windows when a user views the web page.

Panel groups Tools used in developing a website.

Pixel A unit of measurement related to screen resolution.

Property inspector Area of the Dreamweaver workspace that is used to change properties of the selected text or object.

Quitting Dreamweaver The process of removing the Dreamweaver window from the Desktop, which removes the program from the computer's memory.

Tag selector Displays HTML tags used in the current document.

Site definition The process of defining a site which includes specifying a folder name, a server technology, files locations, and remote server options.

Split view A combination of Code and Design view.

Workspace The Dreamweaver application interface, which contains windows, toolbars, and panel groups.

Workspace menu The Dreamweaver application interface, which is used to select a different workspace.

Dreamweaver Commands and Buttons

Change Link command Displays a dialog box used to modify a hyperlink. Found in the Modify menu.

Characters button Displays a menu of special characters to add at the insertion point. Found in the Text category in the Insert panel.

Check Spelling command Finds misspelled words in a web page document. Found in the Text menu.

Clear command Deletes selected content. Found in the Edit menu.

Close command Removes a web page document from the workspace or quits Dreamweaver. Found in the File menu. The button in the upper-right corner of the window can be used instead of the command.

Code view button Displays the code for a document in the Document window. Found in the Document toolbar.

Copy command Duplicates selected content. Found in the Edit menu.

Cut command Moves selected content to the clipboard. Found in the Edit menu.

Design view button Displays the document in the Document window as it will appear in a browser. Found in the Document toolbar.

Dreamweaver Help command Used to display the Adobe Help Viewer. Found in the Help menu.

Exit command Removes the Dreamweaver window from the Desktop.

Manage Sites command Displays a dialog box used to define or edit a website. Found in the Site menu.

Maximize button Expands the Document window in the Dreamweaver window.

Minimize button Reduces the Document window to a button in the Dreamweaver window.

New command Displays a dialog box used to create a new web page document. Found in the File menu on the menu bar.

Open command Displays a dialog box used to open a web page document. Found in the File menu.

Page Properties command Displays a dialog box used to change the page title for a web page document. Found in the Modify menu.

Paste command Places a copy of the clipboard contents at the insertion point. Found in the Edit menu.

Preview in Browser command Displays a submenu used to view the web page document in a browser window. Found in the File menu. The F12 key can be used instead of the command.

Print Code command Prints the code for a web page document. Found in the File menu.

Remove Link command Removes an existing link. Found in the Modify menu.

Repeat command Used to redo an action. Found in the Edit menu.

Save command Displays a dialog box used to save a web page document. Found in the File menu.

Split view button Splits the Document window to display both code and layout of the document. Found in the Document toolbar.

Undo command Cancels the last action performed. Found in the Edit menu.

Chapter 3 Introducing Dreamweaver

Review Questions

1. a) What is Dreamweaver?
   b) What is the Dreamweaver workspace?

2. a) What can be added using the Insert panel?
   b) What does the Files panel display?
   c) What can be changed using the Property inspector?

3. During the site definition process, what is created?

4. List two file name guidelines for web page documents.

5. List the steps required to create a new web page document based on an CSS starter page layout.

6. a) What is the home page?
   b) What file name is used in Dreamweaver to designate a web page document as the home page of a website?

7. Which panel displays all of the files and folders in a website?

8. a) List two places where the page title of a web page document is displayed.
   b) Can page titles contain spaces?
   c) Describe a fast method of changing the page title.

9. a) What view displays a web page document similar to how it will appear in a browser window?
   b) What view displays the code generated for a web page?

10. a) What key is pressed to view a web page document in a browser window?
    b) What is an alternative for viewing a web page document in a browser?

11. What is the information presented in a web page called?

12. a) How is a line break inserted?
    b) How is a © symbol inserted?

13. If a mistake is made, how can the last action be cancelled?

14. Give an example of when you might select Ignore in the Check Spelling dialog box.

15. a) List the steps required to print a web page document from a browser.
    b) List the steps required to determine how many pages will be printed for a web page.

16. What is the difference between closing a web page and quitting Dreamweaver?

17. List two ways a web page document can be opened in Dreamweaver.

18. a) What is the difference between an internal hyperlink and an external hyperlink?
    b) When creating a hyperlink, what is selected in the Target list to display a web page in a new browser window?

19. Describe two methods of locating Dreamweaver help in the Adobe Community Help window.

True/False

20. Determine if each of the following are true or false. If false, explain why.
    a) A website needs to be defined before any web pages are created.
    b) The extension .html indicates that a web page document is a home page.
    c) A web page can be edited in Live view.
    d) Press the F5 key to close all open panels.
    e) A page title can contain spaces.
    f) More than one web page document can be open in Dreamweaver at the same time.
    g) Once a hyperlink is created it cannot be changed.
    h) A link can display a web page in a new browser window.
    i) Press the F1 key to access help.

Exercises

Exercise 1 ———————————————————————— Cooking Herbs

Create a new website about cooking with herbs by completing the following steps:

a) Define a new site named Cooking Herbs in a folder named Cooking Herbs.

b) Using the HTML 2 column fixed, left sidebar CSS layout, add a web page document to the Cooking Herbs website naming it: index.html

c) Create the navigation bar as shown in step (e).

d) Save the modified index.html file. Copy the file and paste two copies of the file in the site root folder. Rename the files: herbs.html and recipes.html

e) Modify the index.html web page document as follows:

   1. Change the page title to: Cooking Herbs.

   2. Add content as shown below:

   3. Link the text Herbs to herbs.html.

   4. Link the text Recipes to recipes.html.

f) Modify the herbs.html web page document as follows:

   1. Change the page title to: Herbs.

   2. Create the appropriate hyperlinks and add content as shown below:

Chapter 3 Introducing Dreamweaver

g) Modify the recipes.html web page document as follows:

   1. Change the page title to: Recipes.

   2. Create the appropriate hyperlinks and add content as shown below:

h) Delete any extra placeholder text and check the spelling.

i) View each web page document in a browser window and test the hyperlinks.

j) Print a copy of each web page document from the browser.

Exercise 2 — Clouds

Create a new website about clouds by completing the following steps:

a) Define a new site named Clouds in a folder named Clouds. Create a default images folder named images.

b) Using the HTML 2 column fixed, left sidebar, header and footer CSS layout, add a web page documents to the Clouds website naming it: index.html

c) In the image placeholder, insert the image clouds.jpg, which is a data file for this text.

d) Create the navigation bar as shown in step (f).

e) Save the modified index.html file. Copy the file and paste three copies of the file in the site root folder. Rename the files: high_clouds.html, middle_clouds.htm, and low_clouds.html

f) Modify the index.html web page document as follows:

1. Change the page title to: Clouds
2. Add content as shown below:

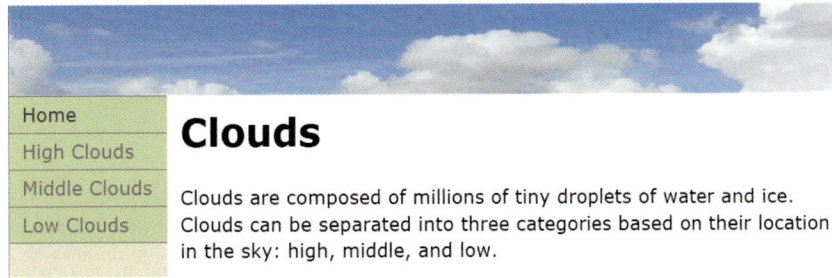

3. Link the text High Clouds to high_clouds.html.
4. Link the text Middle Clouds to middle_clouds.html.
5. Link the text Low Clouds to low_clouds.html.

g) Modify the high_clouds.html web page document as follows:

1. Change the page title to High Clouds.
2. Create the appropriate hyperlinks and add content as shown below:

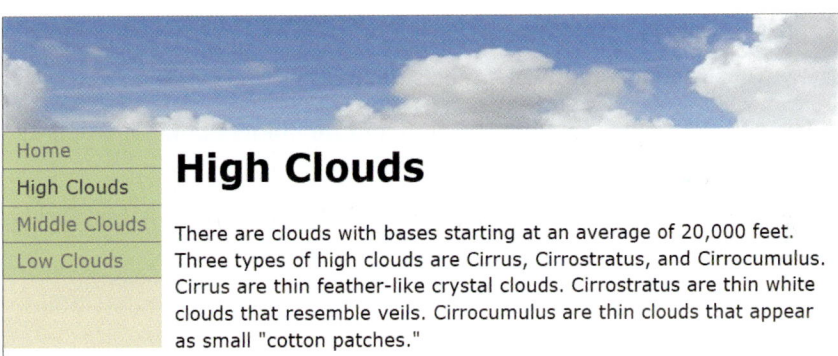

h) Modify the middle_clouds.html web page document as follows:

1. Change the page title to Middle Clouds.
2. Create the appropriate hyperlinks and add content as shown below:

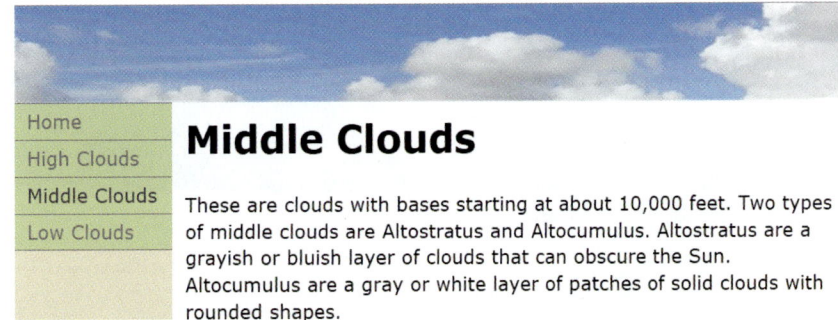

i) Open low_clouds.html and modify the web page document as follows:

   1. Change the page title to Low Clouds.

   2. Create the appropriate hyperlinks and add content as shown below:

j) Delete any extra placeholder text and check the spelling.

k) View each web page document in a browser window and test the hyperlinks.

l) Print a copy of each web page document from the browser.

Exercise 3 ———————————————————— Sharks

Create a new website about sharks that meets the following criteria:

- The site root folder is named Sharks and the folder contains a default images folder named images.

- The web pages are created using the HTML 2 column liquid, left sidebar, header and footer CSS layout.

- The site has four web page documents named index.html, nurse.html, zebra.html, and whale.html.

- The image placeholder on all pages is replaced with the image sharks.jpg, which is a data file for this text. The image width is set to 100% in the Property inspector.

- The navigation bar links the web pages and contains text as shown below.

- All pages have appropriate page titles.

- The index.html page looks similar to:

- The text Shark Research Institute is linked to the URL http://www.sharks.org and the link is set to display in a new window.

- The nurse.html web page document looks similar to:

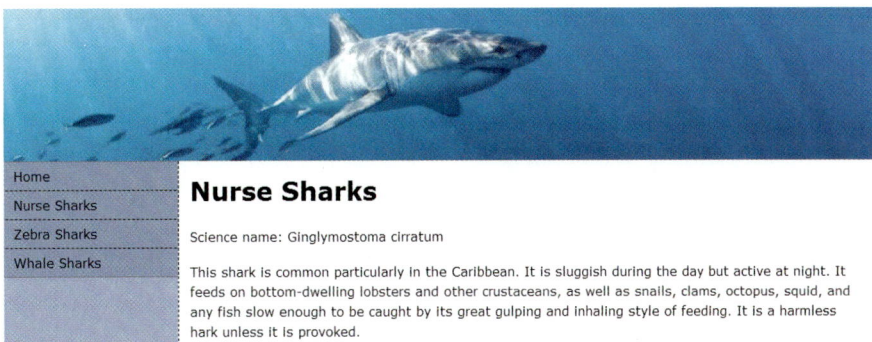

- The zebra.html web page document looks similar to:

- The whale.html web page document looks similar to:

Exercise 4 — E-commerce

Create a new website about e-commerce by completing the following steps:

a) Define a new site named E-commerce in a folder named E-commerce.

b) Using the HTML 2 column fixed, left sidebar CSS layout, add one web page document to the site naming it: index.html

c) Modify the index.html web page document as follows:

   1. Change the page title to E-commerce.

   2. Add the navigation links as shown in step (e), but don't add the content yet!

   3. Save the modified index.html web page document.

d) In the Files panel, copy the index.html file and then paste three copies of the file in the site root folder.

   1. Rename the pasted files: b2c.html, b2b.html, and c2c.html

e) Modify index.html by adding content and creating appropriate hyperlinks:

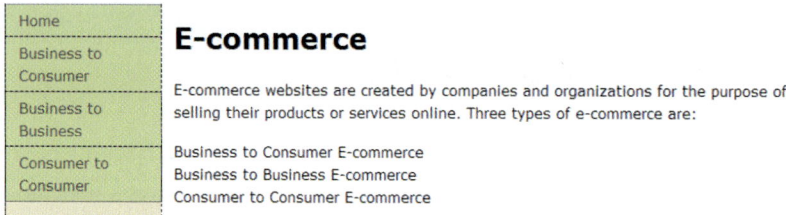

f) Modify the b2c.html web page document as follows:

   1. Change the page title to B2C.

   2. Add content and create the navigation links as shown below:

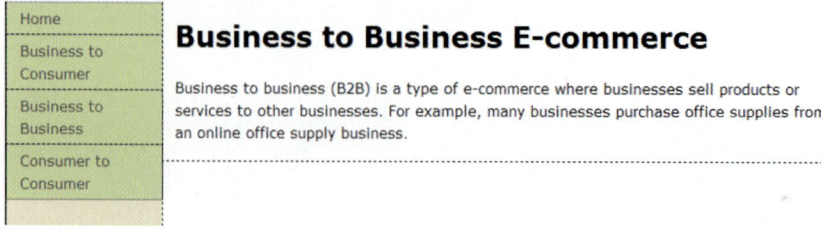

g) Modify the b2b.html web page document as follows:

   1. Change the page title to B2B.

   2. Add content and create the navigation links as shown below:

h) Modify the c2c.html web page document as follows:

   1. Change the page title to C2C.

   2. Add content and create the navigation links as shown below:

   | Home |
   | Business to Consumer |
   | Business to Business |
   | Consumer to Consumer |

   Consumer to Consumer E-commerce

   Consumer to consumer (C2C) is a type of e-commerce where individuals sell items to others using an intermediary website. Online auctions are one example of C2C e-commerce.

i) Modify the b2c.html, b2b.html, and c2c.html web page document as follows:

   1. Using the Internet, find example sites of each of the three types of e-commerce.

   2. Create an external hyperlink with appropriate text that links to the example website for that type of e-commerce.

   3. Set the link to display in a new window.

j) Delete any extra placeholder text and check the spelling.

k) View each web page document in a browser window and test the hyperlinks.

Exercise 5 — Swallowtail Butterflies

Create a new website about swallowtail butterflies by completing the following steps:

a) Define a new site named Swallowtail Butterflies in a folder named Swallowtail Butterflies. Create a default images folder named images. Copy the butterfly_banner.jpg data file to the images folder.

b) Using the HTML 2 column fixed, right sidebar, header and footer CSS layout, add two web page documents to the Swallowtail Butterflies website naming them index.html and black_swallowtail.html.

c) Modify the index.html web page document as follows:

   1. Change the page title to: Swallowtail Butterflies.

   2. Add content and create the navigation links as shown below:

Swallowtail Butterflies

| Home |
| Black Swallowtail |

Swallowtail butterflies are found all over the world but live mostly in the tropics. They are brightly colored and have characteristics tail-like projections from their hind wings. The females look different from the males in many of the species. They are often spotted near flowers and are attracted to wet soil, puddles, or ponds.

There are many Swallowtail species. The one I find the most interesting is the Black Swallowtail.

d) Modify the black_swallowtail.html web page document as follows:

   1. Change the page title to Black Swallowtail.

   2. Add content and create the navigation links as shown below:

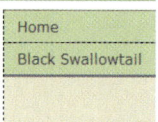

Black Swallowtail

This species of butterfly is usually found in open fields and woodland meadows. They always fly near the ground. They have variable markings, but they are mostly black and blue and yellow coloring along the edge of the wings. Some colored spots on the butterfly may be larger and may be orange instead of yellow.

Home
Black Swallowtail

e) Delete any extra placeholder text and check the spelling.

f) View each web page document in a browser window and test the hyperlinks.

g) Print a copy of each web page document from the browser.

Exercise 6 — Quotations

Create a new website that contains inspirational quotes by completing the following steps:

a) Define a new site named Quotations in a folder named Quotations.

b) Using the HTML 2 column liquid, left sidebar CSS layout, add two web page documents to the Quotations website naming them index.html and inspirational.html.

c) Modify the index.html web page document as follows:

   1. Change the page title to: Quotations.

   2. Use the text below to create the content for the page, arranging it appropriately:

   Qutotations

   A quotation is a phrase spoken or written by another person. This person is usually famous. It is always nice to have an inspirational quote to live by or to remember when times get tough. There are quotes from people about success, commitment, overcoming obstacles, failure, discipline, and knowledge.

   3. Add the appropriate navigation links.

d) Modify the inspirational.html web page document as follows:

1. Change the page title to: Inspirational Quotes
2. Use the text below to create the content for the page, arranging it appropriately:

Success	Mistakes are stepping stones to success. --Charles E. Popplestone The only time you'll find success before work is in the dictionary. --Mary B. Smith
Commitment	Commitment is what transforms a promise into reality. --Abraham Lincoln A somebody was once a nobody who wanted to and did. --Anonymous
Overcoming Obstacles	The greater the difficulty, the more glory in surmounting it. --Epicurus Success is to be measured not so much by the position that one has reached in life as by the obstacles which one has overcome while trying to succeed. --Booker T. Washington
Failure	What would you attempt to do if you knew you would not fail? --Robert Schuller Failure is only the opportunity to more intelligently begin. --Kenny Ford

3. Add the appropriate navigation links.

e) Delete any extra placeholder text and check the spelling.

f) View each web page document in a browser window and test the hyperlinks. Size the browser window smaller and then reflect on whether it is better to use a fixed or liquid layout for this website.

g) Print a copy of each web page document from the browser.

Exercise 7

Select one of the topics listed below. Using the Internet, find at least three websites that provide information on your topic. Create a new website to present your research, and include at least three linked web page documents. Include external hyperlinks to your sources.

- hurricanes
- the Arctic ocean
- earthquakes
- tornadoes
- the ozone layer
- tsunamis

Chapter 4
Website Development

This chapter introduces the overall process of developing a website. The purpose, audience, navigation structure, and content of a website is discussed, as well as modifying HTML formatting in Dreamweaver.

Website Development

In Chapter 3, you learned how to define a site and create web pages using a CSS starter layout. In this chapter, you will learn about the process required to develop a site that meets the needs of your audience.

Website development is the process of planning and creating a website. Planning includes determining the website's purpose, audience, navigation structure, content, and page layout. Dreamweaver is then used to set up the website and create the web pages. Website development can be divided into two stages, planning and implementation:

Planning

1. Define the purpose and target audience.
2. Determine the web pages that will be in the website.
3. Determine the content for each web page.
4. Design the web pages by sketching the page layouts or creating a full-size mock up using Fireworks or Photoshop. Review and revise the sketches, keeping in mind the four design concepts: appropriateness, placement, consistency, and usability.

Implementation

5. Using Dreamweaver, define the website and organize the files and folders.
6. Create the web pages using Dreamweaver.
7. Review the website in a browser and review a printed copy of each web page.
8. Make changes or corrections.
9. Repeat steps 7 and 8 until complete.

Most of the development process is repetitious: start with something, review it, revise it, review it again, and so on. With experience, you may only need to revise once or twice.

Defining the Purpose and Target Audience

purpose

The first step in planning a website is to define the purpose and target audience. The *purpose* is the intent of the website. For example, the purpose of a restaurant's website could be to provide the phone number, location, hours of operation, and menus. Clearly defining the purpose helps to make decisions about the website navigation structure and the content for each web page. Most websites have more than one purpose, so it is best to list as many as possible:

Purposes for a fast-food restaurant's website:

- provide location and contact information
- provide the hours of operation
- provide a fun page for kids
- describe the menus
- provide information about specials and promotions

Purposes for a children's theater website:

- list rehearsal and show times
- describe the theater production company
- provide location and contact information

target audience

Once the purpose is identified, the target audience of the website needs to be defined. The *target audience* is composed of the individuals that are intended to use the website. The content of the website is tailored to the target audience. To define the target audience, describe the intended users. Ask questions such as how old are they, where do they live, what are their interests, and what is their level of education. Answers to these and other questions related to the site can be listed as characteristics which define the target audience, as in the following examples:

Target audience characteristics for a fast-food restaurant website:

- adults, local residents, and travelers
- children who already know and like the restaurant
- people looking for the particular foods offered at the restaurant
- people in a hurry
- people on a budget

Target audience characteristics for a children's theater website:

- parents of children interested in attending or participating in a production
- children interested in attending or participating in a production

Practice: Pasta Restaurant – part 1 of 7

Write your answers on paper.

① DETERMINE THE PURPOSE AND TARGET AUDIENCE FOR A PASTA RESTAURANT

You have been asked to develop a website for a pasta restaurant. The owners want to include the address, hours, phone number, lunch and dinner menus, and a few recipes. The restaurant is unique because the pasta and sauces are made fresh daily. The restaurant is family-owned and is popular with tourists as well as local residents.

a. What are the purposes of the website? List as many as possible.

b. Who is the target audience for the website? List characteristics of the audience.

② DETERMINE THE PURPOSE AND TARGET AUDIENCE FOR A BICYCLING CLUB

You have been asked to develop a website for a local bicycling club. The club meets once a month for a breakfast meeting followed by a group ride. They want to have the club president's contact information and a schedule of events on the home page, and other pages with photos and reviews of past rides.

a. What are the purposes of the website? List as many as possible.

b. Who is the target audience for the website? List characteristics of the audience.

Determining the Web Pages and Navigation Structure

The web pages in a website are determined from the purpose and target audience. The home page typically contains links to web pages of specific topics. The organization of the pages in a website is called its *navigation structure*. Using thumbnails and lines to represent web pages and their relationships, the navigation structure should be sketched during the planning stage of website development. This sketch represents the navigation structure of a restaurant's website:

navigation structure

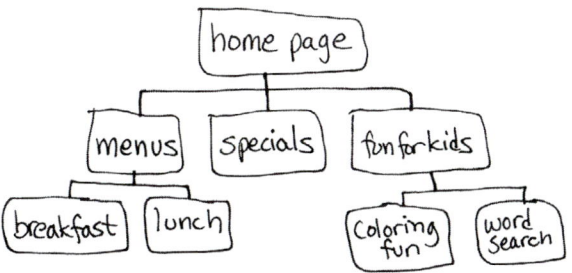

Sticky Notes as a Design Tool

Sticky notes are useful for working on a navigation structure. Using a sticky note for each web page, the notes can be arranged on a table or wall in a hierarchy like a navigation structure sketch. The notes can be rearranged many times to find the best structure.

The arrangement of the pages in a navigation structure should be from general to specific. For example, the menus page is more general than the specific pages for breakfast and lunch. The hierarchy should not be too deep or too shallow and each page should be about one topic.

top-level page

same-level page

The home page is referred to as a *top-level page* because it is at the highest level in the structure. At the second level in the example sketch there are three pages, which are *same-level pages*. This sketch also has web pages at a third level. These third-level pages, such as breakfast and lunch, are also same-level pages with respect to each other.

Chapter 4 Website Development

parent page
child page

In a navigation structure, web pages may also be described in terms of parent and child pages. A *parent page* has at least one page below it, called a *child page*. In the example sketch, the home page is a parent page and pages below it are child pages. The menus page is both a parent page and a child page.

Determining the Content

The *content* of a web page is the text, images, and other objects such as Flash movies that are presented to the user. Content is determined using the navigation structure of a website as a guideline, and then the text and objects for each page are listed on paper. For example, the content of the web pages for a fast-food restaurant's website may be:

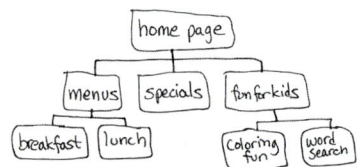

- **Home page** Location, hours of operation, contact information, and a brief introduction about what this website offers. Objects include the restaurant's logo and a picture of the restaurant.

- **Menus page** The hours for breakfast and lunch and links to the breakfast and lunch pages. Objects include the restaurant's logo and pictures of food.

- **Specials page** A listing of the current specials. Objects include the restaurant's logo.

- **Fun for kids page** A brief description of the kids web pages and links to the coloring fun page and word search page. Objects include the restaurant's logo and perhaps a cartoon.

- **Breakfast page** The breakfast menu. Objects include the restaurant's logo and pictures of breakfast menu items.

- **Lunch page** The lunch menu. Objects include the restaurant's logo and pictures of lunch menu items.

- **Coloring fun page** An image that kids can color on a printout of the web page. Objects include the restaurant's logo and the coloring image.

- **Word search page** An image of a word search puzzle that kids can complete on a printout of the web page. Objects include the restaurant's logo and the word search image.

Practice: Pasta Restaurant – part 2 of 7

Write your answers on paper.

① **SKETCH THE NAVIGATION STRUCTURE OF THE PASTA RESTAURANT SITE**

   a. Draw a rectangle and label the rectangle "home page." The home page is at the top level.

   b. Below the home page, draw two rectangles in a row and label them "menus" and "recipes" to represent the pages on the second level.

   c. Below the menus page, draw two rectangles in a row and label them "lunch" and "dinner" to represent pages on the third level.

Check—Your sketch should look similar to:

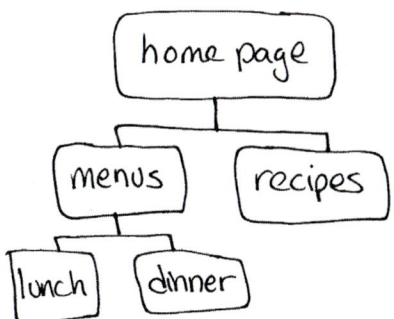

② **DETERMINE THE PAGE CONTENT OF THE PASTA RESTAURANT SITE**
   a. List each of the web pages from the navigation structure created in step 1.
   b. Write down the information each web page should present.
   c. List possible images for each page. Refer to the previous section "Determining the Content" for examples.

Defining Navigation Bars

A *navigation bar* is a set of hyperlinks that give users a way to display the different pages in a website. A website can contain several types of navigation bars and usually contains more than one type for better usability. For example:

top global navigation bar   The *top global navigation bar* typically contains a link to each page on the first and second levels of the website's navigation structure. The links can be text or images. A top global navigation bar can be horizontal like the example above, or vertical like the example sites you created in Chapter 3. A top global navigation bar typically has no more than eight links.

Chapter 4 Website Development

bottom global navigation bar

The *bottom global navigation bar* should appear near the bottom of the page and is often centered. This navigation bar typically uses text links, in a small size and contains links to all of the pages in the website if possible.

the | symbol

Each link in the global navigation bars should be clearly separated. The pipe symbol (|) is often used as a separator when needed. The pipe symbol is created with the | key above the Enter key.

local navigation bar

A *local navigation bar* can be positioned below the top global navigation bar or vertically along the left side of a page. In a large website, a local navigation bar often contains link to the child pages of the current page. It may also contain links to pages at the current level of the navigation structure or to locations on the current page.

breadcrumb trail

A *breadcrumb trail*, also called the *path*, is a navigation bar that displays the page names in order of level, from the home page to the current page, based on the navigation structure. Each of the page names, except for the current page name, is a link to the appropriate page. This path gives the user a point of reference and allows the user to navigate by backtracking through the site. Each page name in the path should be separated by a symbol, most commonly the "greater than" sign (>). A breadcrumb trail does not appear on the home page.

> **Breadcrumb Trails**
>
> Breadcrumb trails can be classified into 3 different types. *Location breadcrumbs* are static and illustrate where the page is located in the website hierarchy. *Path breadcrumbs* are dynamic and show the path that the user has taken to arrive at a page. *Attribute breadcrumbs* give information that categorizes the current page.

There should always be at least one link on each web page to the home page. Users may be directed to a web page in the website by a link at a search engine, and therefore need a way to find the home page. Home page links are always included in the breadcrumb trail and in the bottom global navigation bar. A logo at the top of a web page is also typically a link to the home page.

The Web Page Layout

A *web page layout* refers to the arrangement of the elements on the page. *Elements* can be in the form of text, images, Flash movies, or other media and include navigation bars, a logo or heading, copyright information, and content. A web page layout should be based on usability standards, which dictate the placement of navigation bars and other elements:

> **TIP** A sketch of a web page layout with details such as link names and main headings is referred to as a *wireframe*.

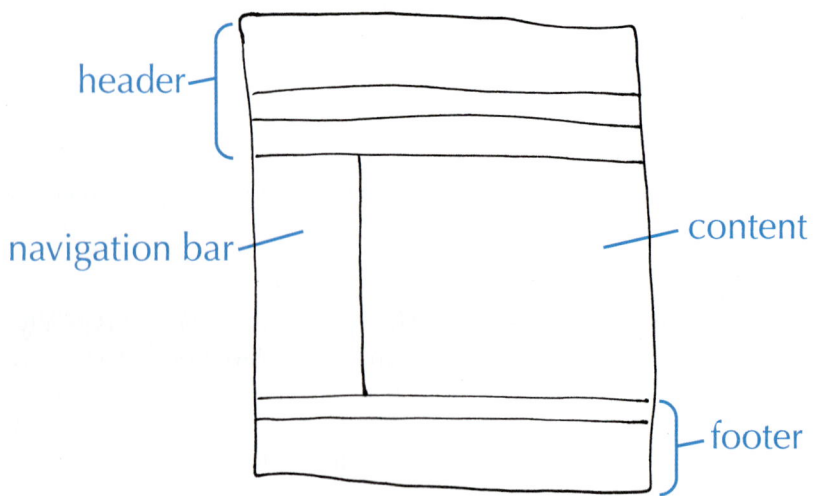

114   *Chapter 4 Website Development*

header The top area of a web page is called the *header* and includes a logo or heading, top global navigation bar, and possibly a breadcrumb trail. The **footer** bottom area of the page is called the *footer* and includes a bottom global navigation bar and other information such as a copyright notice, the date of the last update, and a link to contact the author.

A page layout should be sketched for each page of a website. The sketches should show the general placement of the content elements. The links in the navigation bars can be listed separately or written on the sketch where the links will appear.

Page layout should be similar for each page. By consistently placing elements in the same location, the user quickly becomes familiar with the website and can navigate easily. Because the home page acts as the starting point of a website, it should have a slightly different layout than the other web pages to quickly identify it as the home page.

TIP In Chapter 6, you will learn to modify a CSS starter layout.

Once you have your page layout designed, an efficient way to develop your site is to match one of the existing CSS starter layouts to your design. The CSS starter layouts can be easily modified and adapted to your design, which makes them a good starting point.

Practice: Pasta Restaurant – part 3 of 7

Refer to the navigation structure created in the previous practice to complete this practice. Write your answers on paper.

① SKETCH THE HOME PAGE AND DETERMINE THE NAVIGATION BARS

a. Sketch the home page. The header includes a logo and a top global navigation bar and the footer includes a bottom global navigation bar and copyright notice. Content includes text and a picture.

b. List the links for the top global navigation bar, which are links to the second level pages.

c. List the links for the bottom global navigation bar, which are links to the all the pages.

Check—Your sketch should look similar to:

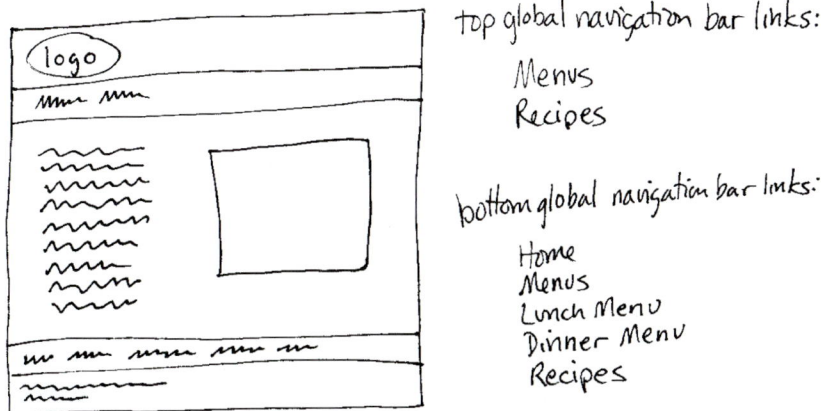

d. Which CSS starter layout would best match the design?

Chapter 4 Website Development

② **SKETCH THE MENUS PAGE AND DETERMINE THE NAVIGATION BARS**

   a. Sketch the menus page. The header includes a logo, top global navigation bar, and a breadcrumb trail. The footer includes a bottom global navigation bar and copyright notice. Content includes text and three pictures.

   b. List the links for the top global navigation bar, which are links to the other pages on the second level of the website and the home page.

   c. List the links for the bottom global navigation bar, which are links to all the pages.

   d. The breadcrumb trail should display Home > Menus, with Home as a link to the home page. Write this information down on your sketch.

③ **SKETCH THE REMAINING PAGES AND DETERMINE THEIR NAVIGATION BARS**

   Refer to "The Web Page Layout" section and steps ① and ② in this practice to sketch the recipes, lunch menu, and dinner menu pages. For each web page sketch, list appropriate links for the navigation bars.

Using Metaphors in a Website

Metaphors can help the user understand concepts in a website. For example, e-commerce websites use a shopping cart metaphor by providing links such as "add to cart" and "view cart" so that users feel as if they were shopping in a retail store. However, metaphors only work if they are obvious to the majority of users. If there is a slight possibility that a user may not understand it, then do not use a metaphor.

Concepts of Design

There are four basic concepts to consider when designing a web page: *appropriateness*, *placement*, *consistency*, and *usability*. Web page design includes the web page's layout and the content elements.

There are no absolute rules for website design, only guidelines that come from design concepts. Although the concepts discussed in this chapter are used frequently to create successful website designs, there are times when they may not yield the best design. With experience, the better choices will become obvious. Keep in mind that a website goes through many changes before it is finished, and good designs result from numerous revisions.

Design Concepts: Appropriateness

The *appropriateness* of a design is how well the elements in the website match the purpose and target audience. Is the text appropriate for the audience? Do the images fit the purpose of the website? Are they appropriate for the audience? What other content would the audience expect to find at this website?

Examine the differences in these two home pages:

Chapter 4 Website Development

Websites are Always Under Construction

The nature of the World Wide Web is change. The content of web pages is always changing and being updated. Adding an "under construction" notation or a construction image is not considered good design and could imply that the content on the page is incomplete or false.

The home page on the left conveys immaturity because of inappropriate wording, wild colors, confusing text hyperlinks, and a childish smiling golf ball image. For example, compare the link in the page on the left that reads Might wanna book a tee time online with the same link in the other page Book your tee time. The wording "Might wanna" is too casual and inappropriate for the target audience of a country club. The page on the right has quiet colors and appropriate wording in the text and links. This page invokes a calm, sophisticated feeling, more appropriate for a country club and golfers.

Design Concepts: Placement

The *placement* or arrangement of web page elements should follow generally accepted standards, with a header, a footer, and content in between. These standards are based on user expectations.

The expectations continue as the user browses the website. After clicking a link, the user expects to see a web page with similar design but different content. If the design suddenly changes, the links are moved, or the placement is different, they may click away from the website.

above the fold

Within the content are additional elements that require careful placement. The most important elements are those that the user should see first. These elements should be near enough to the top of a web page so that they are visible right away, and do not require the user to scroll. This placement is called *above the fold*, which originally referred to the headlines placed on the top half of a newspaper's front page, above where it is folded in half. News items in this location were sure to be seen first. On a web page, any elements that can be viewed without scrolling are seen first and can influence whether the user clicks on a link to another page in the site or leaves the site.

white space

Another factor in the placement of elements is white space. *White space* is any blank area on a page, regardless of the color. Jamming a page full of elements with little space between them causes visual noise and frustrated users may click away, as illustrated in this web page:

Balance

Balance is a design concept that refers to the distribution of optical weight in a web page. Optical weight is the ability of an object to attract the user's eye. An object's size, shape, and color contribute to the optical weight. For example, objects that are large contain more optical weight than smaller objects, colored objects contain more optical weight and are said to be "heavier" than small or black and white objects.

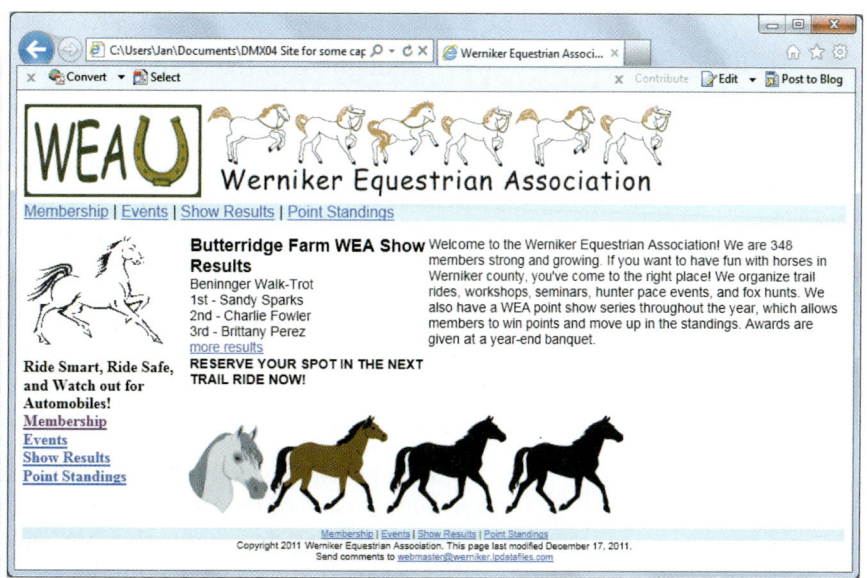

Chapter 4 Website Development

117

> **Testing Window Size**
>
> The appearance of the web page's layout on different monitors can be checked by using the Window Size button. In Design view, click the Window Size button in the status bar to display a menu:
>
>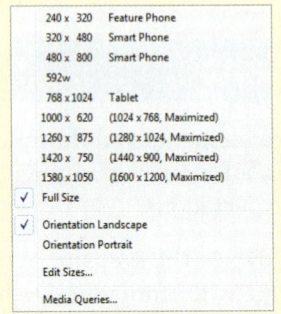
>
> The menu choices correspond to the inside dimensions of a browser window viewed on a monitor of the size given in parentheses. Selecting a size modifies the Document window to reflect how a web page will look when viewed on that monitor.

The shape of white space can emphasize elements and influence the direction that the user's eye travels around the page. Although white space is blank, it is just as important as other elements in the layout of a web page.

Users do not read web pages in a sequential order like a magazine article. Instead, users tend to scan web pages quickly looking for information. If the information is not located, users often jump to a different web page to locate the information instead of scrolling. *Chunking* is presenting and organizing information in small topics, or chunks, that users can easily scan and read in any order.

The concept of chunking is well suited for the computer screen because reading text on a monitor is physically tiring and slower than reading from paper. Online text should have less words than a printed document. The words presented should be easy to read and the number of sentences per paragraph should be limited. Descriptive headings should be used so that users can quickly locate the information they are seeking.

Design Concepts: Consistency

Consistency is achieved by repeating the placement and use of elements in web pages. Repetition in the placement of elements creates and maintains expectations for the user. For example, a breadcrumb trail is repeated on every page except the home page. After viewing a couple of pages, the user expects this as a point of reference. The user also subconsciously uses it as a visual cue to know which pages are not the home page. A *visual cue* is a pattern or object that the user sees and identifies quickly after repeated use.

The importance of consistency increases with the number of pages in a website. In a one-page website, consistent visual cues are not needed. In a website with fifteen pages, consistent visual cues help the user navigate and provide a point of reference.

Design Concepts: Usability

Although all of the design concepts are important, if a website isn't usable, it won't get used. The object is to keep users at a website long enough to find information that is useful to them. The *usability* is indicated by how easily the user navigates through the web pages to find the information. Navigation bars makes the site easier to explore. A breadcrumb trail also helps the user understand the current page location in relation to the rest of the website.

Text content on web pages should be limited to only necessary words and paragraphs. The less text there is for users to scan, the faster they will be able to find what they need. Information should be carefully edited to convey a message clearly but without wordiness.

Will the user be likely to print out the web page? If so, a link to a *printer-friendly version* of the page may be needed. If a web page looks great in the browser but does not look great printed, the user can click the link to display another web page with the same content set up for printing.

> **TIP** Chapter 6, Exercise 4 explores creating a printer-friendly version of a web page.

Practice: Pasta Restaurant – part 4 of 7

Refer to the content determined in the previous practice. Write your answers on paper.

① ANALYZE THE DESIGN OF A WEB PAGE

Based on the navigation structure shown, analyze the design of the Recipes web page in a strawberry farm's website:

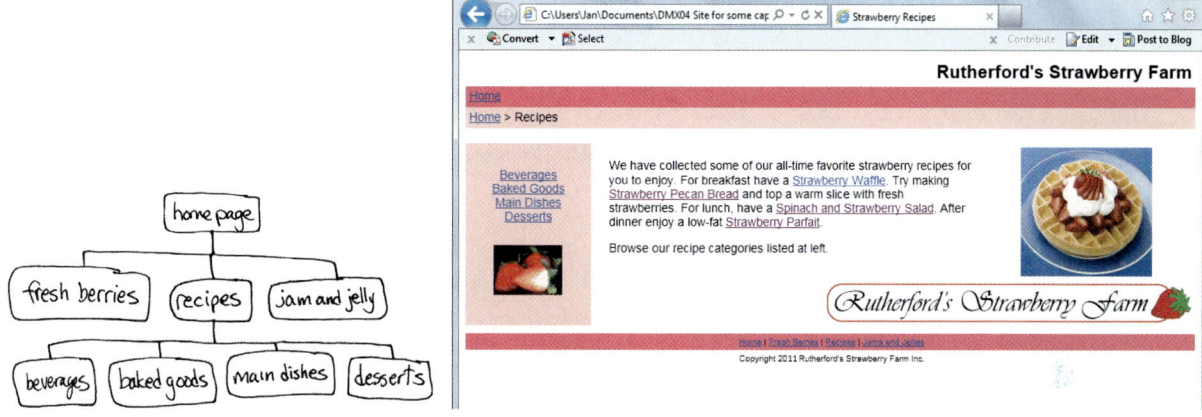

a. Describe the usability and consistency of the top and bottom global navigation bars.
b. Are the links in the local navigation bar appropriate? Explain why or why not.
c. Where is the logo? Where is a more appropriate location for the logo? Why?
d. Describe the appropriateness of the paragraph in the content area.
e. Describe the appropriateness and usability of the links in the content area.
f. How could the footer be improved?

② DESIGN THE PASTA RESTAURANT WEBSITE HOME PAGE

Refine the content layout of the home page for the pasta restaurant. The content of the home page should include:

- a brief statement about the pasta restaurant
- an image related to the restaurant
- the restaurant address, phone number, and hours of business

Check—Your sketch could look similar to:

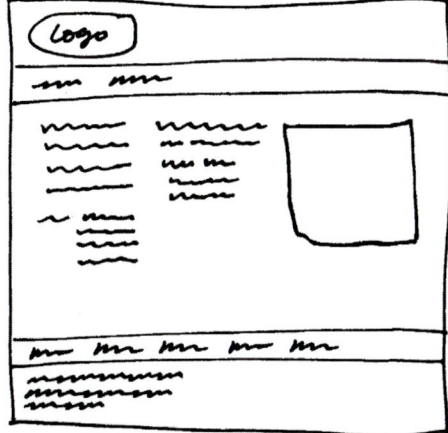

Chapter 4 Website Development

Organizing Files and Folders

root folder

Once the planning stage for a new website is complete, the website can be defined in Dreamweaver as discussed in Chapter 3. The Files panel is then used to organize files and folders for the website. The site *root folder* is created during site definition for storing files and folders. To add a new folder to the website, select the root folder in the Files panel and then select ▦ → File → New Folder in the Files panel group. After adding the new folder, it can be renamed:

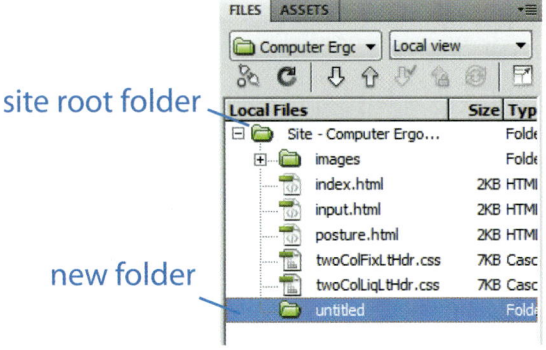

> **Folder Structure**
>
> Large websites may use several folders to organize the files. Use as many folders as needed to maintain organization.

Folders are used to organize files. Web page documents have many elements, including images. For better organization, all the image files for a website should be stored together in a folder named *images*.

An existing file is added to a site by copying it to a folder in the website's root folder. Navigate to an appropriate location from the menu in the Files panel to display a list of files:

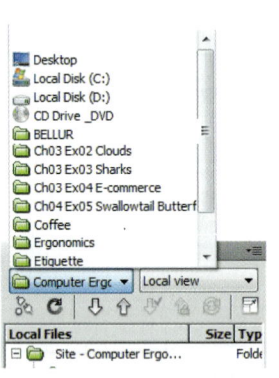 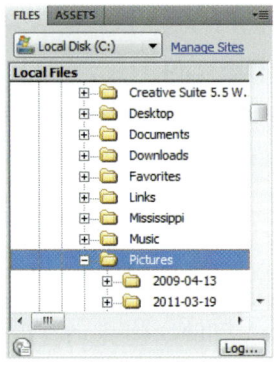

Navigate to a location, such as C: to display a list of files

TIP In the Files panel, website folders are green 📁 and other folders are yellow.

TIP When inserting an image, you will automatically be prompted to copy the file to the website folder.

Navigate to the existing file and select it, then select ▦ → Edit → Copy. A copy of the file is placed in the computer's memory. Select a website from the Files panel pop-up list to display the site's files and folders in the Files panel, and then select ▦ → Edit → Paste to copy the file to the website.

To select several files at once, hold down the Ctrl key while selecting each file. The **Copy** and **Paste** commands can then be used to copy or paste all the selected files.

Practice: Pasta Restaurant – part 5 of 7

① **START DREAMWEAVER**

② **DEFINE A NEW SITE**

    a. Select Site → New Site. A dialog box is displayed.

    b. Select Site if those options are not already displayed.

    c. In the Site Name box type: Pasta Restaurant

    d. Click the Local Site Folder icon. A dialog box is displayed for browsing the local disk.

        1. Navigate to the appropriate location where a folder can be created to store the website files.

        2. Click the Create New Folder button.

        3. A new folder is created. Type Pasta Restaurant to replace the New Folder name and press Enter.

        4. Select Open. The Computer Ergonomics folder appears in the Select list.

        5. Select Select to choose the new folder as the website folder.

    e. Click Advanced Settings:

        1. Click the Default Images folder Browse for folder icon.

        2. If necessary, navigate to the Pasta Restaurant folder.

        3. Click the Create New Folder button:

        4. Type images and then press the Enter key.

        5. Select Open.

        6. Select Select to choose the new folder as the website folder.

    f. Select Save. The Site folder is displayed in the Files panel.

③ **CREATE THE HOME PAGE**

    a. Select File → New. A dialog box is displayed.

        1. Select Blank Page.

        2. In the Page Type list, select HTML and in the Layout list select 3 column fixed, header and footer.

        3. Select Create and then select Save. A web page document is displayed in a Document window.

    b. Select File → Save. A dialog box is displayed.

        1. Use the Save in list to navigate to the Pasta Restaurant folder if it is not already displayed.

        2. In the File name box, replace the existing text with: index.html

        3. Select Save.

    c. On the Document toolbar, in the Title box, replace the text Untitled Document with Pasta Restaurant and press Enter.

④ **CREATE MORE WEB PAGE DOCUMENTS**

    Create four more web page documents naming them: menus.html, lunch.html, dinner.html, and recipes.html.

Check—Your Files panel should look similar to:

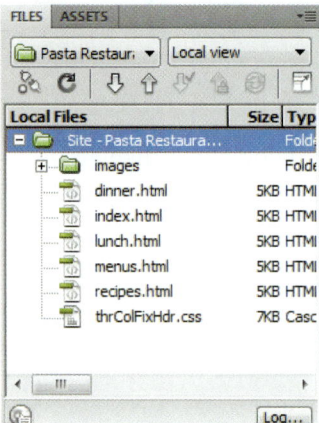

⑤ ADD IMAGE FILES TO THE IMAGES FOLDER
   a. In the Files panel, navigate to the folder that contains the data files for this text.
   b. Click the pasta_drawing.gif file to select it.
   c. Hold down the Ctrl key and click the pasta_logo.gif file. Two files are selected.
   d. In the Files panel group, select ▭ → Edit → Copy.
   e. In the Files panel, select Pasta Restaurant from the pop-up menu.
   f. In the Files panel, click the images folder in the Pasta Restaurant site to select it.
   g. In the Files panel group, select ▭ → Edit → Paste. Two image files are added to the images folder.

Maintaining Consistency in a Website

Assets panel   Dreamweaver includes the *Assets panel* to help maintain consistency in the content throughout a website. The Assets panel, located in the Files panel group, helps website development by listing images and other objects available in the site:

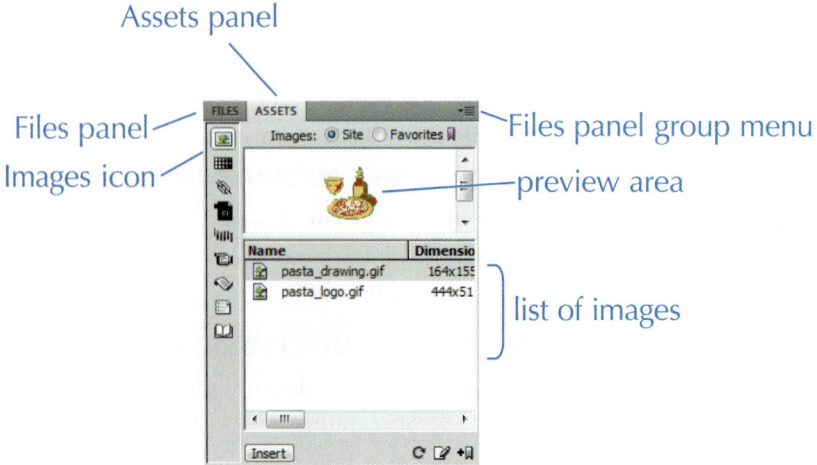

Chapter 4 Website Development

place an image Click the Images icon to display the Images category, which lists all the image files in the site. The selected image, pasta_drawing.gif in the example on the previous page, is displayed in the preview area. It may be necessary to select → Refresh Site List in the Files panel group to update the list of images.

Drag the image from the Assets panel to an open web page document to place the image, or click Insert at the bottom of the Assets panel to place the selected image at the insertion point. The Image Tag Accessibility Attributes dialog box is displayed when an image is placed:

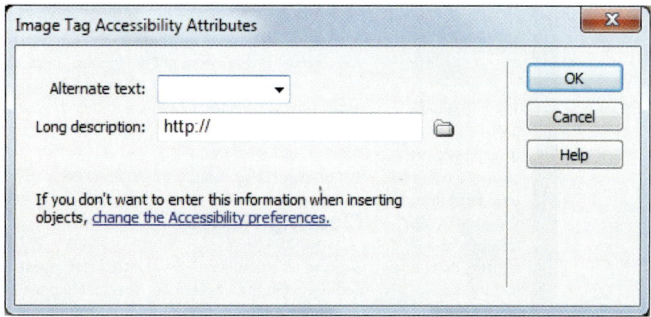

TIP The Long description box is used to provide a URL or file location where the user can locate expanded alternative text content. Alternative text is also discussed in Chapter 5.

Alternative text is added so that if a user is unable to view images, they will at least be able to display a description of the image. This text is also able to be read by a screen reader.

Practice: Pasta Restaurant – part 6 of 7

Dreamweaver should be started and the Pasta Restaurant website should be the working site.

① **INSERT A LOGO**

a. Display the index.html web page.

b. Double-click the logo placeholder in the upper right corner of the web page.

1. Navigate to the images folder and insert the pasta_logo.gif file.
2. Click to select the pasta_logo.gif file and then select OK.

② **VIEW THE ASSETS PANEL**

a. In the Files panel group, click Assets. The Assets panel is displayed.

b. In the Assets panel, click the Images icon if it is not already selected. The images in the site are displayed. If necessary, select → Refresh Site List from the Files panel group.

c. In the Assets panel, click the pasta_drawing.gif file to select it. The image is displayed in the preview area.

Chapter 4 Website Development   **123**

③ USE THE ASSETS PANEL TO INSERT IMAGES

a. Delete the Backgrounds placement heading and text in the third column.

b. Drag the pasta_drawing.gif file name from the Assets panel to third column. A dialog box is displayed.

   1. In the **Alternative** text box, type pasta dinner. Select **OK**. The image appears on the web page:

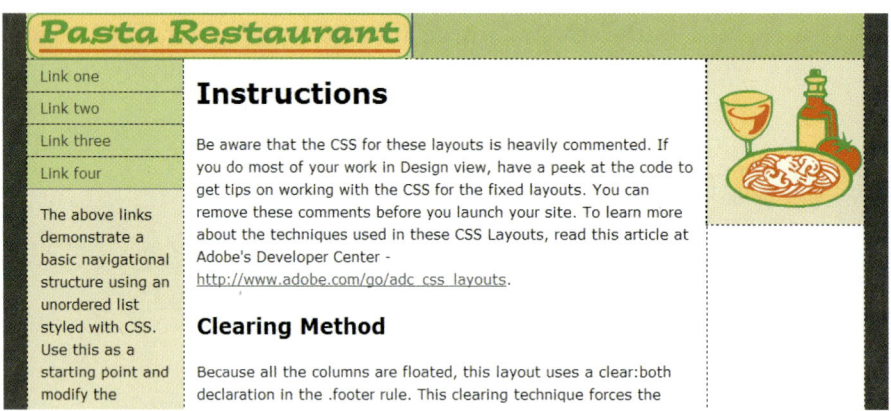

④ SAVE AND CLOSE THE INDEX.HTML WEB PAGE DOCUMENT

a. Save the modified index.html.

b. View the page in Live view.

c. Close the index.html document window.

Creating and Editing Library Items

library item

The Library category in the Assets panel lists the library items that are available in the open website. A *library item* is content in a separate file, with a descriptive name, that is used repeatedly in the website. Using library items helps maintain consistency in a website. For example, a library item that consists of a copyright notice could be created and named copyright. Instead of typing the copyright notice on every web page, this library item can be added to each web page. When the copyright notice needs to be changed, only the library item needs to be edited, and then the occurrences of the library item in the web pages can be updated all at once.

Alternative Select 📋 ➔
New Library Item to create a new, empty library item.

Click the Library icon 📖 in the Assets panel to display the Library. Click the New Library Item button 🗐 at the bottom of the Assets panel to create a new, empty library item:

124   *Chapter 4 Website Development*

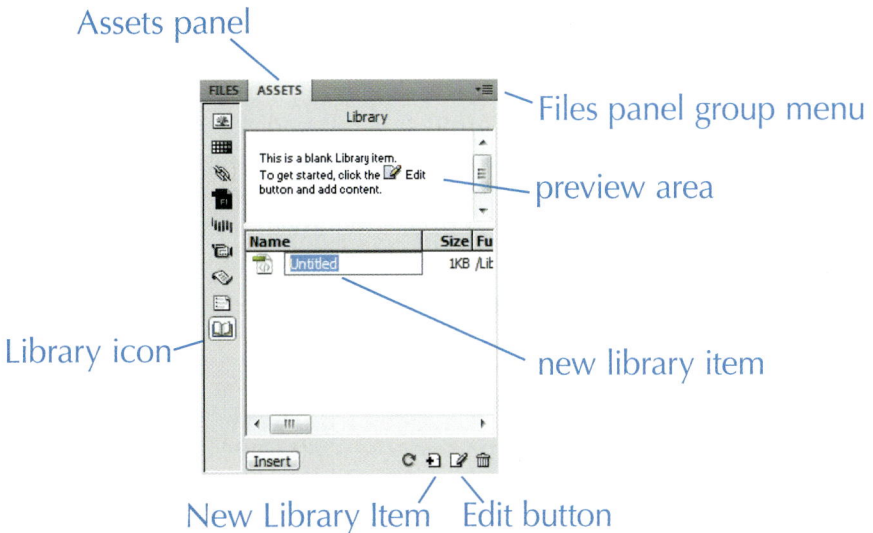

LBI

A library item file is an LBI file. The extension .lbi is automatically added to the file name.

Type a new name for the library item to replace the selected Untitled text. To add content, click the Edit button at the bottom of the Assets panel or double-click the library item. A window is opened and the title bar displays the text <<Library Item>> and the library item name. After adding content in the window, select File → Save to save the changes, then close the window by clicking the Close button. The content of a selected library item appears in the preview area of the Library in the Assets panel. Dreamweaver automatically adds a Library folder to the website root folder when the first library item is created.

A library item may also be created from existing content in a web page document. Select the content and then click the New Library Item button. After the new library item is named, the selected content in the web page has a yellow background to indicate that it is a library item.

Drag a library item from the Library to an open web page document to place it, or click Insert at the bottom of the Assets panel to place the selected library item at the insertion point. In a web page document, a library item appears with a yellow background. Its does not appear with a yellow background in a browser.

Click the Delete button at the bottom of the Assets panel or press the Delete key to delete the selected library item.

To edit an existing library item, select the library item in the Library and then click the Edit button, which opens the item in a window. When changes are saved, a dialog box is displayed that lists all of the web page documents that contain the library item. Click **Update** to update all of the occurrences of the library item in the website.

A library item in a web page document cannot be edited unless the link between it and the Library is broken. To break the link, select the library item in the web page document and then click Detach from original in the Property inspector. In the web page document, the selected library item will no longer have a yellow background and can now be edited in that web page document. Once the link has been broken, the content that was a library item in the web page document will not be updated if the library item in the Library is changed.

Inserting a Date

time stamp

The footer of a web page should contain a date indicating when the web page was last updated to indicate how current the information is to the users. Instead of typing a new date every time the web page is edited, the date can be in the form of a *time stamp* that changes automatically when a page is modified. Select Insert → Date or click the Date button in the Common category in the Insert panel to display the Insert Date dialog box:

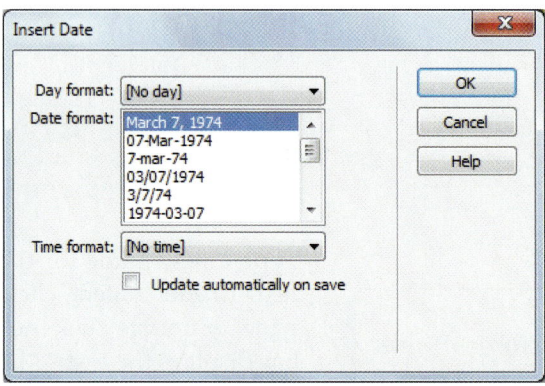

Use the Day format, Date format, and Time format lists to select the format of the date that will appear at the insertion point. The Update automatically on save check box must be selected if the date is to be automatically updated each time the web page document is saved. Select OK to place the time stamp in the web page document at the insertion point.

E-mail Hyperlinks

An *e-mail hyperlink* is a link that allows the user to create and send an e-mail message. When the user clicks an e-mail hyperlink, a new e-mail message window is displayed with the To: address that was specified when the hyperlink was created. After composing the message, the user clicks the Send button to send the message.

An e-mail link to the webmaster is sometimes included in the footer of a web page. This gives the user a chance to provide feedback about the website, so that improvements and corrections can be made to better meet the needs of the website's users.

Alternative Select Insert → Email link.

To create an e-mail hyperlink, select the text that will be the link in the Document window and then type mailto: followed by the e-mail address in the Link box in the Property inspector:

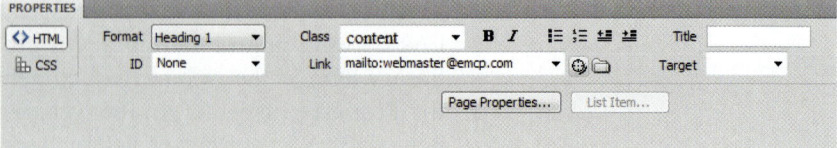

An e-mail hyperlink can be tested in a browser window.

Copyright Information

Certificate of Copyright

A publication, such as a website, can be submitted to the United States Copyright Office to receive an official certificate of copyright. Although not required, this certificate can be used in cases of copyright infringement.

All forms of published work, including a website you may create, are entitled to copyright protection. A web page should include copyright information with a *copyright notice* that contains the text Copyright followed by the year of publication. In addition to a copyright notice, copyright information may also include other statements regarding the use of the website's material and an e-mail hyperlink for sending a request for permission to use the material.

TIP The © symbol may be used in place of the word Copyright.

Published work that displays a copyright notice, in this case a website, is protected work and not intended for the public domain. Copyrighted material can be reproduced only with written permission from the owner. However, a website that does not contain a copyright notice is still entitled to copyright protection. Published work should be treated as copyright protected unless explicitly stated as material for the public domain.

Practice: Pasta Restaurant – part 7 of 7

Dreamweaver should be started and the Pasta Restaurant website should be the working site.

① CREATE A LIBRARY ITEM

a. Close any open Document windows.

b. In the Files panel group, click **Assets** if the Assets panel is not already displayed.

c. In the Assets panel, click the Library icon. The list is empty because no library items exist yet.

d. At the bottom of the Assets panel, click the New Library Item button. A new item is added to the list.

e. Replace the selected library item name with footer and press Enter.

f. At the bottom of the Assets panel, click the Edit button. A window is opened.

g. Type the text: Send us feedback on your dining experience. Last modified

h. Press Shift+Enter after the word "modified" and then type the text:

  Copyright 2012 Pasta Restaurant.

i. Select File → Save. In the Assets panel, the content of the saved selected library item appears in the preview area.

j. Close the library item window.

② EDIT THE FOOTER LIBRARY ITEM

a. In the Assets panel, select the footer library item and click the Edit button at the bottom of the Assets panel. The library item is displayed in a window.

b. Select the text: feedback

c. In the Property inspector, in the Link box type:
  mailto:manager@pasta.emcp.com

d. Press Enter. The text feedback is now an e-mail hyperlink.

e. Place the insertion point at the end of the word modified and type a space.

f. In the Common category in the Insert panel, click the Date button 🗓. A dialog box is displayed.

   1. In the dialog box, set the options to:

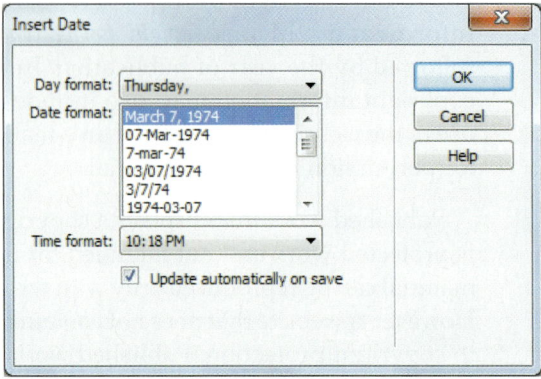

   2. Select OK. A time stamp is placed at the insertion point.

g. Select File → Save. The library item is saved.

h. Close the library item window.

③ CREATE ANOTHER LIBRARY ITEM

a. At the bottom of the Assets panel, click the New Library Item button. A new item is added to the list.

b. Replace the selected library item name with navbar and press Enter.

c. At the bottom of the Assets panel, click the Edit button. A new window is opened.

d. Type the following text, using the | key above the Enter key to create the "pipe" symbol:

Menus | Recipes

e. In the Files panel group, click Files. The list of files in the website is displayed.

f. Link the text Menus to the menus.html web page document.

g. Link the text Recipes to the recipes.html web page document.

h. Select File → Save. The library item is saved.

i. In the Files panel group, click Assets. In the Assets panel, the content of the saved library item appears in the preview area.

j. Close the library item window.

④ PLACE LIBRARY ITEMS

a. In the Files panel group, click Files. The list of files in the website is displayed.

b. Double-click the index.html file name. The web page document is opened.

c. In the Files panel group, click Assets. The Assets panel is displayed.

d. Triple-click to select the placeholder footer text and then press the Delete key.

e. From the Assets panel Library category, drag the navbar library item to the footer area. Click outside the footer area to deselect the library item. Note the yellow background behind the links to indicate a library item.

f. Position the insertion point at the end of the navbar library item in the footer area and press Shift+Enter.

g. From the Assets panel Library category, drag the footer library item to the insertion point in the footer area. The footer appears, with a yellow background:

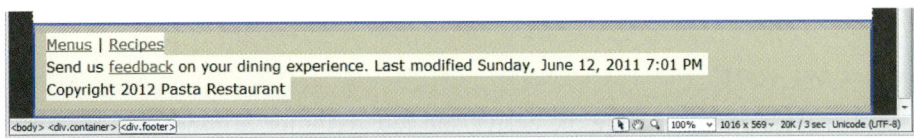

⑤ EDIT A LIBRARY ITEM

a. In the footer area, click the Menus and Recipes links library item to select it.

b. In the Property inspector, click [Detach from original]. Select OK in the warning dialog box. The yellow background no longer appears and the text can be edited.

c. Place the insertion point to the space to the right of Menus and then type:

| Lunch Menu | Dinner Menu

Make sure the navigation items are all separated by a pipe symbol (|) with a space on each side.

d. Link the text Lunch Menu to the lunch.html web page document.

e. Link the text Dinner Menu to the dinner.html web page document.

⑥ SAVE AND CLOSE THE INDEX.HTML WEB PAGE DOCUMENT

a. Save the modified index.html.

b. Press F12. The document is displayed in a browser window. Test the e-mail link.

c. Close the browser window and close all open Dreamweaver documents.

Modifying HTML in Dreamweaver

The Property inspector can be used to apply both HTML and CSS formatting. CSS should be used to apply formatting to a web page and is discussed in Chapter 6. However, you can use the HTML options in the Property inspector to change the document structure:

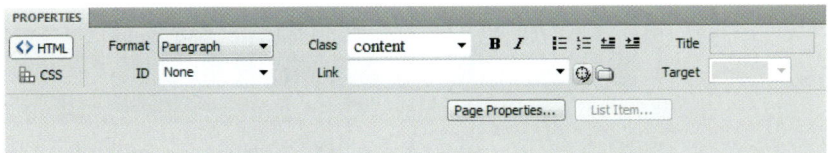

- The Format list sets the paragraph style of the selected text. Select Paragraph to apply the default format for a <p> tag; Heading 1 to apply the default formatting for an <h1> tag, and so forth.
- The Unordered List button creates a bulleted list of the selected text.
- The Ordered List button creates a numbered list of the selected text.
- The Link box is used to create a hyperlink of the selected text.
- The Title box specifies a textual tooltip for a hypertext link.

Chapter 4 Website Development

Practice: Computer Ergonomics

Dreamweaver should be started.

① OPEN A WEBSITE

a. In the Files panel, change the active site to Computer Ergonomics, the site you created in the practices in Chapter 3:

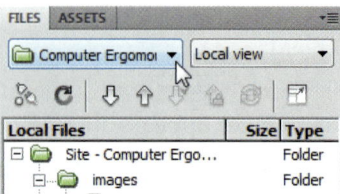

b. Open index.html.

② MODIFY HEADING STYLES

a. Click within the Ergonomics heading.
b. In the Property inspector, click <> HTML if it is not already selected.
c. Click the Format drop-down arrow and select Heading 2.
d. Click within The Workplace heading.
e. Click the Format drop-down arrow and select Heading 3.
f. Save the modified index.html.

③ CREATE AN UNORDERED LIST

a. Open input.html.
b. Place the insertion point to the left of Ergonomic at the start of the second sentence and press the Enter key.
c. In the Property inspector, click the Unordered List button.
d. Move the insertion point to the right of the period after ...keystroke pressure and press the Enter key.

Check—Your page should look similar to:

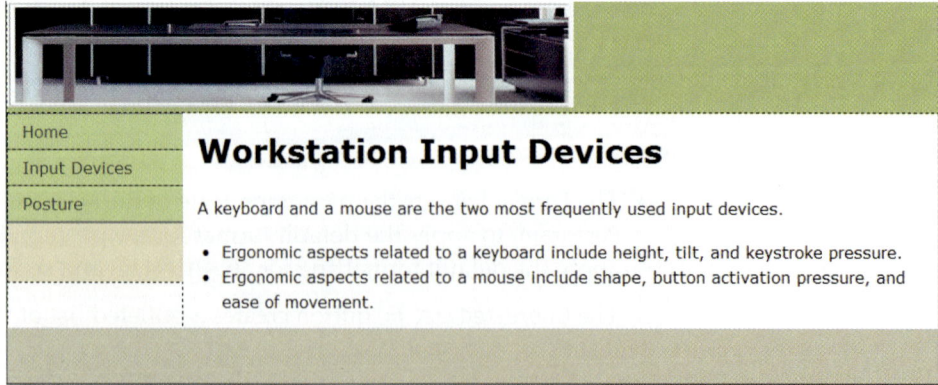

e. Save the modified input.html.

④ QUIT DREAMWEAVER

Chapter Summary

Website development can be divided into two stages, planning and implementation. Planning includes defining the purpose and target audience, determining the web pages in the site, and sketches of the navigation structure and page layouts. Implementation includes creating the website using Dreamweaver, and then reviewing and revising the web pages.

The content of a web page are the elements such as text, images, and navigation bars. Navigation bars help the user navigate through the web pages in a site. Types of navigation bars include the top global navigation bar, bottom global navigation bar, local navigation bar, and breadcrumb trail. A web page layout refers to the placement of the elements on the web page.

There are four basic concepts to consider when designing a web page: appropriateness, placement, consistency, and usability. The appropriateness of a design is how well the elements in the website match the purpose and target audience. The placement of web page elements should follow generally accepted standards, with a header, a footer, and content in between. These standards are based on user expectations. Consistency in placement and use of elements upholds the user's expectations. The usability is indicated by how easily the user navigates through the web pages to find the information.

In Dreamweaver, the Files panel is used to organize files and folders for the website. The root folder and the images folder is created during site setup and additional folders can be added, such as a videos folder. The Assets panel helps website development by listing images and other objects available in the site. The Library category in the Assets panel lists the library items that are available in the open website. A library item is content in a separate file, with a descriptive name, that is used repeatedly in the website.

A date can be added in the form of a time stamp that changes automatically when a web page is modified.

An e-mail hyperlink is a link that allows the user to create and send an e-mail message. An e-mail link to the webmaster is usually included in the footer of a web page.

All forms of published work, including a website you may create, are entitled to copyright protection. A web page should include copyright information with a copyright notice that contains the text Copyright followed by the year of publication. However, a website that does not contain a copyright notice is still entitled to copyright protection.

The Property inspector can be used to apply both HTML and CSS formatting. CSS should be used to apply formatting to a web page and is discussed in Chapter 6. However, you can use the HTML options in the Property inspector to change the document structure.

Vocabulary

Above the fold The placement of the most important elements near the top of a web page so that they are visible without requiring the user to scroll.

Appropriateness A design concept that refers to how well the elements in the website match the purpose and target audience.

Assets panel A panel that helps in website development by gathering a list of objects, such as images, that are available in the site.

Bottom global navigation bar A navigation bar, positioned near the bottom of a web page, that contains links to every page of a website.

Breadcrumb trail A navigation bar that displays the page names in order of level, from the home page to the current page, based on the navigation structure.

Child page A web page that has at least one page above it in the navigation structure of a website.

Consistency A design concept that refers to repetition in the placement and use of elements.

Content The text, images, and other objects presented to the user on a web page.

Copyright notice The text Copyright followed by the year of publication.

Elements Text, images, or other media. Elements on a web page include navigation bars, a logo or heading, copyright information, and content.

E-mail hyperlink A link that allows the user to create and send an e-mail message.

Footer The bottom area of a web page that includes a global navigation bar and other information such as copyright, the date of the last update, and a link to contact the author.

Header The top area of a web page that includes a logo or heading, global navigation bar, and possibly a breadcrumb trail.

Library item Content placed in a separate file, with a descriptive name, that is used repeatedly in a website.

Local navigation bar A navigation bar that typically contains links to the child pages of the current page.

Navigation bar A set of hyperlinks that give users a way to display the different pages in a website.

Navigation structure The organization of the pages in a website.

Parent page A web page that has at least one page below it in the navigation structure of a website.

Path *See* Breadcrumb trail.

Placement A design concept that refers to the arrangement of web page elements.

Printer-friendly version A web page with the same content as another web page, except this page is set up to print.

Purpose The intent of the website.

Root folder The folder created during site definition for storing files and folders.

Same-level page Web pages at the same level in the navigation structure of a website.

Target audience The individuals that are intended to use the website.

Timestamp A date or time that changes automatically when a page is modified.

Top global navigation bar A navigation bar that contains links to the first and second level pages of a website.

Top-level page A web page at the highest level in the navigation structure of a website, usually the home page.

Usability A design concept that refers to how easily the user can navigate through the pages of a website to find information.

Visual cue A pattern or object that the user sees and identifies quickly after repeated use.

Web page design The web page's layout and the content elements.

Web page layout The arrangement of the elements on the page.

Website development The process of planning and creating a website.

White space Any blank area on a page, regardless of the color.

Dreamweaver Commands and Buttons

Copy **command** Places a copy of the selected file in the computer's memory. Found in 🗐 → Edit → Copy.

🗓 **Date command** Inserts a time stamp in a web page document. Found in the Insert menu. The Date button in the Common tab in the Insert panel can be used instead of the command.

🗑 **Delete button** Removes the selected library item from the Library. Found in the Library category in the Assets panel.

[Detach from original] **button** Breaks the link from the selected library item in a web page document to the library item in the Library. Found in the Property inspector.

✏ **Edit button** Opens a window that contains the selected library item. Found in the Library category in the Assets panel.

[<> HTML] Displays HTML options in the Property inspector.

🖼 **Images icon** Displays the Images category in the Assets panel, with a list of all the images in the site. Found in the Assets panel.

[Insert] **button** Places the selected image or library item at the insertion point. Found in the Assets panel.

📖 **Library icon** Displays the Library category in the Assets panel, with a list of all the library items in the site. Found in the Assets panel.

New File **command** Creates a new web page document file and adds it to the list of files in the Files panel. Found in the Files panel group menu.

New Folder **command** Creates a new folder and adds it to the list of files and folders in the Files panel. Found in the Files panel group menu.

🗋 **New Library Item button** Creates a new library item. Found in the Library category in the Assets panel.

Paste **command** Places a copy of the file in the computer's memory in the selected folder. Found in 🗐 → Edit → Paste.

Refresh Site List **command** Updates the list of images in the Assets panel. Found in the Files panel group menu.

Chapter 4 Website Development

Review Questions

1. a) List four steps involved in the planning stage of website development.
   b) List five steps involved in the implementation stage of website development.

2. Consider a website for a competitive soccer team:
   a) List three purposes for the website.
   b) List three characteristics of the target audience for the website.

3. Sketch the navigation structure for an ice cream store's website that contains the following web pages:
   - a home page
   - two second-level pages, one for flavors and one for store hours and other information
   - two child pages of the flavors page, one for ice cream flavors and one for frozen yogurt flavors

4. What is used as a guide when determining web page content?

5. a) List three types of navigation bars used on a web page.
   b) Where should global navigation bars be placed?
   c) How is a breadcrumb trail helpful to the user?

6. List three places on a web page that may have a link to the home page.

7. What does web page layout refer to?

8. a) List three elements that can be found in the header of a web page.
   b) List three elements that can be found in the footer of a web page.

9. List the four basic concepts of design to consider when developing a web page.

10. Would a photograph of a car be appropriate for a web page about gardening? Why or why not?

11. Where do elements need to be placed on a web page in order to be above the fold?

12. a) What is white space?
    b) Why is white space important in the design of a web page?

13. a) How is consistency in a website achieved?
    b) What is a visual cue?

14. a) What is usability?
    b) List two ways to increase the usability of a website.

15. When is the root folder created?

16. a) List the steps required to create a new folder named photos.
    b) List the steps required to add a file named puppies.gif from a folder on your computer's Desktop to the photos folder of a website.

17. a) List the steps required to display a list of the images contained in a website.
    b) What can be done if there are images contained in a website but they are not displayed in the Images category in the Assets panel?

18. List the steps required to place an image in a web page document from the Assets panel.

19. a) List the steps required to create a new library item named contact that contains the text 883-555-0303.
    b) What does Dreamweaver automatically add to the root folder after the first library item is created?

20. a) List the steps required to place a library item in a web page document from the Assets panel.
    b) List the steps required to edit a library item in a web page document.

21. Why should a time stamp be used in a web page document instead of typing the date?

22. What happens when the user clicks an e-mail hyperlink?

23. If a web page does not contain a copyright notice, is the information on the web page entitled to copyright protection?

True/False

24. Determine if each of the following are true or false. If false, explain why.
    a) The navigation structure should be sketched before the purpose and target audience are determined.
    b) Copyright information is typically included in the local navigation bar.
    c) A printer-friendly version of a web page is created in the Assets panel.
    d) If web page elements are above the fold on your computer, they will be above the fold on all computers.
    e) Each web page in a website should contain a link to the home page.
    f) A parent page always has a child page.
    g) Images should be stored in the root folder of a website.
    h) The top area of a web page is called a footer.
    i) Page layout should be different on each page of a website.
    j) The importance of consistency decreases with the number of pages in a website.
    k) Files and folders are organized in the Assets panel.
    l) A library item is edited in the preview area in the Assets panel.
    m) Copyright material can be reproduced only with written permission from the owner.
    n) In a web page document, a library item has a yellow background.
    o) The Property inspector can be used to change an `<h1>` tag to an `<h2>` tag.

Exercises

Exercise 1 — Hockey League

Create a new website for a local hockey league by completing the following steps:

a) Define a new site named Hockey League in a folder named Hockey League. Create a default images folder named images. The purpose of the website is to provide information about the Holyoke Hockey League Association, rules, and a game schedule. The target audience is current and prospective league members and hockey fans of all ages.

b) Into the images folder, copy the following image files from the data files for this text:

- hh_logo.gif
- hh_map.gif
- hh_player.gif

c) Using the HTML 2 column liquid, left sidebar, header and footer CSS layout, add a web page documents to the website, naming it index.html. Elements common to all pages in the website are the hh_logo.gif image in the Insert_logo placeholder and the navigation links shown in step (e). Add these elements to index.html.

d) Copy index.html and paste three copies of the file in the website folder naming them rules.html, schedule.html and location.html.

e) Modify the index.html web page document as follows:

1. Change the page title to: Holyoke Hockey League Association
2. Add content and create the navigation links as shown below:

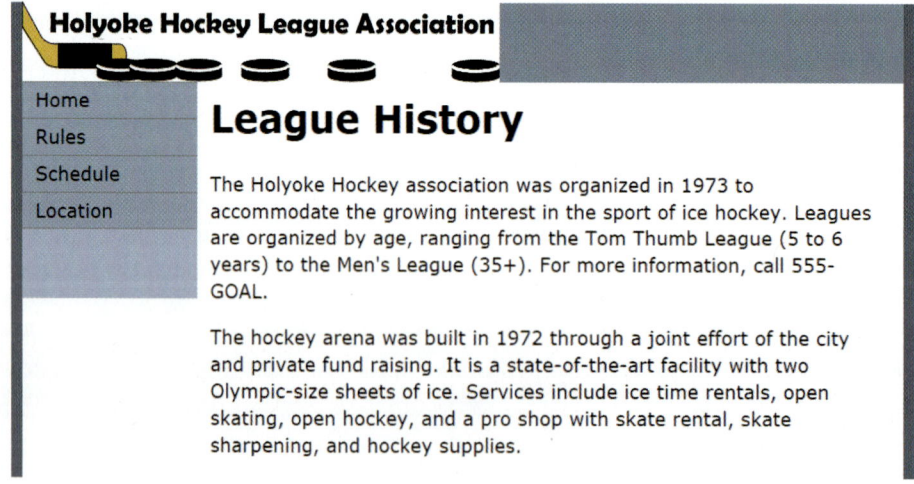

136 Chapter 4 Website Development

f) Create a new library item named footer that is similar to the following text. The date should be a time stamp that will automatically update when the web page document is saved:

Copyright 2012 Holyoke Hockey League Association. Send comments to the webmaster. Last modified March 7, 2012

Link the text webmaster to the e-mail address webmaster@emcp.com.

g) Modify the index.html web page document as follows:

1. Delete the footer placeholder text and insert the footer library item.
2. Apply Heading 2 format to League History.

h) Modify the rules.html web page document as follows:

1. Change the page title to: HHA - Rules
2. Add content as shown below:

   Rules

   Rules are in dispute at this time. Please call Name at (561) 555-GOAL for more information.

3. Create the navigation links.
4. Delete the footer placeholder text and insert the footer library item.
5. Apply Heading 2 format to Rules.

i) Modify the schedule.html web page document as follows:

1. Change the page title to: HHA - Schedule
2. Add content as shown below:

   Schedule

   The new season schedule will be posted any day now. Please call Name at (561) 555-GOAL for more information.

3. Create the navigation links.
4. Delete the footer placeholder text and insert the footer library item.
5. Apply Heading 2 format to Schedule.

j) Modify the location.html web page document as follows:

1. Change the page title to: HHA - Location
2. Add content as shown below:

   Location

3. Insert the hh_map.gif image below the Location heading and insert the hh_player.gif image in the sidebar below the navigation bar.
4. Create the navigation links.

5. Delete the footer placeholder text and insert the footer library item.

6. Apply Heading 2 format to Location.

Check—the location.html page should look similar to:

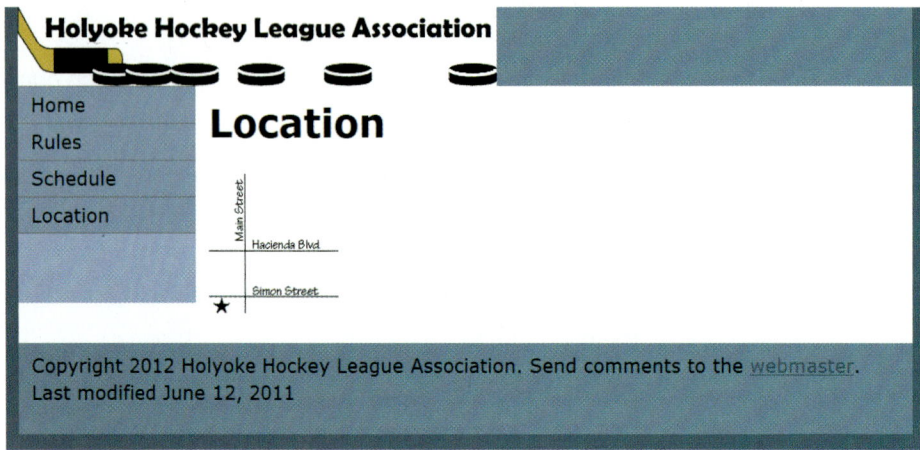

k) Check the spelling in each of the web page documents.

l) View each web page document in a browser window and test the hyperlinks.

m) Print a copy of each web page document from the browser.

Exercise 2 ——————————————— Volcanoes

Create new website about volcanoes by completing the following steps:

a) Define a new site named Volcanoes in a folder named Volcanoes. Create a default images folder named images.

b) Use the HTML 3 column fixed, header and footer CSS layout to create the index.html file. You will add two additional web page documents to the website named lava.html and vol_types.html. Before creating the additional pages, review the steps in the exercise and decide which elements are common to all pages. Add these elements to index.html and then copy the file and create the additional pages.

c) Into the images folder, copy the following image files from the data files for this text:

- vol_close.jpg
- vol_gas.jpg
- vol_logo.gif
- vol_splash.jpg

d) Modify the index.html web page document as follows:

1. Change the page title to: About Volcanoes

2. Insert the vol_logo.gif image in the Insert_logo placeholder.

3. Add content as shown below:

   Volcanoes

   A volcano is a location on the surface of the Earth where magma has erupted out of the interior of the planet. Magma is molten rock, which has melted from the extreme heat and pressure inside the Earth. Molten rock on the Earth's surface is called lava. As lava cools, it builds up and forms mountains.

   Volcanoes are classified as active or inactive. A volcano is active if it is currently erupting or expected to erupt eventually. Inactive volcanoes are older and have usually erupted many times.

   A volcanic eruption occurs when lava, gasses, and other matter come out of a vent. Violent eruptions often include chunks of rock that were blown off the interior walls of the vent. Quiet eruptions consist of lava flowing out of vents.

   Eventually, the volcano reaches the cooling stage. While the volcano cools, it reduces in size from erosion.

e) Add appropriate navigation links to the three pages in the website.

f) Create a new library item named footer that is similar to the following text, replacing Name with your name. The date should be a time stamp that will automatically update when the web page document is saved:

   Copyright 2012 - All rights reserved.

g) Modify the index.html web page document as follows:

   1. Delete the footer placeholder text.

   2. In the footer area, insert the footer library item.

   3. In the third column, delete the placeholder text.

h) Modify the lava.html web page document as follows:

   1. Change the page title to: Types of Lava Rocks

   2. Insert the vol_splash.gif image in the Insert_logo placeholder.

   3. Add content as shown below. Allow the text to wrap:

   Types of Lava Rocks: Basalt, Obsidian, Andesite

   Basalt (pronounced buh-SALT) is rock composed of mostly feldspar and pyroxene. Dark in color, basalt is considered to be a fine-grained rock. Some varieties of basalt contain iron, silica, or aluminum.

   Obsidian (pronounced ub-SID-ee-en) is semi-translucent glass that contains a large amount of silicon. Obsidian is usually black or dark gray in color and occasionally red or brown. Obsidian is formed when lava cools so quickly that it does not have time to crystallize.

   Like basalt, andesite (pronounced AN-deh-site) is composed of feldspar and pyroxene and is a fine-grained rock. Andesite is usually light to medium gray in color. Andesite is one of the most common volcanic rocks.

4. Add appropriate navigation links to the three pages in the website.

5. Delete the footer placeholder text.

6. In the footer area, insert the footer library item.

7. In the third column, delete the placeholder text.

i) Modify the vol_types.html web page document as follows:

1. Change the page title to: Types of Volcanoes

2. Insert the vol_gas.gif image in the Insert_logo placeholder.

3. Add content as shown below. Allow the text to wrap:

   Types of Volcanoes: Cinder Cones, Shield Volcanoes, Composite Volcanoes

   Cinder cone volcanoes are formed from explosive eruptions where materials are ejected high in the air and cool before they hit the ground. Fine-grained rocks are blown away by winds. Coarser rock fragments remain in a cone-shaped pile, which can be hundreds of meters tall.

   Shield volcanoes are formed by frequent, quiet eruptions and are much larger in width than in height. As smooth lava flows build up, a dome shape is formed. Shield volcanoes usually change shape when eruptions become explosive late in the life of the volcano.

   Composite volcanoes are very large and are formed from alternating explosive eruptions and quiet eruptions. This results in layers of ejected material covered by smooth lava flows. Composite volcanoes are usually symmetrical in shape and can be as high as several kilometers.

4. Add appropriate navigation links to the three pages in the website.

5. Delete the footer placeholder text.

6. In the footer area, insert the footer library item.

7. In the third column, delete the placeholder text.

j) Check the spelling in each of the web page documents.

k) View each web page document in a browser window and test the hyperlinks.

l) Print a copy of each web page document from the browser.

Exercise 3 — Lawn Care

Create new website for a lawn care service by completing the following steps:

a) Define a new site named Lawn Care in a folder named Lawn Care.

b) Using the HTML 2 column fixed, header and footer CSS layout, add three web page documents to the website, naming them index.html, services.html, and clients.html.

c) In the website root folder, create a folder named images. Into the images folder, copy the following image files from the data files for this text:
- lawn_happy.gif
- lawn_logo.gif

- lawn_mower.gif
- lawn_wheel.gif

d) Modify the index.html web page document as follows:

1. Change the page title to: Smiley's Lawn Care Service

2. Insert the lawn_logo.gif image in the Insert_logo placeholder.

3. Add content as shown below. Allow the text to wrap:

   Need lawn care services?

   Call me! Hi, I'm Smiley, and I have been working in lawn care for over 10 years. I offer many services to both commercial and residential clients. I have a long list of happy customers, and am quite adept at bringing brown lawns back to life.

   Call Smiley at 903-555-7979 or e-mail any hour of the day.

4. Link the text e-mail to the e-mail address smiley@emcp.com.

5. Add appropriate navigation links for all three pages in the website.

6. Apply Heading 2 format to Need lawn care services?

e) Create a new library item named footer that contains the following text:

   Copyright 2012 - All rights reserved

f) Modify the index.html web page document as follows:

1. Delete the footer placeholder text.

2. In the footer area, insert the footer library item.

3. Delete any remaining placeholder text.

Check—Your page should look similar to:

g) Modify the clients.html web page document as follows:

1. Change the page title to: Smiley's Lawn Care Service - Happy Clients

2. In the top cell, insert the lawn_happy.gif image.

3. Add content as shown below, making the list of customers an unordered list:

   Happy customers include:

   - Jerry's Rib Shack
   - Lake Raton Apartments
   - Bushnell Condominiums
   - Featherton Shopping Plaza
   - Candlewick Mall
   - Renewal Supply Store
   - Terry's Ice Cream
   - Residents in the Tall Oaks neighborhood
   - Residents in the Kendall Highlands neighborhood
   - Residents in the Boynton Ray neighborhood

4. Delete the footer placeholder text and then insert the footer library item.

5. Add appropriate navigation links for all three pages in the website.

6. Delete any remaining placeholder text.

h) Modify the services.html web page document as follows:

   1. Change the page title to: Smiley's Lawn Care - List of Services

   2. In the top cell, insert the lawn_mower.gif image.

   3. Add content as shown below:

      Services Offered

      Lawn Mowing
      Includes trimming, edging, and removal of clippings.

      Tree and Shrub Trimming
      Usually done every three to four months.

      Weeding
      Done by hand, no chemicals used. Includes weeds in plant beds and concrete cracks.

      Mulching
      Cedar or hardwood mulch applied, fertilizer treatment optional.

      Turf Treatments
      Aeration, fertilization, and iron and nitrogen treatments are available.

   4. Delete the footer placeholder text and then insert the footer library item.

   5. Add appropriate navigation links for all three pages in the website.

   6. Delete any remaining placeholder text and apply heading styles as appropriate.

i) Check the spelling in each of the web page documents.

j) View each web page document in a browser window and test the hyperlinks.

Exercise 4 ——————————————————————— METEOROLOGY

Modify the METEOROLOGY website by completing the following steps:

a) Open the METEOROLOGY website for editing, a website provided with the data files for this text.

b) In the website's images folder, copy the following image files from the data files for this text:

- weather_clouds.gif
- weather_logo.gif
- weather_storms.gif
- weather_wind.gif

c) Examine the four pages that make up the website and then complete the website by adding:

1. Proper navigation links.
2. An appropriate logo on each web page using the files in the images folder.
3. A last updated footer with a time stamp.
4. Appropriate page titles.

d) Check the spelling in each of the web page documents.

e) Print a copy of each web page document from the browser.

Exercise 5 ——————————————————————— SEVEN WONDERS

Modify the SEVEN WONDERS of the Ancient World website by completing the following steps:

a) Open the SEVEN WONDERS website for editing, a website provided with the data files for this text.

b) In the website's images folder, copy the following image files from the data files for this text:

- wonder_logo.gif
- wonder_map.gif

c) On all web pages:

1. Complete the navigation bar by adding links to the following pages:
   - Home
   - Temple of Artemis
   - Mausoleum at Halicarnassus
   - Colossus of Rhodes
   - Hanging Gardens of Babylon
   - Pyramid of Egypt
   - Lighthouse of Alexandria
   - Statue of Zeus

Hint: *Create the Home page navigation bar and then copy the HTML to the other pages.*

2. Add appropriate page titles.

3. Insert the wonder_logo.gif in the Insert_logo placeholder.

d) Modify the index.html web page document by inserting the wonder_map.gif image in the content area.

e) Create a new library item named footer that contains the following text:

Copyright 2012 - All rights reserved

f) Insert the footer on each web page.

g) Check the spelling in the index.html web page document.

h) View each web page document in a browser window and test the hyperlinks.

Exercise 6 — Electronic Etiquette

Create new website about electronic etiquette that contains the following:

- Three pages named index.html, written.html, and voice.html.
- An images folder. Into the images folder, copy the following image files from the data files for this text:

    eti_voice.gif
    eti_write.gif

- Appropriate page titles
- A footer with a Last updated time stamp
- Content on each page with tips about electronic etiquette, such as:

    Telephone Calls
    Always state your name and the purpose of the call.

    Cellular Phones
    Refrain from talking on the phone while driving.

    Speakerphone
    Be sure there is no background noise.

    Voicemail
    Speak slowly and clearly.

Exercise 7 ——————————————————————— Local Club

Develop a website that is for a local club, such as a bicycling club or a debate club. The website should include news about the club, club events, and appropriate topics for the club. Complete the following steps to finish the website development, writing the answers to parts a, b, c, and d on paper:

    a) Determine the purpose and target audience.

    b) Determine the web pages and then sketch the navigation structure.

    c) Determine the content and navigation links for each page.

    d) Sketch the design for each page. Match the sketch to the appropriate CSS starter layout.

    e) Create the website naming it Local Club.

    f) Create web page documents, appropriately named, and add the content.

    g) Check the spelling in the web page documents.

    h) View each web page document in a browser window and test the hyperlinks.

    i) Print a copy of each web page document from the browser.

Exercise 8 ——————————————————————— Dentist

Develop a website that is for a dentist. The website should include office hours and location, information about the dentist, and educational information about dental hygiene. Complete the following steps to finish the website development, writing the answers to parts a, b, c, and d on paper:

    a) Determine the purpose and target audience.

    b) Determine the web pages and then sketch the navigation structure.

    c) Determine the content and navigation links for each page.

    d) Sketch the design for each page. Match the sketch to the appropriate CSS starter layout.

    e) Create the website naming it Dentist.

    f) Create web page documents, appropriately named, and add the content.

    g) Check the spelling in the web page documents.

    h) View each web page document in a browser window and test the hyperlinks.

    i) Print a copy of each web page document from the browser.

Chapter 5
Images in Dreamweaver and Fireworks

This chapter introduces graphic file formats and discusses adding graphics to a web page document. Fireworks is introduced, as well as rollover behaviors, exporting HTML, and cropping images.

Graphic File Formats for Web Pages

Images on web pages are usually a GIF or JPG file because these formats are widely supported in browsers. The *GIF* format is best used for graphics that do not contain many colors, such as clip art or logos. GIF graphics are limited to 256 colors. The *JPG* format, also called JPEG, supports millions of colors and is best used for photographs. A third format, PNG, was created in the mid-1990s during a controversy over copyright of the GIF format. The *PNG* format has advantages over GIF and JPG, but it is only supported by the newest browsers.

GIF, JPG, and PNG formats are all *bitmap graphics*, which are composed of tiny squares. Each square is a *pixel* and is one solid color. Many pixels of different colors create a bitmap graphic:

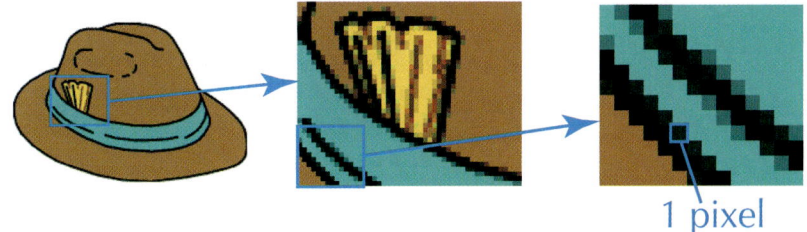

The tiny squares are commonly referred to as "dots." The number of *dots per inch (dpi)* is called the *resolution*. The larger the number of dpi, the better the quality of the graphic.

The GIF format has a *transparency* feature which allows one color in the graphic to be a transparent color, a feature not available for JPGs. A transparent color can be used to blend an image with the background color because it allows the background color to show through:

> **Images and Graphics**
> The terms "images" and "graphics" are both used to refer to pictures. Pictures may be photographs or drawings.

> **GIF, JPG, and PNG**
> GIF (Graphics Interchange Format) format is pronounced either "giff" with a hard g or "jiff." JPG (Joint Photographic Experts Group) format is pronounced "jay-peg." PNG (Portable Network Graphics) format is pronounced "ping."

Two hat GIF graphics on a colored background

In the example above, the GIF on the left has white selected as the transparent color. The GIF on the right does not have any transparent color selected. Transparency is not always used in GIF files, but it is a useful feature to have.

interlaced — GIF files can be *interlaced*, which means that a low-quality version of the graphic appears first and becomes clearer in four horizontal passes as the web page fully loads. This allows the user to see that a graphic is going to be displayed.

compression

lossless, lossy

Compression is a file format feature that reduces file size, which is helpful because smaller files load faster in a browser window. GIF graphics are compressed but retain all of the original information in a process called *lossless compression*. For JPG graphics the compression is *lossy*, which means that some data in the file is removed in order to reduce the file size. The more compression, the smaller the file, but the lower the image quality:

> **Editing Graphics**
> Double-clicking a graphic's file name in the Files panel opens the file in Fireworks or Photoshop.

Two JPG graphics with different levels of compression

In the example above, the JPG on the left has more compression and has a much lower image quality, with a small file size of 2 KB. The JPG on the right has less compression and a higher image quality, but a larger file size of 10 KB.

progressive — JPG files can be *progressive*, which is similar to an interlaced GIF. When a web page is first loaded into a browser window, a low-quality version of a progressive JPG graphic appears. The graphic becomes clearer as the page fully loads. This allows the user to see that a graphic is going to be displayed.

TIP Digital camera images are discussed in Appendix C.

PNG files support lossless compression and image transparency. The PNG format was created to improve upon and replace the GIF format, as an image-file format that does not require a patent license.

Accessibility

The Americans with Disabilities Act (ADA), enacted in 1990, calls for accessibility for all persons with disabilities. In response, the W3C developed guidelines called the Web Accessibility Initiative (WAI). Among other issues, these guidelines call for alternative text to be provided for any content that is not text.

Alternative Text

One consideration for images in a web page is that some users may not be able to view the images. The user may be visually impaired, or they may have a slow modem connection and therefore have turned images off. *Alternative text* is text added to an image that a voice synthesizer "reads" in place of the image. When an image is added to a web page, the Image Tag Accessibility Attributes dialog box is displayed:

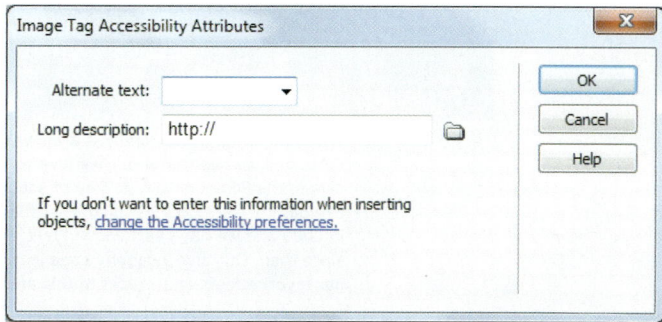

Type the text in the Alternative text box. The Long description box is used to provide a URL or file location where the user can locate expanded alternative text content. Alternative text can be edited by selecting the image in the Document window and typing text in the Alt box in the Property inspector.

TIP Alternative text that ends with a period makes voice synthesizers stop or pause, which helps users understand the content.

TIP Alternative text should be limited to 50 characters or less.

Graphic Hyperlinks

A graphic can be formatted as a hyperlink in the same manner as a text hyperlink, using either the Browse for File icon 📁 or the Point to File icon 🎯 in the Property inspector. When the pointer is moved over a graphic hyperlink in a browser window, the pointer changes to 👆.

Graphic hyperlinks are tested in a browser window. To modify links, select the linked graphic in Dreamweaver and then select Modify → Change Link or Modify → Remove Link.

Practice: SCUBA – part 1 of 7

① **OPEN THE SCUBA WEBSITE FOR EDITING**
   a. Start Dreamweaver.
   b. Open the SCUBA website for editing, which is a website provided with the data files for this text.
   c. Open the index.html web page document and then view the page in a browser.
   d. Click the links to explore the other web pages of the website.
   e. Close the browser window. Dreamweaver is displayed.

② **ADD AN IMAGE TO THE INDEX.HTML WEB PAGE DOCUMENT**
   a. Open the index.html web page document, if it is not already displayed.

Chapter 5 Images in Dreamweaver and Fireworks

b. In the Assets panel, click the Images icon ![]. A list of the images in the website's folder is displayed.

c. Double-click the map placeholder. A dialog box is displayed. The images folder should be the active folder.

   1. Double-click the sketch.gif file.
   2. In the Property inspector, in the Alt text box, type A drawing of a reef, a wreck, and a camera. and press the Enter key.

Check—Your web page document should look similar to:

d. Save the modified index.html.
e. Press F12. The document is displayed in a browser window.
f. Print a copy of the web page.
g. Close the browser window. Dreamweaver is displayed.
h. Close index.html.

③ MAKE A GRAPHIC HYPERLINK

a. Open the photos.html web page document.
b. Click the banner image at the top of the page to select it.
c. In the Property inspector, next to the Link box, drag the Point to File icon to the index.html file name in the Files panel. A graphic hyperlink is created.
d. In the Property inspector, set Alt to Link to home page. and press Enter.
e. Save the modified photos.html.
f. Press F12. The document is displayed in a browser window.
g. Click the logo at the top of the web page to test the hyperlink. The home page is displayed.
h. Close the browser window. Dreamweaver is displayed.
i. Close photos.html.

④ **MAKE ANOTHER GRAPHIC HYPERLINK**
   a. Open the locations.html web page document.
   b. Link the banner image to the index.html web page document.
   c. Set alternative text for the graphic to: Link to home page.
   d. Save the modified locations.html and then test the graphic hyperlink in a browser.
   e. Close the browser window. Dreamweaver is displayed.
   f. Close locations.html.

Creating an Image Map

hotspot   An *image map* is a graphic that contains one or more hotspots. A *hotspot* is an invisible, defined area on a graphic that is a hyperlink. In a browser, when the pointer moves over a hotspot the pointer changes to 👆 and the hotspot's alternative text is displayed:

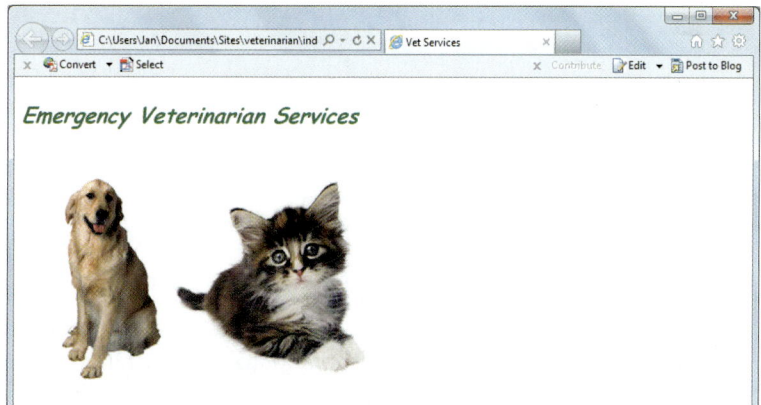

The graphic is an image map with two hotspots

To create an image map, add a graphic to a web page document and then define hotspots on the graphic. Select a graphic in a web page document to display image properties in the Property inspector:

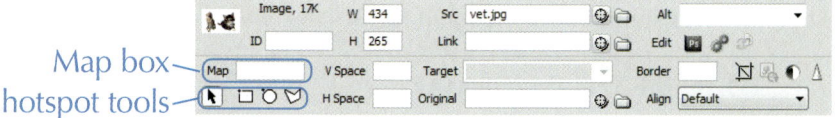

Map box
hotspot tools

- A web page document can have more than one image map, so each image map should be given a unique name in the **Map** box.

- The **hotspot tools** are used to draw or edit hotspots on the selected graphic. Draw hotspots using the Rectangular Hotspot ☐, Oval Hotspot ○, and Polygon Hotspot ✷ tools. Select and edit hotspots once they are created using the Pointer Hotspot tool ▶.

To draw a hotspot on a selected graphic, click a hotspot tool. The pointer changes to ✛ when it is moved over the graphic. If the Rectangular Hotspot or Oval Hotspot tool is selected, drag to draw the hotspot. To draw with the Polygon Hotspot tool, click to create the corner points of a shape. With each click, the area between the clicked locations fills in. Double-click to finish the hotspot. Hotspots do not have to perfectly cover an area of the graphic:

TIP Use the arrow keys to move a selected hotspot.

Hotspot properties are displayed for a selected hotspot in the Property inspector:

- Link is the web page document linked to the hotspot.
- Alt is the alternative text for the hotspot.
- Click the Pointer Hotspot tool ▶ to select the tool, then click a hotspot to select it. Drag the hotspot or use the arrow keys to move it. Drag a handle to change the shape of a selected hotspot. Press the Delete key to delete a selected hotspot.

Hotspots are tested in a browser window.

Practice: SCUBA — part 2 of 7

Dreamweaver should be started and the SCUBA website should be the working site.

① **NAME THE IMAGE MAP**
   a. Open the index.html web page document.
   b. Select the sketch.gif image. Image properties are displayed in the Property inspector.
   c. In the Property inspector, set **Map** to sketch and press Enter.

② **CREATE A RECTANGLE HOTSPOT**
   a. In the Property inspector, click the Rectangular Hotspot tool ▢.
   b. Move the pointer over the image. The pointer changes to +.

c. Starting in the upper-left corner of the image, drag down and to the right to draw a rectangle shape on the top half of the sketch, the part with "Reefs and Wrecks." Do not include the camera. If a dialog box is displayed, select **OK**. If you make a mistake, press the Delete key to delete the shape and try again.

Check—Your image should look similar to:

d. In the Property inspector, next to the Link box, drag the Point to File icon ⊙ to the locations.html file name in the Files panel.

e. In the Property inspector, set **Alt** to Link to dive locations information. and press Enter.

③ CREATE A POLYGON HOTSPOT

a. In the Property inspector, click the Polygon Hotspot tool ▽.

b. Move the pointer over the image. The pointer changes to +.

c. Draw a polygon as follows: click near the "P" at the beginning of the word "Photography". If a dialog box is displayed, click **OK**. Then, click at the tallest point of the camera drawing, then click near the "y" in the word "Photography." A polygon hotspot is created in the shape of a triangle. If you make a mistake, press the delete key to delete the shape and try again.

Check—Your image should look similar to:

d. Link the hotspot to the photos.html web page document.

e. In the Property inspector, set **Alt** to Link to the photo gallery. and press Enter.

④ EDIT HOTSPOTS

a. In the Property inspector, click the Pointer Hotspot tool ▸.

b. In the web page document, click the polygon hotspot. Handles are displayed indicating that it is selected.

c. Drag the polygon hotspot, adjusting its position over the camera drawing. Drag the handles to edit the shape. Move it to cover as much of the camera and the word "Photography" as possible.

d. Save the modified index.html.

Chapter 5 Images in Dreamweaver and Fireworks

⑤ TEST THE IMAGE MAP IN THE BROWSER WINDOW

a. Press F12. The document is displayed in a browser window.
b. Move the pointer over the image, noting where the pointer changes to 👆.
c. Click the top hotspot. The Dive Locations web page is displayed. Click the banner at the top of the page to return to the home page.
d. Click the bottom hotspot. The Photo Gallery web page is displayed. Click the banner at the top of the page to return to the home page.
e. Close the browser window. Dreamweaver is displayed.
f. Close index.html.

⑥ ADD IMAGES AND ALTERNATIVE TEXT TO A WEB PAGE DOCUMENT

a. Open photos.html.
b. Double-click the image1 placeholder.
c. Select the anemone.jpg file from the Select Image Source dialog box and then click OK.
d. In the Alt text box, type Anemone photograph.
e. Double-click the image2 placeholder.
f. Select the sponges.jpg file from the Select Image Source dialog box and then click OK.
g. In the Alt text box, type Purple sponges photograph.
h. Double-click the image3 placeholder.
i. Select the octopus.jpg file and set its alternative text to: Octopus eyes photograph.
j. Save the modified photos.html.

Check—Your web page document should look similar to:

⑦ VIEW IN A BROWSER

a. Press F12. The document is displayed in a browser.
b. Print a copy of the web page.
c. Close the browser window. Dreamweaver is displayed.

Aligning an Image

The horizontal and vertical alignment of a selected image can be changed using the Align drop-down list in the Property inspector:

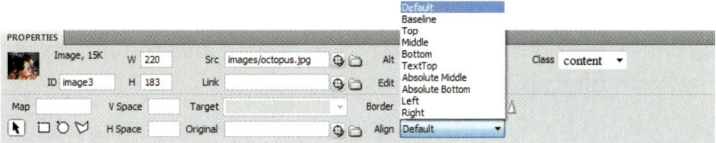

TIP CSS, which is introduced in Chapter 6, should be used to position and align images.

Resizing and Resampling an Image

If the width and height of an image needs to be changed, the image is first resized in the web page document and then resampled. *Resampling* changes the size of the file and correctly adjusts the pixels in the image. An image should not be resized in Dreamweaver and left that way because the image file has not been properly resampled.

To resize an image in a web page document, click the image to select it and display handles:

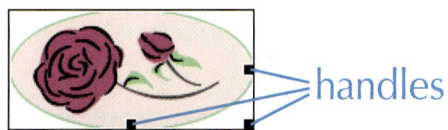

Smaller, not Larger

In general, images should not be sized larger, only smaller. The image quality decreases if the image is sized larger.

Point to a handle until the pointer changes to ↘ and drag to resize the image. Drag the corner handle while pressing the Shift key to *proportionately resize* the image, which keeps the width and height in the same ratio, preventing distortion. Drag any handle without pressing the Shift key to *stretch* the image which causes distortion:

proportionately resize

stretch

A stretched image is distorted

TIP To resample and change the image size, click the Edit image setting button in the Property inspector and then click the File tab. Change the image size and then click OK.

In the Property inspector, bold numbers are displayed in the W and H boxes for a selected image that has been resized but not yet resampled. Click the Reset icon ↻ to restore the dimensions of the image, or click the Resample button to resample the file. Resampling changes the image to the new dimensions, saves the changes to the file, and updates the image in Dreamweaver.

Practice: SCUBA – part 3 of 7

Dreamweaver should be started and the SCUBA website should be the working site.

① **ALIGN AN IMAGE**
   a. Open the photos.html web page document, if it is not already displayed.
   b. Click the octopus image to select it. Handles are displayed.
   c. In the Property inspector, click the Align drop-down list and select TextTop.
   d. Change the alignment of the other two images to TextTop.

② RESIZE AN IMAGE AND RESAMPLE IT

a. Click the anemone image to select it. In the Property inspector, note that W is 200 because this image is 200 pixels wide.

b. Select the octopus image and note the image is 220 pixels wide.

c. Drag the corner handle to make the octopus smaller. In the Property inspector, the W and H values are now bold because the image's size is different from its actual file's size.

d. In the Property inspector, click the Reset icon . The image changes back to its original size and proportions and W and H values are no longer bold.

e. Hold down the Shift key and drag the corner handle of the octopus image until W in the Property inspector is 200. If you have difficulty, click and try again.

f. In the Property inspector, click the Resample button . If a dialog box appears, select OK. The image is resampled to 200 pixels wide, which matches the size of the anemone and sponges images.

g. Save the modified photos.html.

③ VIEW IN A BROWSER

a. Press F12. The document is displayed in a browser window.

b. Print a copy of the web page and then close the browser window.

c. Close photos.html.

④ QUIT DREAMWEAVER

Introducing Fireworks

Fireworks an the image editing application that is part of the Adobe Creative Suite 5 Web Premium. Fireworks is used to create and edit images specifically for use on the Web. Fireworks documents are PNG files, which can be exported in other file formats for use in a web page. Images of other file types, such as GIF and JPG, can also be opened and edited directly in Fireworks.

To create a new document in Fireworks, select File → New, which displays the New Document dialog box:

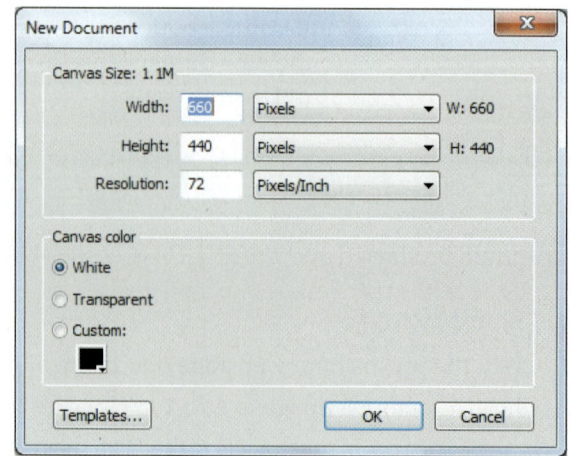

Starting Fireworks

To start Fireworks, select Start → All Programs → Adobe Web Premium CS5 → Adobe Fireworks CS5, or double-click the Fireworks icon on the Desktop:

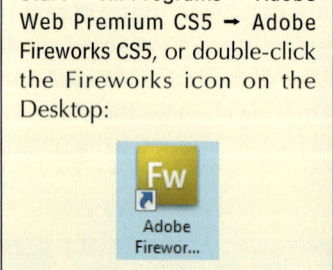

156 *Chapter 5 Images in Dreamweaver and Fireworks*

- The Canvas Size is the size of the area where an image is created. The Width and Height of the canvas are usually specified in pixels.

- The Resolution for an image used in a web page should be 72 Pixels/Inch. A larger number would only increase the file size, and not affect how the image looks when viewed on a monitor.

- The Canvas color can be White, Transparent, or a different color. Transparent is often used for an image that will be exported as a GIF, because the GIF file format supports one transparent color. The JPG file format does not support transparency.

Ideally the canvas is set to the exact size of the image, but the canvas can be initially set larger and later modified to fit the image. Select OK to create a new document and display it in a window:

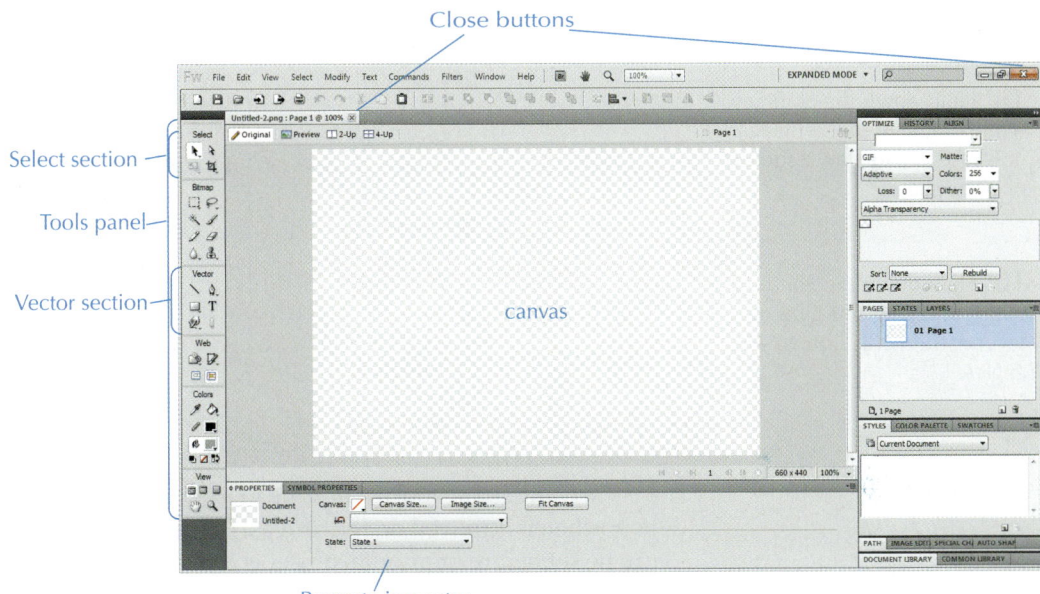

Native File Format

A native file format is the default format in which an application saves files. Files may be saved or exported in other formats, but are worked on in the native file format. The native file format in Fireworks is PNG. A Fireworks PNG document contains additional information than PNG files used in web pages. To create a PNG for use in a web page, the Fireworks document must be exported as a PNG.

- Click a **Close button** to remove the document window or the Fireworks window.

- Create and edit images using tools in the **Tools panel**. The tools are divided into sections.

- Select an image using tools in the **Select section**.

- Draw vector graphics using tools in the **Vector section**. A *vector graphic* is composed of lines connected by points, which allows for smooth resizing and a smaller file size than bitmap graphics. Fireworks can be used to create vector graphics as well as bitmap graphics such as GIF or JPG.

- Create and edit images on the **canvas**. A canvas specified as transparent appears as a checkerboard pattern. The pattern does not appear in an image once it has been exported.

- Change properties of the selected text or object using the **Property inspector**.

Chapter 5 Images in Dreamweaver and Fireworks

TIP Files that are not directly used in a website are best kept in a folder outside the website root folder.

Select File ➡ **Save** to save a Fireworks document. Fireworks documents are automatically saved in PNG format. The PNG file should be saved to a location outside of the website and used to export graphics to the website in JPG or GIF format. If a graphic needs to be edited, the PNG file can be edited and exported again. Exporting is discussed later in this chapter.

Drawing Objects in Fireworks

Lines and shapes can be drawn on the canvas using tools in the Vector section in the Tools panel. To draw a line, click the Line tool and then drag on the canvas. To draw a shape, click and hold down the mouse button on the Rectangle tool to display a menu of shape tools:

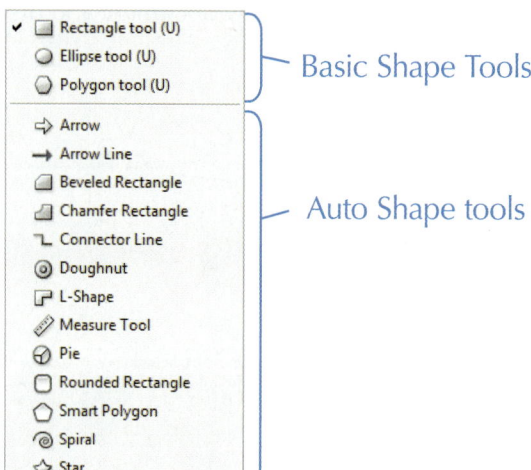

TIP Hold down the Shift key while dragging the Rectangle or Ellipse tool to draw a square or circle shape.

TIP Hold down the Shift key while dragging the Line tool to constrain the line to 45° angles.

When any shape tool or the Line tool is selected, the pointer changes to + when it is moved on the canvas. Properties in the Property inspector can be set before or after an object is drawn:

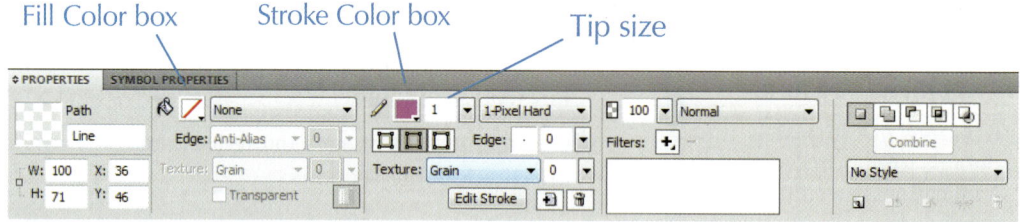

- The **Fill Color box** is the color that fills the shape, and the **Stroke Color box** is the color that outlines the shape. A indicates transparent, or no color. Click a color box to change the stroke or fill color.

TIP Hold down the Alt key and drag to draw the center of the shape at the location of the pointer.

- The **Tip size** affects the thickness of the shape's stroke or line in pixels. Select a different thickness in the list.

When selected, the rectangle and polygon tools have additional options available in the Property inspector:

- For a rectangle, **Roundness** rounds the corners.

Control Points in Auto Shapes

Some Auto Shape objects display control points ◆ when selected. Each control point affects different properties of the object when dragged:

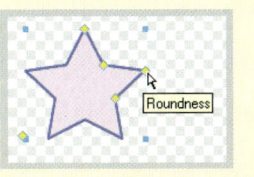

Shapes

The Auto Shapes tab in the Assets panel contains a variety of shapes you can add to the canvas. For example:

- For a polygon, the Shape can be either polygon or star. The number of Sides can be specified, as well as the degrees of Angle between the sides of the polygon.

Most Auto Shape tools also have additional options available in the Property inspector. For example, the fill color of a rectangle can be changed from Solid to a Gradient or Pattern fill.

Once an object is drawn, use the Pointer tool ▶ in the Select section in the Tools panel to click and select an object, or drag to move an object. Changing the values in the X and Y boxes in the Property inspector also moves a selected object.

A selected object can be resized using several methods:

- Change the values in the W (width) and H (height) boxes in the Property inspector.
- Use the Pointer tool ▶ in the Select section in the Tools panel to drag a handle. To proportionately resize an object, hold down the Shift key while dragging a corner handle.
- Use the Scale tool in the Select section in the Tools panel to drag a handle. Dragging a corner handle resizes the object proportionately, and dragging a side handle distorts the shape.

Adding Text in Fireworks

Text can be added to the canvas as a separate object. Select the Text tool T from the Vector section in the Tools panel and then move the pointer over the canvas. The pointer changes to Ị. Click to create a text block that changes size to accommodate text as it is typed:

a new, empty text block   the text block after typing

Properties in the Property inspector can be changed before a text block is created, or after text is typed:

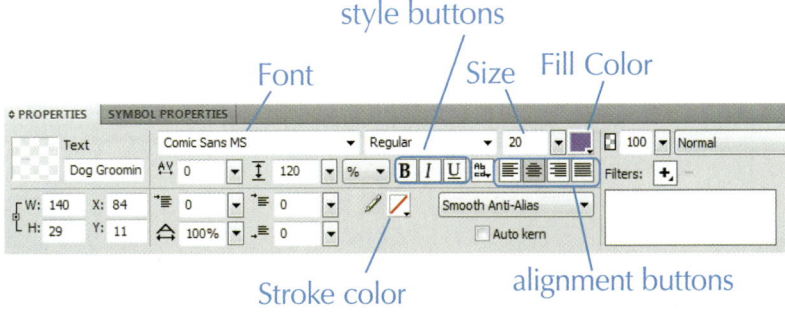

- The Font list is the name that describes the shape and style of the letters in the text. A new font can be selected from the list.
- The Size box is the size of the text. A new size can be typed or set using the slider.

TIP Fonts, sizes, and text color are discussed in Chapter 6.

Chapter 5 Images in Dreamweaver and Fireworks   159

- The Fill Color box is the text color. Click the Fill Color box and select a different color to change the fill color.
- The style buttons **B** *I* U indicate **bold**, *italic*, and underlined text. Click a style button to apply the style. Click the same style button again to remove the style.
- The alignment buttons are used the same way style buttons are used. Alignment buttons indicate the arrangement and position of text in the text block:

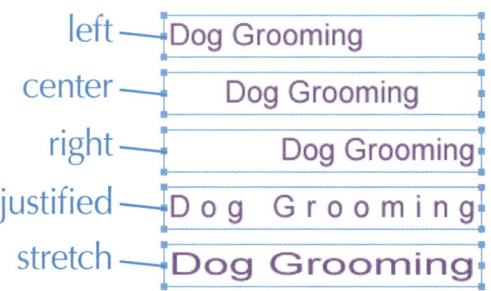

Text blocks are objects that are moved and resized in the same manner as shapes. Resizing a text block by dragging a corner handle changes the text block to a fixed width block, and it will no longer change size as more text is typed. However, it can be resized repeatedly by dragging on its handles.

Select the Text tool and click in the text block to place the insertion point and edit text.

Aligning Objects in Fireworks

Selected objects can be aligned with respect to each other using commands in the Modify → Align submenu. Multiple objects are selected using the Pointer tool in the Select section in the Tools panel. Drag the pointer to draw a rectangle that touches all of the objects to select them, or hold down the Shift key and click each object:

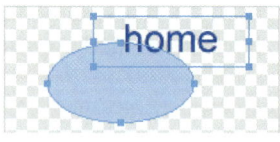

TIP Select Window → Align to display the Align panel, which can be used to align objects.

Select Modify → Align → Center Vertical to align the centers of the objects on a vertical axis:

Select Modify → Align → Center Horizontal to align the centers of the objects on a horizontal axis:

Additional alignment commands include Left, Right, Top, and Bottom.

Modifying the Canvas

When an image is finished, select Modify → Canvas → Trim Canvas to reduce the canvas to exactly fit the objects. Other commands in the Modify → Canvas submenu can also be used to modify the canvas:

- Fit Canvas is used to increase the size of the canvas enough to fit all of the objects.
- Canvas Size is used to change the dimensions of the canvas size in pixels.
- Canvas Color is used to change the canvas color, such as white or transparent.

Optimizing and Exporting a Fireworks Document

To use a Fireworks document in Dreamweaver, it should be optimized and then exported in a format other than PNG. An *optimized* image has the best possible quality and the smallest possible file size. A small file size allows a web page to load faster in a browser window.

The Export Wizard is used to choose the best optimization settings and to then export the document. Select File → Export Wizard to display a dialog box. Select the Select an export format option:

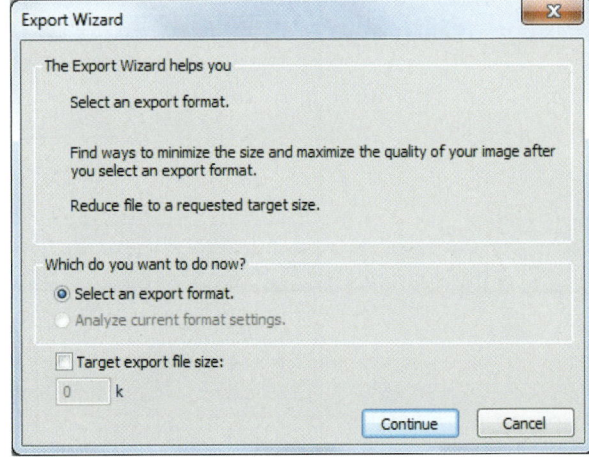

> **Target File Size**
>
> The target file size is the size, in kilobytes, of the exported file. If an approximate file size is known, select **Target export file size** in the first Export Wizard dialog box and type the number of kilobytes in the k box.

Select Continue to display the next dialog box. Select Dreamweaver because the file will be used in Dreamweaver:

Chapter 5 Images in Dreamweaver and Fireworks

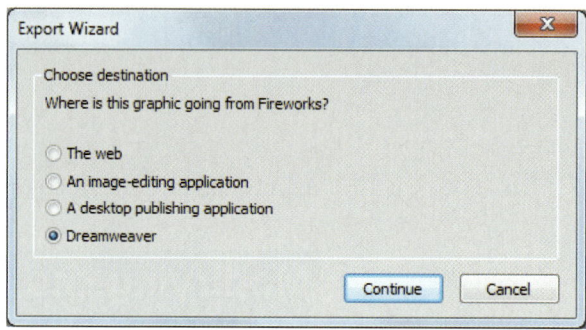

Select Continue to display recommended file formats:

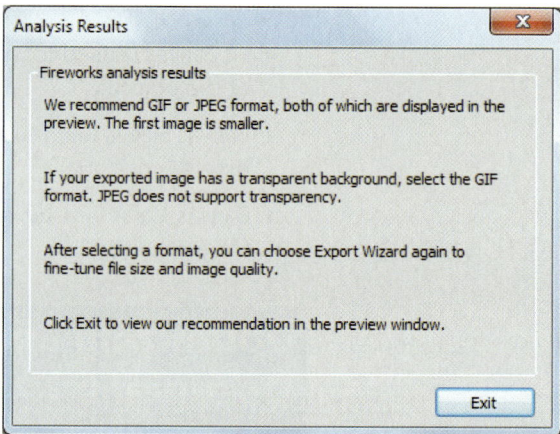

Select Exit to display the Image Preview window:

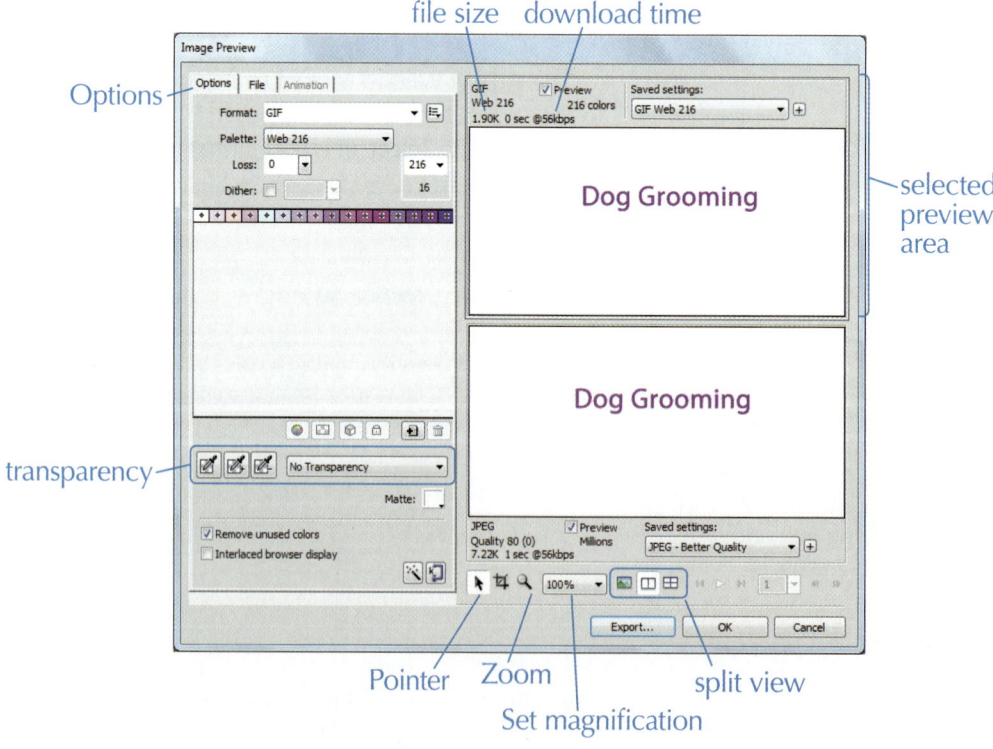

- The **file size** and **download time** are displayed in each preview area and should be considered when choosing between suggested file formats.

Chapter 5 Images in Dreamweaver and Fireworks

- The **preview areas** display the image in the suggested file formats. Settings can be changed in the preview areas, but remember that the window opens with the best choices.

- The **split view buttons** change the number of preview areas that are displayed to one, two, or four. The window opens with the number of preview areas needed to display the suggested file formats.

- The **Set magnification** list changes the magnification of the preview areas with precision. 100% is the best choice when viewing an image for quality.

- Click the **Zoom button** to change the pointer to ⊕ when moved over a preview area. Click to magnify the preview areas. Hold down the Alt key to change the pointer to ⊖. Click to zoom out.

- Click the **Pointer button** and then drag an image to move it in the preview area.

- Click a **transparency button** to change the pointer to ✐ when it is moved over a color in the color list, and clicking a color selects the transparency color, adds the color to the transparency, or removes the transparency color.

- Select Index transparency in the **Transparency list** if the image should have a transparent background. In the example on the previous page, the image should have a transparent background, so GIF would be the best file format choice and the transparency should be changed to Index transparency.

- Triple-click a preview area to display the optimization settings in the Options tab, where the options can be changed.

With the best preview selected, click **Export** to display the Export dialog box with a file name already selected:

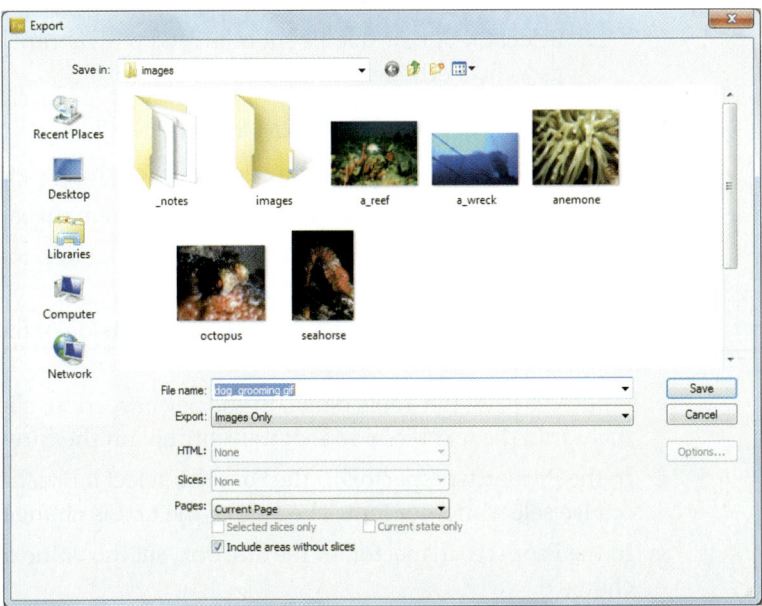

The extension .gif indicates that the document will be exported as a GIF

Chapter 5 Images in Dreamweaver and Fireworks   163

The Save in list and the contents box below it are used to navigate to the location where the file is to be saved. A Fireworks image exported for use in a website should be saved in the website's images folder. Type a descriptive name for the image in the File name box, and set Export to Images Only. Select Save to export the image. In Dreamweaver, the exported image can then be inserted into a web page document.

Practice: SCUBA – part 4 of 7

① **START FIREWORKS**

Ask your instructor for the appropriate steps to start Fireworks. Note the canvas, Tools panel, and Property inspector.

② **CREATE AND SAVE A NEW FIREWORKS DOCUMENT**

Select File → New. A dialog box is displayed.

1. In the dialog box, specify the following:

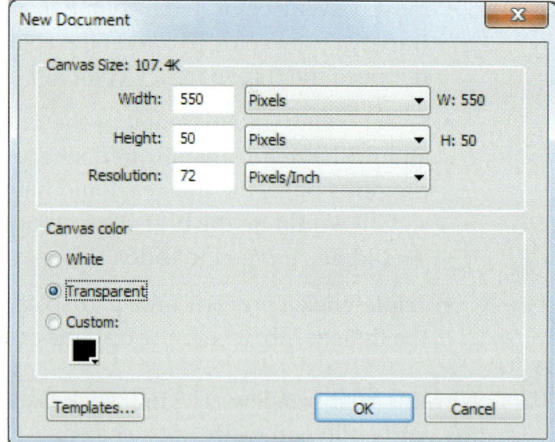

2. Select OK. A new document is created with a transparent canvas that appears as a checkerboard pattern.

③ **ADD A TEXT OBJECT AND FORMAT THE TEXT**

a. In the Tools panel, in the Vector section, click the Text tool T .

b. Move the pointer over the canvas. The pointer changes to I.

c. On the canvas (not the gray document area), click to create a new, empty text block.

d. Type Favorite Reefs and click in the canvas outside of the text block. The text block is selected.

e. If necessary, in the Tools panel, in the Select section, click the Pointer tool and then drag the text block so that it is entirely on the canvas.

f. In the Property inspector, in the Font list, select a Brush Script font if it is available or else select another font. The font of the text is changed.

g. In the Property inspector, in the Size box, set the value to 28. The size of the text is changed.

h. In the Property inspector, click the Fill Color box and select the color that corresponds to #0099FF:

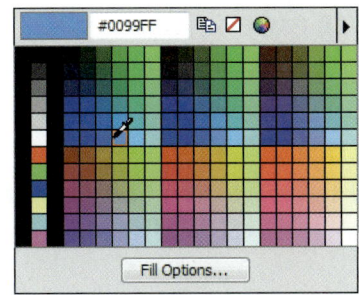

i. In the Property inspector, click the Bold button **B**. The text is bold.

j. In the Property inspector, set the stroke color to transparent ✎ ⃞, if it is not already set.

Check—Your canvas should look similar to:

④ MODIFY THE CANVAS AND SAVE THE DOCUMENT

a. Select Modify → Canvas → Trim Canvas. The canvas now exactly fits the text.

b. Select File → Save.
   1. Use the Save in list to navigate to a folder that is outside of any website folder.
   2. In the File name box, replace the existing text with: fav_reefs
   3. Select Save. Fireworks automatically adds the .png extension, so the document is saved with the file name fav_reefs.png.

⑤ EXPORT THE IMAGE

a. Select File → Export Wizard. A dialog box is displayed.

b. Select the Select an export format option and then select Continue. The next dialog box is displayed.

c. Select Dreamweaver because the file will be used in Dreamweaver, and then select Continue. The next dialog box is displayed.

d. Read the information in the dialog box and then select Exit. The Export Preview window is displayed. The top preview area has GIF settings and the bottom preview area is JPG. The GIF preview is selected, and the GIF settings appear in the Options tab in the left side of the Export Preview window.
   1. In the Transparency list, select Index Transparency.
   2. Click the Zoom button 🔍.
   3. Click the top preview area. Both preview areas are zoomed in and the transparent background of the GIF image is more apparent.
   4. Select Export. The Export dialog box is displayed.
      a) Use the Save in list to navigate to the images folder in the SCUBA folder.
      b) In the File name box, type the file name fav_reefs.gif if it is not already there.
      c) Check that in the Export list the Export Wizard has already selected Images Only, then select Save. A GIF is exported to the SCUBA website.

Chapter 5 Images in Dreamweaver and Fireworks

⑥ ADD AN IMAGE TO A WEB PAGE

a. Start Dreamweaver. The SCUBA website should be the working website.

b. Open the locations.html web page document.

c. Delete the text: FAVORITE REEFS

d. In the Assets panel, click the Images icon ▣ if it is not already selected. The images in the site are displayed. Select ▤ → Refresh Site List . The fav_reefs.gif image is displayed in the list.

e. Drag the fav_reefs.gif file from the Assets panel to the location that contained the deleted text. A dialog box is displayed. Add appropriate alternative text.

Check—Your document should look similar to:

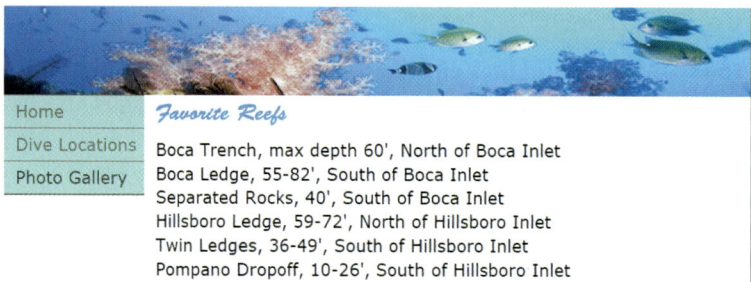

⑦ CREATE A SECOND GIF

a. Switch back to Fireworks.

b. Follow steps ② through ⑤ to create a second Fireworks document named fav_wrecks.png that looks similar to:

c. Save the document and then export it to the images folder of the SCUBA website naming it: fav_wrecks.gif

d. Follow step ⑥ to insert the fav_wrecks.gif image into the locations.html web page:

e. Save the modified locations.html.

Creating a Button Symbol in Fireworks

In a web page document, a *button* is an element that indicates to the user that it is a graphic hyperlink by its appearance. A button can be created easily in Fireworks, and then several copies placed together in a Fireworks document to form a navigation bar that can be exported to Dreamweaver.

A button is created by drawing the objects that make up the button or inserting a button from the common library:

The objects are then selected together and made into a single object called a *symbol*. A symbol is similar to a library item in Dreamweaver, except a symbol placed on a canvas does not have to have its link broken to be edited. In Fireworks, symbols appear in the Library panel in the Assets panel group.

Select Modify → Symbol → Convert to Symbol to display a dialog box where a descriptive name should be typed for the symbol:

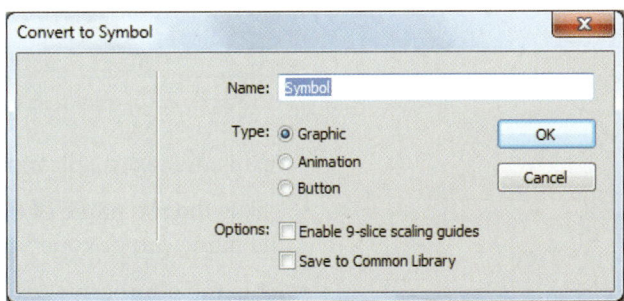

Select **Button** and then **OK** to convert the selected objects to a button symbol and add the symbol to the Document Library:

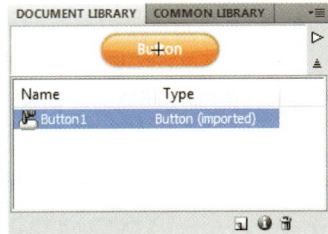

Items in the Library are stored with the open Fireworks document.

instance — When a symbol is created, the selected objects on the canvas are changed into an *instance* of the symbol, which is a copy of the button symbol:

Styles

The **Styles** tab in the Assets panel contains a variety of styles that can be applied to a button. For example:

TIP Symbols are useful when graphics need to be used more than once.

slice   A symbol is also automatically sliced. *Slicing* is the way Fireworks divides an image so that interactivity can be assigned. The red lines on the canvas are slice boundaries. A button symbol has only one slice—the entire object itself. Therefore interactivity is assigned to the entire button object.

Navigation bars usually have more than one button. More instances can be added to the canvas by dragging the button symbol from the Library to the canvas. Another way to create an instance is to select an instance on the canvas and then select Edit → Clone, which places another button on top of the selected one. The arrow keys can then be used to position the button, or the Pointer tool can be used to drag the button. A document can contain many clones of a symbol:

Each instance of a symbol can be selected individually and its properties changed in the Property inspector:

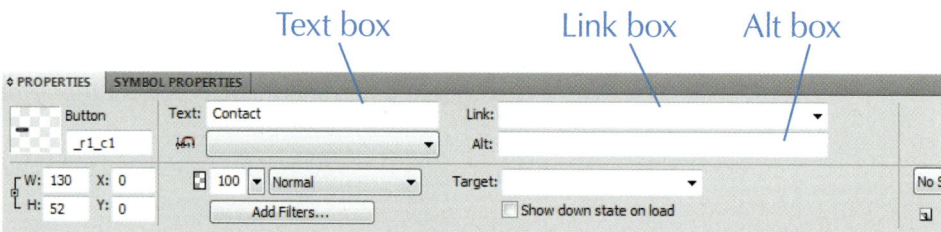

- Text is the text displayed on the button. New text can be typed.
- Link is the file name of the document linked to the button. A new file name can be typed or selected from the list.
- Alt is the alternative text for the button. New alternative text can be typed.

Click Preview at the top of the Document window to display the button as it will appear in a website. The preview is interactive, so moving the pointer over or clicking a button displays the interactivity. Click Original to return to the editing view.

Button Symbol Rollover Behavior

A *behavior* is how a symbol interacts with the user. The default behavior for a button symbol is a *rollover*, which allows each state of a button symbol to display a different image. In Fireworks, a button symbol has four states:

- The *Up state* is also called the normal state. A button is in this state when a pointer is not over it or it is not clicked.
- The *Over state* is when the pointer is moved over a button.
- The *Down state* is when a button is clicked.
- The *Over While Down state* is when the pointer is moved over a button that is in the Down state.

JavaScript

Rollover behavior is defined with JavaScript code. Fireworks automatically generates the JavaScript for a button.

To modify the images for each state of a button symbol, double-click a button instance on the canvas or the button symbol's preview in the Library panel.

Each **state** is edited separately. Click the State button to select a state option, either Up, Over, Down, or Over While Down:

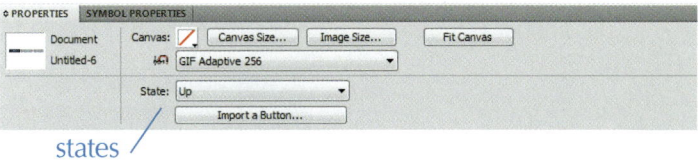

states

Select a state option to display the button as it will appear in that state. If the work area is empty, click the Copy Up Graphic button to copy the button from the previous state into the work area, then make any edits such as color changes. Click to make the changes to the button symbol and to all the instances on the canvas. Edits made in the Button Editor window do not affect text, alternative text, and links that were set for each button instance on the canvas.

Click Preview at the top of the Document window to display the button as it will appear in a website. The preview is interactive, so moving the pointer over or clicking a button displays the images for each button state. Click Original to return to the editing view.

Practice: SCUBA – part 5 of 7

Fireworks should be started.

① CREATE AND DRAW OBJECTS

a. In Fireworks, close any open documents.
b. Select File → New. A dialog box is displayed.
  1. In the dialog box, set the options to:

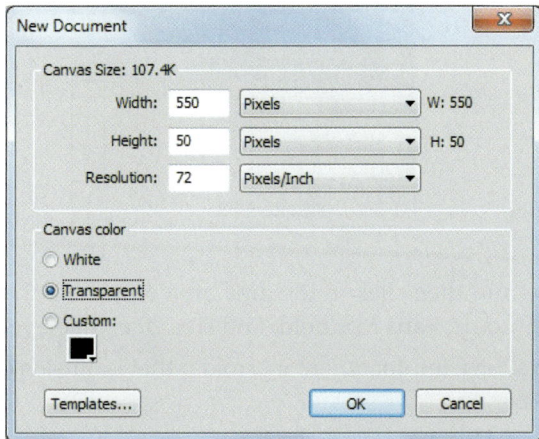

  2. Select OK. A new document is created with a transparent canvas.

c. In the Tools panel, in the Vector section, click the Rectangle tool.
d. On the canvas, draw a rectangle of any size.
e. In the Property inspector, set W to 150 and H to 30 and press Enter. The rectangle is resized. Note that you may have to click the Constrain proportions button to the left of the W and H boxes.
f. In the Property inspector, click the Fill Color box and select the color that corresponds to #0000CC:

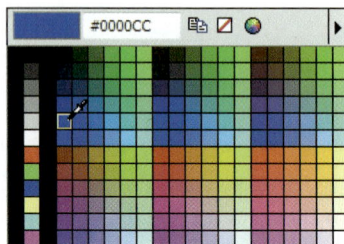

Check—Your canvas should look similar to:

g. In the Tools panel, in the Vector section, click the Text tool T.
h. On the rectangle on the canvas, click to create a new, empty text block.
i. In the Property inspector:
   1. In the Font box, select Comic Sans MS if it is available or else select Arial.
   2. In the Size box change the value to 20 and press Enter.
   3. Click the Center alignment button if it is not already selected.
   4. Click the Bold button B if it is not already selected.
   5. Click the Fill Color box and select the color that corresponds to #FFFFFF:

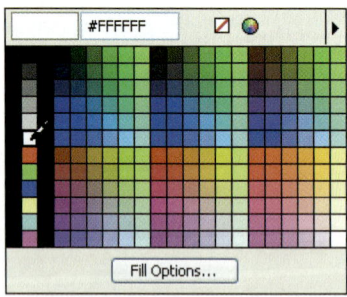

j. Type button text and then click in the gray area outside of the canvas. Text that is white, centered, Comic Sans MS, bold, and size 20 is displayed.
k. Select File → Save. Save the document in a folder that is outside of any website folder, naming it: divebar.png

② ALIGN THE OBJECTS

a. In the Tools panel, in the Select section, click the Pointer tool.
b. On the canvas, click the rectangle to select it.
c. Hold down the Shift key, and on the canvas, click the text block to select it. Both objects are selected.

d. Select Modify → Align → Center Vertical. The objects are aligned vertically.
e. With both objects still selected, select Modify → Align → Center Horizontal. The objects are aligned horizontally.
f. With both objects selected, drag the objects to the left side of the canvas.
   Check—Your canvas should look similar to:

g. Save the modified divebar.png.

③ CONVERT THE OBJECTS TO A BUTTON SYMBOL
a. Select the rectangle and the text block if they are not already selected. Handles are displayed for both objects:

b. Select Modify → Symbol → Convert to Symbol. A dialog box is displayed.
   1. In the **Name** box, type: blue button
   2. Select **Button**.
   3. Select **OK**. The objects are converted to a Button symbol, which is added to the Document Library. The canvas displays an instance of the button symbol and slice boundaries are displayed.

④ PREVIEW THE BUTTON AND CREATE MORE INSTANCES OF THE BUTTON
a. At the top of the Document window, click ⬚Preview. A preview of the button with correct colors is displayed.
b. At the top of the Document window, click ✏Original. The editing view is displayed.
c. On the canvas, select the instance if it is not already selected.
d. Select Edit → Clone. Another instance is added to the canvas.
e. Hold down the right arrow key until the two instances are next to each other:

f. Select Edit → Clone. Another instance is created.
g. Hold down the right arrow key until the three instances are in a row:

⑤ CHANGE THE PROPERTIES OF EACH INSTANCE
a. On the canvas, click the far-left instance to select it.
b. In the Property inspector, set **Text** to Home and press Enter.
c. In the Property inspector, set **Link** to index.html and press Enter.
d. In the Property inspector, set **Alt** to Link to home page. and press Enter.

e. On the canvas, select the middle button instance and in the Property inspector set the properties to:
      - Text: Dive Locations
      - Link: locations.html
      - Alt: Link to dive locations information.
   f. On the canvas, select the far-right button instance and set the properties to:
      - Text: Photo Gallery
      - Link: photos.html
      - Alt: Link to the photo gallery.

⑥ EDIT THE OVER BUTTON STATE IMAGES
   a. On the canvas, double-click the button symbol instance.
   b. In the Property inspector, click the **State** button and select **Over**. No image yet exists for this state.
   c. In the Property inspector, click **Copy Up Graphic**. The Up state image is copied to the Over state.
   d. Click the text block to select it.
   e. In the Property inspector, click the Fill Color box and select the color that corresponds to #33FFFF:

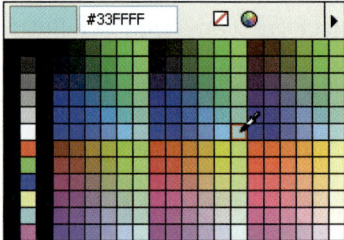

   The text is now light blue for the Over state.

⑦ EDIT THE DOWN STATE AND THE OVER WHILE DOWN STATE
   a. In the Document Library, double-click the button symbol instance.
   b. In the Property inspector, click the **State** button and select **Down**. No image yet exists for this state.
   c. Click **Copy Over Graphic**. The Over state image is copied to the Down state.
   d. Click the text block to select it.
   e. In the Property inspector, click the Fill Color box and select the color that corresponds to #FFFFFF (white). The text is now white for the down state.
   f. Click the rectangle to select it.
   g. In the Property inspector, change the Fill Color to #33FFFF:

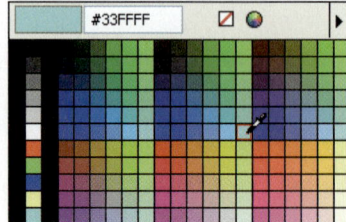

   The rectangle is now light blue for the Down state.

h. In the Document Library, double-click the button symbol instance.

i. In the Property inspector, click the **State** button and select **Over While Down** tab. No image yet exists for this state.

j. Click **Copy Down Graphic**. The Down state image is copied to the Over While Down state. This state will remain as is so that nothing changes when the pointer is moved over a button displayed in the Down state.

k. Click the **Page 1** link.

⑧ MODIFY THE CANVAS

Select Modify → Canvas → Trim Canvas. The canvas is reduced in size to exactly fit the instances.

⑨ PREVIEW THE BUTTONS

a. At the top of the Document window, click [Preview]. A preview is displayed.

b. Move the pointer over the buttons and click each one.

c. At the top of the Document window, click [Original]. The editing view is displayed.

d. Save the modified divebar.png.

Exporting HTML and Images from Fireworks

Exporting a Fireworks document with symbol instances generates many files, including a set of image files for rollover behavior states and an HTML file that arranges the objects in the Fireworks document. Also in the HTML file is the code that controls the rollover behavior of the clones. For example, a Fireworks document with a button symbol and three clones generates an HTML document and up to 12 image files, one image file for each state of each button instance.

The Export Wizard can be used to optimize and automatically generate all the files associated with a Fireworks document. Select File → Export Wizard to display the same dialog boxes as shown in the "Optimizing and Exporting" section earlier in this chapter. When the Export Preview dialog box is displayed, select **Export** to display a dialog box with HTML and Images as the file type:

Chapter 5 Images in Dreamweaver and Fireworks

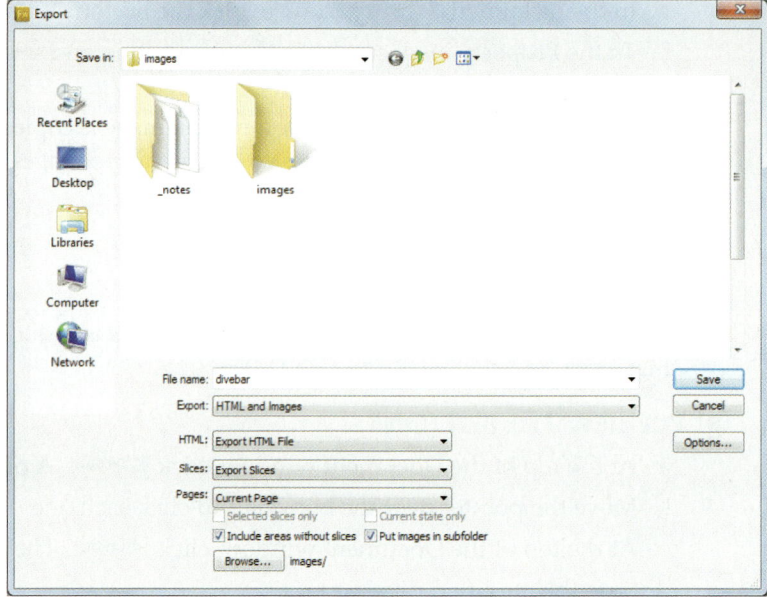

- Use the Save in list and the contents box below it to navigate to the location of the website root folder where the HTML document is to be saved.
- Type a descriptive file name in the File name box.
- The Export list is set to HTML and Images by the Export Wizard.
- The HTML and the Slices lists should be set as shown in the dialog box above.
- Select the Include Areas without slices check box to ensure that the entire document is exported.
- Select the Put Images in subfolder check box to place image files into the images folder of the website root folder specified in the Save in list.
- Select Save to create an HTML document and the image files associated with all the button states.

Using an Exported HTML Document in Dreamweaver

A Fireworks document exported as HTML and Images to a Dreamweaver website is used by following these steps:

1. Open the HTML document that was exported from Fireworks.
2. Select <body> in the Tag selector to select everything in the body of the document.
3. Select Edit → Copy to make a copy of the HTML.
4. Open a web page document and place the insertion point where the exported document should appear.
5. Select Edit → Paste to add the HTML to the document.

source file

In Dreamweaver, a selected image from Fireworks can be edited by clicking the Edit button in the Property inspector. Fireworks is started and the PNG *source file*, the PNG file that was created in Fireworks, is displayed. After edits are made and the modified PNG is saved, select Done in the Fireworks document window to close the PNG file. Changes are automatically made to the exported HTML document in Dreamweaver. The HTML that was copied and pasted in Dreamweaver is also updated. Note that changes to links need to be made in Dreamweaver.

Changing Behaviors in Dreamweaver

In Dreamweaver, behaviors for a selected button are listed in the Behaviors panel in the Tag panel group. Select Window → Behaviors to display the Behaviors panel:

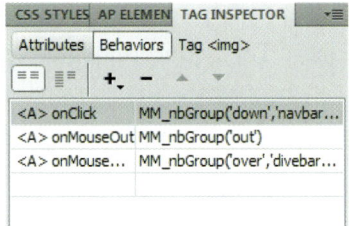

Click the behavior to display a list of options:

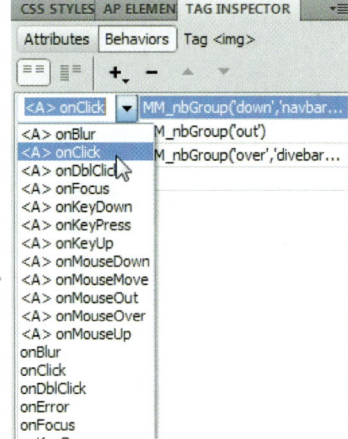

Change the behavior by selecting a different option in the list.

Chapter 5 Images in Dreamweaver and Fireworks

Practice: SCUBA – part 6 of 7

Fireworks should be started and divebar.png should be open.

① **OPTIMIZE AND EXPORT THE NAVIGATION BAR**

a. Select File ➡ Export Wizard. A dialog box is displayed.

b. Select the Select an export format option and then select Continue. The next dialog box is displayed.

c. Select Dreamweaver because the file will be used in Dreamweaver, and then select Continue. The next dialog box is displayed.

d. Read the information in the dialog box and then select Exit. The Export Preview window is displayed. The top preview area has GIF settings and the bottom preview area is JPG. The GIF preview is selected, and the GIF settings appear in the Options tab in the left side of the Export Preview window.

e. In the Transparency list, select Index Transparency.

f. Select Export. The Export dialog box is displayed. Set the options to:

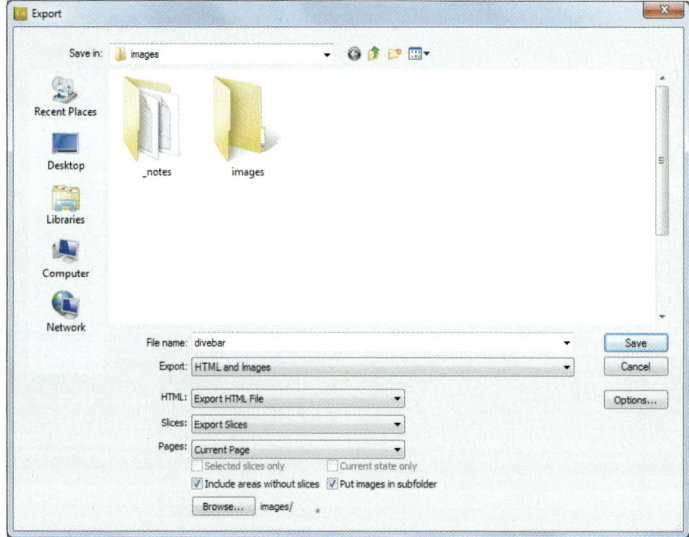

Select Browse. A dialog box is displayed. Navigate to the images folder in the root folder of the SCUBA website and then select Open.

g. Select Save. An HTML document named divebar.html is created in the SCUBA website folder and all the images used in divebar.html are added to the images folder of the website.

② **SAVE THE MODIFIED DIVEBAR.PNG AND QUIT FIREWORKS**

③ **EDIT THE SCUBA WEBSITE**

a. Start Dreamweaver. The SCUBA website should be the working website.

b. In the Files panel, check that the divebar.html document is in the website's folder.

c. In the Assets panel, display the Images category. Additional images have been added. If only the few images from earlier practices are displayed, select 🗐 ➡ Refresh Site List.

④ OPEN DIVEBAR.HTML AND COPY THE HTML TO ANOTHER DOCUMENT

a. In the Files panel, double-click the divebar.html web page document. The document contains the three buttons created in Fireworks in the previous practice.

b. Select the <body> tag in the Tag selector at the bottom of the Document window. The entire document is selected.

c. Select Edit → Copy. A copy is created of the selected content.

d. Open the index.html web page document.

e. Click in the footer area to place the insertion point.

f. Select Edit → Paste. The navigation bar is pasted in the footer area.

g. Save and the modified index.html.

⑤ TEST THE BUTTONS IN A BROWSER WINDOW

a. Press F12. The document is displayed in a browser window.

b. Move the pointer over the buttons and observe the text changing to light blue for the Over state.

c. Click the Dive Locations button. The locations.html web page document is displayed in the browser window.

d. Press the Back button and then test the other two buttons.

e. Close the browser window. Dreamweaver is displayed.

f. Close index.html.

Cropping an Image in Fireworks and in Dreamweaver

There may be occasions when only part of an image is needed. *Cropping* an image trims away areas that are not needed. To crop an image that is open in Fireworks, click the Crop tool ⊞ in the Select section in the Tools panel. Move the pointer over the canvas to change the pointer to ⊞ and then drag to draw a cropping box:

Chapter 5 Images in Dreamweaver and Fireworks

Adjust the cropping box by dragging any handle or by setting the W (width) and H (height) properties in the Property inspector. The arrow keys can also be used to move the cropping box. Double-click in the cropping box or press Enter to crop the image:

The canvas is resized to the cropped image. If a mistake is made, select Edit → Undo Crop Document. Select File → Save to save the changes. Once a cropped image is saved, the trimmed areas cannot be restored.

Instead of using Fireworks to crop images, an image in a web page document can be cropped directly in Dreamweaver. Select the image in the web page document then click the Crop tool ⬚ in Property inspector. A cropping box appears in the image. Adjust the cropping box by dragging handles and using the arrow keys to move the box. Double-click in the box or press Enter to crop the image:

The canvas is resized to include only the cropped image. If a mistake is made, select Edit → Undo Crop. The cropped image can be restored using the Undo command until Dreamweaver is quit.

Editing an Image in Fireworks from Dreamweaver

There may be occasions when an image in a web page document needs to be edited. In Dreamweaver, select an image and then click ▣ in the Property inspector to start Fireworks and display a dialog box:

TIP By default, jpg files are set to be edited in Photoshop. For this chapter, select **Edit → Preferences** and then click **File Types/Editors** in the **Category** list. Select the .jpg extension and then select **Fireworks** and click the **Make Primary** button.

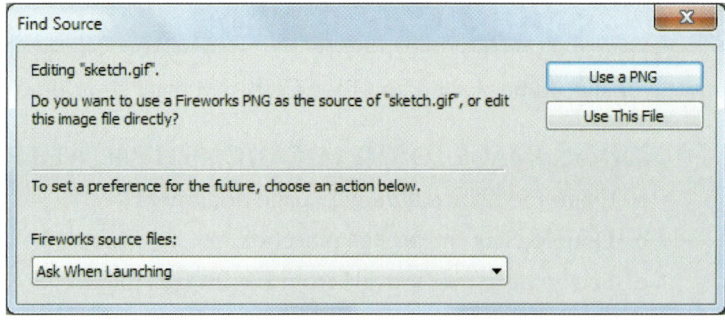

Select Use This File to open the image in Fireworks. After edits such as cropping are made to the image, click **Done** in the Document window to save the changes to the image, close the file, and update the image in Dreamweaver in the web page document. If the size of the image changed, click ⟳ in the Property inspector in Dreamweaver to adjust the size.

Swap Images

The Swap Image action exchanges one image on a web page for another when the mouse rolls over the image. For this behavior to work properly, both images must be the same width and height.

To add a swap image action, select the image and give it a name in the ID box in the Property inspector:

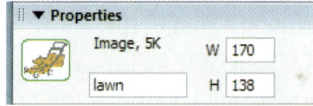

Image is named lawn

Then, select **Window → Behaviors** to display the Behaviors panel, click ➕, and select **Swap Image** to display a dialog box:

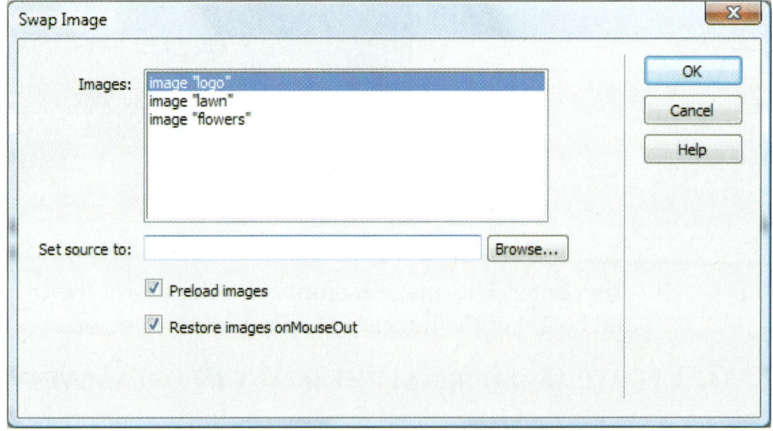

- In the Images list, select the name of the starter image.
- In the **Set source to** list, click Browse and navigate to the image that will be swapped in.
- Click **Preload images** to ensure that the swap action is not slow.

Practice: SCUBA – part 7 of 7

Dreamweaver should be started and the SCUBA website should be the working site.

① **ADD AN IMAGE TO THE LOCATIONS.HTML WEB PAGE DOCUMENT**
   a. Open the photos.html web page document.
   b. Double-click the image4 placeholder.
   c. Select the a_reef.jpg file from the images folder.
   d. In the Alt text box, type reef.
      Note that the image is quite large.

② **OPEN THE IMAGE FOR EDITING IN FIREWORKS**
   a. Click the image to select it if it is not already selected.
   b. In the Property inspector, click . A dialog box is displayed.
   c. Select Use This File. The image is displayed in a Document window in Fireworks.

③ **CROP THE IMAGE IN FIREWORKS**
   a. Click the image to select it if it is not already selected.
   b. In the Tools panel, in the Select section, click the Crop tool .
   c. Move the pointer over the canvas. The pointer changes to .
   d. Drag the pointer. A cropping box is drawn.
   e. In the Property inspector, set W to 250 and press Enter. The width of the cropping box is changed.
   f. In the Property inspector, set H box to 200 and press Enter. The height of the cropping box is changed.
   g. Use the arrow keys to move the cropping box to only include the bright fish and the corals beneath it:

   h. Press Enter. The image is cropped to the size of the cropping box. Note the width and height of the image in the Property inspector.

④ **UPDATE AND FORMAT THE IMAGE IN DREAMWEAVER**
   a. In the Document window above the image click Done. The Document window is closed and Dreamweaver is again displayed.
   b. In the Property inspector, click . The image changes to the new size.

⑤ CROP AN IMAGE IN DREAMWEAVER

a. Double-click the image5 placeholder.

b. Select the a_wreck.jpg file from the images folder.

c. In the Alt text box, type ship wreck.

d. Click the image to select it if it is not already selected.

e. In the Property inspector, click the Crop tool . Click OK if a dialog box is displayed. A cropping box appears in the image.

f. Drag the handles of the cropping box so that the diver is <u>not</u> included inside the cropping box:

g. Press Enter. The image is cropped.

h. Save the modified photos.html.

⑥ SWAP AN IMAGE

a. In the photos.html page, select the a_reef.jpg image.

b. In the Property inspector, in the ID box, name the image: reef

c. In the Behaviors panel, click , and select Swap Image. A dialog box is displayed.

　　1. In the Images list, select image "reef" if it is not already selected.

　　2. Click Browse and navigate to FISH.jpg, which is a data file for this text.

　　3. Select OK.

d. Save the modified photos.html

⑦ VIEW THE DOCUMENT IN A BROWSER

a. Press F12. The document is displayed in a browser window. Note you may have to click an Allow Blocked Content button. Move the mouse over the reef image. The image is swapped with the FISH image.

b. Print a copy.

c. Close the browser window. Dreamweaver is displayed.

d. Close photos.html.

⑧ QUIT DREAMWEAVER

Creating a Web Photo Album

Adobe Bridge

Previous versions of Dreamweaver included a feature called Create Web Photo Album. This feature is now part of *Adobe Bridge CS5*, which is installed automatically with a default installation of Dreamweaver CS5. Adobe Bridge is a program that lets you organize your visual assets, such as photographs, illustrations, PDFs, and Flash movies. The screen capture below illustrates a Web photo album that can be created using this feature:

To use this feature, first organize image files in a single folder. Then, create a new site and add a blank web page. Select File → Browse in Bridge. When the Adobe Bridge window is displayed, select Window → Workspace → Output. Adobe Bridge will display the Output panel at the right side of the window and the Folders panel at the left side. Select the folder containing the photos in the Folders panel and the Content panel will display the selected photos at the bottom of the window. Click a photo to display it in the Preview area:

Select Web Gallery in the Output panel. A Template and Thumbnail style can then be selected from the Output panel. Options can also be selected in the Site Info, Color Palette, and Appearance areas of the Output panel. Once options are set, click the Refresh Preview button or click the Preview In Browser button to preview the gallery in your default web browser.

To save the gallery on your hard drive, scroll the Output panel and select Save To Disk. Navigate to the appropriate website folder for the gallery, and then click Save. The gallery is saved with the index.html file name. The index.html file can then be opened in Dreamweaver and previewed in a browser.

Practice: Web Photo Album

① **CREATE A NEW WEBSITE**
   a. Select Site → New Site. The Site Setup dialog box is displayed.
   b. Select Site if those options are not already displayed.
   c. In the Site Name box type: Photo Album.
   d. Click the Local Site Folder icon 📁. A dialog box is displayed for browsing the local disk.
      1. Navigate to the appropriate location where a folder can be created to store the website files.
      2. Click the Create New Folder button:
      3. A new folder is created. Type Photo Album to replace the New Folder name and press Enter.
      4. Select Open.
      5. Select Select to choose the new folder as the website folder.
   e. Click Advanced Settings:
      1. Click the Default Images folder Browse for folder icon 📁.
      2. If necessary, navigate to the Photo Album folder.
      3. Click the Create New Folder button:
      4. Type images and then press the Enter key.
      5. Select Open.
      6. Select Select to choose the new folder as the website folder.
   f. Select Save. The Site folder is displayed in the Files panel:

② **CREATE A WEB PHOTO ALBUM**
   a. File → Browse in Bridge. The Adobe Bridge window is displayed.
   b. Select Window → Workspace → Output. Note the Output panel at the right side of the window and the Folders panel at the left side.
   c. In the Folders panel, navigate to the FLOWERS folder, which is a data files folder for this text.
   d. In the Content panel, click one of the images to display the selected photo in the Preview area.

e. Set options as shown in the Output panel:

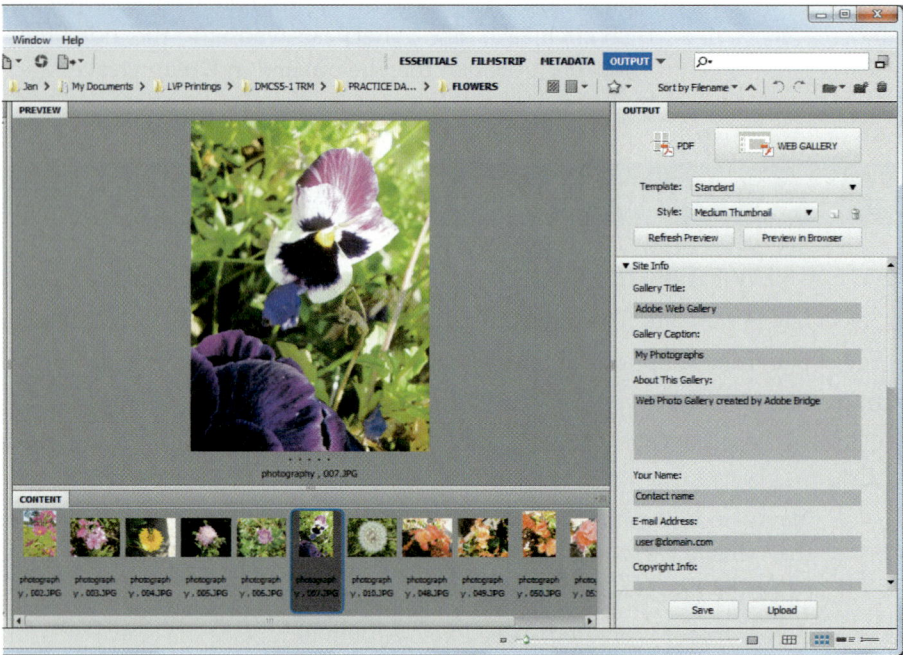

f. In the Content panel, select all of the images.
g. Scroll the Output panel to the Create Gallery section and then click the **Browse** button.
h. Navigate to the Photo Album website folder and click **OK**.
i. In the Output panel, click the **Save** button.
j. Click **OK**.

③ OPEN THE WEB PHOTO ALBUM IN DREAMWEAVER

a. Switch to Dreamweaver. Photo Album should be the active site. The Files panel should look similar to:

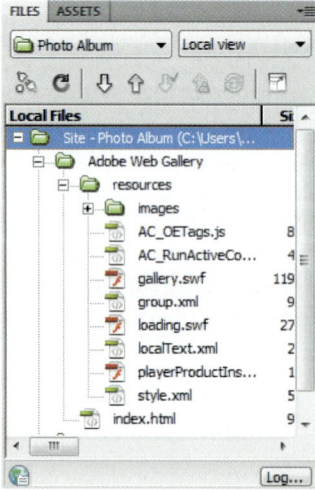

b. In the Files panel, double-click the index.html file. The web page appears similar to:

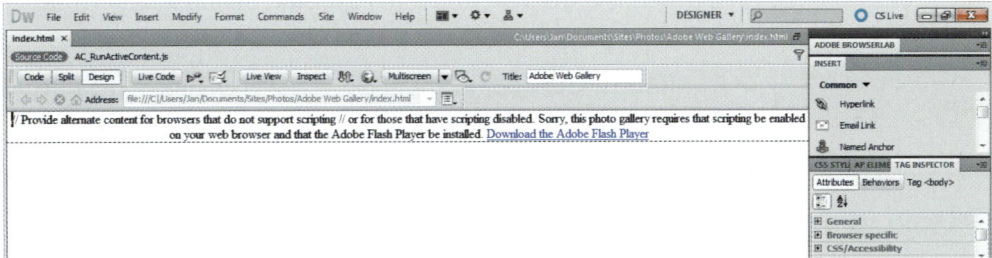

④ VIEW THE WEB PHOTO ALBUM IN A BROWSER

a. Press the F12 key. If a warning dialog box is displayed, click the Close button. The Web Photo Album appears similar to:

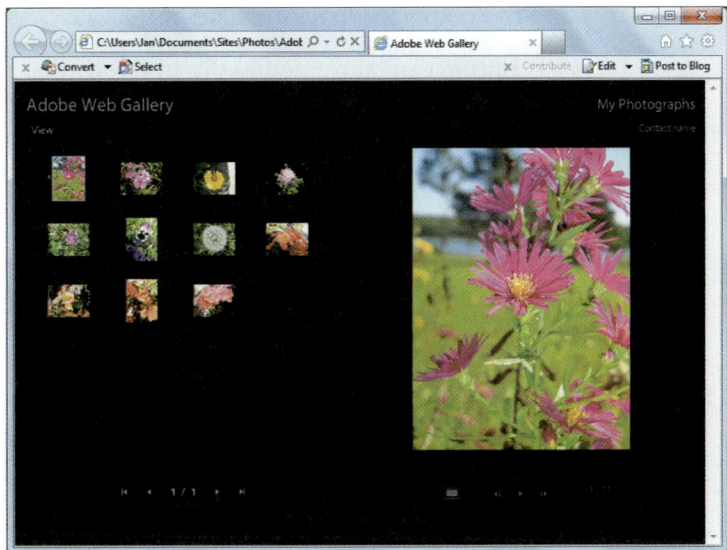

b. Scroll the images.

⑤ CLOSE THE BROWSER WINDOW

⑥ QUIT DREAMWEAVER

Chapter Summary

Images on web pages are usually a GIF or JPG file because these formats are widely supported in browsers. The GIF format is best used for graphics that do not contain many colors, and the JPG format is best used for photographs. GIF, JPG, and PNG formats are all bitmap graphics made up of pixels.

Alternative text provides text for a voice synthesizer to "read" in place of the image and is displayed as the screen tip that appears when the pointer is paused over an image. Alternative text is typed in the Alt box in the Property inspector.

A graphic can be formatted as a hyperlink in the same manner as a text hyperlink. An image map is a graphic that contains one or more hotspots, which is a defined area on a graphic that is a hyperlink. Hotspots are created using tools in the Property inspector.

If the width and height of an image is changed, the image needs to be resampled which changes the size of the file and correctly adjusts the pixels in the image.

Fireworks is used to create and edit images specifically for use on the web. Fireworks documents are PNG files, which should be saved to a location outside of the website and used to export graphics to the website in JPG or GIF format. In a Fireworks document, lines and shapes can be drawn on the canvas using tools in the Vector section in the Tools panel. Text can be added as a separate object by selecting the Text tool.

To use a Fireworks document in Dreamweaver, it should be optimized and then exported in a format other than PNG using the Export Wizard.

A button can be created easily in Fireworks, and then several copies placed together in a Fireworks document to form a navigation bar that can be exported to Dreamweaver. A button is created by making several objects into a button symbol. Instances of the symbol are then added to the canvas to create a navigation bar. A behavior is how a symbol interacts with the user, and the default behavior for a button symbol is a rollover.

The Export Wizard is used to optimize and automatically generate all the files associated with a Fireworks document. A Fireworks document exported as HTML and images to a Dreamweaver website is used by copying and pasting the HTML.

Cropping an image trims away areas that are not needed. Images can be cropped in Fireworks or in Dreamweaver. A selected image in a web page document in Dreamweaver can be opened and edited in Fireworks by clicking in the Property inspector.

Images can also be swapped and used to create a web photo album.

Vocabulary

Adobe Bridge A program that lets you organize your visual assets, such as photographs, illustrations, PDFs, and Flash movies.

Alternative text Text added to an image that a voice synthesizer "reads" in place of the image.

Behavior How a symbol interacts with the user.

Bitmap graphic A graphic based on rows and columns of tiny squares.

Button An element that indicates to the user that it is a graphic hyperlink by its appearance.

Canvas In Fireworks, the rectangular area in which an image is created and edited.

Compression A file format feature that reduces file size.

Crop To trim away areas of an image that are no longer needed.

Dots per inch (dpi) The number of pixels in an inch. Measures the resolution of a bitmap graphic.

Down state The button state when a button is clicked.

GIF A file format best used with graphics that do not contain many colors, such as clip art or logos.

Hotspot An invisible, defined area on a graphic that is a hyperlink.

Image map A graphic that contains one or more hotspots.

Instance A copy of a symbol.

Interlaced A GIF file format feature in which a low-quality version of the graphic appears first and becomes clearer in four horizontal passes as the web page fully loads.

JPG A file format that supports millions of colors and is best used for photographs.

Lossless compression Type of compression in which all of the original file information is retained. Used for GIF graphics.

Lossy compression Type of compression in which some data in the file is removed in order to reduce the file size. Used for JPG graphics.

Optimized image The best quality images with the smallest possible file size.

Over state The button state when a pointer is moved over a button.

Over While Down state The button state when a pointer is moved over a button in the Down state.

Pixel A square in a bitmap graphic.

PNG A file format created in the mid-1990s during a controversy over copyright of the GIF format. It is only supported by the newest browsers.

Progressive A JPG file format feature in which a low-quality version of the JPG graphic appears when a web page is first loaded and then becomes clearer as the page fully loads.

Proportionate size The width and height of a graphic are in the same ratio as the original graphic to prevent distortion.

Resample Correctly adjust the pixels in an image.

Resolution The number of dots per inch (dpi) in a graphic.

Rollover The default behavior for a button symbol, which allows each state of a button symbol to display a different image.

Slice The way Fireworks divides an image so that interactivity can be assigned.

Source file The PNG file created in Fireworks that is used to export images to Dreamweaver.

Stretch To distort an image by dragging a handle without holding the Shift key.

Symbol A single object that is similar to a library item in Dreamweaver, except a symbol placed on a canvas does not have to have its link broken to be edited.

Transparency A color that allows the background color to show through.

Up state The button state when a pointer is not over it or it is not clicked. Also called the normal state.

Vector graphic A graphic composed of lines connected by points, which allows for smooth resizing and a smaller file size than bitmap graphics.

Dreamweaver Commands and Buttons

Align button   Displays a drop-down list with options for aligning an image. Found in the Property inspector.

Behaviors command   Displays the Behaviors panel. Found in the Window menu.

Browse for File icon   Displays a dialog box used to locate a destination file for a hyperlink. Found in the Property inspector.

Browse in Bridge command   Opens Adobe Bridge where a web photo album page can be created. Found in the File menu.

Change Link command   Modifies an existing link. Found in the Modify menu.

Copy command   Makes a copy of selected HTML. Found in the Edit menu.

Crop tool   Trims parts of an image that are no longer needed. Found in the Property inspector.

Oval Hotspot tool   Creates an oval shaped hotspot. Found in the Property inspector.

Paste command   Pastes copied HTML at the insertion point. Found in the Edit menu.

Point to File icon   Points to a destination file for a hyperlink. Found in the Property inspector.

Pointer Hotspot tool   Selects a hot spot. Found in the Property inspector.

Polygon Hotspot tool   Creates an polygon shaped hotspot. Found in the Property inspector.

Rectangular Hotspot tool   Creates a rectangular shaped hotspot. Found in the Property inspector.

Remove Link command   Removes an existing link. Found in the Modify menu.

Swap Image command   Swaps an image during a mouse rollover. Found in the Behaviors panel menu.

Fireworks Commands and Buttons

Center Horizontal command   Aligns selected objects so that they are horizontally centered with respect to each other. Found in Modify → Align.

Center Vertical command   Aligns selected objects so that they are vertically centered with respect to each other. Found in Modify → Align.

Clone command   Creates an instance from a selected instance. Found in the Edit menu.

Convert to Symbol command   Displays a dialog box used to create a symbol. Found in Modify → Symbol.

Crop tool   Trims parts of an image that are no longer needed. Found in the Select section in the Tools panel.

Export Wizard command   Displays a series of dialog boxes used to select the best optimization settings and to export a document. Found in the File menu.

Line tool   Draws a line on the canvas. Found in the Vector section in the Tools panel.

New command   Displays a dialog box used to create a new document. Found in the File menu.

Pointer tool   Moves and resizes an object. Found in the Select section in the Tools panel.

Rectangle tool   Draws a rectangle to the canvas. Found in the Vector section in the Tools panel.

Save command   Saves the open Fireworks document. Found in the File menu.

Scale tool   Resizes a shape. Found in the Select section in the Tools panel.

Text tool   Adds text to the canvas. Found in the Vector section in the Tools panel.

Trim Canvas command   Reduces the canvas to exactly fit the objects. Found in Modify → Canvas.

Review Questions

1. a) Why are images on web pages usually a GIF or JPG file?
   b) What file format is best used with graphics that do not contain many colors?
   c) How many colors are GIF graphics limited to?
   d) What file format is best used with graphics that are photographs?

2. a) What is a bitmap graphic composed of?
   b) In a bitmap graphic, how is the quality of the graphic measured?

3. What file format allows one color in a graphic to be transparent?

4. Describe how an interlaced GIF graphic is displayed as a web page is loaded.

5. a) What is compression?
   b) What is lossless compression?
   c) What is lossy compression?
   d) What file format has lossless compression?
   e) What file format has lossy compression?

6. Describe how a progressive JPG file is displayed as a web page is loaded.

7. Why should alternative text be added to an image?

8. a) What is an image map?
   b) What is a hotspot?

9. a) List the three tools that can be used to create hotspots.
   b) List the steps required to delete a hotspot.

10. Describe a web page scenario where an image map could be used.

11. List the steps required to change the horizontal alignment of an image to center.

12. If the width and height of an image in a web page document is changed, what should then be done to the image?

13. How can an image be sized proportionately in Dreamweaver?

14. a) What is Fireworks?
    b) What is the file format of a Fireworks document?

15. What should the resolution be set to for an image used in a web page?

16. a) What is a vector graphic composed of?
    b) What is the canvas?

17. Where should a Fireworks document be saved?

18. Describe how shapes and lines are drawn in Fireworks.

19. a) What is the Stroke Color box used to change?
    b) What does the Tip size change?

20. List the steps required to add text to the canvas in Fireworks.

21. List the steps required to align objects so that they are centered vertically with respect to each other.

22. How can the canvas size be reduced to exactly fit the objects?

23. a) What is an optimized image?
    b) What can be used to choose the best optimization settings and to then export the document?

24. a) In a web page document, what does a button represent to a user?
    b) List the steps required to convert two objects to a single symbol.

25. What is an instance of a symbol?

26 What is slicing?

27. a) What is a behavior?
    b) What is the default behavior for a button symbol?

28. List and describe the four states a button symbol has in Fireworks.

Chapter 5 Images in Dreamweaver and Fireworks

29. List the steps required to use an exported HTML document in Dreamweaver.

30. What program is used to create a web photo album?

31. a) Why would you crop an image?
    b) List the steps required to crop an image in Dreamweaver.

True/False

32. Determine if each of the following are true or false. If false, explain why.
    a) Alternative text is displayed as an alternative if the image cannot be displayed.
    b) A hotspot is a behavior.
    c) An image should be sized by dragging a middle handle.
    d) Resampling an image changes the size of the file.
    e) The font in a Fireworks document can be changed after the text is typed.
    f) A small file allows a web page to load faster in a browser window.
    g) A graphic hyperlink has a blue underlined border.
    h) The Down State appears when the pointer is moved over a button.
    i) If an image is proportionately resized, the width and height remain in the same ratio.
    j) A document can contain many instances of a symbol.
    k) Cropped parts of an image can be restored after the cropped image is saved.
    l) When swapping images, the images have to be the same size.

Exercises

Exercise 1 ———————————————————————— GREECE

Use Fireworks and Dreamweaver to modify the GREECE website by completing the following steps:

a) In Dreamweaver, open the GREECE website for editing, which is a website provided with the data files for this text.

b) Modify the index.html web page document as follows:

   1. Select the map_greece.gif image and add alternative text: Map of Greece.

   2. Resize the image to 280 pixels wide, and then resample the image.

c) Modify the photos.html web page document as follows:

   1. In the image1 placeholder, insert the image hydra_cats.jpg and add alternative text: Cats on Hydra.

   2. Edit the image in Fireworks to crop it. Use a cropping box of 250 pixels wide and 154 pixels high that includes at least two cats in the image. Save the changes and then update the image in Dreamweaver.

   3. In the other image placeholders, insert images and add alternative text as follows:

image placeholder	insert the image	and add alternative text
image2	hydra_view.jpg	Island of Hydra.
image3	diros.jpg	Inside the Diros caves.
image4	goat.jpg	One of the many goats.
image5	monemvasia.jpg	The city of Monemvasia.
image6	road_to_kosmas.jpg	Winding road to Kosmas.

d) Switch to Fireworks and create a new document with a width of 660 pixels, a height of 100 pixels, a resolution of 72 pixels/inch, and a transparent canvas. Save the document outside of any website folder naming it: greeknav.png

e) Create a button symbol as follows:

   1. Draw a rectangle with a width of 160 pixels and a height of 36 pixels.

   2. Apply a fill color of #3399FF and a transparent stroke color to the rectangle.

   3. Create a text box with the text button formatted as Verdana font, 24 points in size, center aligned, and #FFFFFF in color.

   4. Align the rectangle and the text block horizontally and vertically.

   5. With both the rectangle and text block selected, convert them to a button symbol named: greek button

f) Create instances of the button symbol and modify them as follows:

   1. Create two more instances of the button symbol on the canvas and then position all three instances next to each other.

2. Change the properties of each instance, from left to right, as follows:

Text	Link	Alt
Home	index.html	Link to home page.
Photos	photos.html	Link to photo page.
Itinerary	itinerary.html	Link to itinerary page.

Your buttons should look similar to:

| Home | Photos | Itinerary |

g) Double-click any instance to display the button symbol in the Button Editor. Edit the states of the button symbol as follows:

1. Edit the Over state to be identical to the Up state except change the text color to #FFCCFF.

2. Edit the Down state to be identical to the Over state except change the rectangle fill color to #3300FF.

3. Edit the Over While Down state to be identical to the Down state.

h) Finish and export the navigation bar as follows:

1. Modify the canvas to exactly fit the buttons and then save the modified document.

2. Use the Export Wizard to export an HTML file named greeknav.html to the GREECE website. Make sure the images are exported as GIF files, with Index Transparency, to the images folder.

i) In Dreamweaver, modify the GREECE website as follows:

1. Open greeknav.html and click the <body> tag to select the entire document.

2. Copy the HTML.

3. Paste the HTML in the yellow navigation area in the index.html, photos.html, and itinerary.html web page documents.

j) In the photos.html and itinerary.html web page documents, link the logo to index.html.

k) View each web page document in a browser window and test the hyperlinks.

l) Print a copy of each web page document from the browser.

Exercise 2 ———————————————————— CACTUS

Use Fireworks and Dreamweaver to modify the CACTUS website by completing the following steps:

a) In Dreamweaver, open the CACTUS website for editing, which is a website provided with the data files for this text.

b) Modify the index.html web page document as follows:

   1. In the image1 placeholder, insert the cactus.gif image and add alternative text: Cactus image.

   2. Crop the image in Fireworks using a cropping box of 140 pixels wide that only includes one cactus in the image. Save the changes and then update the image in Dreamweaver.

c) Modify the gallery.html web page document as follows:

   1. In the image1 placeholder, insert the image prickly_pear.jpg and add alternative text: Prickly pear cactus.

   2. Resize the image proportionately to 300 pixels wide, and then resample the image.

   3. In the image2 placeholder, insert the image agave.jpg and add alternative text: Agave or century plant.

   4. Resize the image proportionately to 300 pixels wide, and then resample the image.

   5. In the two remaining image placeholders, insert images and add alternative text as follows:

insert the image	and add alternative text
saguaro.jpg	Saguaro cactus.
cholla.jpg	Cholla cactus.

d) Switch to Fireworks and create a new document with a width of 660 pixels, a height of 100 pixels, a resolution of 72 pixels/inch, and a transparent canvas. Save the document outside of any website folder naming it: cactusnav.png

e) Create a button symbol as follows:

   1. Draw an ellipse with a width of 180 pixels and a height of 40 pixels.

   2. Apply a fill color of #009900 and a transparent stroke color to the ellipse.

   3. Create a text box with the text button formatted as Arial font, 18 points in size, center aligned, bold, and #CCFFCC in color.

   4. Align the ellipse and the text block horizontally and vertically.

   5. With both the ellipse and text block selected, convert them to a button symbol named: cactus button

f) Create instances of the button symbol and modify them as follows:

   1. Create two more instances of the button symbol on the canvas and then position all three instances next to each other.

   2. Change the properties of each instance, from left to right, as follows:

Text	Link	Alt
Home	index.html	Link to home page.
Photo Gallery	gallery.html	Link to photo page.
Cactus Types	types.html	Link to page about cactus types.

Your buttons should look similar to:

g) Double-click any instance to display the button symbol in the Button Editor. Edit the states of the button symbol as follows:

   1. Edit the Over state to be identical to the Up state except change the ellipse fill color to #00CC33.

   2. Edit the Down state to be identical to the Over state except change the text color to #FFFFFF.

   3. Edit the Over While Down state to be identical to the Down state.

h) Finish and export the navigation bar as follows:

   1. Modify the canvas to exactly fit the buttons and then save the modified document.

   2. Use the Export Wizard to export an HTML file named cactusnav.html to the CACTUS website. Make sure the images are exported as GIF files, with Index Transparency, to the images folder.

i) In Dreamweaver, modify the CACTUS website as follows:

   1. Open cactusnav.html and click the <body> tag to select the entire document.

   2. Copy the HTML.

   3. Paste the HTML under the logo in the index.html, gallery.html, and types.html web page documents.

j) In the gallery.html and types.html web page documents, link the logo to index.html.

k) View each web page document in a browser window and test the hyperlinks.

l) Print a copy of each web page document from the browser.

Exercise 3 ——————————— COMPUTER MAINTENANCE

Use Fireworks and Dreamweaver to modify the COMPUTER MAINTENANCE website by completing the following steps:

a) In Dreamweaver, open the COMPUTER MAINTENANCE website for editing, which is a website provided with the data files for this text.

b) Modify the index.html web page document as follows:

   1. In the image1 placeholder, insert the com_maint.gif image and add alternative text: Computer maintenance home page.
   2. In Dreamweaver, crop the fish out of the image.

c) Modify the cleaning.html web page document as follows:

   1. In the image1 placeholder, insert the com_cleaning.gif image and add alternative text: Cleaning the computer.
   2. In Dreamweaver, crop the fish out of the image.

d) Modify the disks.html web page document by inserting the com_disks.gif image in the image placeholder and adding alternative text: Disk maintenance.

e) Modify the updates.html web page document by inserting the com_updates.gif image in the image placeholder and adding alternative text: Software updates.

f) Switch to Fireworks and create a new document with a width of 660 pixels, a height of 100 pixels, a resolution of 72 pixels/inch, and a transparent canvas. Save the document outside of any website folder naming it: maint_nav.png

g) Create a button symbol as follows:

   1. Draw a rectangle with a width of 150 pixels and a height of 55 pixels.
   2. Apply a fill color of #FF9900 and a transparent stroke color to the rectangle.
   3. Create a text box with the text button formatted as Verdana font, 18 points in size, center aligned, bold, and #FFFFFF in color.
   4. Align the rectangle and the text block horizontally and vertically.
   5. With both the rectangle and text block selected, convert them to a button symbol named: maintenance button

h) Create instances of the button symbol and modify them as follows:

   1. Create three more instances of the button symbol on the canvas and then position all four instances next to each other, with a little space in between.
   2. Change the properties of each instance, from left to right, as follows:

Text	Link	Alt
Home	index.html	Link to home page.
Cleaning	cleaning.html	Link to computer cleaning page.
Disks	disks.html	Link to disk maintenance page.
Updates	updates.html	Link to software update page.

Your buttons should look similar to:

i) Double-click any instance to display the button symbol in the Button Editor. Edit the states of the button symbol as follows:

1. Edit the Over state to be identical to the Up state except change the text color to #333399.

2. Edit the Down state to be identical to the Over state except change the text color to #FFFFFF and the rectangle fill color to #333399.

3. Edit the Over While Down state to be identical to the Down state.

j) Finish and export the navigation bar as follows:

1. Modify the canvas to exactly fit the buttons and then save the modified document.

2. Use the Export Wizard to export an HTML file named maint_nav.html to the COMPUTER MAINTENANCE website. Make sure the images are exported as GIF files, with Index Transparency, to the images folder.

k) In Dreamweaver, modify the COMPUTER MAINTENANCE website as follows:

1. Open maint_nav.html and click the <body> tag to select the entire document.

2. Copy the HTML.

3. Paste the HTML under the logo in the index.html, cleaning.html, disks.html, and updates.html web page documents.

l) View each web page document in a browser window and test the hyperlinks.

m) Print a copy of each web page document from the browser.

Exercise 4 — SEVEN WONDERS

The SEVEN WONDERS website was last modified in Chapter 4, Exercise 5. Use Dreamweaver to further modify the SEVEN WONDERS website by completing the following steps:

a) In Dreamweaver, open the SEVEN WONDERS website for editing.

b) Modify the index.html web page document as follows:

1. Select the wonder_map.gif image and in the Property inspector set **Map** to locations and press Enter.

2. Create seven rectangular hotspots, one on each word and its corresponding bullet on the wonder_map.gif image, linking each hotspot and adding alternative text as follows:

The hotspot	should link to	and have alternative text
Ephesus	temple.html	Temple of Artemis at Ephesus.
Halicarnassus	mausoleum.html	Mausoleum at Halicarnassus.
Rhodes	colossus.html	Colossus of Rhodes.
Babylon	hanging.html	Hanging Gardens of Babylon.
Giza	pyramids.html	Pyramids of Egypt.
Alexandria	lighthouse.html	Lighthouse of Alexandria.
Olympia	statue.html	Statue of Zeus at Olympia.

c) View the index.html web page document in a browser window and test the hyperlinks and alternative text.

d) Print a copy of index.html from the browser.

Exercise 5 — Photographer

Create a personal photo album using Dreamweaver's photo album feature. Be sure to organize your images into a folder before starting to create your page.

Exercise 6 — Entrepreneur

If you were an entrepreneur, what business would you open? Decide on a business and then use Fireworks to design a logo and navigation bar that could be used in the website.

Chapter 6
Typography, Style Sheets, and Color

This chapter discusses CSS style sheets and formatting web page documents. Typography, controlling images with CSS, and CSS layouts are also discussed.

Typography

Typography refers to the arrangement, shape, size, style, and weight of text. Typography affects the navigation and usability of a website and helps to convey a specific message to the audience.

Making typography choices for a website is more complicated than for a print document. When creating a print document, the text can be presented in any format that is supported by the local monitor and printer. Whereas, web page text has to be formatted so that it appears similarly on various monitor sizes, in different screen resolutions, and in different browsers.

typeface A *typeface* is a set of letters drawn in a specific style. Examples of *font* typefaces include **Arial**, Times New Roman, and **Verdana**. The word *font* technically refers to a specific size and weight of a typeface, such as 10 point Verdana bold.

Design Considerations: Choosing Fonts

In order for a font to display correctly in a browser, the user must have the font installed on their computer. Dreamweaver only lists commonly available fonts:

Fonts

To ensure that logos and other fancy fonts are displayed as intended on a web page, a graphic is created of the logo and then inserted on the web page.

Dreamweaver also groups fonts so that if a user does not have the first font installed, the next font in the group will be used, and so forth. This is one way to ensure a web page will display similarly on different computers.

The end of each group of fonts lists a font category. If the user doesn't have any of the fonts in the group, a font from the font category is used. Fonts categories include *serif* and *sans serif*. Serifs are small extensions at the ends of the strokes of a character:

TIP *sans* is the French word for "without."

serif **The**   sans serif **The**

Fonts can also be categorized as monospace, cursive, and fantasy.

When designing print documents, serif fonts tend to be easier to read. Because the serifs extend towards the neighboring letters, serif fonts appear closer together, scan easier, and are more readable than sans serif. However, serif fonts are not the best choice for web pages. The clean strokes of sans serif fonts are easier to read on a monitor. Monitor resolution is coarse, which results in serif fonts appearing fuzzy especially if the text is small.

Monospace, Cursive, and Fantasy Fonts

`Courier` is a common monospace font that most users have installed on their computer. The cursive and fantasy font categories include fonts that are not as common, such as **Comic Sans** and **Impact**.

A website should be as readable as possible, allowing the user to scan the text for information. One way to make the text readable is to limit the number of fonts used on the page. Two different fonts should be the maximum for a single web page. More than two fonts decreases usability. Users will also find that text in all capital letters is more difficult to read because our eyes scan for shapes:

EXAMPLE   example

Design Considerations: Font Size

points   The size of printed text is measured vertically in *points*, where one point is 1/72 of an inch. The text in this paragraph is 10 point. In Dreamweaver, text size may be specified as an absolute value in a unit of measure, such as pixels, as a relative size, such as smaller, or as a fixed size, such as x-small:

Ems

Ems is a relative measurement. One em is equal to the default font size. Ems allow users to control the size of onscreen text. If the size is too small, the user can increase the default font size in their browser settings.

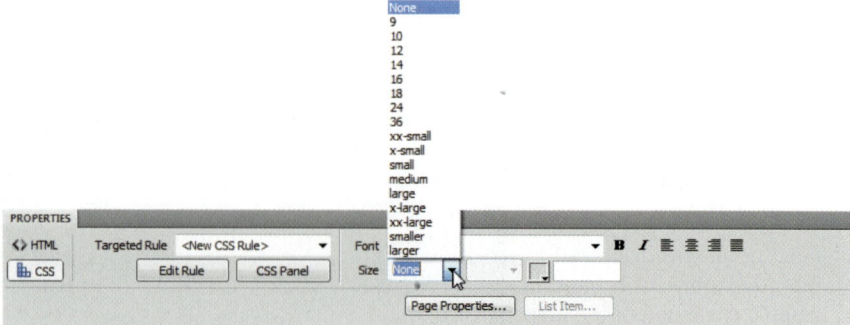

Monitors display in pixels. Therefore, many web designers specify the font size as an absolute value in pixels because pixels are a way to prevent

Chapter 6 Typography, Style Sheets, and Color

> **Text Size in Internet Explorer**
>
> To change the display size of relative fonts in Internet Explorer, users can select **View → Text Size** and then select an appropriate size, such as **Smaller**. This setting will not alter any fixed fonts. However, other browsers do allow fixed fonts to be resized.

distortion and achieve a consistent look across a variety of web browsers. Fonts set using this method are referred to as "fixed fonts."

Usability is a consideration when choosing sizes for the text on a web page. The font size should be big enough so that the user can easily read the text, but not so big that it appears loud. Sizes from 12 pixels to 16 pixels are a good choice for paragraphs of text, and 14 pixels to 24 pixels for headings. Other size considerations are:

- Text in the top global navigation bar should be in the same size as the text or slightly larger.
- Text in the breadcrumb trail and local navigation bar should be slightly smaller than the top global navigation bar.
- Page footer elements, including the bottom global navigation bar, can be much smaller.
- Serif fonts become difficult to read at small sizes, so use sans serif fonts for any text in a very small size.

Design Considerations: Line Height

Line height is the distance from one line of text to another. Text with greater line height will have more space below it, which gives more separation to lines of text. Line height affects the readability of a document. Lines of text need enough space between them to allow the reader's eye to focus and scan.

The line height is determined by the type size and the line length. The greater the type size, the greater the line height and the longer the lines of text, the greater the line height. Line height is also used to visually connect items on a web page:

> **Heading**
> Subhead
>
> **Heading**
> Subhead

The line height in the example on the right connects the heading to the subhead better

In Dreamweaver, line height can be specified as a value in a unit of measure, such as pixels or as "normal," which automatically calculates the line height.

> **Leading**
>
> For printed material, l*eading* (pronounced "ledding") is the typography term that refers to line height.

Design Considerations: Type Styles

Plain type is referred to as normal, regular, roman, or book style. Type styles, such as *italic* and **bold**, can be applied to normal type to make text stand out and to indicate a heading hierarchy. However, type styles can visually change the meaning of words and should be used with care.

Bold type is said to visually "weigh" more than normal type. Italic style should only be applied to larger text (at least 12 pixels), because it is much more difficult to read on a screen at a smaller size. Underline style should not be applied to text unless it is a hyperlink.

Design Considerations: Alignment

Alignment is a paragraph format that refers to the position of the lines of text relative to the sides of a cell: left, centered, right, and justified:

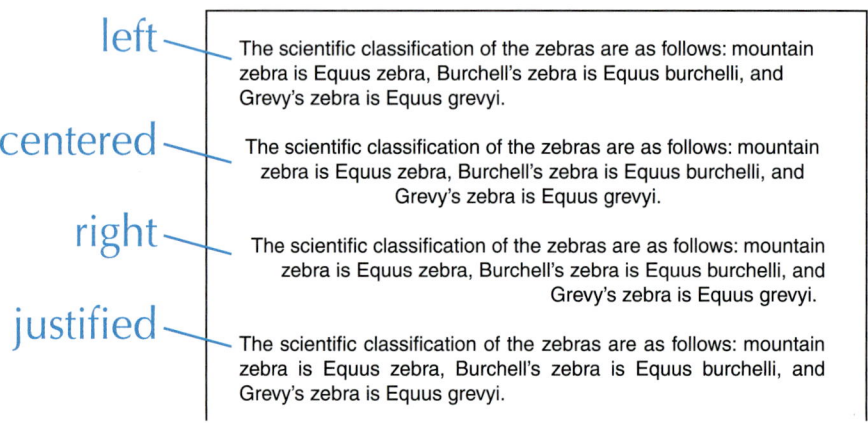

Left alignment is the most readable and therefore provides the highest degree of usability. Right alignment is difficult to read in long paragraphs of text. Long paragraphs of centered text are difficult to read, so centered alignment should be used only for headings or short amounts of text. Justified alignment is not recommended because browser support for this format varies.

Links in top and local navigation bars are most readable and usable when left aligned. However, centered alignment is also an acceptable and usable choice for formatting the links in navigation bars. The bottom global navigation bar is often formatted as centered.

Style Sheets

TIP Mastering style sheets requires a basic understanding of HTML, which is covered in Chapter 2.

The websites that you have been creating throughout the text have been based on a CSS starter layout. The layout along with the formatting specifications have been saved in a separate CSS file. The CSS file defines the type, paragraph, and page formats for a web page document. A single style sheet can be applied to all the pages in a website to achieve a consistent look. Changing the text format of all the web pages in a website is as easy as modifying a single style sheet because updates to the style sheet are automatically applied to linked documents. Multiple style sheets can be applied to a single web page, with the rules in one style sheet layering, or *cascading*, those in another style sheet.

A CSS style sheet is saved as a separate file in the website folder. Select File → Save All to save the style sheet and any open web page documents. When opened, a style sheet is displayed in a Document window in Code view:

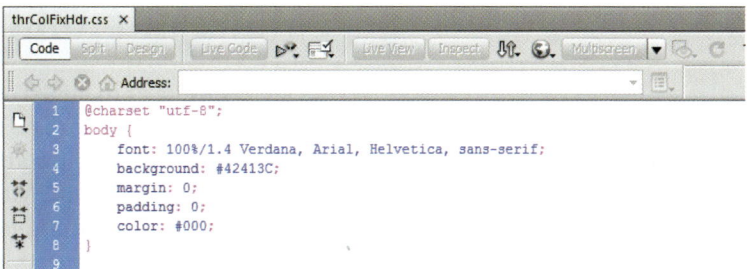

In Dreamweaver, the CSS Styles panel is used to link, create, and modify style sheets:

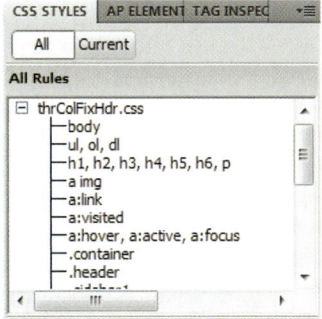

TIP Select Window → CSS Styles to display the CSS Styles panel.

To link a style sheet to the open web page document, click the Attach Style Sheet button . The Attach External Style Sheet dialog box is displayed:

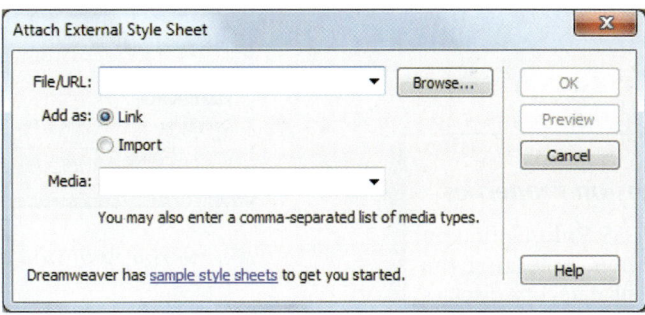

> **Publishing Style Sheets**
>
> Style sheets are saved in the website's folder and posted along with a website.

- To link an existing style sheet to the open web page document, click Browse, which displays another dialog box where the style sheet name is selected. The selected style sheet is automatically copied to the website root folder.

- To use a predesigned Dreamweaver style sheet, click sample style sheets, which displays a dialog box with sample style sheets. Select a style sheet and OK.

To create a new CSS style sheet, select File → New and then select CSS in the Page Type list. Click Create to display a blank style sheet. The style sheet should then be saved with a .css extension.

Chapter 6 Typography, Style Sheets, and Color   **203**

Creating and Applying a CSS Rule

A CSS style sheet can include rules. A *rule* modifies an HTML element and is comprised of a selector and declarations. The *selector* is the HTML element being redefined and the *declarations* are the formats to be applied. Rules are defined using the HTML element name. For example, the rule below modifies the paragraph element (<p>) to automatically display paragraphs in 14 px Georgia:

selector
declaration

```
p {
    font-family: Georgia, "Times New Roman", Times, serif;
    font-size: 14px;
}
```

To add a new style to a style sheet, click the New CSS Rule button , which displays a dialog box. To create a rule, select Tag (redefines an HTML element) and then select a tag from the Selector Name list:

TIP The selector can be any HTML element.

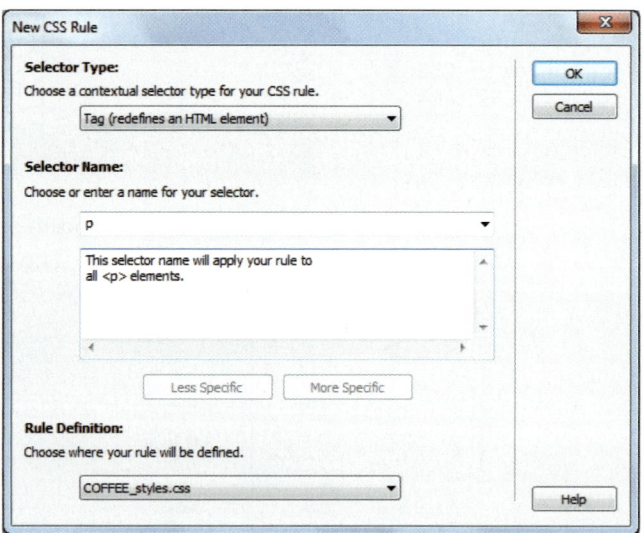

A new rule will be created for the paragraph tag (<p>)

Select **OK** to display a dialog box where formats for a paragraph and text within a paragraph are set:

Extension Properties

In the CSS Rule Definition dialog box, selecting the Extensions category displays options for specifying page breaks before or after certain elements and customizing the appearance of the insertion point when it is moved over the specified element.

The Apply Button

The **Apply** button can be used to preview the style while keeping the dialog box open for modifications. If necessary, move the dialog box by dragging the title bar.

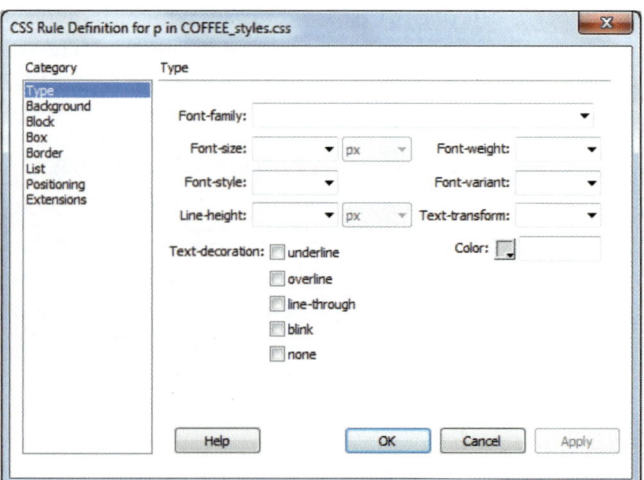

Chapter 6 Typography, Style Sheets, and Color

Each Category in the dialog box contains a different set of attributes. Not every attribute affects the tag being redefined. For example, the List category of attributes has no effect on paragraph text. For the p tag, the Type and Block categories of attributes can be set. The Type attributes include:

- Font-family for selecting a font family.
- Font-size for specifying a type size. Selecting a value enables the units list where pixels should be selected.
- Font-weight for selecting the thickness of text.
- Font-style for selecting normal, italic, or oblique.
- Line-height for selecting the line height.

> **Oblique vs. Italic Style**
> Oblique style slants letters. Italic style is an actual different font because it creates structural changes to letters to alter their appearance.

The Block category displays attributes that include the Text-align list for selecting a paragraph alignment of left, center, right, or justified. Once attributes are selected, select OK to create the style. Rules are automatically applied to any text on the web page document that is within the tags that were redefined.

Creating and Applying a CSS Class

A *class* is a set of declarations that can be applied to different tags. Class names must begin with a dot (.). For example:

```
.para_with_space {
    font-family: Georgia, "Times New Roman", Times, serif;
    font-size: 14px;
    line-height: 28px;
    text-align: center;
}
```

The class above can be applied to individual paragraphs to format the paragraph in 14px Georgia with a line-height of 28 px.

A new class is added to a style sheet the same way a rule is created, except that Class (can be applied to any HTML element) is selected and then a class name typed in the Selector Name box:

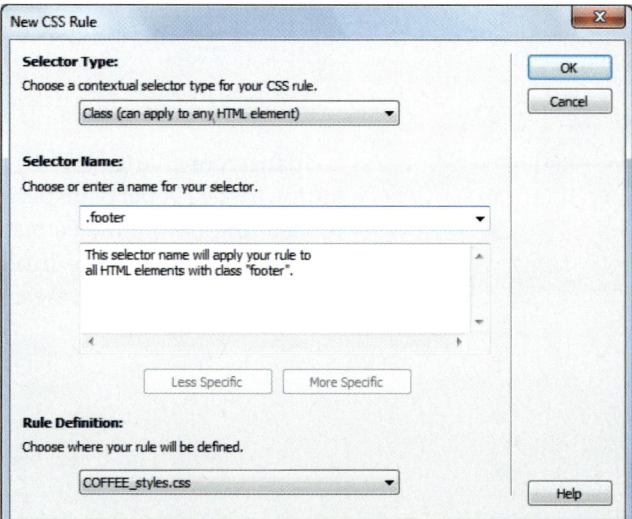

> **Class Attributes**
> It is important to keep in mind what the class will be used for. For example, a class that will modify paragraphs should only include attribute settings that apply to paragraphs of text.

Chapter 6 Typography, Style Sheets, and Color

Select OK to display a dialog box where attributes are set. The class style can then be applied to selected text. Classes are not automatically applied like rules because classes are created to modify tags, not redefine specific tags. Classes override rules. To apply a class, select the text or table cell and then select the style name in the Targeted Rule list in the Property inspector:

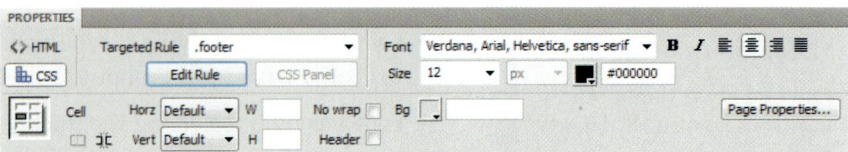

The footer style is selected

Editing HTML Code

Dreamweaver provides a visual environment that allows a page to be designed in Design view while the HTML code is generated in the background. However, when attaching a style sheet, there may be cases, such as formatting inconsistencies, where HTML tags need to be checked in Code view and then modified. For example, Code and Design view can be used to determine if paragraphs of text are enclosed by <p> and </p>:

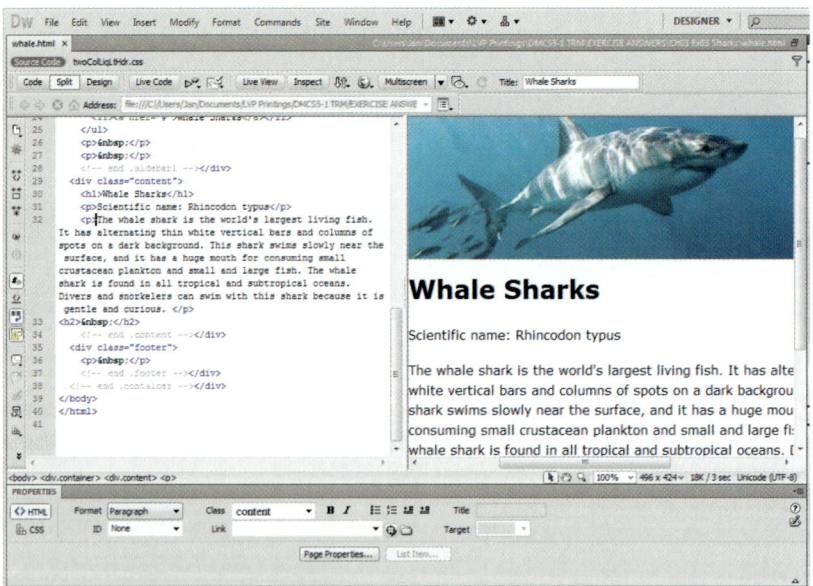

To insert or change HTML tags, select the text and then click the HTML button in the Property inspector. Next, select an option, such as paragraph or Heading 1 from the Format list. Alternatively, select a tag button from the Text category in the Insert panel The Text category includes many commonly used HTML tags:

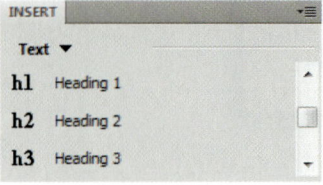

Chapter 6 Typography, Style Sheets, and Color

Practice: COFFEE – part 1 of 6

① OPEN THE COFFEE WEBSITE FOR EDITING

a. Start Dreamweaver.
b. Open the COFFEE website for editing, which is a website provided with the data files for this text.
c. Familiarize yourself with the files and folders in this website.
d. Open the index.html web page document and view the page in a browser.
e. Click the links to explore the other web pages of the website.
f. Close the browser window. Dreamweaver is displayed.
g. Open the footer library item.
h. Replace the text Name with your name.
i. Save and close the library item, allowing Dreamweaver to update all the files.

② ATTACH A NEW STYLE SHEET TO INDEX.HTML

a. Display the index.html web page document, if it is not already displayed.
b. Select Window → CSS Styles if the CSS Styles panel is not already visible.
c. In the bottom of the CSS Styles panel, click the Attach Style Sheet button. A dialog box is displayed.
d. In the File/URL box, click Browse and select COFFEE_styles.css.
e. Select OK.

③ CREATE A NEW STYLE

a. In the bottom of the CSS Styles panel, click the New CSS Rule button. A dialog box is displayed.
   1. Select Tag (redefines the look of a specific tag).
   2. In the Selector Name list, select p.
   3. In the Rule Definition list, select COFFEE_styles.css.
b. Select OK and then select Yes. A dialog box is displayed..
c. In the Type category, set attributes to:

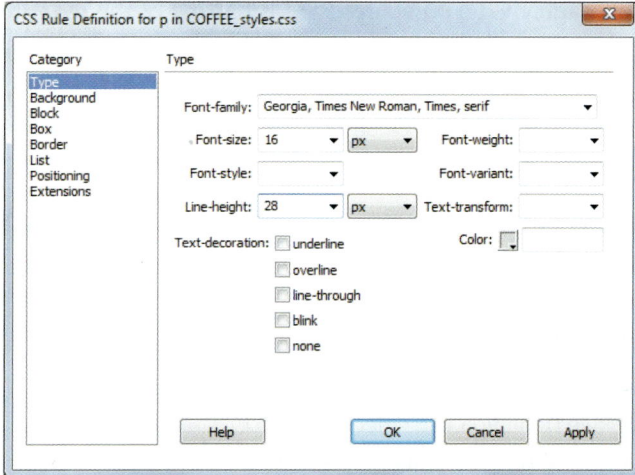

Chapter 6 Typography, Style Sheets, and Color   **207**

d. In the Block category, set attributes to:

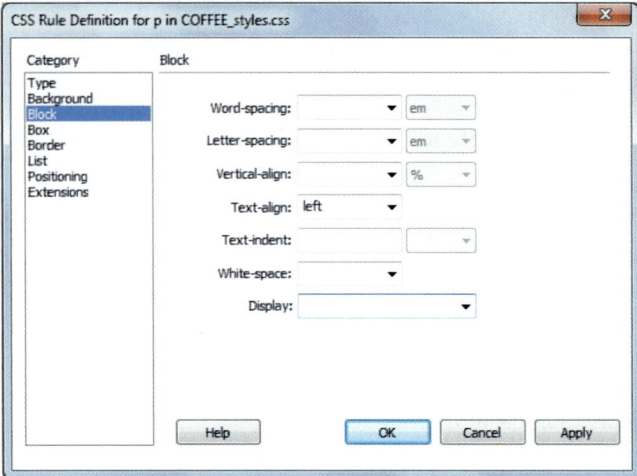

e. Select **OK**. A rule is created and applied to the web page document.

④ CHECK THE HTML TAGS AND EMPHASIZE TEXT

a. Scroll the web page document window and note that the sentence that begins "Tips for brewing…" has not changed to reflect the new rule. Place the insertion point in the sentence.

b. Switch to Split view to display the HTML for the web page document. Note the text is not enclosed by <p> and </p>.

c. In the Property inspector, click <> HTML and then select **Paragraph** in the Format drop-down list. <p> and </p> enclose the text, similar to:

```
27      <p>Tips for brewing that perfect cup:
28      </p>
29      <ol>
30        <li>Use fresh, high quality coffee.</li>
31        <li>Select the correct grind.</li>
32        <li>Use the proper amount of coffee.</li>
33        <li>Add pure water.</li>
```

In the Design pane, the text displays the formatting of the redefined p tag.

d. In the Design pane, select the entire sentence that begins "Tips for brewing…."

e. In the Text category in the Insert panel, click the Emphasis button *em*. <em> and </em> enclose the text. In the Design pane, the text is emphasized.

f. Switch to Design view.

⑤ REDEFINE THE EM TAG

a. In the bottom of the CSS Styles panel, click the New CSS Rule button. A dialog box is displayed.

   1. Select **Tag** (redefines the look of a specific tag).

   2. In the **Selector Name** list, select em.

   3. In the **Rule Definition** list, select COFFEE_styles.css.

b. Select **OK**. A dialog box is displayed.

c. In the Type category, set **Font-style** to italic.

d. Select **OK**. A rule is created and applied to the web page document.

⑥ CREATE AND APPLY A STYLE

a. In the bottom of the CSS Styles panel, click the New CSS Rule button. A dialog box is displayed.
   1. Select **Class (can apply to any tag)**.
   2. In the **Selector Name** box, type: .footer
   3. In the **Rule Definition** list, select COFFEE_styles.css.

b. Select **OK**. A dialog box is displayed.

c. In the **Type** category, set attributes to:

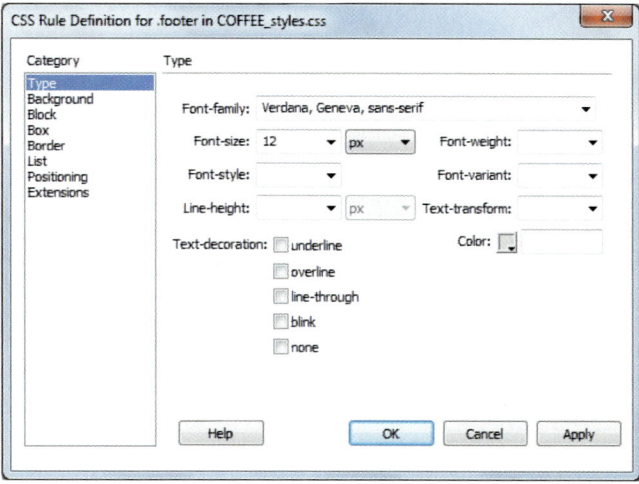

d. In the **Block** category, set **Text align** to center.
e. Select **OK**. A class is created.
f. In the Document window, select the entire bottom navigation bar.
g. In the Property inspector, click CSS.
h. Select **footer** from the **Targeted Rule** list. The style is applied.
i. In the Document window, place the insertion point to the left of the library item in the last row of the table.
j. In the Property inspector, select **footer** from the **Targeted Rule** list. The library item is formatted.

⑦ CREATE AND APPLY A SECOND STYLE

a. In the CSS Styles panel, click the New CSS Rule button. A dialog box is displayed.
   1. Select **Class (can apply to any tag)**.
   2. In the **Selector Name** box, type: .topnavbar
   3. In the **Rule Definition** list, select COFFEE_styles.css.

b. Select **OK**. A dialog box is displayed.

c. In the Type category, set the options to:

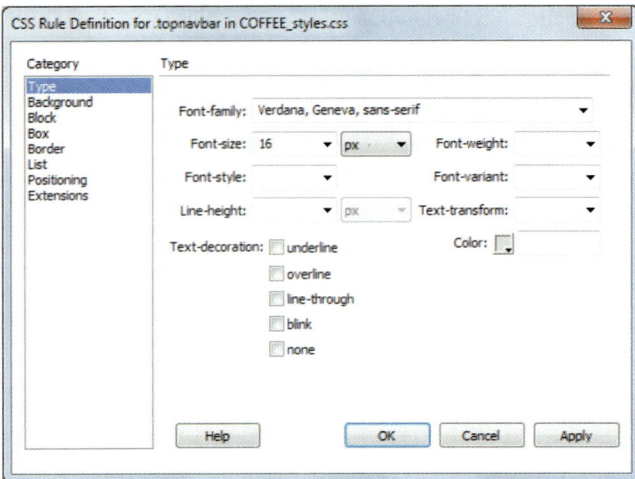

d. In the Block category, set Text align to left.
e. Select OK. A class is created.
f. In the Document window, select the entire top navigation bar.
g. In the Property inspector, select topnavbar from the Targeted Rule list. The navigation bar is formatted.

⑧ VIEW AND SAVE THE STYLE SHEET

a. In the Files panel, double-click COFFEE_styles.css. The style sheet is displayed in a Document window.
b. Select File ➞ Save All. The style sheet and all open web page documents are saved.

Working with CSS Styles

The CSS Styles panel is used to edit, duplicate, delete, and remove styles from a document:

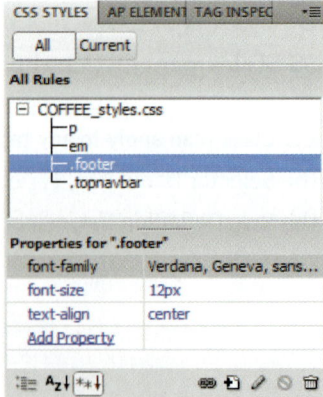

To modify a style, select the style and then click the Edit Style Sheet button, which displays a dialog box where attributes can be modified. You can also edit a rule by selecting the rule from the Targeted Rule list and then clicking the Edit Rule button in the Property inspector.

A style can be duplicated to create a new, similar style. To duplicate a style, right-click the style in the CSS Styles panel and select Duplicate to display a dialog box where the new style is given a name. The style can then be edited to customize it.

To remove a class style that has been applied to text, select the text and then select None from the Style list in the Property inspector. To remove a rule, the style must be deleted. To delete a style, select the style name in the CSS Styles panel and then click the Delete CSS Rule button 🗑.

Formatting Headings

Headings are used in text to indicate a hierarchy and help with readability. Different levels of headings can be used to further enhance readability. For example, two heading levels are shown below:

Recipes

Vanilla Iced Coffee

A user can more easily scan a long page of text if topics are divided by headings.

HTML includes six headings tags, ranging from <h1> through <h6>. Each heading level has specific formatting associated with it, which includes font size, bold text, and space above and below the heading. The largest font size is typically applied to <h1> to represent the highest level or the topic of greatest importance. <h6> typically has the least importance and the smallest font size.

Only one heading level can be applied to a line of text. To apply a heading tag, place the insertion point in the line of text and select a heading tag button from the Text category in the Insert panel:

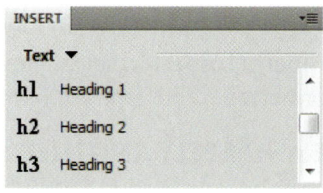

The Text category contains buttons for heading level 1, 2, and 3 only. Other heading tags are inserted by clicking [<> HTML] in the Property inspector and then selecting a heading level from the Format list or by selecting Text → Paragraph Format, which displays a menu with all six heading levels.

CSS styles should then be used to redefine the heading tags so that heading formats compliment the paragraph styles. In the CSS Rule Definition dialog box, both the Type and Block categories have attributes that can apply to headings.

> ### Antialiasing
> Some web designers create headings in a graphics program because large size fonts can appear jagged on a monitor. The jagged appearance results because web fonts do not have antialiasing, which is a feature that blends pixel edges with the background color to make letters look smoother.

Practice: COFFEE – part 2 of 6

Dreamweaver should be started and the COFFEE website should be the working site.

① ATTACH THE STYLE SHEET AND APPLY STYLES

a. Display the recipes.html web page document.
b. Display the CSS Styles panel if it is not already displayed.
c. In the CSS Styles panel, click the Attach Style Sheet button. A dialog box is displayed.
d. Select OK. The COFFEE_styles.css style sheet is linked to the recipes.html web page document.
e. In the Document window, select the entire top navigation bar.
f. In the Property inspector, click [CSS] and then select topnavbar from the Targeted Rule list. The navigation bar is formatted.
g. Select the entire bottom navigation bar.
h. In the Property inspector, select footer from the Targeted Rule list. The bottom navigation bar is formatted.
i. Place the insertion point to the left of the library item.
j. In the Property inspector, select footer from the Targeted Rule list. The library item is formatted.

② DUPLICATE A STYLE

a. In the CSS Styles panel, click the All button if it is not already selected. Next to COFFEE_styles.css click the plus sign if all the styles are not already displayed.
b. Right-click the .topnavbar style and then select Duplicate. A dialog box is displayed.
c. In the Selector Name box, replace the current name with: .btrail
d. Select OK. The new style is listed in the CSS Styles panel.
e. Right-click the new .btrail style and select Edit. A dialog box is displayed.
f. In the Type category, set Font-size to 12 pixels.
g. Select OK.
h. In the recipes.html Document window, select the entire breadcrumb trail.
i. In the Property inspector, select btrail from the Targeted Rule list. The breadcrumb trail is formatted.

③ DUPLICATE AND APPLY ANOTHER STYLE

a. In the CSS Styles panel, right-click the .btrail style and then select Duplicate. A dialog box is displayed.
b. In the Selector Name box, replace the current name with: .localnavbar
c. Select OK. The new style is listed in the CSS Styles panel.
d. Right-click the new style and select Edit. A dialog box is displayed.
e. In the Type category, set Line-height to 35 pixels.
f. In the Block category, set Vertical alignment to top.
g. Select OK.
h. In the recipes.html Document window, select the local navigation bar.
i. In the Property inspector, select localnavbar from the Targeted Rule list. The local navigation bar text is formatted.

④ **FORMAT HEADINGS**
   a. In the Design pane, click in the text "Recipes" above "Vanilla Iced Coffee."
   b. In the Text category in the Insert panel, click the Heading 1 button [h1]. In the Code pane, the "Recipes" text is now enclosed by <h1> and </h1> instead of <p> and </p>.
   c. Below the "Recipes" heading text, place the insertion point in the Vanilla Iced Coffee text.
   d. In the Property inspector, click [<> HTML] and then select Heading 2 from the Format list. In Code view, the text is now enclosed by <h2> and </h2>.
   e. Switch to Design view.
   f. Scroll down and apply the Heading 2 tags to the "Cappuccino" text.
   g. Scroll down and apply the Heading 2 tags to the "Cafe au Lait" text.

⑤ **CREATE HEADING STYLES**
   a. In the bottom of the CSS Styles panel, click the New CSS Rule button. A dialog box is displayed.
      1. Select Tag (redefines the look of a specific tag).
      2. In the Selector Name list, select h1.
      3. In the Rule Defintion list, select COFFEE_styles.css.
   b. Select OK. A dialog box is displayed.
   c. In the Type category, set attributes to:

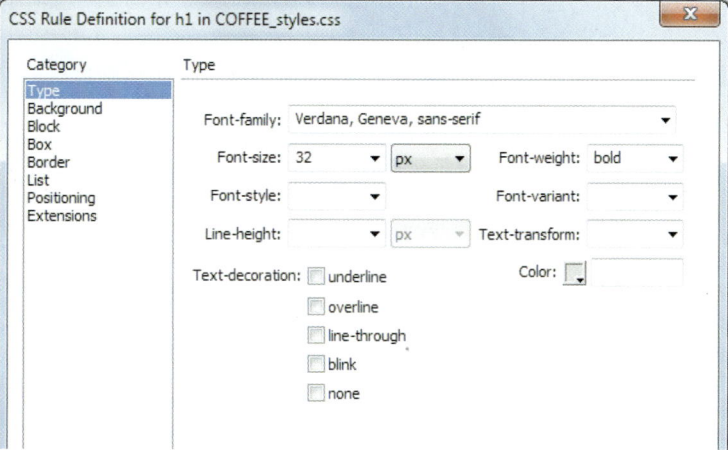

   d. In the Block category, set Text align to left.
   e. Select OK. The dialog box is removed and the heading is formatted.
   f. Create a new style that redefines the h2 tag so that the font family is Verdana, Arial, Helvetica, sans-serif, the font size is 18 pixels, the font weight is "bold", the line height is "normal", and the text alignment is left.
   g. Select File → Save All. The style sheet and all open web page documents are saved.
   h. Display the index.html web page document. The heading was automatically formatted because the style sheet is already attached.

⑥ **VIEW INDEX.HTML AND RECIPES.HTML IN A BROWSER**

Indenting with Blockquotes

A paragraph that should be set off from other paragraphs, such as a quotation, can be indented. In a web page document, a paragraph is indented by making it a blockquote:

> The Global Bean's mission is to educate coffee lovers about the coffees of the world.
>
> "A morning without coffee is like sleep."
>
> Coffee tastes are a matter of individual preference. The differences in coffees are found in the country or region of original and the quality of

The second paragraph is a blockquote

A blockquote is a paragraph enclosed by <blockquote> and </blockquote>. To apply a blockquote tag to a selected paragraph, click the Block Quote button in the Text category in the Insert panel or click the Text Indent button in the Property inspector. Multiple blockquote tags can be inserted to increase the indentation.

Blockquotes are removed from a paragraph by clicking the Text Outdent button in the Property inspector. The button may used multiple times to remove levels of blockquotes.

Typographer's Quotes

Typographer's quotes (" and ") have a more professional appearance than straight quotes. In Dreamweaver, press Alt+0147 and Alt+0148 to create left and right typographer's quotes.

Lists

Lists are used to indicate features, to-do items, or steps in a procedure. *Numbered lists* show a priority of importance for each step:

1. Use fresh, high quality coffee.
2. Select the correct grind.
3. Use the proper amount of coffee.
4. Add pure water.
5. Drink within half an hour of brewing.
6. Store coffee grinds or beans in a cool, dark, airtight container.

To convert selected paragraphs to a numbered list, click the Ordered List button in the Property inspector. Ordered list (<ol>) and list item (<li>) tags replace any tags originally enclosing the text.

A *bulleted list* contains a set of items where each item is equally important. A solid circle (•) called a bullet is typically used to denote each item. To convert selected paragraphs to a bulleted list, click the Unordered List button in the Property inspector. Unordered list (<ul>) and list item (<li>) tags replace any tags originally enclosing the text.

Lists are formatted by creating and then applying a CSS class style. The Type category in the CSS Style Definition dialog box is used to set attributes to match paragraph text. The List category contains attributes that will apply to list items:

Nested Lists

A sublist, or nested list, can be created within another list. Select the list items to be nested and then select Text → Indent to indent the items and numbers.

bulleted list

Chapter 6 Typography, Style Sheets, and Color

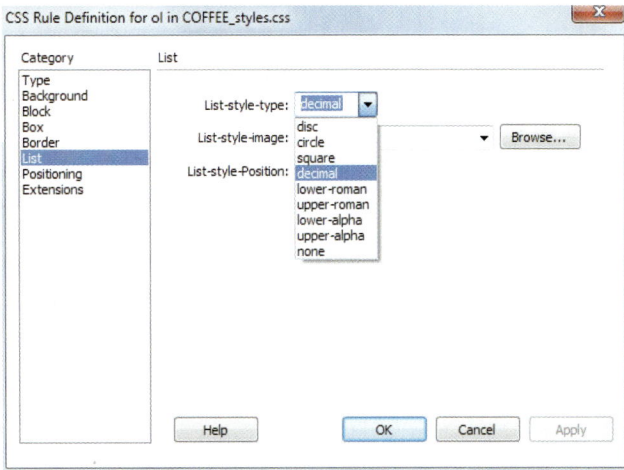

Bullet shapes and number formats can be selected from the Type list.

Practice: COFFEE – part 3 of 6

Dreamweaver should be started and the COFFEE website should be the working site.

① CREATE A BLOCKQUOTE

a. Display the index.html web page document.

b. Click in the paragraph that starts "A morning without coffee…"

c. In the Property inspector, click <> HTML and then click the Text Indent button. The paragraph is indented.

d. Click the Text Indent button again. The paragraph is indented farther.

② CREATE A NUMBERED LIST

a. Display the recipes.html web page document.

b. Scroll to the Vanilla Iced Coffee recipe directions that begin "Combine ingredients…" and select all the text in the directions:

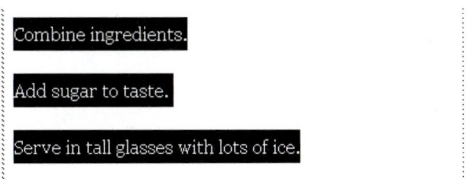

c. In the Property inspector, click the Ordered List button. The paragraphs are now a numbered list.

③ CREATE AND APPLY A RULE

a. In the CSS Styles panel, click the New CSS Rule button. A dialog box is displayed. Set options as shown:

Chapter 6 Typography, Style Sheets, and Color

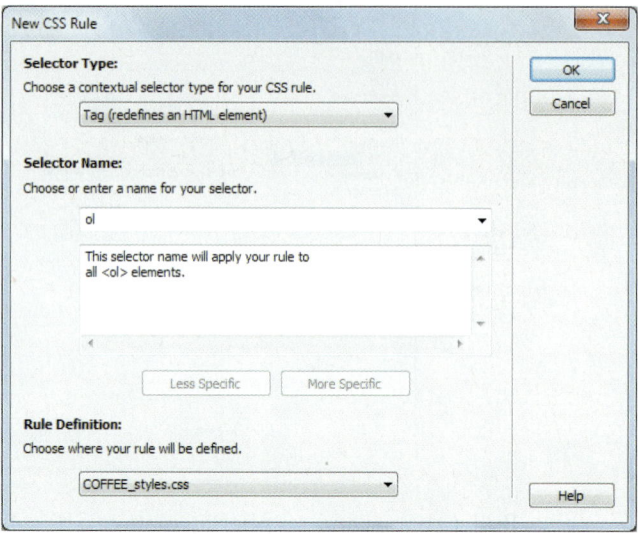

b. Select OK. A dialog box is displayed.
c. In the Type category, set attributes to:

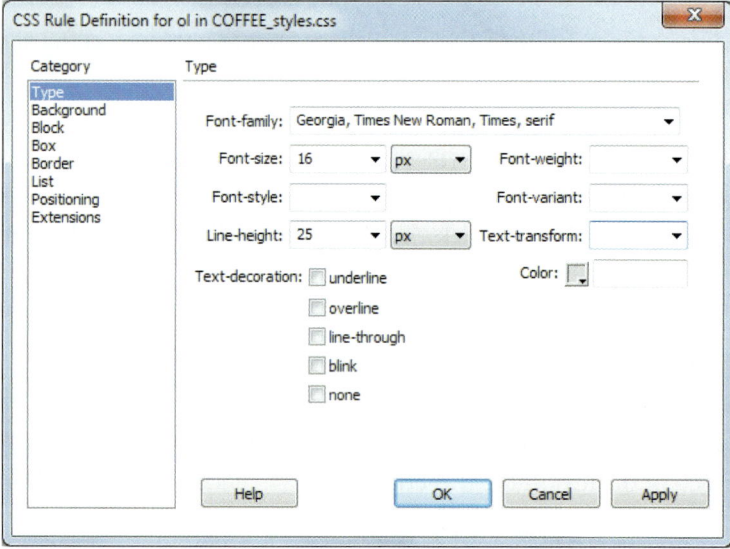

d. In the List category, set List-style-type to decimal.
e. Select OK. The dialog box is removed and the recipe steps are formatted.

④ **CREATE TWO MORE LISTS**

a. In the recipes.html web page document, scroll to the Cappuccino recipe directions that begin "Add the expresso…" and select all the text in the directions:

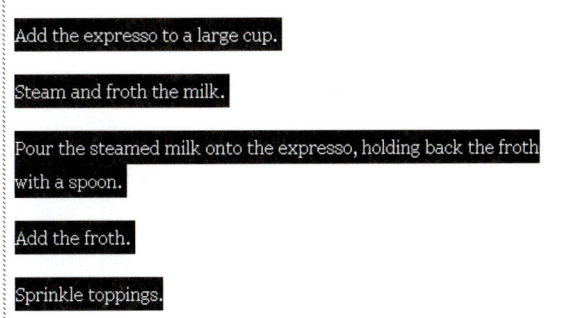

b. In the Property inspector, click the Ordered List button ≔. The paragraphs are now a numbered list.

c. In the recipes.html web page document, locate the Cafe au Lait recipe directions and format the four recipes steps as an ordered list.

d. Select File → Save All. The style sheet and all open web page documents are saved.

e. View the recipes.html web page document in a browser and then print a copy.

f. Display the index.html web page document. The ordered list is formatted because the style sheet is attached.

Using Color in a Website

Color can be added to a web page in many ways: text, page background, and table cells. However, using too many colors can make a web page visually annoying, causing users to click off the site. Color should be used to enhance the design and increase the usability of a website by guiding the user through the navigation aids and making the content more visually scannable.

color wheel   Colors that go together well can be determined with a *color wheel*. On the color wheel, colors from red to violet are arranged chromatically in a circle:

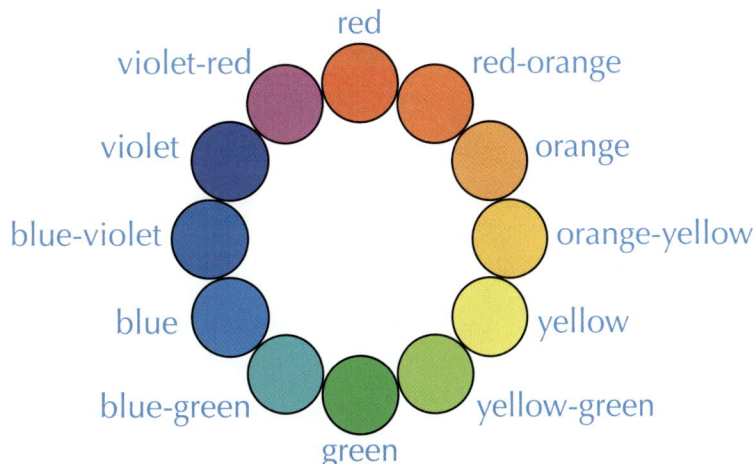

Chapter 6 Typography, Style Sheets, and Color

Color Wheel

Occupations that use color wheels include graphic artists, painters, interior designers, and web designers.

The position of a color on the wheel represents its relationship to other colors:

- Colors that are directly opposite each other are **complementary**, such as red and green.
- Three adjacent colors are called **analogous**, such as red, red-orange, and orange.
- Three equally-spaced colors are called **triads**, such as red, blue, and yellow.

Colors are also grouped by temperature:

- Reds, oranges, and yellows are **warm** colors.
- Blues, greens, and violets are **cool** colors.

Choosing two or three colors from the color wheel using one of these methods will ensure that the colors go well together.

Other elements on a web page should also be considered when choosing colors. For example, a company logo may be red, and cannot be changed, so the other colors chosen should go well with red. Also consider the effect of the color on the user. For example, red is a bright, energetic color, and does not appear soothing or relaxing. Therefore, red is usually not the best color choice for a background or text.

Color interactions should be considered when choosing text and background colors. Black text on a white background is the easiest to read, and white text on a black background is also a readable combination. Colored text can be difficult to read depending on the background color, especially with light-colored text on a light background, or dark on dark:

some color combinations can be difficult to read

Colored text needs to be large enough and contrast with the background enough to be easily read. For example, yellow text can be eye-catching and effective, but it has to be in large letters on a dark background to be readable. However, if all the text is yellow, it would get tiring for the user to read. A bright color, for any element, also is tiring for the user to view. The text and background colors should enhance the usability of a web page, not reduce it.

One possible application of background color is the navigation bar. Navigation bars should be in a different color than the background for maximum usability. However be careful that the color does not conflict with the hyperlink colors.

Changing Background and Text Color

The background of a web page document is changed by redefining the body tag. The **Background** category in the CSS Rule Definition dialog box includes the **Background color** attribute:

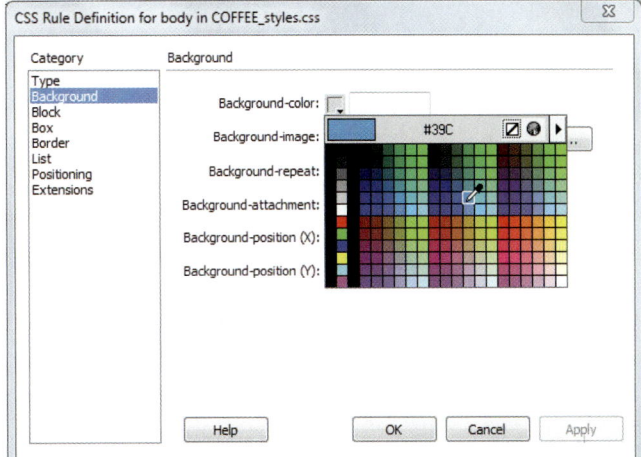

> **Hexadecimal Colors**
>
> Dreamweaver uses shorthand hexadecimal colors, Nearly all newer browsers support shorthand hexadecimal colors.

The color picker displays a grid of colors to choose from. In addition, the eyedropper can be moved into the document to match a color from the screen. To change the background color for the entire web page, select a color and then select OK.

The body tag should be redefined with a background color even if the color is white. If the color is not formatted and left as Automatic, the web page will display with whatever the user has chosen as the default background color for their browser.

The background color of a cell is changed with a CSS class style. The **Text** category contains the **Color** attribute that will apply to cells.

Text can be displayed in a different color by changing the **Color** option in the **Type** category of a CSS style:

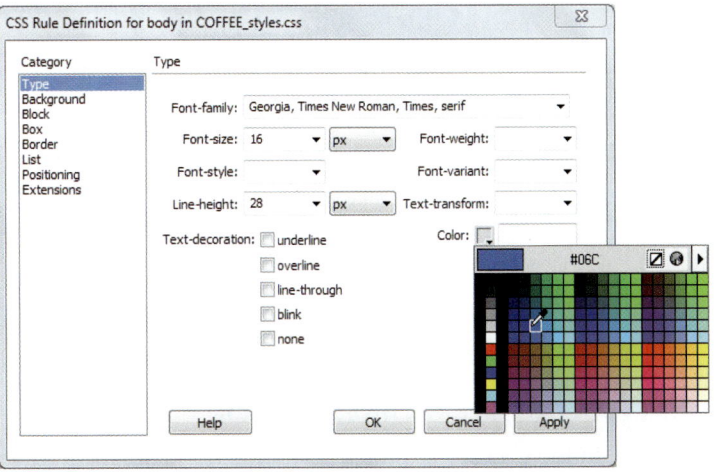

Select a color to change the color of text with the applied CSS style.

Chapter 6 Typography, Style Sheets, and Color

Practice: COFFEE – part 4 of 6

Dreamweaver should be started and the COFFEE website should be the working site.

① **CHANGE THE WEBSITE BACKGROUND COLOR**

   a. Display the recipes.html web page document.
   b. In the CSS Styles panel, click the New CSS Rule button. Set options as shown:

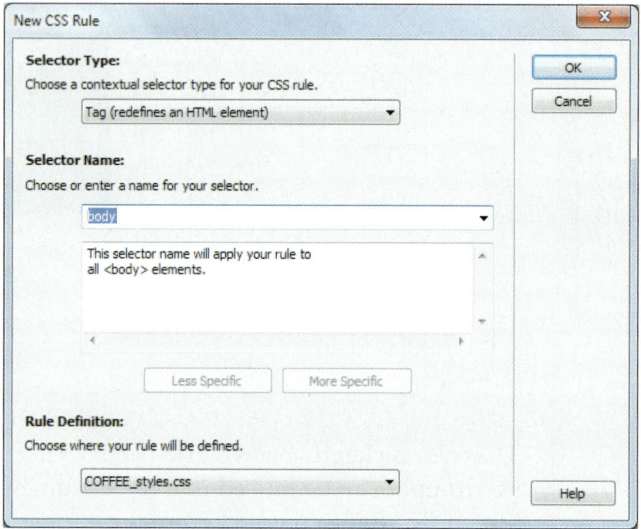

   c. Select OK. A dialog box is displayed.
   d. In the Background category, click the Background color box and select the color that corresponds to #FFC:

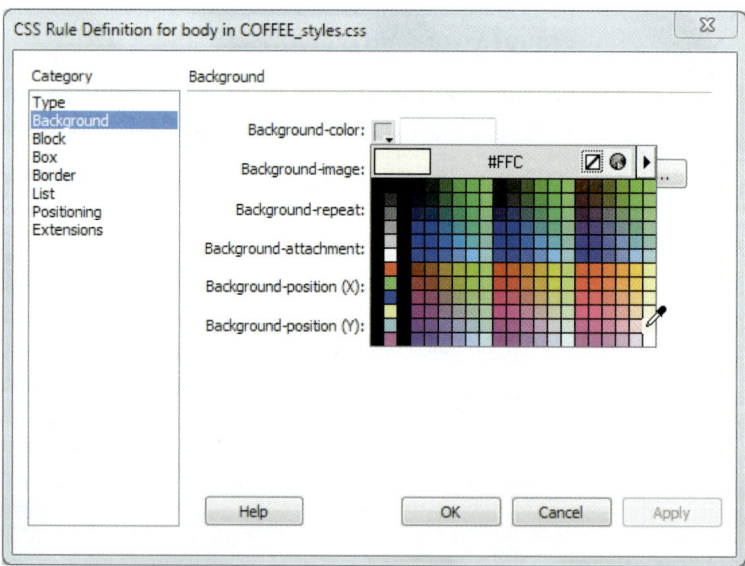

   e. Select OK. A rule is created and applied to the website.

② **CHANGE THE HEADING 2 COLOR**

   a. In the CSS Styles panel, select the h2 class rule and then click the Edit Rule button. A dialog box is displayed.

Chapter 6 Typography, Style Sheets, and Color

b. In the Type category, set attributes to:

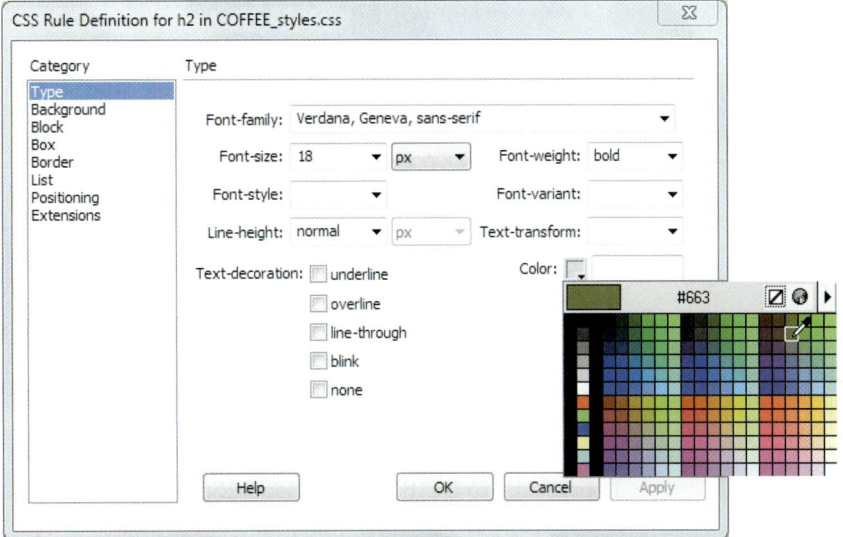

c. Select OK. The Heading 2 text color is changed.
d. Select File ➜ Save All. The style sheet and all open web page documents are saved.

③ **VIEW RECIPES.HTML IN A BROWSER**

Hyperlinks to Named Anchors

A long web page is easier to navigate if hyperlinks are provided to different parts of the page. For example, hyperlinks in a local navigation bar can link to sections in a web page. Hyperlinks to different parts of the same page are linked to a *named anchor* that has been created in the page. To create a named anchor, place the insertion point in the location of the anchor and click the Named Anchor button in the Common category in the Insert panel. A dialog box is displayed:

TIP Anchor names must start with a letter, are case-sensitive, and cannot contain spaces.

Type a descriptive name for the anchor and then select OK. An anchor icon is added at the insertion point:

TIP The anchor icon is not visible when the web page is viewed in a browser.

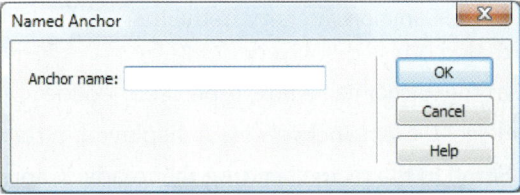

To link selected text to a named anchor, click the Browse for File icon in the Property inspector and type the anchor name in the Select File dialog box. Selected text can also be linked to a named anchor by dragging the Point to File icon to the anchor icon:

Chapter 6 Typography, Style Sheets, and Color

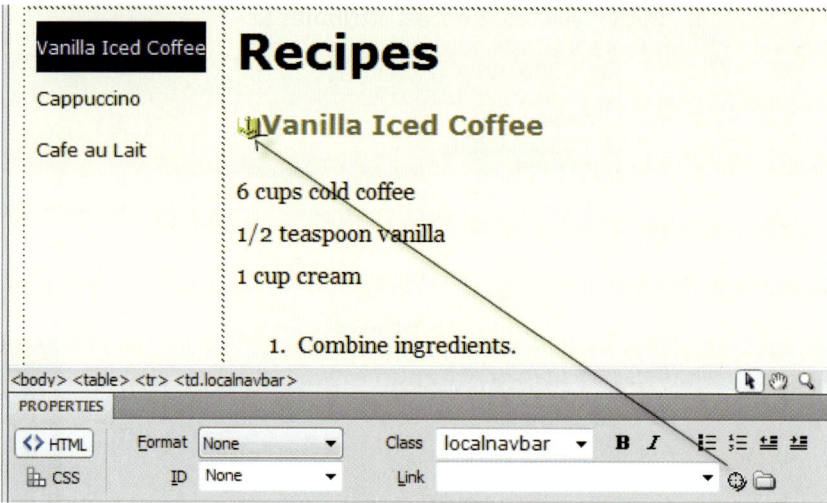

The Link list in the Property inspector displays the anchor name when the insertion point is in a hyperlink.

Links should be tested in a browser window. Links are modified in Dreamweaver by selecting the link text and then selecting Modify → Change Link or Modify → Remove Link.

A link to a named anchor typically causes a page to scroll. To increase usability, there should be another link that takes the user back to the original link location. For example, include a link such as top or Back to top that links to a named anchor near the position of the original hyperlink.

Practice: COFFEE – part 5 of 6

Dreamweaver should be started and the COFFEE website should be the working site.

① **CREATE NAMED ANCHORS**
   a. Display the recipes.html web page document.
   b. Place the insertion point to the left of the recipe heading that reads "Vanilla Iced Coffee."
   c. In the Common category in the Insert panel, click the Named Anchor button. A dialog box is displayed.
   d. In the Anchor name box, type: iced_coffee
   e. Select OK. An anchor icon is displayed in the web page document.
   f. Scroll to the recipe heading that reads "Cappuccino" and insert an anchor named cappuccino to the left of the heading.
   g. Scroll to the recipe heading that reads "Cafe au Lait" and insert an anchor named cafe_au_lait to the left of the heading.

② **CREATE HYPERLINKS TO ANCHORS**
   a. In the local navigation bar, select the text: Vanilla Iced Coffee
   b. In the Property inspector, drag the Point to File icon to the anchor next to the "Vanilla Iced Coffee" recipe. A hyperlink is created and the anchor name is displayed in the Link box in the Property inspector.
   c. In the local navigation bar, select the text: Cappuccino

d. Scroll to the recipe heading that reads "Cappuccino" and then drag the Point to File icon to the anchor next to that recipe. A hyperlink is created.

e. In the local navigation bar, select the text: Cafe au Lait

f. Scroll to the recipe heading that reads "Cafe au Lait" and then drag the Point to File icon to the anchor next to that recipe. A hyperlink is created.

③ CREATE A BACK TO TOP HYPERLINK

a. Scroll to the top of the recipes and place the insertion point to the left of the "Recipes" heading.

b. Insert an anchor named: top

c. Scroll to the last step of the last recipe, place the insertion point just after the period in "…the foam." and then insert a line break.

d. Type and then select the text: Back to top

e. Drag the Point to File icon to the anchor next to "Recipes."

f. Save the modified recipes.html.

④ VIEW RECIPES.HTML IN A BROWSER AND TEST THE HYPERLINKS

Changing Hyperlink Colors

A lot of design consideration should go into the decision to change hyperlink colors. Users recognize the standard colors: blue for a link and purple for a visited link. However, when appropriately done, nonstandard hyperlink colors can enhance a design.

Hyperlink colors are changed by creating a *CSS selector style*, which defines a style for a tag and attribute combination. Click the New CSS Rule button, which displays a dialog box. Select Compound (based on your selection) and then make a selection from the Selector list:

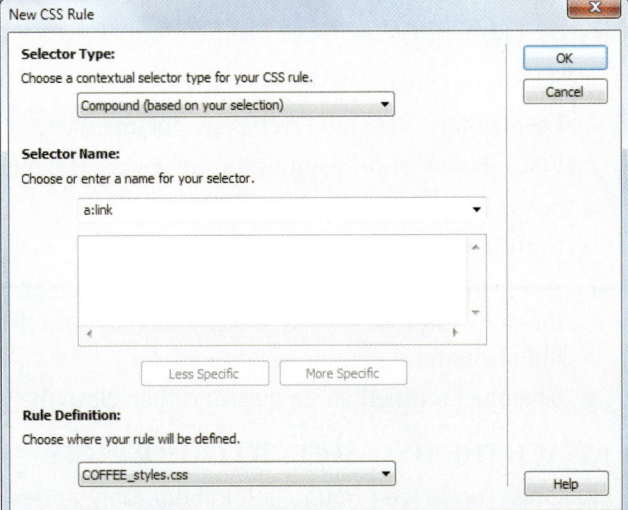

> **Selector Options**
>
> link="value" is the HTML attribute that sets the color of links and vlink="value" sets the color of previously visited links.

Select OK to display a dialog box where color and other formats can be selected from the Type category.

Chapter 6 Typography, Style Sheets, and Color   223

Using Content from Other Sources

Web development often involves collaborating with others to get the content for a website. For example, one person or department may have the responsibility of providing the images for a site, while others are responsible for the copy. *Copy* is a term that refers to text content.

Files that contain copy are typically in text or TXT format to avoid having formatting copied with the text. Notepad is a text editor that can be used to open a text file and then copy and paste text to a Dreamweaver web page document:

1. Open the TXT file, which has the .txt extension, in Notepad.
2. Select the text to be placed in a web page document.
3. Select Edit → Copy. The text is placed on the Windows clipboard.
4. Display the web page document in Dreamweaver and place the insertion point where the text should be placed.
5. Select Edit → Paste. The copy is pasted at the insertion point.

You can also import text from a Word document by selecting File → Import → Word Document.

TIP Notepad was introduced in Chapter 2.

Practice: COFFEE – part 6 of 6

Dreamweaver should be started and the COFFEE website should be the working site.

① ADD COPY FROM A TEXT FILE

a. Start Notepad.
b. Open the AFRICA.txt file, a text file provided with the data files for this text.
c. Select Edit → Select All. All the text is selected.
d. Select Edit → Copy. The text is copied to the Windows Clipboard.

② PASTE THE TEXT

a. Switch to Dreamweaver.
b. Display the africa.html web page document.
c. Place the insertion point in the empty paragraph below the "Africa" heading.
d. Select Edit → Paste. The text is pasted.
e. In the CSS Styles panel, attach the COFFEE_styles.css style sheet.
f. Apply the topnavbar, localnavbar, btrail, and footer styles appropriately. Remember the footer style will need to be applied to both the bottom navigation bar and the library item.
g. Save the modified africa.html and then close the web page document.

③ ATTACH THE STYLE SHEET TO OTHER PAGES

a. Open the coffee_around_world.html, latin_america.html, and indonesia.html web page documents and link the COFFEE_styles.css style sheet.
b. Apply the topnavbar, localnavbar, btrail, and footer styles appropriately. Remember the footer style will need to be applied to both the bottom navigation bar and the library item.

④ CHANGE HYPERLINK COLORS

a. Display the index.html web page document.
b. In the CSS Styles panel, click the New CSS Rule button. A dialog box is displayed. Set options as shown:

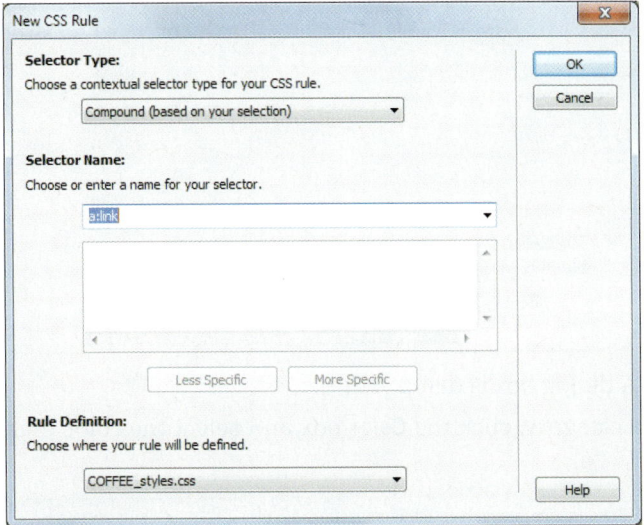

c. Select OK. A dialog box is displayed.
d. In the Type category, click the Color box and select the color that corresponds to #663:

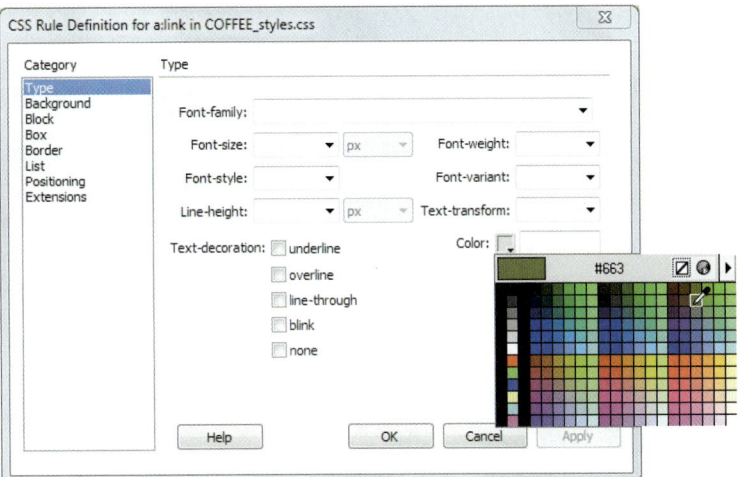

e. Select OK. The hyperlink color is changed.
f. In the CSS Styles panel, click the New CSS Rule button. A dialog box is displayed. Set options as shown:

Chapter 6 Typography, Style Sheets, and Color   225

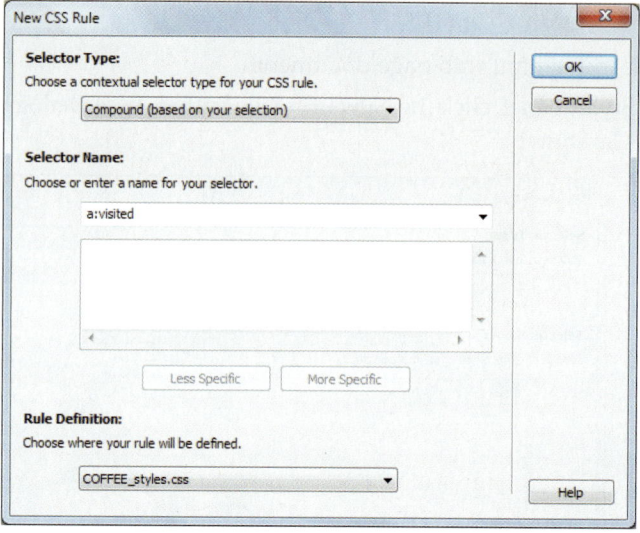

g. Select **OK**. A dialog box is displayed.

h. In the **Type** category, click the **Color** box and select the color that corresponds to #930:

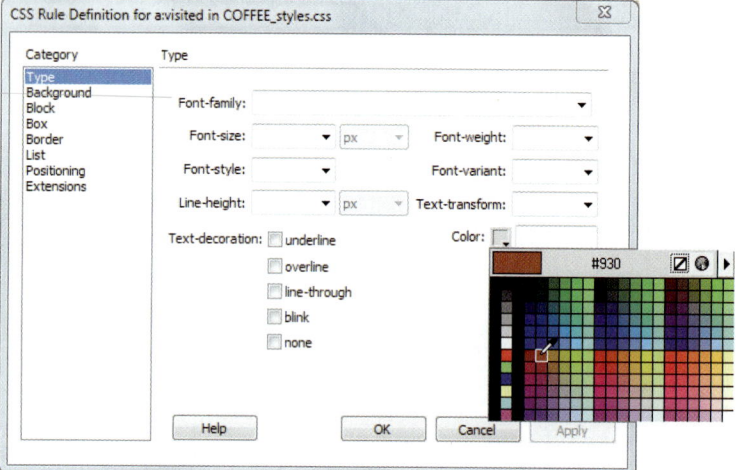

i. Select **OK**. The visited hyperlink color is changed.

j. Select **File → Save All**. All open web page documents are saved.

⑤ VIEW THE WEBSITE IN A BROWSER

a. View the website in a browser. Note the consistency between the pages.

b. Print a copy of each web page from the browser.

c. Close the browser window.

d. Quit Notepad and close all open Dreamweaver documents.

Controlling Images with CSS

CSS styles can be used to add a border to an image and to force text to wrap around an image. In general, it is not a good idea to redefine the <img> tag because not all images in a site typically require the same settings. Instead, a class style should be used. To wrap text around an image, the **Float** property in the Box category is set. For example, to place a graphic to the left of the text and add space around the graphic use settings similar to:

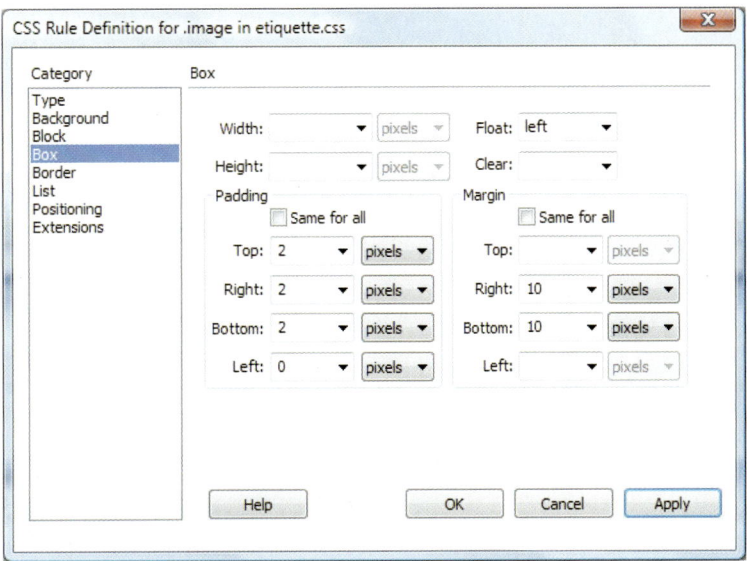

TIP You can think of CSS as being between the HTML and the browser, defining how elements should be displayed. CSS puts a 'box' around each element and then allows the box to be formatted.

The Padding property adds space between the content and any borders around the element. The Margin property adds space between elements, such as the image and the text wrapping around the image.

Borders can be added to images to give them a 'framed-finish'. Borders can also help define a series of thumbnail images. Select the **Border** category to display style, width, and color options:

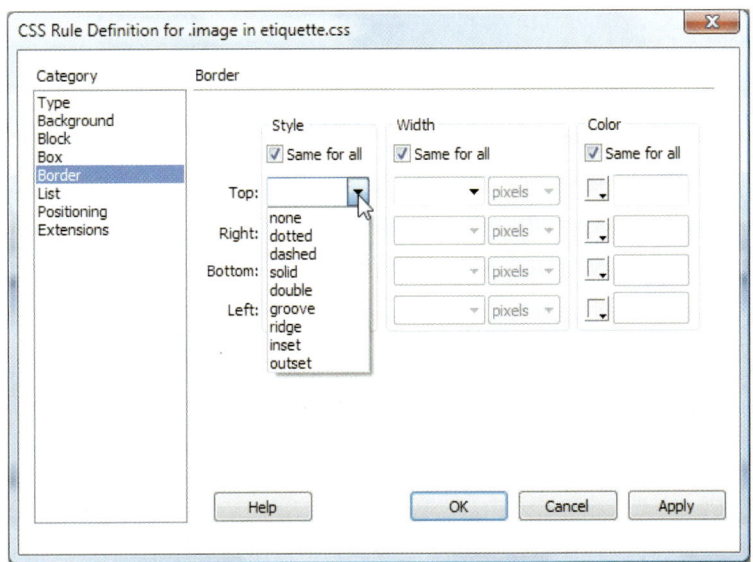

Chapter 6 Typography, Style Sheets, and Color

227

You can also use the Property inspector to control the alignment of an image if you use one of the CSS starter layouts. For example, an image has been inserted to the left of the first sentence:

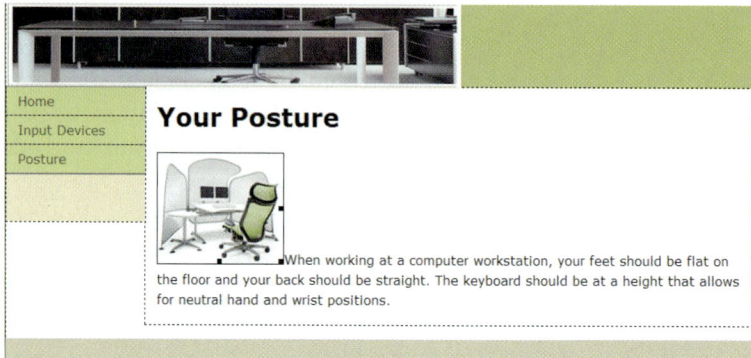

With the image selected, select *fltrt* (float right) from the Class pop-up menu in the Property inspector:

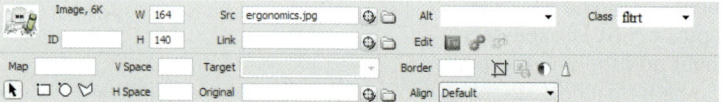

The image is aligned to the right side of its container with text wrapping around it to the left:

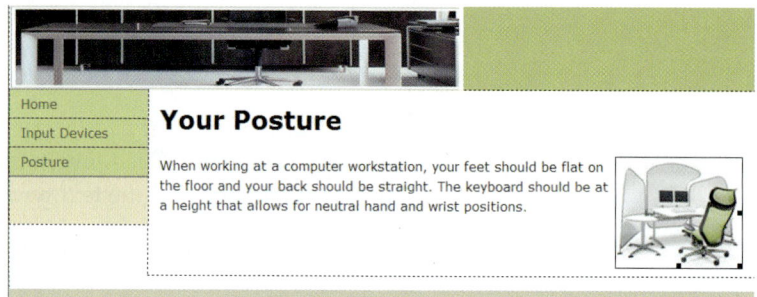

CSS Layouts

The start of this chapter explained how typography choices are more complicated for a web page than for a print document. Placement issues are also more complicated. CSS layouts allows block-level element to be placed at a specific location on a web page. For example, h1, p, and div tags all produce block-level elements on a page. You can set margins and borders, position them in a specific location, float text around them, and so forth.

CSS page layouts requires a CSS rule to be defined and then the rule is applied to a <div> tag, which represents a specific area on a page. The Practice below illustrates how to create a simple page layout.

Practice: Time Management

In this practice, a simple CSS page layout will be created from a blank page that will appear similar to:

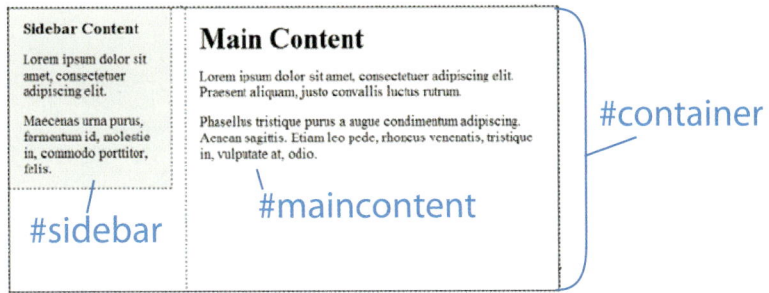

① **DEFINE A NEW SITE NAMING IT TIME MANAGEMENT**

② **CREATE A NEW BLANK WEB PAGE DOCUMENT**

   a. Change the page title to: Time Management
   b. Save the web page naming it: index.html

③ **CREATE A NEW STYLE SHEET**

   a. Select File → New. A dialog box is displayed.
      1. Select CSS in the Page Type list.
      2. Click Create.

④ **CREATE THE STYLE SHEET**

   a. In the CSS Styles panel, click the New CSS Rule button. A dialog box is displayed.
      1. Select ID (applies only to one HTML element).
      2. In the Selector Name box, type: #container
         Note that the # sign creates an ID attribute in the div tag and is used to assign a unique name to the element.
      3. Select OK. A dialog box is displayed.
   b. In the Background category, set Background color to: #FFF
   c. In the Block category, set Text align to: left
   d. In the Box category, set Width to: 780 pixels and Margin to 0 pixels. Select Same for all if it is not already selected.
   e. In the Border category, set Style to solid and Width to: 1 pixel. In both settings, select Same for all if it is not already selected and then select OK.
   f. In the CSS Styles panel, click the New CSS Rule button. A dialog box is displayed. Set options as shown:
      1. Select ID (applies only to one HTML element).
      2. In the Selector Name box, type: #sidebar

Chapter 6 Typography, Style Sheets, and Color

g. Select OK. A dialog box is displayed. Set options as shown:

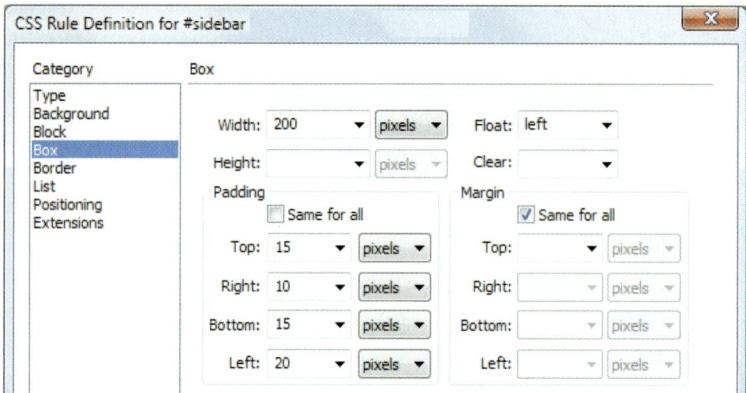

h. Select OK.
i. In the CSS Styles panel, click the New CSS Rule button. A dialog box is displayed.
   1. Select ID (applies only to one HTML element).
   2. In the Selector list, type: #maincontent
j. Select OK. A dialog box is displayed. Set options as shown:

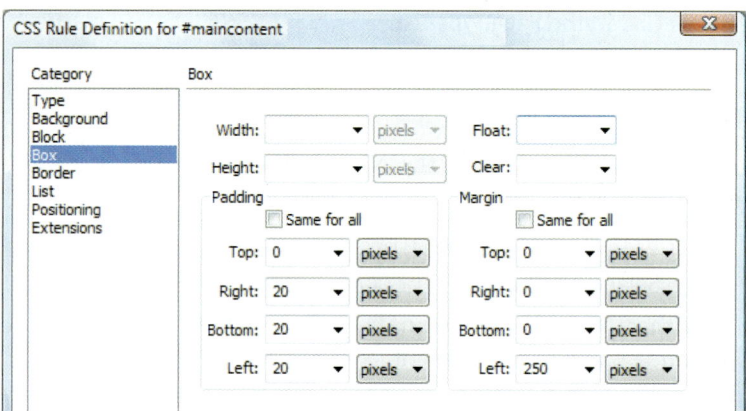

k. Select OK.
l. Save the style sheet naming it: timemgt.css
m. Display index.html.
n. Attach the timemgt.css style sheet.

⑤ APPLY THE STYLE TO A <DIV> TAG

a. Position the insertion point in the top left corner of the index.html page.
b. In the Layout category in the Insert panel, click the Insert Div Tag button. A dialog box is displayed.
   1. In the ID list, select container.
   2. Select OK. The container for the web page is displayed. With the placeholder text selected, press Enter twice. The placeholder text is deleted and the container outline is visible.
c. Position the insertion point in the top left corner of the container.

230   *Chapter 6 Typography, Style Sheets, and Color*

d. In the Layout category in the Insert panel, click the Insert Div Tag button. A dialog box is displayed. Set options as shown:

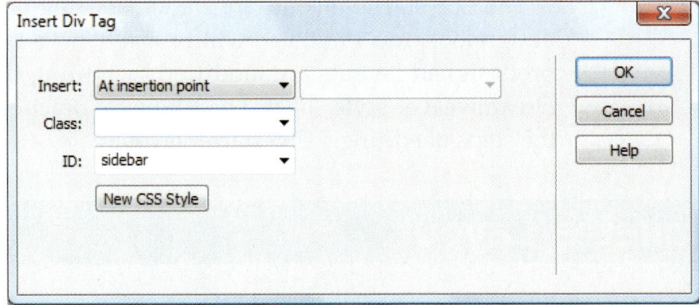

e. Select **OK**. A sidebar element is displayed on the page.
f. Place the insertion point to the right of the sidebar.
g. In the Layout category in the Insert panel, click the Insert Div Tag button. A dialog box is displayed.
   1. In the ID list, select maincontent.
   2. Select **OK**. The maincontent placeholder is displayed. Add content relevant to time management and apply additional CSS formatting rules to produce a web page similar to:

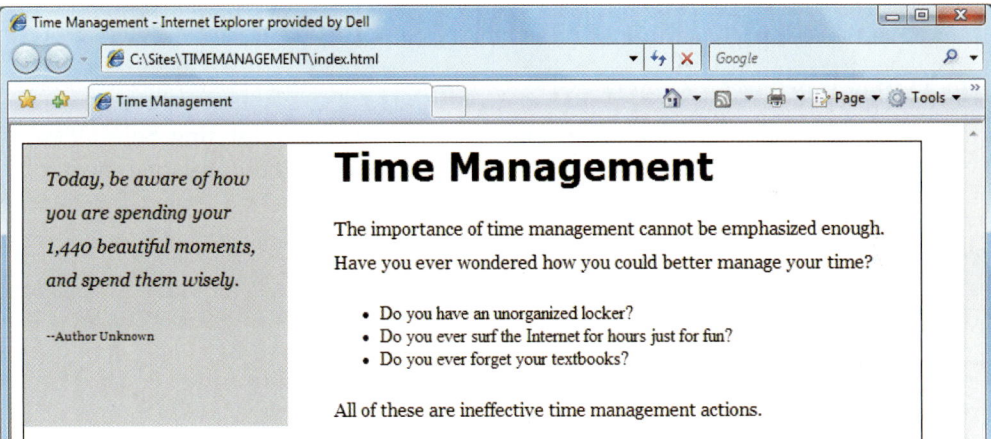

⑥ VIEW INDEX.HTML IN A BROWSER
a. Save and then view index.html in a browser.
b. Close the browser window and in Dreamweaver, close index.html

Editing CSS Starter Layouts

The CSS starter layouts are a good starting point. However, to get the design look you want, you will probably have to modify the layout. The predesigned layouts are modified by editing the styles defined in the Dreamweaver style sheet. The Etiquette practice will take you through the steps of editing a CSS starter layout.

Practice: Etiquette/Layout

① **DEFINE A NEW SITE NAMING IT ETIQUETTE**

② **CREATE A NEW WEB PAGE DOCUMENT**

    a. Select File → New. A dialog box is displayed.

        1. Select Blank Page.

        2. In the Page Type list, select HTML.

        3. In the Layout list, select 1 column fixed, centered, header and footer.

        4. Select Create.

        5. Select Save.

    b. Change the page title to: Electronic Etiquette

    c. Save the web page naming it: index.html

③ **EXAMINE THE PAGE LAYOUT**

    a. To understand the design of the page, you will turn of CSS styling. Select View → Style Rendering → Display Styles. The page is displayed without the style sheet:

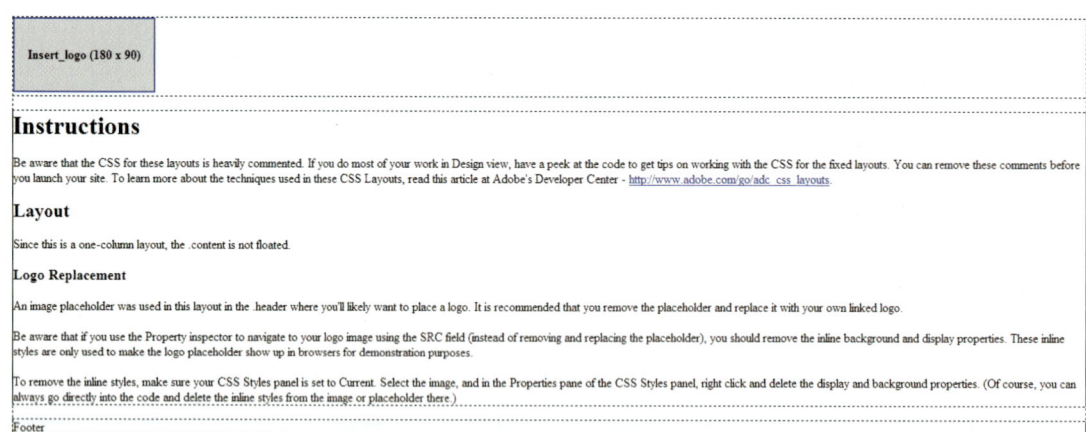

    b. The layout has been created with three content <div> elements (header, footer, and content) and one <div> that wraps around the others (container).

Chapter 6 Typography, Style Sheets, and Color

c. Switch to Code view and locate the <div> tags:

```
<!DOCTYPE html PUBLIC "-//W3C//DTD XHTML 1.0 Transitional//EN" "http://www.w3.org/TR/xhtml1/DTD/xhtml1-transitional.dtd">
<html xmlns="http://www.w3.org/1999/xhtml">
<head>
<meta http-equiv="Content-Type" content="text/html; charset=utf-8" />
<title>Untitled Document</title>
<link href="file:///C|/Users/Jan/Documents/LVP Printings/DMCS5-1 TRM/PRACTICE ANSWERS/Layout/oneColFixCtrHdr.css" rel="stylesheet" type="text/css" />
</head>

<body>
<div class="container">
  <div class="header"><a href="#"><img src="" alt="Insert Logo Here" name="Insert_logo" width="180" height="90" id="Insert_logo" style="background: #C6D580; display:block;" /></a>
    <!-- end .header --></div>
  <div class="content">
    <h1>Instructions</h1>
    <p>Be aware that the CSS for these layouts is heavily commented. If you do most of your work in Design view, have a peek at the code to get tips on working with the CSS for the fixed layouts. You can remove these comments before you launch your site. To learn more about the techniques used in these CSS Layouts, read this article at Adobe's Developer Center - <a href="http://www.adobe.com/go/adc_css_layouts">http://www.adobe.com/go/adc_css_layouts</a>.</p>
    <h2>Layout</h2>
    <p>Since this is a one-column layout, the .content is not floated. </p>
    <h3>Logo Replacement</h3>
    <p>An image placeholder was used in this layout in the .header where you'll likely want to place  a logo. It is recommended that you remove the placeholder and replace it with your own linked logo. </p>
    <p> Be aware that if you use the Property inspector to navigate to your logo image using the SRC field (instead of removing and replacing the placeholder), you should remove the inline background and display properties. These inline styles are only used to make the logo placeholder show up in browsers for demonstration purposes. </p>
    <p>To remove the inline styles, make sure your CSS Styles panel is set to Current. Select the image, and in the Properties pane of the CSS Styles panel, right click and delete the display and background properties. (Of course, you can always go directly into the code and delete the inline styles from the image or placeholder there.)</p>
    <!-- end .content --></div>
  <div class="footer">
    <p>Footer</p>
    <!-- end .footer --></div>
  <!-- end .container --></div>
</body>
</html>
```

d. Switch to Design view.

e. Select View → Style Rendering → Display Styles. The page is displayed with the style sheet.

④ ADD A BACKGROUND TO THE IMAGE HEADER

a. Select the image placeholder and press the Delete key. The empty header collapses because it has no CSS height specification.

b. In the CSS Styles panel, double-click the .header rule. A dialog box is displayed.

   1. Click the **Background** category.

   2. Click the **Browse** button next to the Background-image box.

   3. Navigate to banner.gif, which is a data file for this text.

   4. Select banner.gif and click **OK**.

   5. It is important to note that background images repeat both vertically (y) and horizontally (x) by default, which can affect the way they are displayed in different browsers. In this case, you will select the **repeat-x** option so that the banner fills the width of the header:

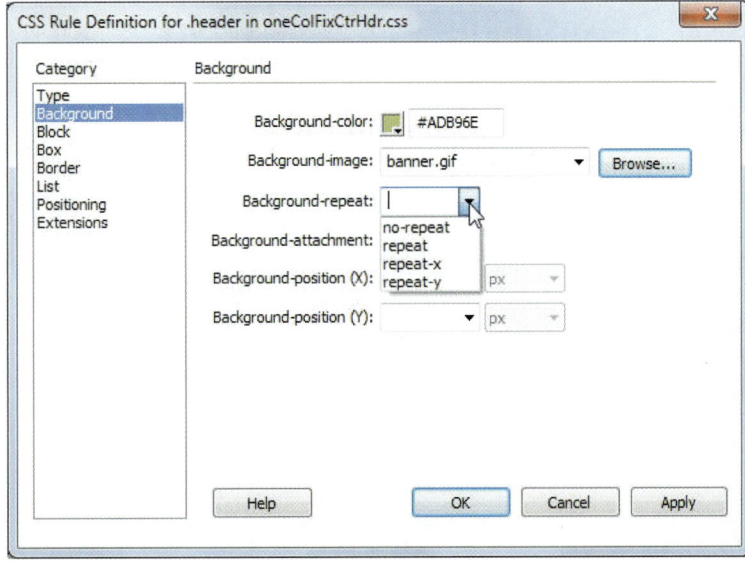

   6. Click **Apply** to view the results.

Chapter 6 Typography, Style Sheets, and Color

7. Currently the header isn't tall enough to display the banner. To change the height, click the Box category.
8. In the Height box, type 90 and click Apply. Note that the width of the page is set in the .container rule so you don't need to change the width in this dialog box.
9. Click the Background category.
10. Notice the default background color. If the background image doesn't display, the background color will be displayed. Therefore, you should select a color that will match the color scheme of the page. Click a green or blue background color.
11. Click OK.

⑤ ADD A DIV TAG
a. Place the insertion point in the header.
b. Click the <div.header> tag selector.
c. Press the right arrow key.
d. In Code view, the insertion point should now be after the ending </div> tag of the header:

```
10
11  <div class="container">
12    <div class="header"><!-- end .header --></div>
13    <div class="content">
14      <h1>Instructions</h1>
```

e. Switch to Design view and select Window → Insert if the Insert panel is not displayed.
f. Select the Layout category in the Insert panel.
g. Click Insert Div Tag. A dialog box is displayed.
   1. Set the following options:

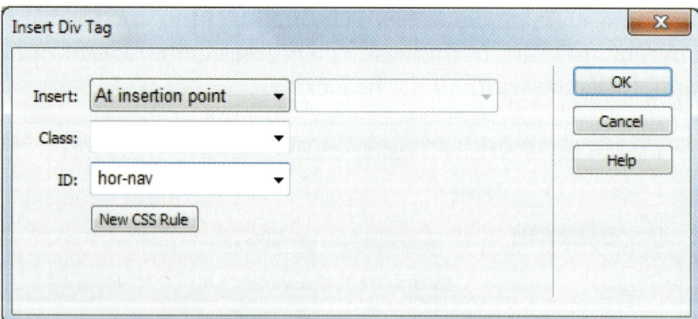

   2. Click the New CSS Rule button. The New CSS Rule dialog box is displayed. Notice that #hor-nav has been automatically entered in the Selector Name box.
   3. Click OK. A dialog box is displayed. Set the following options:

Chapter 6 Typography, Style Sheets, and Color

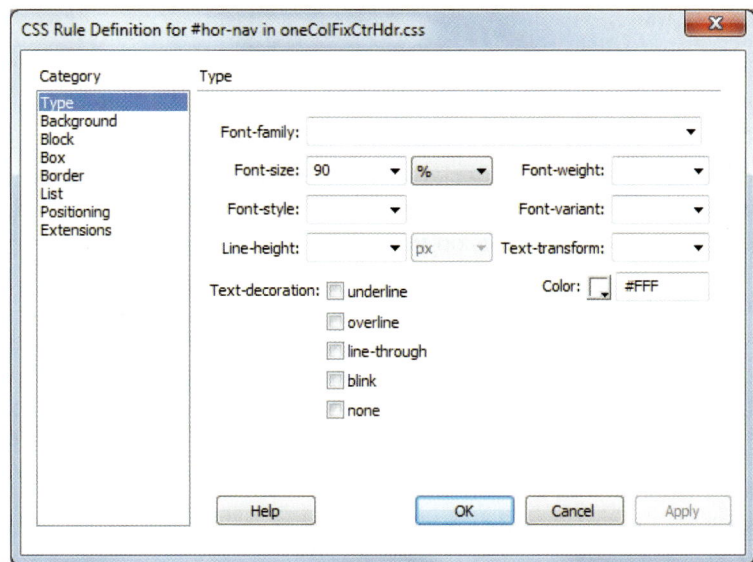

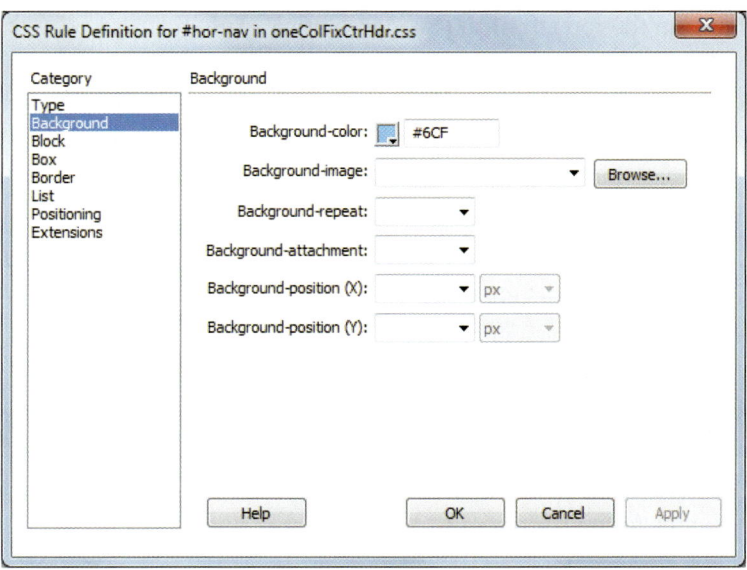

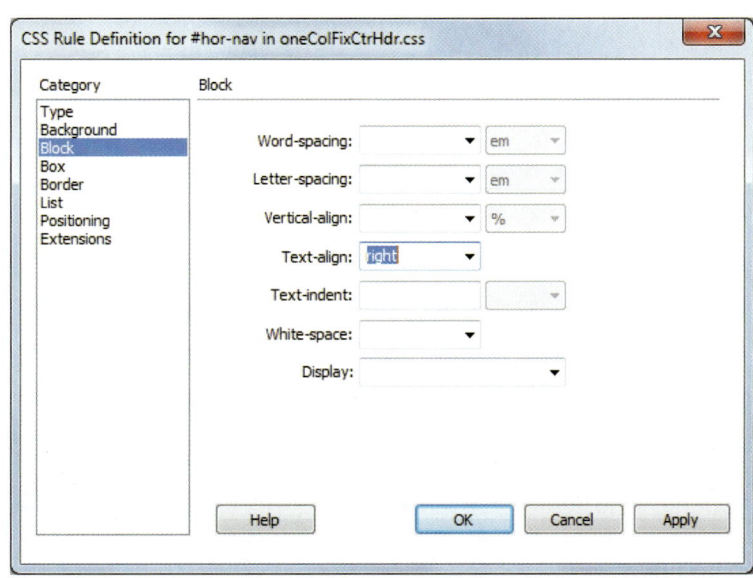

Chapter 6 Typography, Style Sheets, and Color

4. Click **OK**.

5. Click **OK**. The div tag has created an area for a horizontal navigation bar.

h. Replace the content placeholder text with Home | Etiquette Tips | Contact Us. This text can then be used to create hyperlinks to appropriate pages.

i. The colors selected for the horizontal navigation bar can be edited by double-clicking #hor-nav in the CSS Styles panel and selecting different color options. You can experiment with this on your own.

⑥ INSERT ANOTHER DIV TAG

a. A div tag will be used to place an image that will overlap the header and the horizontal navigation bar. In order to achieve this effect, you will use an absolutely positioned <div>. Start by placing the insertion point in the header.

b. Click the <div.header> tag selector.

c. Press the left arrow key.

d. In Code view, the insertion point should now be before the starting <div> tag of the header.

e. Switch to Design view and select Insert → Layout Objects → AP Div. An AP div is displayed in the top left of the header. Notice a rule has also been added in the Targeted Rule box.

f. Click the <div#apDiv1> tag selector. Notice the width and height settings in the Property inspector.

g. Place the insertion point in the <div#apDiv1>.

h. Select Insert → Image. A dialog box is displayed.

1. Navigate to the globe.gif image, which is a data file for this text.

2. Click **OK** and then click **Yes**.

3. Click **Yes** and then click **Cancel** when the Alternative text box is displayed. The image is inserted.

i. The size of the AP div is different than the size of the image. It is a good idea to match the container dimensions to those of the image. Double-click the #apDiv1 rule in the CSS Styles panel. A dialog box is displayed.

1. Set the following options:

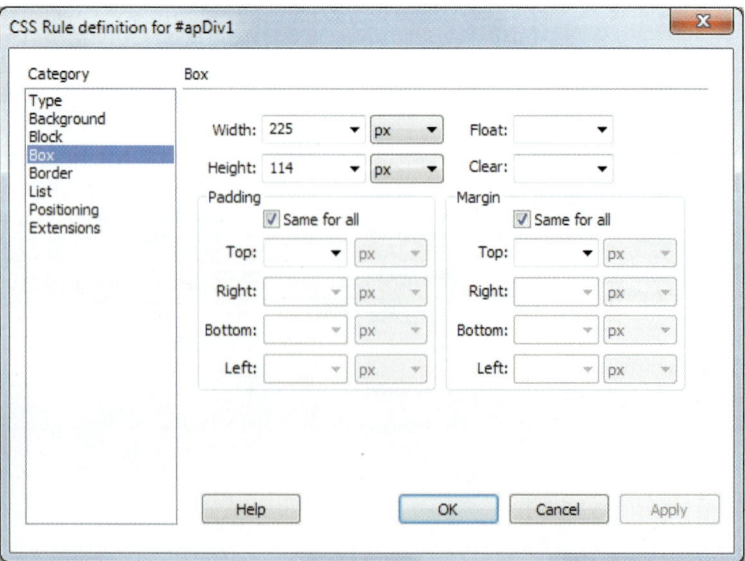

2. Click **OK**.

Chapter 6 Typography, Style Sheets, and Color

⑦ EXAMINE THE CSS STYLES PANEL

a. Display the CSS Styles panel and drag the top border to size the panel appropriately.

b. Click body and notice the properties for the <body> tag are displayed:

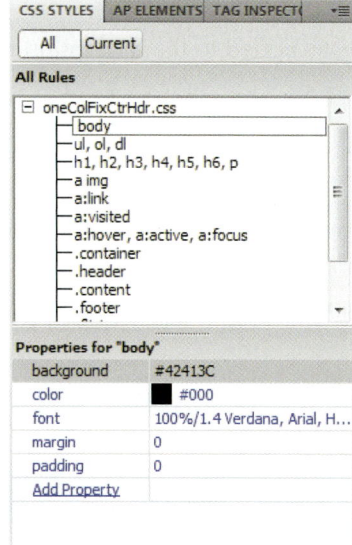

c. In the tag selector, click the <body> tag. All text that is affected by this tag is highlighted.

d. Click a blank area of the page to remove the highlighting.

e. In the CSS Styles panel, click the color button and then select a different text color. Notice all the body text changes color. (*except text that was defined with an over-riding rule*)

f. Save the modified index.html.

g. Close index.html.

⑧ CREATE A NEW SITE

a. Create a new site named Layout in a folder named Layout.

b. Add a new page with the 2 column, fixed, left sidebar, header and footer starter layout.

⑨ ADD A NAVIGATION LINK

a. By default, this CSS starter layout, contains a navigation bar with four links. You will add an additional link.

b. Place the insertion point at the end of the Link four text and then switch to Split view.

c. In the Code window, notice the HTML used to create the navigation links.

d. In the Code window, select <li><a href="#">Link four</a></li> and press Ctrl+C to copy the selected code.

e. Move the insertion to the end of the selected line of code and press the Enter key.

f. Press Ctrl+P to paste the code.

g. Edit the pasted code to read Link five:

Chapter 6 Typography, Style Sheets, and Color   237

```
15    <ul class="nav">
16      <li><a href="#">Link one</a></li>
17      <li><a href="#">Link two</a></li>
18      <li><a href="#">Link three</a></li>
19      <li><a href="#">Link four</a></li>
20      <li><a href="#">Link five</a></li>
21    </ul>
```

An additional link has been added to the navigation bar.

⑩ EXAMINE THE SIDEBAR

a. Switch to Design view.

b. In the CSS Styles panel, double-click .sidebar1.

c. Experiment with the appearance of the sidebar by changing the style settings including the Height setting in the Box category.

d. Save the modified web page document naming it: index.html

e. Quit Dreamweaver.

Chapter Summary

Typography refers to the arrangement, shape, size, style, and weight of text. A typeface is a set of letters drawn in a specific style. The word font technically refers to a specific size and weight of a single typeface. In order for a font to display correctly in a browser, the user must have the font installed on their computer.

Font categories include serif and sans serif font. When choosing sizes for the text on a web page, keep usability in mind. Type styles indicate variations of the characters. Line height is the distance from one line of text to another. In a paragraph, left alignment is the most readable and therefore provides the highest degree of usability.

A style sheet defines the type, paragraph, and page formats for a web page document. A single style sheet can be applied to all the pages in a website to achieve a consistent look. The CSS Styles panel is used for linking, creating, and modifying style sheets. A CSS document can have rules, which modify HTML elements and classes, which are a set of declarations that can be applied to different tags.

Headings are used in text to indicate a hierarchy and help with readability. HTML includes six headings tags, ranging from `<h1>` through `<h6>`. A paragraph that should be set off from other paragraphs, such as a quotation, can be indented using a blockquote. A numbered list shows a priority of importance for each step. A bulleted list contains a set of items where each item is equally important.

Color can be added to a web page in many ways: text, page background, and table cells. Colors that go together well can be determined with a color wheel. Colored text needs to be large enough and contrast with the background enough to be easily read.

A long web page is easier to navigate if hyperlinks are provided to different parts of the page. Hyperlinks to different parts of the same page are linked to a named anchor. Hyperlink colors can be changed. However, a lot of design consideration should go into the decision to change hyperlink colors because users recognize the standard blue and purple colors.

The CSS starter layouts can be modified by editing the styles defined in the Dreamweaver style sheet. This is a quick and efficient way to achieve the layout you want.

Vocabulary

Alignment A paragraph format that refers to the position of the lines of text relative to the sides of a cell. Paragraph alignments include left, centered, right, and justified.

Analogous Three adjacent colors on the color wheel.

Bulleted List A list of items where each item is equally important.

Cascading The effect of applying rules from one style sheet in addition to those in another style sheet.

Class A set of declarations that can be applied to different tags.

Color wheel Colors from red to violet that are arranged chromatically in a circle. Used to determine colors that go together well.

Complementary Colors that are directly opposite each other on the color wheel.

Cool colors Blue, green, and violet colors.

Copy Refers to text content.

CSS Selector Style Defines a style for a tag and attribute combination. Used to change hyperlink colors.

Declarations The formats to be applied in a rule.

Font A specific size and weight of a single typeface.

Line Height The distance from one line of text to another.

Named Anchor A hyperlink destination that is located on the same web page document as the hyperlink.

Numbered List A list of items where each item has a priority of importance.

Point Unit used to measure the size of printed text. One point is 1/72 of an inch.

Regular Text that has no style applied to it.

Rule A selector and its declaration(s) which are used to modify an HTML element.

Sans serif Characters without the small extensions (serifs) on their ends.

Selector The HTML element being redefined in a rule.

Serif The small extensions on the ends of the strokes of a character.

Style Variations of characters including bold and italic.

Style Sheet Used to define the type, paragraph, and page formats for a web page document.

Triad Three equally-spaced colors on the color wheel.

Typeface A set of letters drawn in a specific style.

Typography The arrangement, shape, size, style, and weight of text.

Warm colors Red, orange, and yellow colors.

Dreamweaver Commands and Buttons

AP Div command Inserts an absolutely positioned <div> tag. Found in Insert → Layout Objects.

Attach Style Sheet button Links a style sheet to the open web page document. Found in the CSS Styles panel.

Block Quote button Indents a paragraph. Found in the Text category in the Insert panel.

Bold button Creates strong text, which is displayed as bold text. Found in the Text category in the Insert panel.

Change Link command Displays a dialog box used to modify a hyperlink. Found in the Modify menu.

Copy command Copies selected text. Found in the Edit menu.

Delete CSS Style button Deletes a style. Found in the CSS Styles panel.

Edit Style Sheet button Displays a dialog box used to modify attributes or duplicate styles. Found in the CSS Styles panel.

Emphasize button Creates emphasized text, which is displayed as italic text. Found in the Text category in the Insert panel.

Heading 1 button Formats the selected text in heading 1. Found in the Text category in the Insert panel.

Insert Div Tag button Inserts a <div> tag. Found in the Layout category in the Insert panel.

Italic button Creates emphasized text, which is displayed as italic text. Found in the Text category in the Insert panel.

Named anchor button Creates a named anchor at the location of the insertion point. Found in the Common category in the Insert panel.

New CSS Rule button Adds a new style or a new class to a style sheet. Found in the CSS Styles panel.

Ordered list button Converts selected paragraphs to a numbered list. Found in the Property inspector.

Paragraph button Inserts <p> and </p> around selected text. Found in the Text category in the Insert panel.

Paragraph Format command Displays a submenu used to insert heading tags. Found in the Text menu.

Paste command Pastes copied text. Found in the Edit menu.

Remove Link command Removes an existing link. Found in the Modify menu.

Save All command Saves all open documents.

Strong button Creates strong text, which is displayed as bold text. Found in the Text category in the Insert panel.

Text Indent button Indents a paragraph. Found in the Property inspector.

Text Outdent button Removes blockquotes from a paragraph. Found in the Property inspector.

Unordered list button Converts selected paragraphs to a bulleted list. Found in the Property inspector.

Review Questions

1. What does typography refer to?

2. a) What is a typeface?
   b) What is a font?

3. a) Why does Dreamweaver only list commonly available fonts?
   b) List four fonts that are available on most computers.
   c) Why are fonts grouped?
   d) What is the difference between a serif and a sans serif font?

4. List three ways text size can be specified in Dreamweaver.

5. What is line height?

6. a) What can bold type be used to indicate?
   b) What font size should italic style be applied to?

7. a) What does the alignment of text in a paragraph refer to?
   b) List the four paragraph alignments.

8. What does a style sheet define?

9. List the steps required to create a new style sheet named school_styles.css.

10. a) What does a rule modify?
    b) What is a rule comprised of?

11. List the steps required to create a rule for the p tag that sets the size attribute to 14 pixels.

12. What is a class?

13. List the steps required to create and apply a new class named .footer to selected text.

14. List the step required to insert `<p>` and `</p>` around selected text.

15. Why is it often faster to duplicate a style than to create a new one?

16. What are headings used to indicate and help with?

17. List the steps required to indent a paragraph.

18. a) What are complementary colors?
    b) What are analogous colors?

19. Which color combination would be easier for the user to read: red text on a pink background, or black text on a white background?

20. List the steps required to change the background color of a web page to #CF6.

21. a) What is a named anchor?
    b) What type of web page would be most likely to use hyperlinks to named anchors?

22. Why should a lot of design consideration go into the decision to change hyperlink colors?

23. Why is it a good idea to copy content from a TXT file as opposed to a word processing file into a web page document?

True/False

24. Determine if each of the following are true or false. If false, explain why.
    a) Serifs are the small extensions found on the end of letters.
    b) Text written in all capital letters is easier to read than text written in lowercase letters.
    c) Left alignment is the most readable for paragraph text.
    d) A style sheet can only be applied to the home page of a website.
    e) Class names must begin with a dot.
    f) There are twelve HTML heading tags.
    g) The Unordered List button creates a numbered list.
    h) Red is a warm color.
    i) The background of a web page document is changed by redefining the head tag.
    j) The .container rule sets the page width.
    k) `<div>` tags define an area on the page.
    l) CSS starter layouts cannot be modified.

Exercises

Exercise 1

Select two of the websites developed in the exercises of Chapters 3 through 5 and modify the CSS starter layout and styles to improve the appearance of site. Possible websites to select include:

Website	Last Modified
Clouds	Chapter 3
Sharks	Chapter 3
E-commerce	Chapter 3
Hockey League	Chapter 4
Volcanoes	Chapter 4
Lawn Care	Chapter 4
METEOROLOGY	Chapter 4

Possible modifications include:

- Redefine the body tag if a background color is appropriate for the website
- Redefine the p tag to format paragraph text with an appropriate font, font size, line height, and paragraph alignment
- Create selector styles that redefine hyperlink colors where appropriate
- Create class styles to format navigation bars, breadcrumb trails, and footer text
- Create additional <div> tags
- Position and size images

Exercise 2 ——————————————————Workplace Safety

Research safety in the electronic workplace and present your research in a website. Design the site to have a horizontal navigation bar. Topics to research include:

- causes of workplace accidents
- ergonomics
- virus threats
- importance of having an emergency back-up plan

Refer to the website development steps in Chapter 4 when creating this site.

Chapter 6 Typography, Style Sheets, and Color

Exercise 3 — Entrepreneur

In Chapter 5, Exercise 6 you created a navigation bar and logo for a new business website. Using these graphics, create a website to promote your new business idea. Use your knowledge of CSS to apply appropriate formatting and to modify the page layout.

Exercise 4 — Enrichment

Use the Internet and Dreamweaver help to research how to create a 'print-friendly' version of a site. This may involve creating a separate style sheet or linking to a PDF file. Be sure to look at the **Style Rendering** options in the **View** menu as well. Apply your research by creating a print-friendly version of an existing site.

Chapter 7
Introducing Flash

This chapter introduces Flash and explains how to create Flash movies. Exporting and using a Flash movie file in Dreamweaver is also discussed.

Flash

Flash technology is used to create a movie file for a website. A *Flash movie file* can be an animated button, animated text, or an entire web application. For example, the interactive web application shown below was created with Flash:

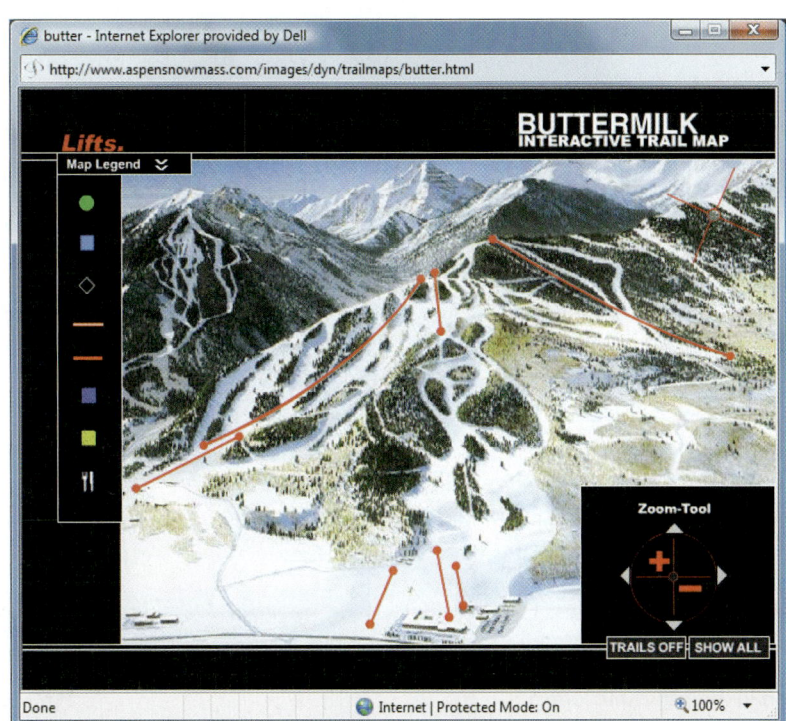

Courtesy of Aspen Skiing Company

Pointing to a symbol in the Map Legend changes the displayed information in the map

Flash is an interactive authoring application that is part of the Adobe Creative Suite 5 Web Premium.

The Flash Player

Download the Flash Player at: www.adobe.com.

What is Animation?

Animation is the result of many images shown quickly one after the other to create the effect of movement. For example, the following images shown quickly one after the other create the effect of a skateboarder going down a hill:

A Flash movie animation can be broken into components. A *Timeline* correlates images to a particular moment in the movie. At any point in a movie, there is a *frame* with an image. The frame can be several images that are layered. Layers are used because from frame to frame there may be different animation techniques applied. For example, an animation of a skateboarder going down a hill requires only the position of the skateboarder to change. The hill remains unchanged from frame to frame. The hill can be on one layer and the skateboarder on another.

Introducing Flash

TIP ActionScript is an object-oriented programming language used to add interactivity to a Flash movie.

Websites are often designed to include animations beyond rollover text and buttons with special effects. The Flash application, which is part of the Adobe Creative Suite 5 Web Premium, is used to create custom animations that can include video and sound.

To create a new Flash document, select File → New, which displays a dialog box:

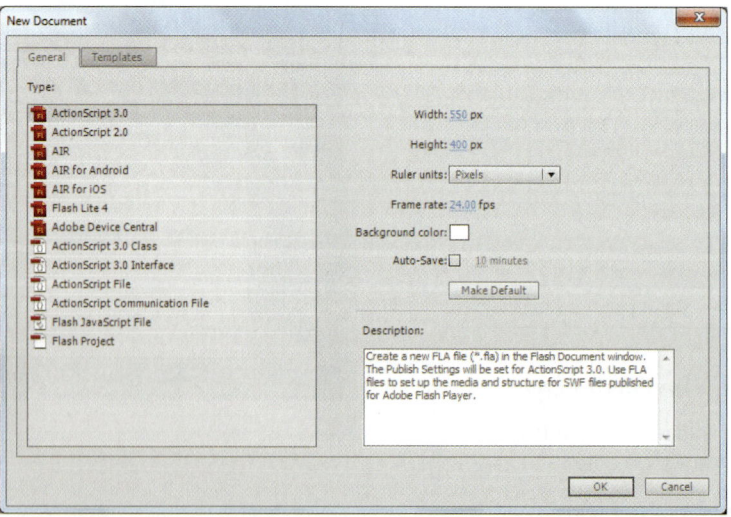

Flash Native File Format

The native file format in Flash is FLA. A native file format is the default format in which an application saves files. Files may be saved or exported in other formats, but are worked on in the native file format.

Select **ActionScript 3.0** in the **General** tab and then **OK** to create a new FLA file in the Flash Document window:

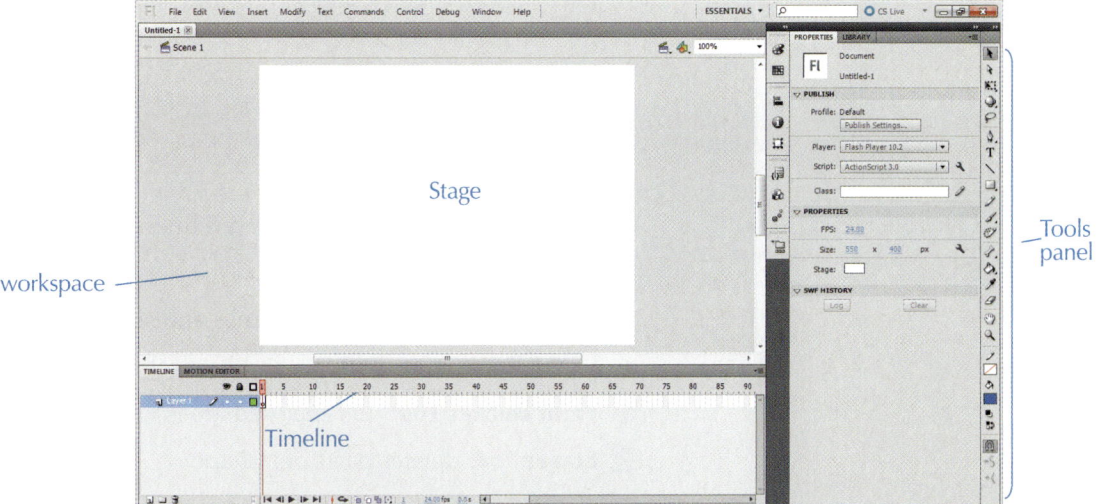

- The **Tools panel** contains tools for drawing, painting, and selecting.
- The **Timeline** correlates images to a frame in the movie.
- The **Stage** is the area used to create a Flash movie.
- The **workspace** is the gray area around the Stage, which can be used as a temporary storage area while working.
- Change properties of selected objects in the **Properties panel**.

Select File → Save to save a Flash document. Flash documents are automatically saved in FLA format. The FLA file should be saved to a location outside of the website's root folder and used to export a movie file to the website in SWF format. The FLA file cannot be used in a web page document. If an SWF movie file needs to be changed, the FLA file can be edited and exported again. Exporting is discussed later in this chapter.

TIP Files that are not directly used in a website are best kept in a folder outside the website root folder.

The Flash Tools Panel

vector graphic

Images drawn in Flash are vector graphics. A *vector graphic* is composed of lines connected by points, which allows for smooth resizing and a smaller file size than bitmap graphics.

The tools in the Tools panel are used to create images. Tools include:

Selection Tool selects objects.

anchor points

Subselection Tool adjusts *anchor points*, which define sections of a line or shape.

Line and **Rectangle Tools** draw basic shapes. Click the arrow in the Rectangle tool to display a menu of shapes:

Chapter 7 Introducing Flash 247

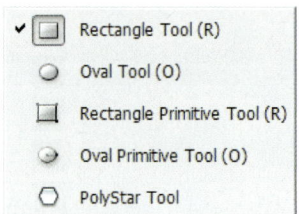

- **Pen Tool** draws straight or curved lines.
- **Text Tool** creates a text block.
- **Pencil Tool** draws free-form lines and shapes.
- **Brush Tool** paints with brush-like strokes.
- **Paint Bucket Tool** fills enclosed areas with a selected color.
- **Eraser Tool** deletes parts of a shape.
- **Hand Tool** moves the Stage within the workspace.
- **Zoom Tool** changes the magnification level of the Stage.
- **Stroke Color** changes the outline color of the tool.
- **Fill Color** changes the fill color of the tool.

Creating a Flash Movie

The process of creating a Flash movie includes:

- Set Flash document properties.
- Create images.
- Use the Timeline to lay out the sequence of the images.
- Preview the animation.
- Export the document.

When a new Flash document is created, the Properties panel displays the properties for the current Flash document:

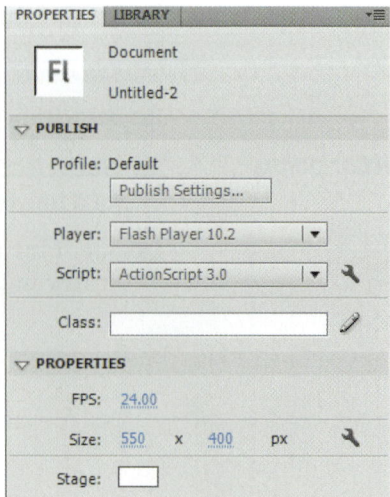

Chapter 7 Introducing Flash

- Size is the Stage size, in pixels, which is representative of the size of the movie. Change the Stage size by clicking the Edit document properties button to display a dialog box:

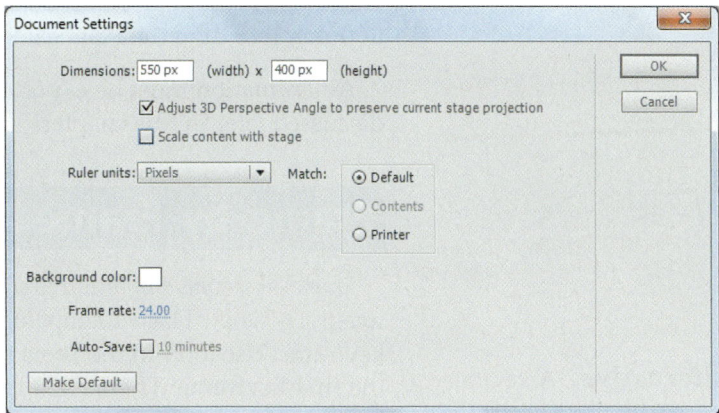

- Select Contents to resize the Stage to just accommodate the objects on the Stage.

- Background color is the color of the Stage and of the background of the movie. To change the color, click the box and select a color.

- Frame Rate is the number of animation frames to be displayed every second. The default frame rate is 24 frames per second (fps).

Images are created using the Tools panel. To help precisely place objects, rulers and a grid can be displayed. Select View → Rulers to display rulers along the top and left side of the work area. Rulers are scaled in pixels by default. Select View → Grid → Show Grid to display a set of gridlines.

The Timeline is used to lay out the sequence of images:

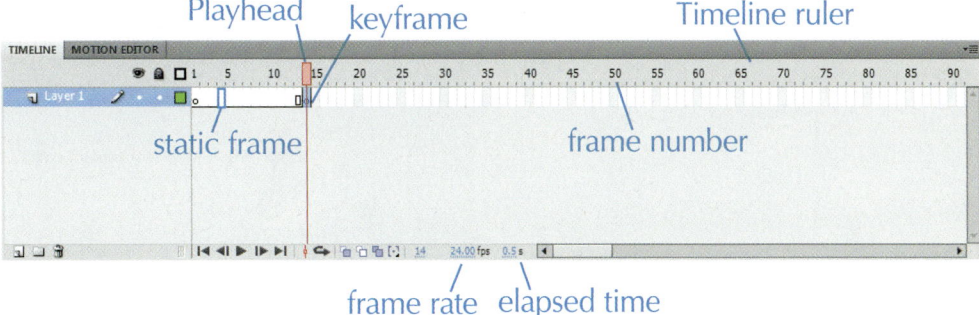

- Drag the **Playhead** to a frame to display the frame's image on the Stage. When the animation is played, the Playhead moves through the Timeline.

- A **frame** is a point on the Timeline. A **keyframe** is a frame that contains an image that can be edited. A **static frame** contains the same image as the previous frame.

- The **elapsed time** is the time of the animation up to the Playhead.

- The **frame rate** is the rate at which an animation plays in frames per second (fps).

Alternative Press Enter to play a movie from the selected frame.

An animation should be previewed to test it. Select **Control → Play** to preview an animation. Previewing shows if an animation is moving too slowly or too quickly and demonstrates the smoothness of transitions from one image to another. Select **Control → Rewind** to move the Playhead back to frame 1, or drag the Playhead.

An animation must be exported to be used in a website. Exporting is discussed later in this chapter.

Frame-by-Frame Animation

Frame-by-frame animation is a movie created from a set of specified images. In a new Flash document, the first frame in the Timeline is a blank keyframe. Use tools in the Tools panel to create an image on the Stage for the first keyframe. Then, right-click a frame on the Timeline and select **Insert Keyframe** from the displayed menu to add a keyframe and create static frames between the two keyframes. The existing image is included in the new keyframe. The image in the new keyframe can then be modified to progress the animation:

Alternative A keyframe can also be added by selecting **Insert → Timeline → Keyframe**.

Repeat the process and continue the progress of the animation:

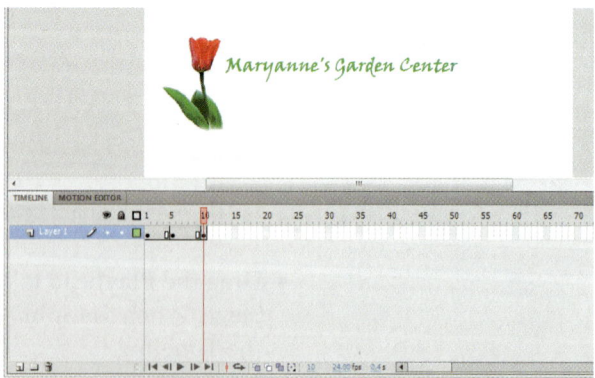

The rest of the flower was added at frame 10

The gray static frames are needed to control the rate of animation so that the animation does not play too quickly for the viewer to comprehend. The process of inserting keyframes and modifying the image is repeated until the final frame of the animation.

Editing Techniques

To speed up a slow-moving animation, delete a few static frames. The same number of static frames should be removed between each keyframe to keep the animation smooth. Right-click a static frame and select **Remove Frames** from the menu to delete the frame. To slow down an animation, right-click a frame and select **Insert Frame** from the menu to add a frame.

onion skinning

To help position and edit images, two or more frames can be displayed at the same time using a technique called *onion skinning*. Click the Onion Skin button at the bottom of the Timeline to display Onion Skin markers. Drag the right marker in the Timeline ruler to display keyframe images between the markers:

> **Importing Images**
>
> Artwork created in other applications can be imported and used in Flash. Supported file formats include JPG, GIF, PNG, BMP, EMF, EPS, AI, PIC, and WMF. Select **File → Import → Import to Stage** to display a dialog box where a file is selected.

The current keyframe is darker than the other keyframes

Images that are dimmed cannot be edited, but the Playhead can be dragged to change the current keyframe for editing purposes.

Common ways to modify an image include scaling, rotating, and skewing objects. To modify a selected object, select **Window → Transform**, which displays the Transform panel:

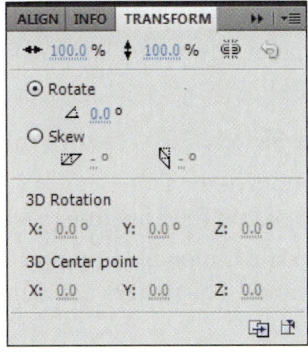

> **The Selection Tool**
>
> The Selection tool is used to select objects. Click once on a shape to select the fill, or double-click a shape to select both the fill and stroke. Multiple shapes can be selected by holding down the Shift key while selecting.

- Click **Rotate** and type an angle to rotate the object.
- Click **Skew** and type an angle in the Skew Horizontal or Skew Vertical box to slant the object.

Chapter 7 Introducing Flash

Click the INFO tab to display the Info panel:

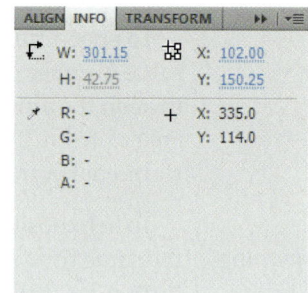

- Type a value in the W and H boxes to adjust the width or height.

Practice: SAMPLER – part 1 of 7

① START FLASH

Ask your instructor for the appropriate steps to start Flash. Note the Stage, Tools panel, gray workspace, Timeline, and Properties panel.

② OPEN A FLASH DOCUMENT

a. Select File → Open. A dialog box is displayed.
   1. Use the Look in list to navigate to the folder containing data files for this text.
   2. Select the PURPLE_BALL.fla file.
   3. Select Open. The Flash document is opened and the first frame is displayed on the Stage.

③ PLAY THE FRAME-BY-FRAME ANIMATION

a. Select Control → Play. The animation plays and a purple ball bounces but does not quite land because the animation is not complete.
b. In the Timeline, drag the Playhead back to frame 1. The image for the first keyframe is displayed.

④ USE ONION SKINNING TO VIEW THE FRAMES

a. At the bottom of the Timeline, click the Onion Skin button . Onion Skin markers are displayed on the Timeline ruler.
b. Drag the right Onion Skin marker to the last keyframe (frame 15) to display all of the keyframes. The images are dimmed except the image from frame 1:

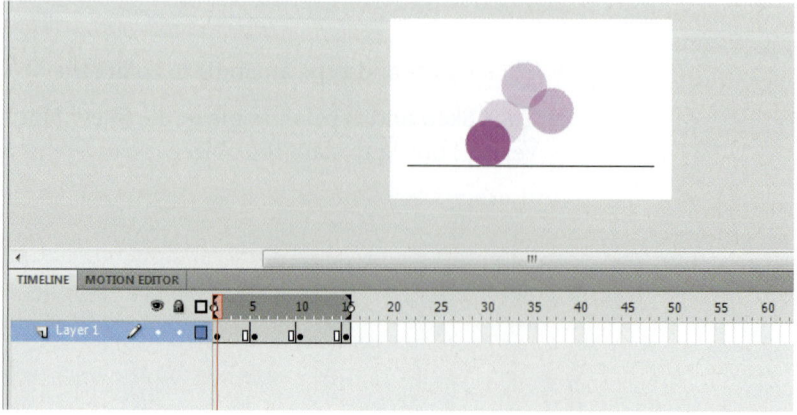

Chapter 7 Introducing Flash

c. Drag the Playhead to the last keyframe. The image in the last frame is in full color and editable.

5 ADD A KEYFRAME

a. In the Timeline, below the Timeline ruler, right-click frame 20 and select Insert Keyframe. A keyframe is added to the animation. The image from the last keyframe is now displayed on the Stage, and the Onion Skin has advanced to the last frame:

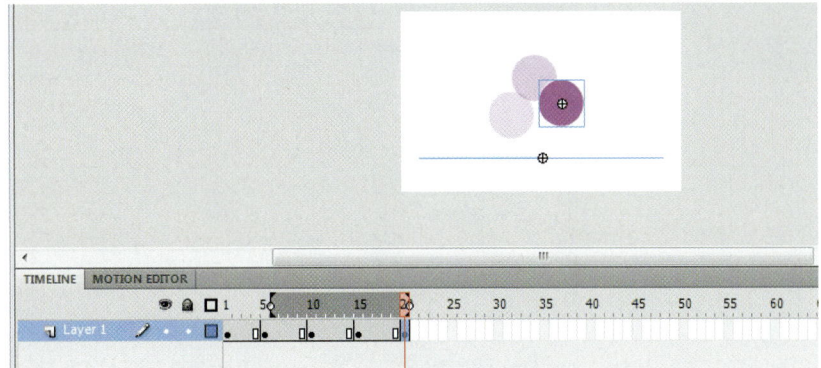

b. Click anywhere in the gray workspace to remove the selection from the ball and surface object.

c. Drag the ball object so that it is just on the surface and slightly to the right:

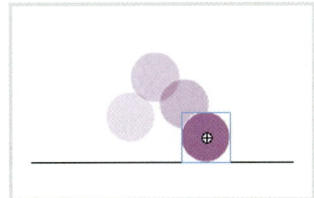

d. Select File → Save. The modified PURPLE_BALL.fla is saved.

6 PLAY THE ANIMATION

a. Click the Onion Skin button to deselect it. The Onion Skin images are no longer displayed.

b. Select Control → Play. The animation plays. The ball bounces from the left to the right.

7 MODIFY THE ANIMATION

a. In the Timeline, right-click frame 2 and select Remove Frames. A static frame is removed.

b. Remove one static frame after each of the other keyframes, so that your Timeline looks similar to:

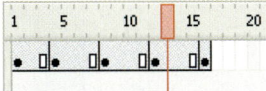

c. Save the modified PURPLE_BALL.fla.

d. Select Control → Rewind. The Playhead moves back to frame 1.

e. Select Control → Play. The animation is faster.

Chapter 7 Introducing Flash   **253**

Exporting a Flash Document

To use a Flash document in Dreamweaver, it must be exported in SWF format so that it can be played with the Flash Player plug-in. Select File → Export → Export Movie, which displays the Export Movie dialog box:

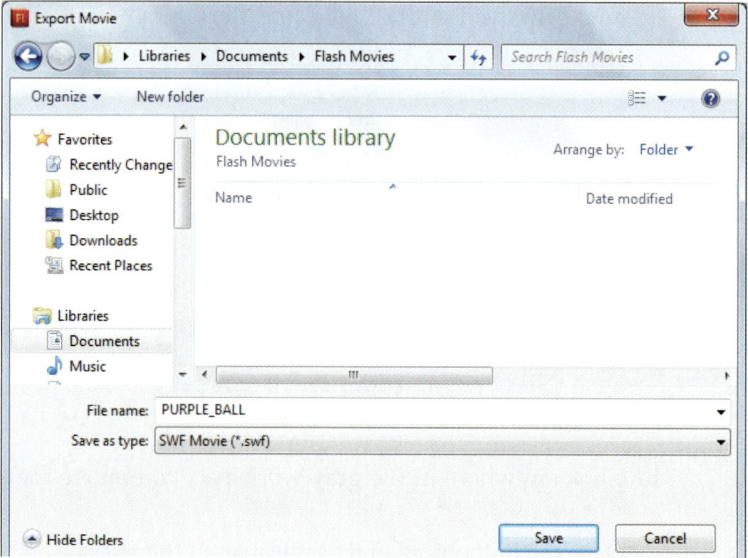

Use the Save in list and the contents box below it to navigate to the location where the file is to be saved. A Flash movie exported for use in a website should be saved in a folder named media in the site. Type a descriptive file name for the movie in the File name box, and make sure the Save as type is Flash Movie. Select Save to export the movie.

Flash Movie Files

Flash movies in a website are listed in the Flash category in the Assets panel. Click the Flash icon in the Assets panel to display the list:

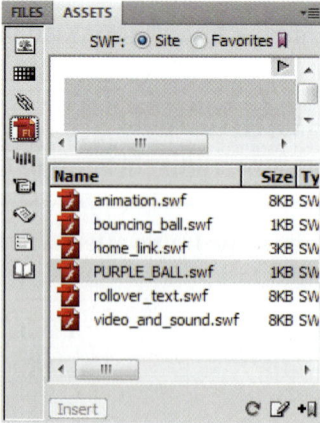

TIP It may be necessary to select → Refresh Site List in the Files panel group to update the list of movies.

The selected image, PURPLE_Ball.swf in the example above, is displayed in the preview area. Click the button in the preview area to play the Flash movie and display the button. Click the button to end the movie.

254 Chapter 7 Introducing Flash

Drag a Flash movie from the Assets panel to an open web page document to place it, or click [Insert] at the bottom of the Assets panel to place the selected movie at the insertion point. The Object Tag Accessibility Attributes dialog box will be displayed when inserting a Flash button.

Organizing and Using Flash Movie Files in Dreamweaver

For better organization, Flash movies created in Flash for a website should be stored together in a media folder that is created in the website root folder.

In Dreamweaver, Flash movie files are displayed in the Flash category in the Assets panel. Select a movie in the Assets panel to display it in the preview area. Click the ▶ button in the preview area to play the Flash movie and display the ■ button. Click the ■ button to end the movie. Select ▤ → Refresh Site List in the Files panel group to update the list of movies in the Assets panel.

Drag a Flash movie from the Assets panel to an open web page document to place it, or click [Insert] at the bottom of the Assets panel to place the selected movie at the insertion point. When a movie created in Flash is added to a web page document, a placeholder is displayed:

A Flash placeholder varies in size depending on the Stage size

Click the Flash placeholder to display the Flash movie properties in the Property inspector:

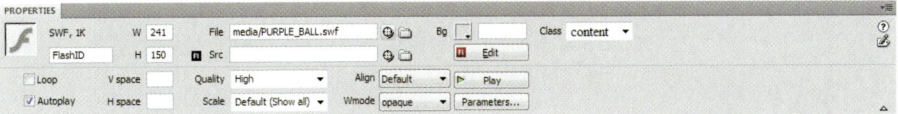

- Select the Loop check box to have the movie play continuously. Clear the Loop check box to have the Flash movie play only once when the web page loads in a browser.

- Select the placeholder and then click [▶ Play] in the Property inspector to preview the Flash movie in Design view. Click [■ Stop] in the Property inspector to end the preview. The Flash movie can also be previewed by viewing the web page document in a browser.

- Click [Edit...] to display a dialog box from which the FLA file corresponding to the movie can be opened for editing in Flash.

Practice: SAMPLER – part 2 of 7

① **START DREAMWEAVER**

Open the SAMPLER website, which is a website provided with the data files for this text.

② **CREATE A MOVIE**

a. Switch to Flash. The PURPLE_BALL.fla document is displayed.

b. Select File → Export → Export Movie. A dialog box is displayed.

1. Use the Save in list to navigate to the SAMPLER website folder.
2. At the top of the dialog box, click the Create New Folder button. A folder is added to the website folder. Change the folder name to: media
3. Open the media folder.
4. In the File name box, type: bouncing_ball
5. Select Save. A dialog box is displayed.
6. Select OK. The default options are applied and the purple ball animation is exported as an SWF file to the SAMPLER website.

c. Save and close the PURPLE_BALL.fla document.

③ **INSERT A FLASH MOVIE IN DREAMWEAVER**

a. Switch to Dreamweaver and open the index.html web page document.

b. In the Assets panel, click the Flash icon. If bouncing_ball.swf is not listed, select → Refresh Site List from the Files panel group.

c. Drag the bouncing_ball.swf file from the Assets panel to the blank paragraph below the title. A dialog box is displayed:

1. Type bouncing ball animation. in the Title box.
2. Click OK.

A Flash placeholder is displayed:

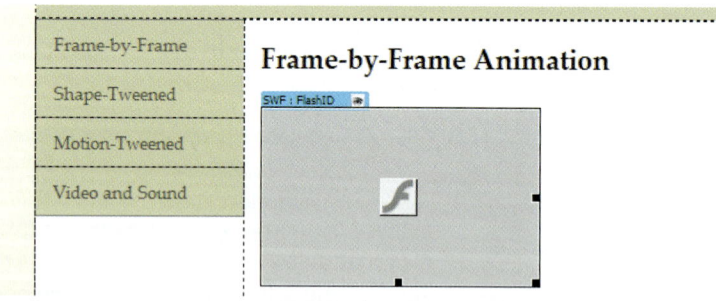

d. Save the modified index.html.

④ **PREVIEW THE FLASH MOVIE**

a. In the Property inspector, click Play. The animation runs and the bouncing ball animation plays continuously.

b. In the Property inspector, clear the Loop check box.

c. Save the modified index.html and then in the Property inspector, click Play. The movie plays just once.

Shape Tweening

tweened animation

morphing

A *tweened animation* is an animation where Flash generates the keyframes between the first keyframe and the last. One form of tweened animation is *shape tweening*, which is similar to morphing an image. *Morphing* is a technique that turns one shape into another. For example, a square can be turned into a circle:

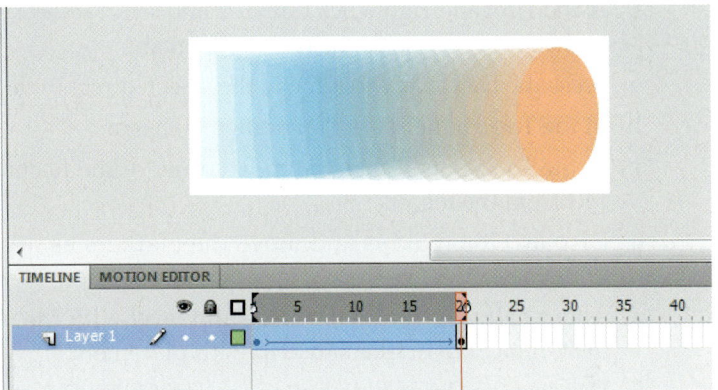

TIP Shape tweening can only be applied to images that are composed of simple lines and fills.

Onion Skin markers show the frames generated by Flash

The steps for creating a shape tweened animation are:

1. Create an image in the first keyframe.
2. Create an end keyframe, delete the image from the first keyframe, and draw a second image.
3. Right-click any frame between the keyframes.
4. Select **Create Shape Tween**.
5. Preview the animation.
6. Export the document.

Shape tweening is indicated by green shading and an arrow in the Timeline:

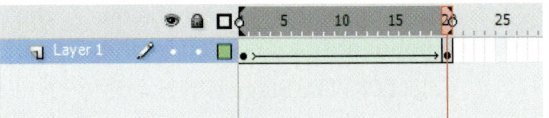

Practice: SAMPLER – part 3 of 7

① CREATE A NEW FLASH DOCUMENT

a. Start Flash if it is not already running.
b. In Flash, close any open documents, saving if necessary.
c. Select **File → New**. A dialog box is displayed.
d. Select **ActionScript 3.0** in the **General** tab and then select **OK**. A new document with a blank Stage is displayed.

② CREATE THE SHAPE-TWEENING ANIMATION

a. Scroll the workspace so that the upper-left corner of the Stage is visible.
b. In the Tools panel, select a blue Fill color.
c. In the Tools panel, select a transparent Stroke color.
d. In the Tools panel, click the Rectangle Tool.
e. Near the top-left corner of the Stage draw a rectangle.
f. In the Timeline, right-click frame 20 and select Insert Keyframe. A keyframe is added to the animation with the rectangle image.
g. Press the Delete key to remove the selected rectangle from the Stage.
h. In the Tools panel, select an orange Fill color.
i. In the Tools panel, click the right corner of the Rectangle Tool and select Oval Tool from the menu.
j. Display Onion Skins and move the markers as necessary to see the complete Timeline.
k. About half way across the stage and level with the rectangle, draw an oval. Use the Onion Skin markers to help with placement.
l. Deselect the Onion Skin button. The Onion Skins are no longer displayed.
m. In the Timeline, right-click frame 10.
n. Select Create Shape Tween. The static frames are green, an arrow is displayed between the keyframes on the Timeline and the shape in frame 10 is displayed.

③ PLAY THE ANIMATION

a. Save the document in a folder that is outside of any website folder, naming it: morph_demo.fla
b. Rewind and then play the animation.

④ CREATE A MOVIE

a. Select the Selection tool.
b. Click anywhere in the gray workspace. Document properties are displayed in the Properties panel.
c. In the Properties panel, click the Edit document properties button. A dialog box is displayed.
   1. Select Contents. The dimensions of the Stage are recalculated based on the amount of space needed by the animation.
   2. Select OK. The Stage is resized.
d. Save the modified morph_demo.fla.
e. Select File → Export → Export Movie. A dialog box is displayed.
   1. Navigate to the media folder in the SAMPLER website folder.
   2. In the File name box, type: morphing
   3. Select Save. A dialog box is displayed.
   4. Select OK. The default options are applied and the shape-tweened animation is exported as an SWF file to the SAMPLER website.
f. Close morph_demo.fla.

⑤ INSERT A FLASH MOVIE IN DREAMWEAVER

   a. Switch to Dreamweaver.
   b. Open the SAMPLER website for editing if it is not the working website.
   c. Display the shape.html web page document.
   d. In the Assets panel, display the Flash category. If morphing.swf is not listed, select ▦ → Refresh Site List from the Files panel group.
   e. Drag the morphing.swf file from the Assets panel to the blank paragraph below the heading. A dialog box is displayed.
      1. Type shape tweened animation in the Title box.
      2. Click OK.
   f. Save the modified shape.html.

⑥ PREVIEW THE FLASH MOVIE

In the Property inspector, click 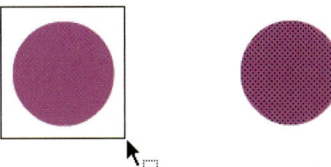. The animation runs.

Creating Symbols to Optimize a Flash Movie

A Flash movie file should be as small a file size as possible to keep web page load times as short as possible. Techniques for optimizing an animation for size include using symbols for images that appear more than once, using tweened animation, and using layers for objects that do not change from frame to frame. Layers are discussed in later in this chapter.

symbols
instance

Symbols are stored in a Flash Library and used to create instances on the Stage. An *instance* is a reference to a symbol, rather than a copy of an image. Any image that is used more than once in a movie file should be converted to symbol. This allows the movie file size to be much smaller. A symbol can be created from a single object or multiple objects selected together. Use the Selection tool and drag to marquee select the object:

Dragging the Selection tool selects the objects enclosed by the box (the marquee). On the right, the object is selected.

Select Modify → Convert to Symbol to display a dialog box. Type a descriptive name for the symbol and select Graphic to create a graphic symbol:

Chapter 7 Introducing Flash   **259**

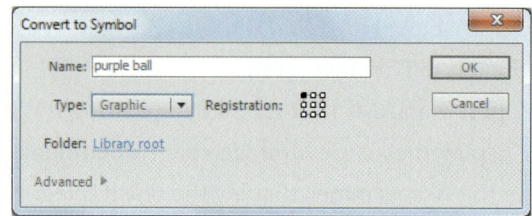

Select OK to convert the selected objects on the Stage to an instance of the symbol. An instance displays a registration point (○) in the center:

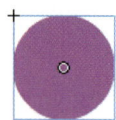

Select Window → Library to display the Flash Library. Click the symbol name in the Library to view the preview area:

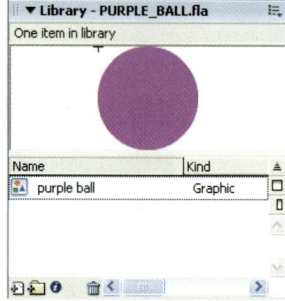

Drag the symbol name from the Library to the Stage to create an instance of the symbol.

Motion Tweening

In *motion tweening*, a single symbol is tweened to move from a start location to an end location:

The steps for creating a motion tweened animation are:

1. Create or import an image and convert it to a graphic symbol.

2. Create a start keyframe with an instance at the starting position.

260   *Chapter 7 Introducing Flash*

TIP You can also create a motion tween by selecting **Create Motion Tween** and then creating the motion path.

3. Create an end keyframe with an instance at the ending position.
4. Right-click a frame between the keyframes.
5. Select **Create Classic Tween**.
6. Preview the animation.
7. Export the document.

Classic motion tweening is indicated by lavender shading and an arrow in the Timeline:

Flash uses the shortest, most direct path from the start position to the end position to fill in the motion tweening. To change the path of the motion, click a frame and then drag the instance in that frame to a new position. For example, in the animation below, frame 20 was clicked and the instance was dragged upwards to change the straight-line path:

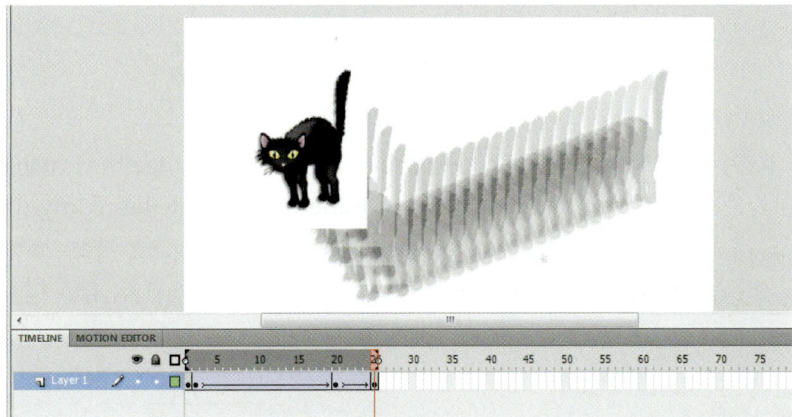

Flash makes each frame that changes the path a keyframe and recalculates the motion path.

Practice: SAMPLER – part 4 of 7

① CREATE A NEW FLASH DOCUMENT

a. In Flash, close any open documents, saving if necessary.
b. Select File → New. A dialog box is displayed.
c. Select **ActionScript 3.0** and then select **OK**. A new document with a blank Stage is displayed.

② CREATE AN IMAGE

a. Scroll so that the upper-left corner of the Stage is visible.
b. Select View → Rulers to display rulers, if they are not already displayed.
c. In the Tools panel, change the Stroke color and Fill color to a bright yellow:

Chapter 7 Introducing Flash

d. In the Tools panel, click the right corner of the Rectangle Tool  and select **Oval Tool** from the menu.

e. Hold down the Shift key and drag on the Stage to create a small circle about 50 pixels in diameter.

f. In the Tools panel, change the Stroke and Fill colors to black.

g. In the Tools panel, click the Brush tool .

h. In the Tools panel, set brush options to:

i. Draw eyes and a smile onto the yellow circle to create a smiley face:

Note: Select **Edit → Undo** as necessary. Change the brush size if needed.

j. Save the document in a folder that is outside of any website folder, naming it: smiley.fla

③ CREATE A SYMBOL

a. In the Tools panel, click the Selection tool and then marquee select the smiley face:

b. Select **Modify → Convert to Symbol**. A dialog box is displayed:
   1. In the **Name** box, type: smiley_face
   2. Select **Graphic**.
   3. Select **OK**. The selected image is converted to a symbol and replaced by an instance of the symbol.

c. Select **Window → Library** if the Library is not displayed. Note the smiley_face symbol.

④ CREATE KEYFRAMES

a. In the Timeline, note that the first frame is already a keyframe. Drag the smiley_face instance on the Stage, leaving some room above the image:

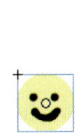

    b. In the Timeline, right-click frame 40 and select Insert Keyframe.

    c. Drag the smiley_face instance directly across to the right side of the Stage.

⑤ APPLY MOTION TWEENING

    a. In the Timeline, right-click frame 12.

    b. Select **Create Classic Tween**. An arrow is displayed between the starting and ending frames on the Timeline.

    c. Save the modified smiley.fla.

    d. Select **Control → Rewind** and then select **Control → Play**. The smiley face moves across the Stage horizontally.

⑥ MODIFY THE PATH

    a. In the Timeline, click the Onion Skin button. Onion Skin markers are displayed on the Timeline ruler.

    b. Drag the Onion Skin markers to display the entire animation. Note the straight path.

    c. Deselect the Onion Skin button. The Onion Skins are no longer displayed.

    d. Click frame 20. Drag the smiley face up near the top of the Stage. The frame is automatically converted to a keyframe and a symbol is displayed.

    e. Display Onion Skins and move the markers as necessary to see the complete motion path. The path is no longer a straight line.

    f. Save the modified smiley.fla.

    g. Deselect the Onion Skin button. The Onion Skins are no longer displayed.

    h. Select **Control → Rewind** and then select **Control → Play**. The smiley face moves across the stage along the new motion path.

⑦ CREATE A MOVIE

    a. Click anywhere in the gray workspace and display the Properties panel.

    b. In the Properties panel, click the Edit document properties button. A dialog box is displayed.

        1. Select **Contents**.

        2. Select **OK**. The Stage is resized.

    c. Save the modified smiley.fla.

    d. Select **File → Export → Export Movie**. A dialog box is displayed.

        1. Navigate to the media folder in the SAMPLER website folder.

        2. In the **File name** box, type: smiley.swf

        3. Select **Save**.

    e. Save and close smiley.fla.

⑧ INSERT A FLASH MOVIE IN DREAMWEAVER

a. Switch to Dreamweaver.
b. Open the SAMPLER website for editing if it is not the working website.
c. Display the moton.html web page document.
d. In the Assets panel, display the Flash category and refresh the list.
e. Drag the smiley.swf file from the Assets panel to the blank paragraph below the heading. The Object Tag Accessibility Attributes dialog box is displayed. Select Cancel. A Flash placeholder is displayed.
f. Save the modified motion.html.

⑨ PREVIEW THE FLASH MOVIE

In the Property inspector, click ▶ Play . The animation runs.

Using Layers

Flash documents of any complexity should be divided into layers. *Layers* can be thought of as transparent sheets of paper with images drawn on them and the sheets placed one on top of the other. The image on one layer can be modified without changing the images on other layers. In animation, an image on one layer can be tweened without affecting the other layers. This allows multiple objects to be motion-tweened and for both motion- and shape-tweening in one document. The document below is divided into layers:

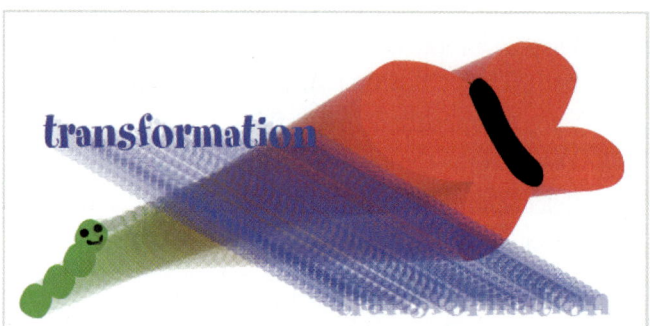

A caterpillar is shape tweened into a butterfly on one layer, and a word is motion tweened from top to bottom on another layer.

Click the Insert layer button 🗔 in the bottom-left corner of the Timeline to add a layer to a document. Layer names appear in the Layers list:

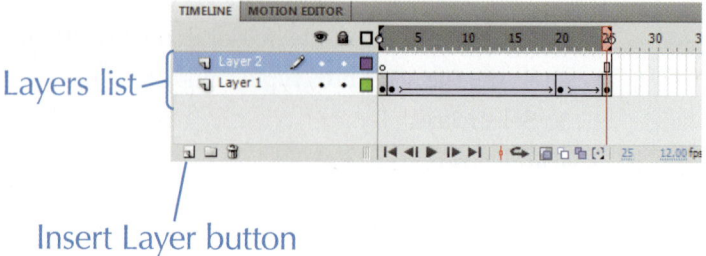

Chapter 7 Introducing Flash

By default, layers are named Layer 1, Layer 2, and so on. To change a layer name, double-click a name in the Layers list and type a more descriptive name.

The layers in the Layers list are ordered top to bottom, with the top layer Layer 1. Images on Layer 1 appear on top of any images in the layers below. The order of the layers is changed by dragging a layer to a different location in the list:

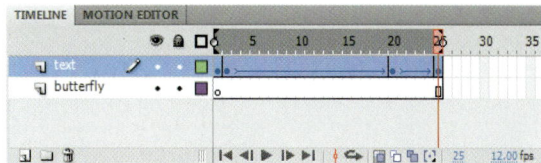

It may be to work on one layer if other layers are temporarily hidden from view. To hide a layer, click to the right of the layer name in the Eye column . An is displayed in the column:

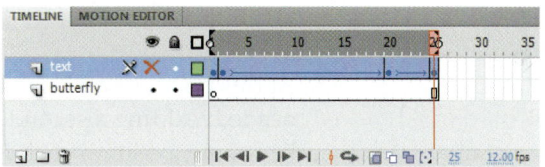

The text layer is hidden

To display a hidden layer, click the .

To lock a layer, which prevents it from being edited, click to the right of the layer name in the Lock column .

To delete a layer, click the layer name in the Layers list and then click the Delete Layer button below the Layers list.

Animating Text

Text can be broken apart into individual characters and then placed onto layers so that a word or phrase can be motion tweened. For example, each letter in a word can move onto the Stage from a different direction or the letters of a word could "dance" on Stage.

To create a text block in Flash click the Text tool in the Tools panel and then click the Stage and type a word or phrase. Use the Properties panel to change font, size, and color properties:

To be animated, the text must be broken up into separate objects, one for each character. Select the text block and then select Modify ➔ Break Apart:

To allow motion tweening for smooth animation of the text, the characters must be distributed to layers. Select Modify → Timeline → Distribute to Layers to automatically distribute each character to an individual layer with an appropriate name:

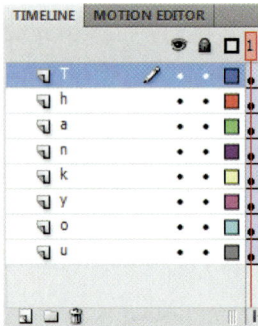

At this point, Layer 1 can be deleted because the entire word is no longer needed. Adding a second keyframe creates the end keyframe. In the first keyframe, position each letter to starting position off the stage. Finally, motion tweening is applied to each layer. Below is the animated "Thank you" as the letters move from off the stage to a centered location:

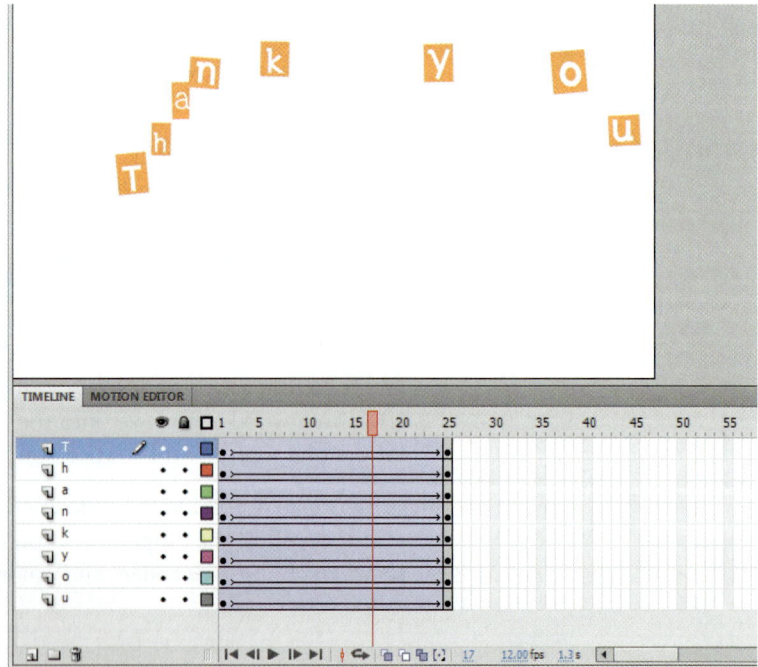

The steps for creating animated text are:

1. Create a text block.

2. Break apart the text block into separate layers.

3. Distribute the separate objects to layers.

266   Chapter 7 Introducing Flash

4. Delete Layer 1.
5. Insert the last keyframe for each layer.
6. In the first keyframe, position the characters in a start position.
7. Apply motion tweening to each layer.
8. Preview the animation.
9. Export the document.

Practice: SAMPLER – part 5 of 7

① CREATE A NEW FLASH DOCUMENT AND SIZE THE STAGE

a. In Flash, close any open documents, saving if necessary.
b. Select File → New. A dialog box is displayed.
c. Select ActionScript 3.0 and then select OK. A new document with a blank Stage is displayed.
d. In the Properties panel, click the Edit document properties button next to the Size option. A dialog box is displayed.
   1. Set the Dimensions options to 400 px for the width and 200 px for the height.
   2. Select OK. The Stage is resized.

② CREATE A TEXT ANIMATION

a. In the Tools panel, click the Text tool T.
b. Click the Stage to create a text block.
c. In the Properties panel, select Tahoma for the Family (font), a Size of 72, and a dark green color for the Color.
d. Type: Hola!
e. In the Tools panel, click the Selection tool and then drag the text block to the center of the Stage.
f. Select Modify → Break Apart. Characters are selected as separate objects.
g. Select Modify → Timeline → Distribute to Layers. A named layer is created for each character in the word Hola!
h. In the Layers list, click Layer 1 to select it.
i. At the bottom of the Layers list, click the Delete Layer button. Layer 1 is deleted.
j. In layer H, right-click frame 20 and select Insert Keyframe. A keyframe is added.
k. Add a keyframe at frame 20 for each of the remaining layers.
l. In the Timeline, drag the Playhead back to the first frame.
m. Drag each of the characters to a starting position off the Stage, similar to the example of "Thank you" in the previous section.
n. In the H layer, click a frame between the keyframes and select Create Classic Tween in the Property inspector.
o. Set motion tweening for the remaining layers.

③ SAVE THE FLASH DOCUMENT

Save the document in a folder that is outside of any website folder, naming it: hola.fla

④ REWIND AND THEN PLAY THE ANIMATION

Importing Sound Files

Sound can be added to a Flash movie by importing a sound file and then adding the file to a layer. Flash supports sound file formats that include WAV and MP3. Other file formats are available if QuickTime or DirectX is installed on your computer.

Sound files are imported to the document's Library to allow the sound file to be used repeatedly without increasing the Flash movie file size. To import a sound file, select File → Import → Import to Library, which displays the Import to Library dialog box. Select All Sound Formats and then use the Look in list and the contents box below it to navigate to the file. Select the file and then Open to import the file to the Library.

In an animation, a sound file needs to be on a separate layer with a descriptive name. To add the sound file to the animation, create the start keyframe, drag the sound file from the Library to the Stage, then create the end keyframe. A sound wave is displayed in the Timeline between the keyframes:

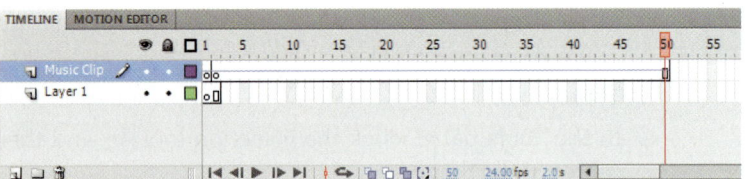

The steps for adding sound to an animation are:

1. Import the sound file to the Library.
2. Create a layer and give it a descriptive name.
3. Create the start keyframe in the sound layer.
4. Display the Library and drag the sound file to the Stage.
5. Create an end keyframe.
6. Preview the animation.
7. Export the document.

When the frames that contain sound are selected, the Properties panel displays their properties:

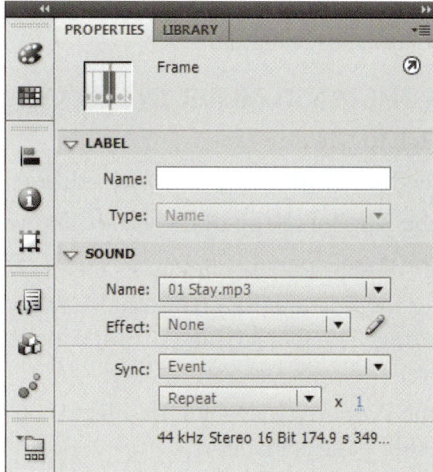

- Select a sound effect such as Fade Out from the **Effect** list.
- In the Sync options, select **Repeat** and type the number of times to repeat the sound, or select Loop to play the sound continuously.

Practice: SAMPLER – part 6 of 7

This practice assumes you have speakers or headphones and a sound card in your computer.

① ADD SOUND TO THE HOLA ANIMATION
  a. Open the hola.fla document in Flash if it is not already displayed.
  b. Select File → Import → Import to Library. A dialog box is displayed.
   1. Use the **Look in** list to navigate to the folder containing data files for this text.
   2. Select All Sound Formats.
   3. Select the HOLA.wav file.
   4. Select **Open**.
  c. Select Window → Library if the Library panel is not already displayed.
  d. Select the H layer and then click the Insert layer button below the Layers list.
  e. In the Layers list, double-click the new layer's name and rename it: greeting
  f. In the Timeline, in the greeting layer, click the first keyframe.
  g. From the Library, drag the HOLA.wav file onto the Stage.
  h. In the greeting layer, right-click frame 20 and select **Insert Keyframe**.
  i. Save the modified hola.fla.

② PLAY THE ANIMATION

③ CREATE A MOVIE
  a. Click anywhere in the gray workspace. Document properties are displayed in the Properties panel
  b. In the Properties panel, click the Edit document properties button next to the Size option. A dialog box is displayed.
   1. Set the **Dimensions** options to 400 px for the width and 200 px for the height.
   2. Select **Contents** and then select OK. The Stage is resized.

Chapter 7 Introducing Flash

c. Save the modified hola.fla.
d. Export the movie as an SWF file to the media folder in the SAMPLER website folder, naming it: hola.swf
e. Save and close hola.fla.

④ **INSERT THE FLASH MOVIE IN DREAMWEAVER**
a. Switch to Dreamweaver.
b. Open the SAMPLER website for editing if it is not the working website.
c. In the Files panel, open the video.html web page document.
d. In the Assets panel, display the Flash category and refresh the list.
e. Drag the hola.swf file from the Assets panel to the blank paragraph below the heading. The Object Tag Accessibility Attributes dialog box is displayed. Select Cancel.
f. In the Property inspector, deselect Loop. The sound file will play just once when the web page is loaded.
g. Save the modified video.html.

⑤ **PREVIEW THE FLASH MOVIE**
In the Property inspector, click ▶ Play . The animation runs.

Importing Video

Video can be imported to Flash and then exported as a Flash movie. Supported video file formats include FLV, F4V, and MPEG. If you want to use video in another format, use the separate Adobe Media Encoder application to convert other video formats to FLV and F4V.

To import a video into a Flash document, select File → Import → Import to Stage, which displays the Import dialog box. Navigate to the file and then select Open to display the Import Video dialog box:

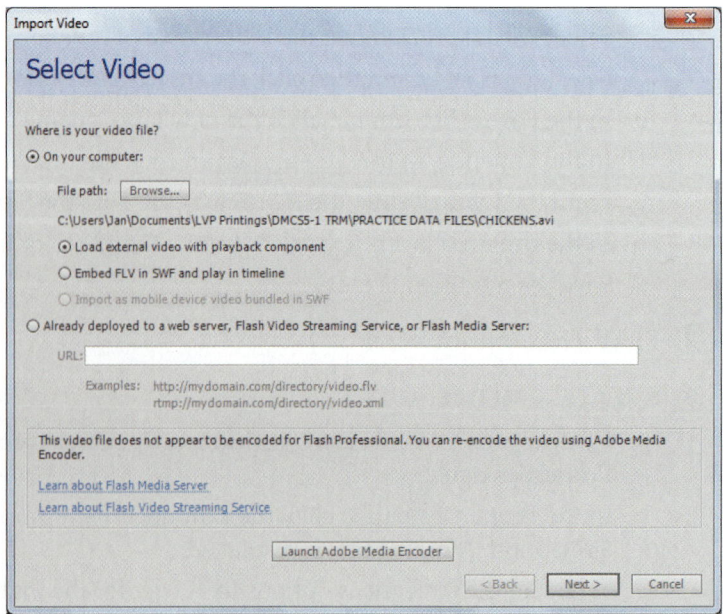

Chapter 7 Introducing Flash

Select a deployment options and then select Next to display skinning options:

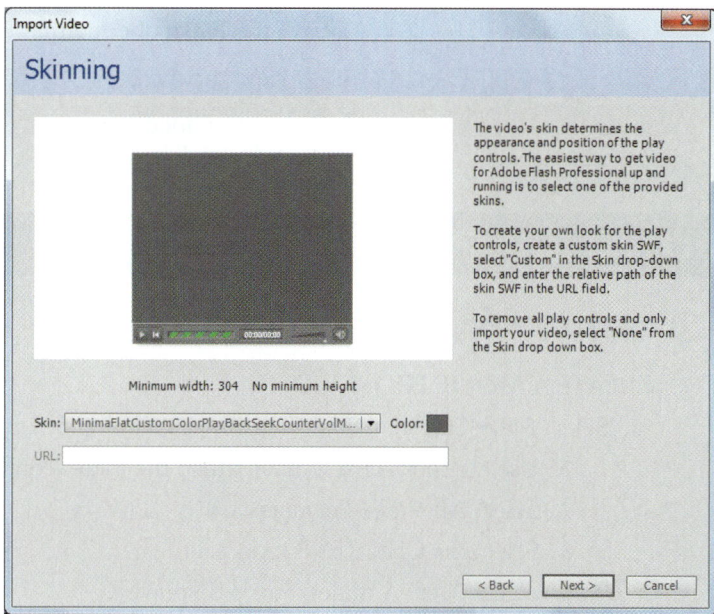

Select a skinning options and then select Next to display the Finish Video Import dialog box:

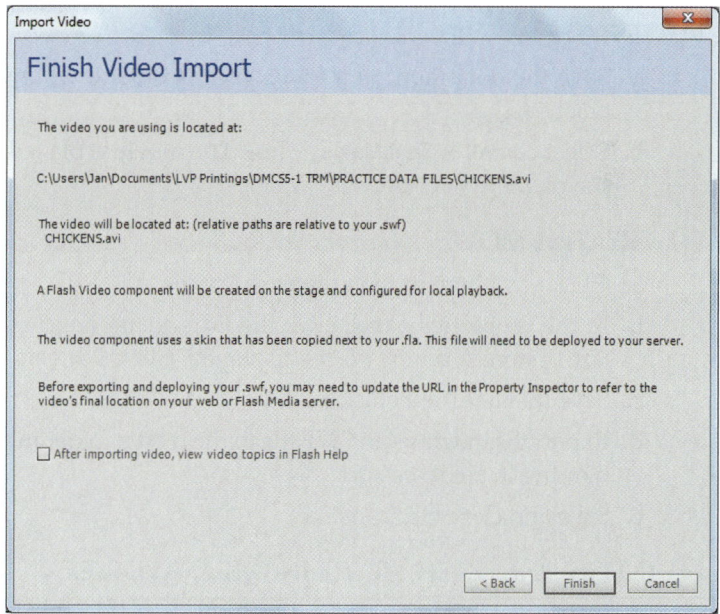

Select Finish.

To use a video in Dreamweaver, it must be exported in the SWF format, so that it can be played with the Flash Player plug-in. A video exported to the SWF format is considerably smaller than the native file format of the video. Select File → Export Movie to export a movie.

The steps for creating a Flash movie from video are:

1. Import the video file to a new Flash document.
2. Save the Flash document.
3. Preview the movie.
4. Export the document.

Practice: SAMPLER – part 7 of 7

① **CREATE A NEW FLASH DOCUMENT**

② **CREATE A MOVIE FROM VIDEO**
   a. Select File → Import → Import to Stage. A dialog box is displayed.
      1. Use the Look in list to navigate to the folder containing data files for this text.
      2. Select All Video Formats.
      3. Select the CHICKENS.mpeg-4 file.
      4. Select Open. A dialog box is displayed.
         a) Select Load external video wth playback component. Select Next.
         b) Explore the skinning options and select a skin. Select Next.
         c) Select Finish. The video is imported.

③ **TEST THE MOVIE**
   a. Save the document in a folder that is outside of any website folder, naming it: chickens.fla
   b. Select Control → Test Movie → Test. The movie is played in a separate window. Close the preview window.

④ **CREATE A MOVIE**
   a. Click anywhere in the gray workspace.
   b. In the Properties panel, click the Edit document properties 🔧 button next to the Size option. A dialog box is displayed. Click Contents and then select OK.
   c. Save the modified chickens.fla.
   d. Export the movie as an SWF file to the media folder in the SAMPLER website folder, naming it: chickens.swf
   e. Save and close chickens.fla.

⑤ **INSERT THE FLASH MOVIE IN DREAMWEAVER**
   a. Switch to Dreamweaver and open the SAMPLER website for editing.
   b. In the Files panel, open the video.html web page document.
   c. Place the insertion point to the right of the existing Flash placeholder and press the Enter key.
   d. In the Assets panel, display the Flash category and refresh the list.
   e. Drag the chickens.swf file from the Assets panel to the insertion point. If the Object Tag Accessibility Attributes dialog box appears, select Cancel.
   f. Save the modified video.html.

⑥ PREVIEW THE FLASH MOVIE

a. Press F12. The web page document is displayed in a browser with the movie.

b. Close the browser window. Dreamweaver is displayed.

⑦ QUIT DREAMWEAVER AND FLASH

Chapter Summary

This chapter introduces Flash, which can be used to create animations for websites. Animation is the result of many images shown quickly one after the other to create the effect of movement. In Flash, a Timeline correlates images to a particular moment in the movie. Flash documents are automatically saved in FLA format, which should be saved to a location outside of the website's root folder and used to export a movie file to the website in SWF format. In Dreamweaver, Flash movie files are displayed in the Flash category in the Assets panel.

Images drawn in Flash are vector graphics. The process of creating a Flash movie includes setting document properties, creating images, and using the Timeline to lay out the sequence of the images. The animation is previewed and then the document is exported. Onion Skins can be used to help in the placement of objects.

In a new Flash document, the first frame in the Timeline is a blank keyframe. Use tools in the Tools panel to create an image on the Stage for the first keyframe, then add another keyframe which creates static frames between the two keyframes. The image in the new keyframe can then be modified to progress the animation. To speed up or slow down an animation, delete or add static frames.

A tweened animation is an animation where Flash generates the keyframes between the first keyframe and the last. In shape tweening, one shape changes into a different shape. In motion tweening, a single symbol moves from a start location to an end location on the Stage.

A Flash movie file should be as small a file size as possible to keep web page load times as short as possible. Techniques for optimizing an animation for size include using symbols for images that appear more than once, using tweened animation, and using layers for objects that do not change from frame to frame. Symbols are stored in a Flash Library and used to create instances on the Stage. An instance is a reference to a symbol, rather than a copy of an image.

Flash documents of any complexity should be divided into layers so that the image on one layer can be modified without changing the images on other layers. In animation, an image on one layer can be tweened without affecting the other layers. Layer names can be changed and layers can be hidden to help work with the animation.

Sound can be added to a Flash movie by importing a sound file to the document's Library and then adding the file to a layer. Video can also be imported to Flash and then exported as a Flash movie.

Chapter 7 Introducing Flash

Vocabulary

Anchor points Points that define sections of a line or shape in an object.

Animation The result of many images shown quickly one after the other to create the effect of movement.

Flash movie file An animated button, animated text, or an entire web application.

Frame A Flash movie component that shows an image.

Frame-by-frame animation A movie created from a set of specified images.

Instance A reference to a symbol.

Layers A component of a Flash document that can be compared to images drawn on transparent sheets of paper placed one on top of the other.

Morphing A technique that turns one shape into another.

Motion tweening A form of tweened animation where a symbol is tweened to move from a start location to an end location.

Onion skinning Displaying two or more frames at the same time to help position and edit images.

Properties panel Area of the Flash window that contains options to modify object properties.

Shape tweening A form of tweened animation that turns one shape into another.

Stage The area used to create a Flash movie.

Symbols Stored in a Flash Library and used to create instances on the Stage.

Timeline A Flash movie component which correlates images to a particular moment in the movie.

Tools panel Area of the Flash window that contains tools for drawing, painting, and selecting.

Tweened animation An animation where Flash generates the keyframes between the first keyframe and the last.

Vector graphic A graphic that is composed of lines connected by points.

Workspace The gray area around the Stage, which is used as a temporary storage area while working.

Dreamweaver Commands and Buttons

button Clicked to play the selected Flash movie. Found in the Assets panel.

button Clicked to stop the playing of the selected Flash movie. Found in the Assets panel.

Flash icon Displays a list of all the Flash files in the website. Found in the Assets panel.

Insert button Inserts the selected movie at the insertion point. Found in the Assets panel.

Play button Previews a Flash button, Flash text, or a Flash movie. Found in the Property inspector.

Stop button Stops a Flash button, Flash text, or Flash movie preview. Found in the Property inspector.

Flash Commands and Buttons

Break Apart command Breaks text into separate letter objects. Found in the Modify menu.

Brush tool Paints with brush-like strokes. Found in the Tools panel.

Convert to Symbol command Displays a dialog box used to convert a selected object to a symbol. Found in the Modify menu.

Create Classic Tween command Creates a classic motion animation. Found by right-clicking a frame.

Create Shape Tween command Creates a shape tween animation. Found by right-clicking a frame.

Delete Layer button Deletes a selected layer. Found below the Layers list.

Distribute to Layers command Automatically distributes separate letter objects to an individual layer and names the layer. Found in Modify → Timeline.

Eraser tool Deletes parts of a shape. Found in the Tools panel.

Export Movie command Displays a dialog box used to export a Flash movie in SWF format. Found in File → Export.

Fill Color Changes the fill color of the tool. Found in the Tools panel.

Hand tool Moves the Stage within the workspace. Found in the Tools panel.

Import to Stage command Displays a dialog box used to import a video into a Flash document. Found in File → Import.

Import to Library command Displays a dialog box used to import a sound file into the Flash Library. Found in File → Import.

Insert Keyframe command Adds a new keyframe and creates static frames between two keyframes. Found in the menu displayed by right-clicking a frame.

Insert Layer button Adds a layer to a document.

Library command Displays the Flash Library. Found in the Window menu.

Line tool Draws a line. Found in the Tools panel.

Onion Skin button Displays Onion Skin markers. Found in the Timeline.

Paint Bucket tool Fills enclosed areas with a selected color. Found in the Tools panel.

Pen tool Draws straight or curved lines. Found in the Tools panel.

Pencil tool Draws free-form lines and shapes. Found in the Tools panel.

Play command Previews an animation. Found in the Control menu.

Rectangle tool Draws a rectangular shape. Found in the Tools panel.

Rewind command Moves the Playhead to frame 1. Found in the Control menu.

Rulers command Displays rulers along the top and left side of the work area. Found in the View menu.

Selection tool Selects objects. Found in the Tools panel.

Show Grid command Displays a set of gridlines on the Stage. Found in the Grid submenu in the View menu.

Stroke Color Changes the outline color of the tool. Found in the Tools panel.

Subselection tool Adjusts anchor points, which define sections of a line or shape. Found in the Tools panel.

Test Movie command Previews a Flash movie in a separate Flash window. Found in the Control menu.

Text tool Creates a text block. Found in the Tools panel.

Transform command Displays a window used to scale, rotate, and skew an object. Found in Window → Design Panels.

Zoom tool Changes the magnification level of the Stage. Found in the Tools panel.

Review Questions

1. In Dreamweaver, where are Flash movies listed?

2. What is animation?

3. a) What function does a Timeline perform in an animation?
   b) Why is layering used in an animation?

4. a) What is the Stage?
   b) What is the workspace?

5. a) Where should a Flash document be saved?
   b) What format is a Flash document saved in?
   c) What format must a Flash document be exported in so that it can be used in a web page document?

6. a) What is a vector graphic?
   b) How does the file size of a vector-based graphic compare to the file size of a bitmap graphic?

7. What are the tools in the Tools panel used for?

8. List the five steps involved in the process of creating a Flash movie.

9. What is the frame rate?

10. a) What is the Timeline used for?
    b) What does a keyframe contain?
    c) What does a static frame contain?
    d) What is the elapsed time?

11. What does previewing an image show and demonstrate?

12. What is frame-by-frame animation?

13. a) List the steps required to add a keyframe.
    b) Why are static frames needed?

14. What should be done if an animation is moving too slowly?

15. What is onion skinning?

16. List three common ways to modify an image.

17. Where should Flash movies exported in SWF format for a website be stored?

18. What is displayed when a movie created in Flash is added to a web page document?

19. a) What is a tweened animation?
    b) List one type of tweened animation.
    c) What is morphing?

20. Why should Flash movie files be a small file size?

21. a) Where are symbols stored?
    b) What is an instance?

22. a) What is motion tweening?
    b) What can motion tweening be applied to?

23. What can layers be compared to?

24. Why are sound files imported to the document's Library?

25. List three video file formats supported by Flash.

True/False

26. Determine if each of the following are true or false. If false, explain why.
    a) Flash can be used to create a movie file for a website.
    b) In Dreamweaver, Flash movie files can be previewed in the Assets panel.
    c) The Timeline is used to control the rollover behavior of Flash text.
    d) Flash documents are automatically saved in SWF format.
    e) The Text tool is used to create a keyframe.
    f) A Flash document is exported in FLA format.
    g) At least two keyframes are required to create a shape tweened animation.
    h) Symbols are stored in the Assets panel.
    i) An instance is a Flash movie file.
    j) A sound file needs to be on a separate layer.
    k) A video exported to SWF format is larger than the video in the native file format.

Exercises

Exercise 1 ———————————————————— gumball.fla

Create a Flash file that uses motion tweening and layers to recreate a gumball machine that has the gumballs roll out of it through the dispenser opening. Save the Flash file naming it gumball.fla. The gumball machine could look similar to:

Exercise 2 ———————————————————————— car.fla

In Flash, draw a car , similar to the example below or import an image of a car and then animate the car using motion-tweening.

Exercise 3 ———————————————————— banner_ad.fla

Expand your knowledge of Flash by reading Appendix A - Banner Ads and ActionScript at the end of the text. Then, in Flash create a banner ad for a previously created website.

Exercise 4 ———————————————————— lavalamp.fla

Create a lava lamp animation by completing the following steps:

a) In Flash, create a new document. Create the container of the lava lamp as follows:

1. Click the Rectangle tool and draw a tall rectangle in the middle of the Stage with a white Fill color and a black Stroke color.

2. Click the Line tool and draw a vertical guide line through the middle of the rectangle overlapping the edges of the rectangle.

3. Click the Line tool and, two-thirds from the top of the rectangle, draw a horizontal guide line across the width of the rectangle overlapping the edges of the rectangle.

4. Click the Subselection tool and drag the intersection points of the lines to shape the container similar to:

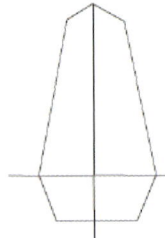

5. Delete the vertical and horizontal guide lines and rename Layer 1: container

b) Create a gradient fill for the container as follows:

1. Select Window → Color to display the Color panel.

2. In the Color panel, select Linear in the Type list and set the fill color by experimenting with the R, G, and B settings.

3. Drag the Gradient pointers to create a gradient fill of your choice.

4. Click inside the container and convert it to a graphic symbol named: container

c) Create the lamp base as follows:

1. Create a new layer named: lampbase

2. Click the Rectangle tool and then select a black Fill and a black Stroke color.

3. Draw a square shape that fits onto the bottom of the container.

4. Click the Line tool and then select a green Stroke color.

5. To make the base look three dimensional, draw a vertical guide line through the middle of the square overlapping the edges of the square.

6. Use the Subselection tool to drag the intersection of the vertical line and the top line of the square down a few pixels.

7. Drag the intersection of the vertical line and the bottom line of the square down a few pixels. and delete the green vertical guide line.

8. Draw a horizontal line between the square's top left edge and the top right edge.

9. Fill the top part of the oval with black.

10. Convert the base to a graphic symbol named: lampbase

278   Chapter 7 Introducing Flash

d) Create a new layer named: lamptop and then use the appropriate tools and modifier buttons to create the top of the lamp. Hint: draw the top of the lamp away from the lamp and base, convert it to a symbol named: lamptop and then move it to the appropriate location.

e) Create a new layer named: lava1 and use shape tweening to create the moving lava in the lamp. Note that each piece of lava should be on a separate layer, and it is a good idea to view a real or animated lava lamp on the Internet to watch the speed of motion and different shapes that are created. Hint: shapes can be modified with the Subselection tool. The lamp should look similar to:

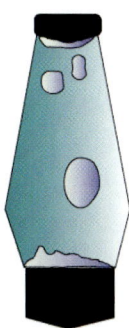

f) Save the Flash file naming it: lavalamp.fla and test the movie.

Exercise 5 — fireworks.fla

Create a Flash file that uses shape tweening to create fireworks. Start by creating a dot in in the first frame and then creating numerous dots in the ending frame. Save the Flash file naming it fireworks.fla.

Exercise 6 — puzzle.fla

Create a Flash file that uses frame-by-frame animation to assemble shapes into a large image. For example, a few squares of varying sizes could fit together to make a large square. Another example would be squares and circles that move into a round formation. Save the Flash file naming it puzzle.fla.

Exercise 7 — CAT TOYS

Use Flash and Dreamweaver to modify the CAT TOYS website by completing the following steps:

a) In Dreamweaver, open the CAT TOYS website for editing, a website provided with the data files for this text.

b) Modify the copyright info library item by replacing Name with your name. Allow Dreamweaver to update all occurrences of the library item.

c) In the CAT TOYS root folder, create a folder named media.

d) Start Flash and create a new document.

e) Save the document outside of any website folder naming it cattoysinc.fla. Create animated text with sound as follows:

1. Create animated text with letters that start in the left side of the Stage in a pile (on top of each other) and move to the right to recreate the text Cat Toys Inc. in a font and color of your choice and a size of 60.
2. Import the MEOW.wav sound file to the Library. Place the sound file in a new layer named kitty, creating keyframes as necessary.
3. Change the dimensions of the stage to just accommodate the objects.
4. Export the Flash movie to the CAT TOYS media folder naming it: cattoysinc.swf

f) In Flash, create a new document. Save the document outside of any website folder naming it ani_roll.fla. Create a motion-tweened animation as follows:
1. Draw a solid circle in a red color and convert it to a Graphic symbol named toy.
2. Create keyframes and apply motion tweening so that the circle moves in a straight line from the left to the right on the Stage and back again.
3. Change the dimensions of the stage to just accommodate the objects.
4. Export the Flash movie to the CAT TOYS media folder naming it: ani_roll.swf

g) In Flash, create a new document. Save the document outside of any website folder naming it ani_bounce.fla. Create a motion-tweened animation as follows:
1. Draw a solid circle in a red color and convert it to a Graphic symbol named toy.
2. Create keyframes and apply motion tweening so that the circle moves in a straight line from the top to the bottom on the Stage and back again.
3. Change the dimensions of the stage to just accommodate the objects.
4. Export the Flash movie to the CAT TOYS media folder naming it: ani_bounce.swf

h) In Dreamweaver, modify the index.html web page document by inserting the cattoysinc.swf file above the paragraph of text. With the Flash movie placeholder selected, clear the Loop check box in the Property inspector.

i) In Dreamweaver, modify the roll.html web page document as follows:
1. Insert the cattoysinc.swf file above the first paragraph of text and, with the Flash movie placeholder selected, clear the Loop check box in the Property inspector.
2. Insert the ani_roll.swf file below the last paragraph of text.

j) In Dreamweaver, modify the bounce.html web page document as follows:
1. Insert the cattoysinc.swf file above the first paragraph of text and, with the Flash movie placeholder selected, clear the Loop check box in the Property inspector.
2. Insert the ani_bounce.swf file below the last paragraph of text.

k) View each web page document in a browser window.

l) Print a copy of each web page document from the browser.

Exercise 8 — Video_Clips

Develop a website that showcases an upcoming event. Create a short video about the event. Import the video into a Flash document and then export it so that it can be used on the website.

Chapter 8
Website Content, Forms, and Dynamic Web Pages

This chapter discusses various website categories including electronic portfolios. Site maps, forms, and behaviors are also introduced.

Electronic Portfolios

A *portfolio* is a collection of work that clearly illustrates effort, progress, knowledge, achievement, and skills. Traditional portfolios typically take the form of a file folder or a three-ring binder. An *electronic portfolio* stores and presents portfolio content in a digital format such as a website:

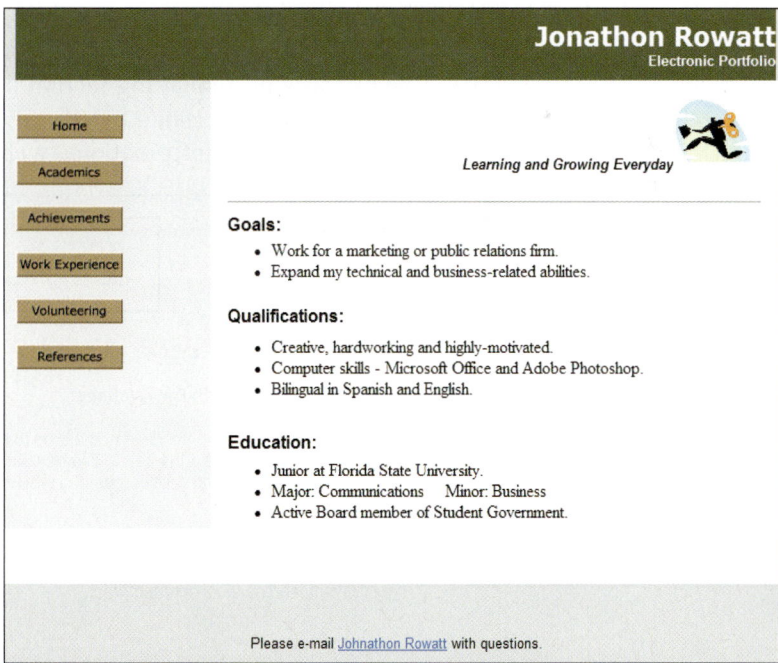

TIP Electronic portfolios are also called e-portfolios and Webfolios.

Electronic portfolios are preferred over traditional portfolios because they:

- are interactive
- can include sound, video, and digital images
- are easy to access, distribute, and share
- take up less space than a binder or stack of work samples

Personal Information

An electronic portfolio website contains personal information and therefore should only be posted to a secure server with limited access.

> **College Admission Requirement**
>
> Some colleges and universities require an electronic portfolio as part of their admissions process.

- can be updated easily
- demonstrate technical knowledge

The content and design of electronic portfolios will vary depending on the purpose and target audience. For example, an electronic portfolio for admission to college would have a design that reflects individuality and creativity and could include detailed academic and athletic information as well as samples of work. An electronic portfolio for a job search would have a professional appearance and include career objectives, résumé information, work samples, and links to related websites.

In general, the home page of an electronic portfolio website should include an introduction, contact information, and appropriate links. Additional content and design considerations for an electronic portfolio include:

- **Résumé information**
- An **e-mail link** to allow portfolio reviewers to send comments
- **Work samples,** which may be scanned images or links to files

Website Categories

As discussed in Chapter 1, websites can be classified into general categories, such as social media, commercial, informational, media, and portal. The category is determined by the website purpose and type of content on the site. For example, *informational websites* are created for the purpose of displaying factual information about a particular topic and are typically created by educational institutions, governments, and organizations. An informational website can have a variety of content:

- a **site map** for easier navigation
- a **search form** so that users can search the site for information
- a **list of links** to websites that contain related information
- tables of **tabular data**
- **banner ads** or other advertising to help pay for site maintenance

> **Banner Ads**
>
> Banner ads are discussed in Appendix A, Banner Ads and ActionScript.

The purpose of an informational website is to provide factual information, and therefore the site should be updated frequently to keep the content accurate. The target audience varies for informational websites, but all users of this type of website are looking for information that is easy to find.

commercial websites
corporate presence websites

Commercial websites include corporate presence websites and e-commerce websites. *Corporate presence websites* present information about a company's products or services, but do not have online ordering capabilities. The corporate presence website is a form of branding. *Branding* is the technique of raising awareness about a company by making a company logo visible in many places. Successful branding means the user will recognize the logo at a later time, such as when deciding which product to purchase at a store. The Bellur website includes a distinctive logo:

branding

A corporate presence website typically includes:

- a **company history**
- a **list of products** or services
- a **FAQ** page
- a **site map**
- **search** capabilities
- a description of **employment opportunities**
- a **feedback page**
- a **promotion** or contest to keep users returning to the site

The purpose of a corporate presence website is to make users aware of the products and services offered by a company. The target audience varies greatly, but users may be looking for product or contact information.

e-commerce websites

E-commerce websites are created by businesses for the purpose of selling their products or services to consumers online:

Chapter 8 Website Content, Forms, and Dynamic Web Pages

Amazon.com Inc.

amazon.com is a well known e-commerce website. Founded by Jeff Bezos in 1994, Amazon.com Inc. is an Internet retailer of books, music, toys, electronics, software, and other products.

An e-commerce website typically includes:

- product and service **visuals** and **descriptions**
- **search** capabilities and/or a **site map**
- **contact** and **return** information
- a **promotion** or coupon to keep users returning to the site
- **personalized user account** information and a **shopping cart**

Creating a FAQ Page

A *FAQ* (pronounced *fak*) page is a web page that contains frequently asked questions and their answers, such as where to find a company's products and how to use a certain product. The intent is to answer commonly asked questions quickly without the user having to call or send an e-mail. For example:

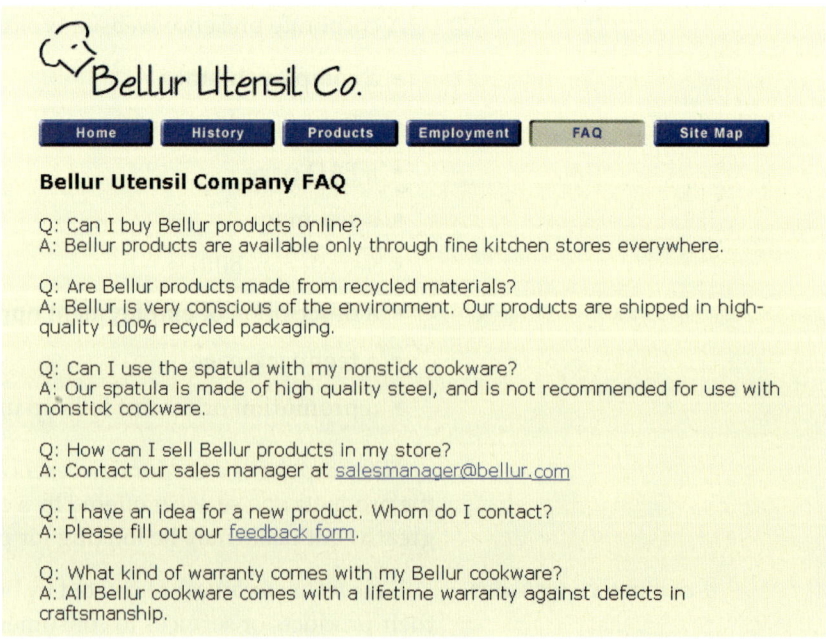

Depending on the type of company, a FAQ may also list known problems and their solutions or other technical support questions.

Practice: BELLUR – part 1 of 6

① OPEN THE BELLUR WEBSITE FOR EDITING

a. Start Dreamweaver.

b. Open the BELLUR website for editing, which is a website provided with the data files for this text.

c. Open the index.html web page document and view the page in a browser.

d. Click the links to explore the other web pages of the website.

e. Close the browser window. Dreamweaver is displayed.

f. Close index.html.

② MODIFY THE FAQ PAGE

a. Open the faq.html web page document.

b. At the bottom of the list of questions and answers, place the insertion point after the period in craftsmanship. and press Enter.

c. Type the following text, allowing the text to wrap:

Q: What materials are used to make the very comfortable, long-lasting handles of the spoons and spatulas?

d. Insert a line break and then type the following text, allowing the text to wrap:

A: We use a special compound called Typlak, which was developed and is produced by the NowPont Chemical Company.

e. Select all of the questions and answers in the list and apply the faqtext CSS style.

f. Save the modified faq.html.

③ PREVIEW AND PRINT THE WEB PAGE

a. Press the Live View button. The document is displayed similar to how it will appear in a browser window.

b. Press the Live View button.

c. Close faq.html.

Importing Tabular Data

In the early days of website design, tables were often used for web page layout. Tables for web page layout are problematic because they look different in different browsers, take a long time to load, and make changes to the design time consuming and therefore expensive.

Tables still have a purpose in web page design. They can be used to display tabular data, such as schedules, directories, and product lists Dreamweaver allows you to create tables from scratch, to copy and paste tables from another application, or to create them from data supplied by a database or spreadsheet application.

To create a table, select Insert → Table. The Table dialog box is displayed:

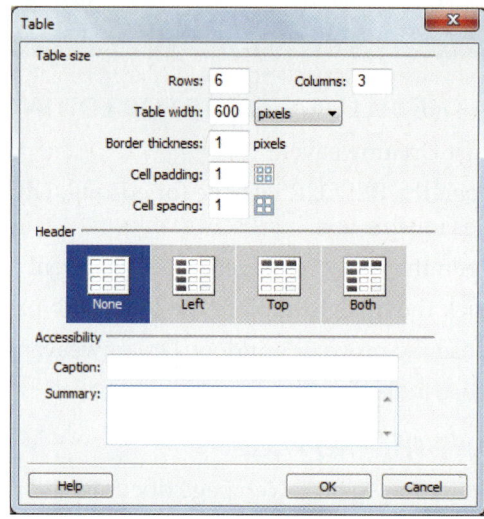

Enter table specifications in the Table dialog box and then click OK to create the table:

Use the Tab key to move from cell to cell as data is entered.

Tables can also be copied from a spreadsheet application such as Excel by copying selected data in Excel and then in Dreamweaver, selecting Edit → Paste Special. The Paste Special dialog box is displayed with options for pasting the spreadsheet data:

TIP Paste Special can also be used to copy and paste data from Microsoft Word.

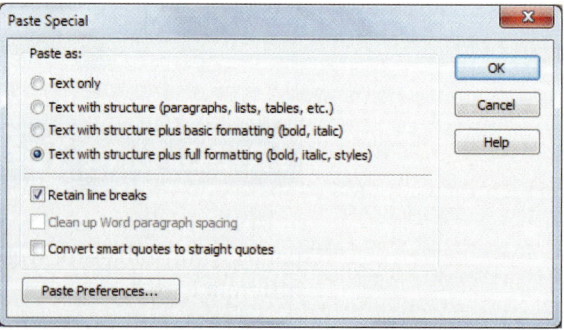

Select an option for pasting the data and then click OK to display the Excel data in the web page:

Customer	Total Sales
Harbor Manufacturing	$ 131,600.00
Timberlake Designs	$ 80,345.00
Cascade Plastics	$ 313,318.00
Avalon Clinic	$ 210,600.00
Gravelly Lake Plumbing	$ 1,150,074.00
Bavarian Productions	$ 227,253.00
Stealth Media	$ 8,250.00
Robinson Group	$ 835,658.00

tab-delimited

You can also import tabular data that has been created in another application and saved in a delimited text format, such as a text (TXT) file. *Tab-delimited* data indicates that each item in each row is separated by a tab character. For example, the tabular data shown below is displayed in a table with nine rows and three columns and a border of 1, which makes the data easier to read. The event, location, and time data was separated by tabs and saved in a delimited text format before it was imported:

Event	Location	Time
Bird House and Bird Feeder projects	Craft Tent	10:00 a.m.
Performance by The Nature Chorus	Amphitheatre	10:30 a.m.
Endangered Wildlife Show	Pavilion	11:00 a.m.
Rain Stick project	Craft Tent	11:00 a.m.
Performance by The Nature Chorus	Amphitheatre	1:00 p.m.
Paper Making and Recycling Bin Projects	Craft Tent	1:30 p.m.
Endangered Wildlife Show	Pavilion	2:30 p.m.
Earth Day Celebration Closing Ceremony	Amphitheatre	4:00 p.m.

Home | Events | Projects | History | Site Map | Volunteer Sign Up | Comments

To import tabular data and automatically create a table for the data, select Insert → Table Objects → Import Tabular Data. A dialog box is displayed:

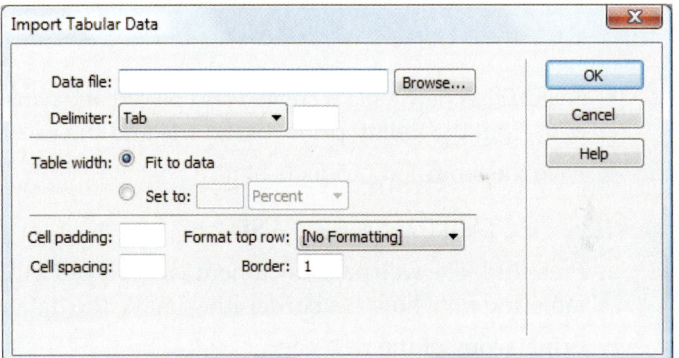

- Use the Browse button to navigate to the file that is to be imported and display the file name in Data File box.

- Select Tab in the Delimiter box for tab-delimited data.

- The Fit to data option sizes the table to fit all the imported data.

- Set the Cell padding, Cell spacing, and Border options for the new table. It is recommended to include a border of at least 1 for a table of data to make the table more readable.

- Use the Format top row list to format the data in the top row of the table if the top row of the imported data contains column headings.

Select OK to create the table at the insertion point. The tables can then be styled with CSS.

Chapter 8 Website Content, Forms, and Dynamic Web Pages

Practice: BELLUR – part 2 of 6

Dreamweaver should be started and the BELLUR website should be the working site.

① ADD A TABLE OF DATA

a. Open the products.html web page document.
b. Place the insertion point below the text Price List.
c. Select Insert → Table Objects → Import Tabular Data. A dialog box is displayed.
d. Click Browse. A dialog box is displayed.
   1. Navigate to the root folder of the BELLUR site if it is not already displayed.
   2. Select bellur_price_list.txt and then select Open.
e. In the Import Tabular Data dialog box, set the rest of the options to:

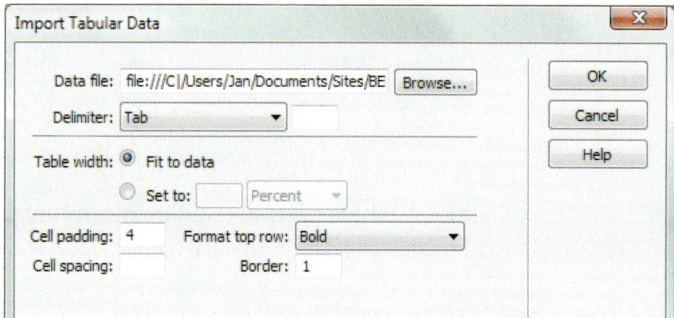

f. Select OK. A new table is created and placed at the insertion point. The table contains data from the bellur_price_list.txt file and the text in the top row is bold.
g. Save the modified products.html.

② VIEW THE TABLE IN A BROWSER

a. Press F12. The web page document is displayed in a browser window. Scroll to the table and note how the border lines make the data more readable.
b. Print a copy of the web page.
c. Close the browser window. Dreamweaver is displayed.
d. Close products.html.

Creating a Site Map

A *site map* is a web page that contains links to information on other pages of the website. Site maps are often used on large websites. The links are usually arranged in alphabetical order or grouped by subject, as in the Earth Day site map:

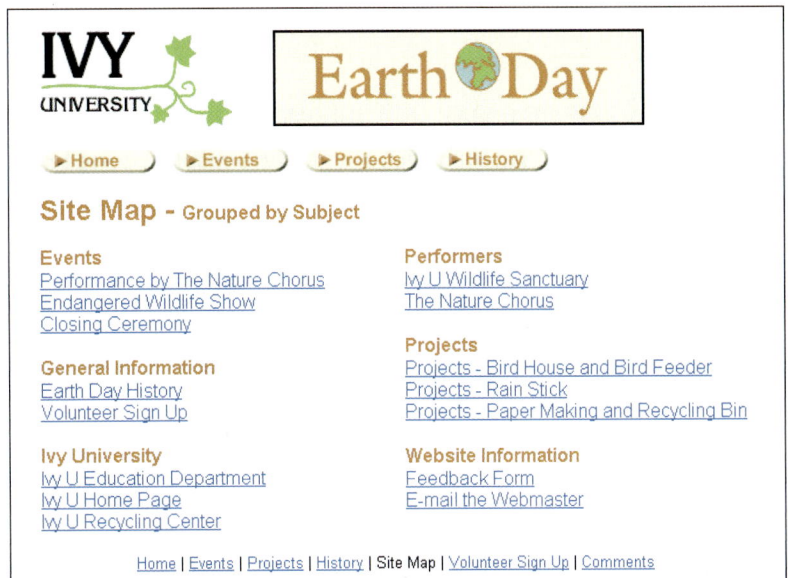

A site map helps users find the web page they are looking for if they cannot find the web page using the navigation bars. The links on a site map web page also provide an overview of the website's contents.

Practice: BELLUR – part 3 of 6

Dreamweaver should be started and the BELLUR website should be the working site.

① ADD THE LINKS TO THE SITE MAP WEB PAGE DOCUMENT

a. Open the site_map.html web page document.

b. Place the insertion point below the top global navigation bar.

c. Type the following text, pressing Enter at the end of each line:

> Bellur Utensil Company Site Map
> Company History
> Employment Opportunities
> FAQ Page
> Feedback Form
> Products and Prices
> Sweepstakes

d. Select the text Bellur Utensil Company Site Map and apply the sitemaptitle CSS style.

e. Link text to web page documents as follows:

Link the text	to the web page document
Company History	history.html
Employment Opportunities	employment.html
FAQ Page	faq.html
Feedback Form	feedback.html
Products and Prices	products.html
Sweepstakes	sweeps.html

Chapter 8 Website Content, Forms, and Dynamic Web Pages

f. Select all the link text and apply the sitemaptext CSS style.

g. Save the modified site_map.html.

② VIEW THE SITE MAP IN A BROWSER

a. Press F12. The web page document is displayed in a browser window. Test the links in the site map.

b. Print a copy of the web page.

c. Close the browser window. Dreamweaver is displayed.

d. Close site_map.html.

Adding Jump Menus

A *jump menu* is a navigation tool that takes the user immediately to a different online location. Jump menus provide a list of links in a drop-down list:

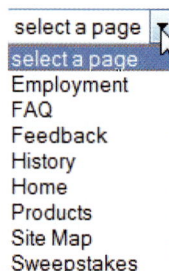

Jump menus are a way to provide a list of hyperlinks without taking up a lot of room on the web page.

To add a jump menu at the insertion point, click the Jump Menu button in the Forms category in the Insert panel:

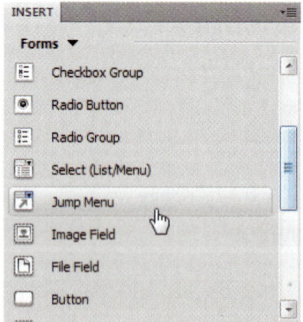

Chapter 8 Website Content, Forms, and Dynamic Web Pages

A dialog box is displayed:

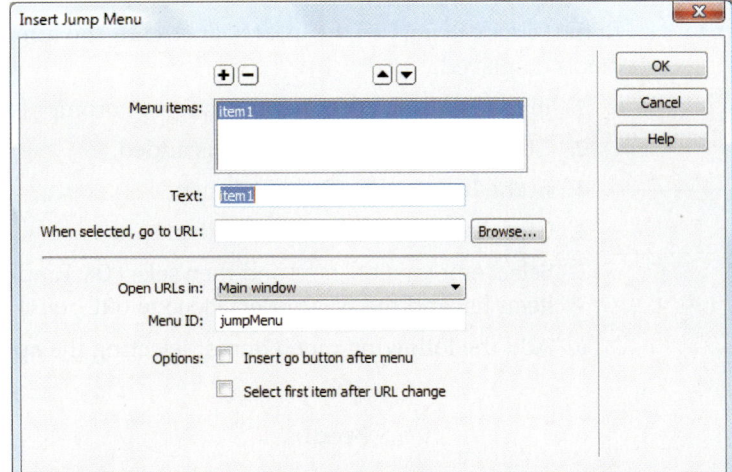

TIP It is a good design to include either a Go button or a first item prompt in a jump menu.

- The text and target URL for the selected menu item are set in the Text box and the When selected, go to URL box.
- Click ➕ or ➖ to add or delete Menu items.
- Click ▲ and ▼ to move a selected item up or down.
- Select Insert go button after menu to add a Go button Go next to the jump menu in the form.
- Select Select first item after URL change to have the list automatically return to the first item, which should be a prompt. A *prompt* is text in the first menu item that guides the user to select an item from the menu, for example Choose One or Select a Page. A prompt is not a list item that is a link.

Select OK to create the jump menu. A jump menu can be tested in a browser window.

To edit a selected jump menu, double-click the Jump Menu action in the Behaviors panel:

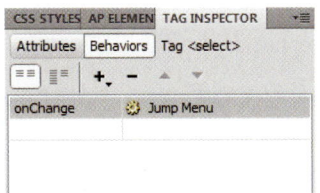

Alternatively, click List Values... in the Property inspector to edit items in the list.

Practice: BELLUR – part 4 of 6

Dreamweaver should be started and the BELLUR website should be the working site.

① **ADD A JUMP MENU**
   a. Open the *index*.html web page document.

b. Place the insertion point to the left of the dark blue "10th Annual Bellur Utensil Sweepstakes" image.
c. In the Forms category in the Insert panel, click the Jump Menu button. A dialog box is displayed.
   1. In the Text box, type: select a page. A prompt is added.
   2. Click +. Another menu item is added.
   3. In the Text box, type: Employment
   4. Click Browse. A dialog box is displayed.
   5. Select employment.html and then select OK. Employment is added to the Menu items list and the When selected, go to URL box displays employment.html.
   6. Add the following menu items, selecting the appropriate URLs:
      FAQ
      Feedback
      Home
      History
      Products
      Site Map
      Sweepstakes
   7. In the Menu items list, click the History menu item and then click ▲ to move History above Home.
   8. Select the Select first item after URL change check box.
   9. Select OK. The red outline indicates that the jump menu has been created within a form. Forms are discussed in the next section.
d. Save the modified index.html.

② **VIEW THE FORM IN A BROWSER**
a. Press F12. The web page document is displayed in a browser window.
b. Print a copy of the web page.
c. Test the jump menu links.
d. Close the browser window. Dreamweaver is displayed.
e. Close index.html.

Creating a Form

A *form* allows users to communicate and interact with a web server. Forms are used extensively on websites for tasks such as surveys, polls, online ordering, and guest books. The web page on the next page contains a form for a guest book:

TIP The design of a form should be simple to use, easy to understand, and as short as possible.

TIP The size of a form is determined by the form objects that are added. Therefore, a form cannot be sized by dragging.

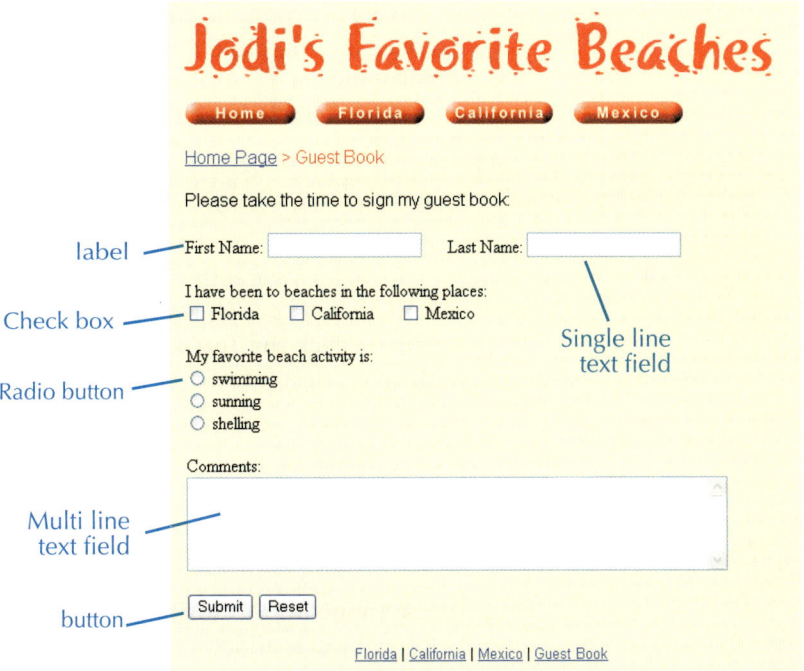

Labels

When the Label button [abc] is clicked, Dreamweaver automatically displays the page in Split view. Typed label text is enclosed in <label> and </label> tags. The <label> tag can then be defined in a style sheet for consistent label formatting.

Form objects are used to obtain information from the user in a structured manner:

- **Single line text field** allows the user to type a short amount of text
- **Labels** describe the purpose of a form object
- **Check boxes** and **radio buttons** allow the user to select options
- **Multi line text field** allow the user to type one or more lines of text
- **Buttons** are used to send the form results to a file or to an e-mail address, and to clear the form entries

A form and form objects are created using buttons in the Forms category in the Insert panel:

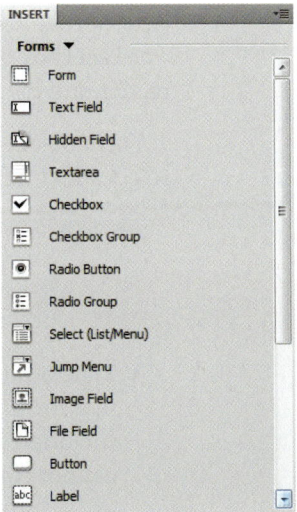

Chapter 8 Website Content, Forms, and Dynamic Web Pages   293

A form should be created in a table cell to control the form layout. To create a form, place the insertion point in a table cell and then click the Form button in the Insert panel. A form indicated by a dashed red outline is created and the insertion point is placed in the form:

To add objects at the insertion point, click a button in the **Forms** category in the Insert panel. For example, click the Label button, type First Name:, click the Text Field button, and then click the Button button to create a form similar to:

First Name: [   ]
[Submit]

The Input Tag Accessibility Attributes dialog box is displayed when a form object is added:

> **Accessibility Settings**
>
> The Input Tags Accessibility Attributes dialog box is used to make a form easier to use for all of the visitors to your site. For example, the **Access key** option lets you create a keyboard shortcut for each of the form items.

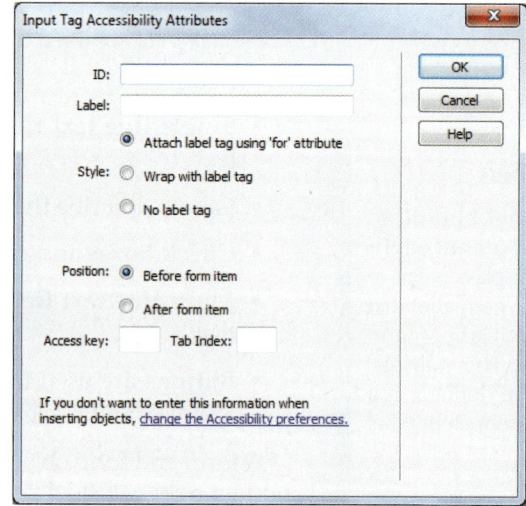

Appropriate accessibility information should be added for all form objects. The **Label** box is used to enter descriptive text that can be read by a screen reader and by default also appears on the form before the form object.

Form object properties are set in the Property inspector. For example, select a text field to display the following properties:

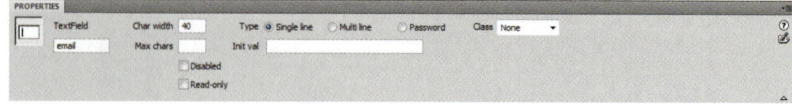

- Type a name for the form object in the **TextField** box. Each object in a form should have a descriptive name because the names are included in the file containing the form results. Object names cannot contain spaces.
- Select **Multi line** to change the field to a multi-line text field.

Chapter 8 Website Content, Forms, and Dynamic Web Pages

- Select **Password** to allow users to enter data, such as a password, secretly. A character, such as •, is displayed on the screen to represent the characters the user is typing.
- Type a value greater than 0 in the **Char width** box to indicate the number of characters that can be displayed in the text field.
- Type a value greater than 0 in the **Max Chars** box to indicate the maximum number of characters that the field can accept. The value may be more or less than the number of characters that can be displayed.
- **Init val** is text that should appear in the text field when the form loads. This property is often left empty. Text can be typed by the user to set the initial value.

A Button form object has the following properties:

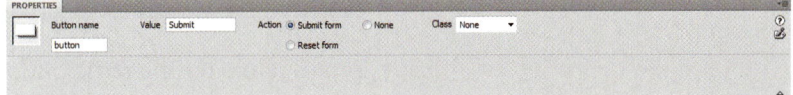

- **Button name** is the form object name.
- **Value** is the text that appears on the button. The Button form object automatically resizes to accommodate the text.
- **Action** is used to determine what action is taken when the user clicks the button. **Submit form** sends the form contents to the server. **Reset form** clears the form fields and allows the user to start over again. **None** indicates no action.

Form objects can be tested in a browser window. However, the form will not interact with a server unless a server-side script or application has been defined.

Check Boxes and Radio Buttons

A *Check Box form object* allows the user to select an option by clicking a check box. More than one check box can be selected at the same time. The *Radio Group form object* allows the user to only select one radio button from each group.

Click the Checkbox button in the **Forms** category in the Insert panel to add a check box form object. Properties include:

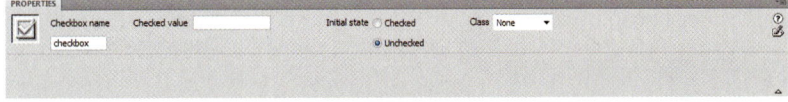

- **CheckBox name** is the form object name
- **Checked value** indicates the value returned if the user selects the check box, which can be text or a numeric value
- **Initial state** sets the check box to checked or unchecked when the form loads

Chapter 8 Website Content, Forms, and Dynamic Web Pages

Radio button form objects should be added in groups. Click the Radio Group button in the **Forms** category in the Insert panel, which displays a dialog box:

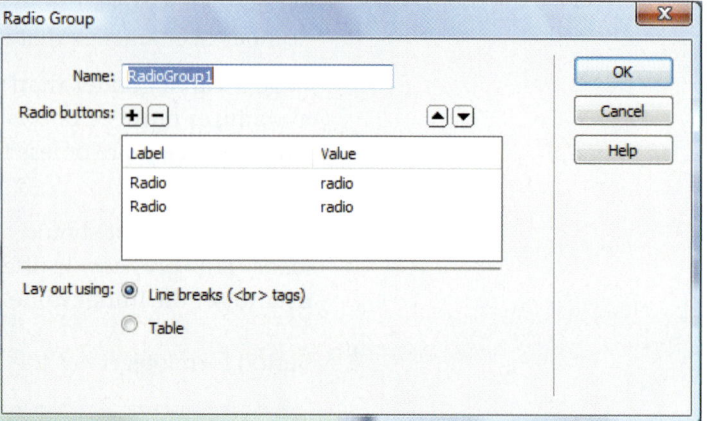

TIP For easy data entry, use the Tab key to move from Item Label to Value.

- Type a name for the radio button group in the **Name** box.
- The radio button group is created with at least two buttons, which are already listed in the **Radio buttons** list and include labels Radio and the values radio. Select each one and type a new label and value to change the radio buttons. Click + to add more radio buttons. Click − to delete a selected radio button.
- The **Lay out using** options indicate the way the radio buttons will be separated in the web page document. Select Line breaks (
 tags) to add a line break after each radio button. The **Table** value creates a one-column table with each radio button in a separate cell.

Select **OK** to create the radio buttons in the form at the insertion point.

Scrolling Lists and Drop-Down Menus

Forms often include a scrolling list or a drop-down menu, which allow users to easily select from a list of predetermined choices rather than typing responses. With limited choices, a form is more likely to be completed by the user and the form results are easier to evaluate. A *scrolling list* allows the user to select an option from a list of items by scrolling the list using a scroll bar:

Scrolling Lists vs. Drop-down Menus

A scrolling list differs from a drop-down menu in that it has scroll arrows, it can be enabled so that the user can select more than one option, and the height can be set.

scrolling list

A *drop-down menu* allows the user to select an option from a list of items that appear when the user clicks the 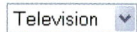 next to the list:

Select product of interest:

Television

drop-down menu

To add a scrolling list, click the Select (List/Menu) button in the Forms category in the Insert panel. A scrolling list is created by selecting List in the Property inspector. A name for the list should be typed in the Select box. Click List Values... to display a dialog box. The list items are added in this dialog box. Each item should have an Item Label, which is the text that is displayed in the scrolling list, and a value, which is returned to the server:

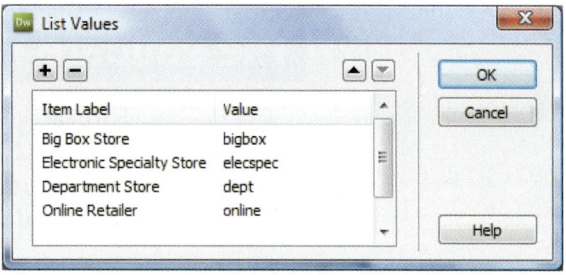

Click + to add an item and click − to delete the selected item. The ▲ and ▼ are used to move a selected item up or down in the list. Select OK to add the items to the form object.

In the Property inspector, the scrolling list can be further modified:

- Height is the number of items that should be displayed in the list. The rest of the items will be displayed when the list is scrolled.
- Select Allow multiple to enable the user to select more than one list item.
- Initially selected is the list item that will appear selected in the form object when the web page loads.

To create a drop-down menu, add a List/Menu form object and select Menu in the Property inspector. A name for the menu should be typed in the List/Menu box. Click List Values... to display a dialog box. The menu items are added in this dialog box. Each item should have an Item Label, which is the text that is displayed in the menu, and a value, which is returned to the server:

Chapter 8 Website Content, Forms, and Dynamic Web Pages

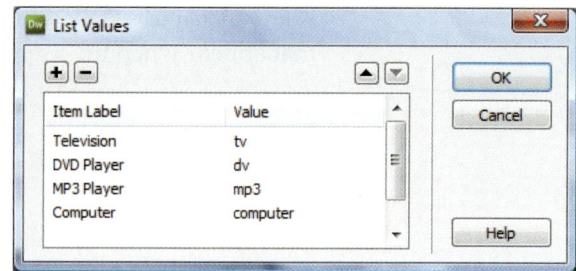

Click + to add an item and click − to delete the selected item. The ▲ and ▼ are used to move a selected item up or down in the list. Select OK to add the items to the form object.

In the Property inspector, one menu item can be selected in the Initially selected list, and that item will be selected in the form object when the web page loads.

The Validate Form Action

The Validate Form action can be applied to a form to check the contents of a field for the correct type of data and to see if a value falls within a specified range. For example, a field could be checked to see if the data entered was numeric and in the range of 1 through 10.

To validate a field, name the field in the Property inspector and then select the form's Submit button. Select Window → Behaviors to display the Behaviors panel, click +, and select Validate Form to display a dialog box:

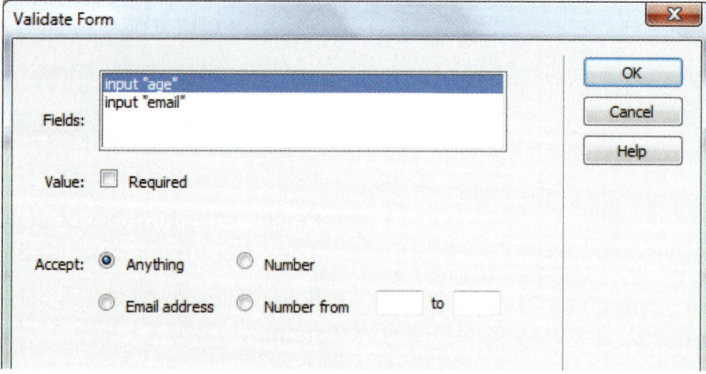

TIP The Validate Form Action only works with HTML forms.

Select the field to validate and then select the Value Required check box to indicate that the field cannot be left blank. The Accept section includes additional options:

- Anything indicates the field can contain any type of data.
- Number indicates the field is to contain only numerals.
- Email address indicates the field will contain the @ symbol.
- Number from is used to specify a numeric range.

onBlur and onChange Events

The Validate Form action can also be triggered by an onBlur or onChange event, which both occur when the user moves away from the validated field.

Select OK to apply the validation criteria to the field. The Validate Form action will be triggered by an onClick event, which occurs when a user clicks the Submit button.

Pop-up Messages

The Popup Message behavior can be used to communicate important messages to the user. For example:

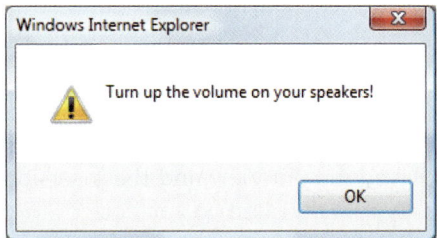

To create a Popup message, select the tag that the message will be attached to. For example, select the <body> tag to have a message display when a user loads the page. Then, in the Behaviors panel, click ➕, and select **Popup Message** to display a dialog box where the message is typed.

Practice: BELLUR – part 5 of 6

Dreamweaver should be started and the BELLUR website should be the working site.

① ADD CHECK BOX FORM OBJECTS

a. Open the feedback.html web page document. A form, labels, and text fields have already been added to this web page document.

b. Place the insertion point to the right of the e-mail address text field and press Enter.

c. In the Forms category in the Insert panel, click the Label button 🔡. The page is displayed in Split view and the insertion point is between <label> and </label> tags. Type: What Bellur utensils do you own? (check all that apply)

d. Switch to Design view and insert a line break.

e. In the **Forms** category in the Insert panel, click the Checkbox button ☑. The Input Tag Accessibility Attributes dialog box is displayed.

  1. In the ID box, type utility
  2. In the Label box, type: Utility Spoon
  3. In the **Position** area, select **After form item**.
  4. Select **OK**. A Check Box form object and label is inserted in the form.

f. Select the check box and in the Property inspector, set **Checked Value** to: utility spoon

g. Insert a line break after the check box label.

h. In the **Forms** category in the Insert panel, click the Checkbox button ☑. The Input Tag Accessibility Attributes dialog box is displayed.

  1. In the ID box, type perforated
  2. In the Label box, type: Perforated Spoon
  3. In the **Position** area, select **After form item**.
  4. Select **OK**. A Check Box form object and label is inserted in the form.

i. In the Property inspector, set **Checked Value** to: perforated spoon

j. Place the insertion point to the right of the check box, type and insert a line break.

k. Insert another Check Box form object with the ID spatula and the Label Spatula. In the Property inspector, set Checked value to: spatula
l. Place the insertion point to the right of the check box and insert a line break.
m. Insert a Check Box form object with the ID none and the Label None. In the Property inspector, set Checked value to: none
n. Press Enter and then save the modified feedback.html.

② ADD A RADIO BUTTON GROUP FORM OBJECT

a. In the Forms category in the Insert panel, click the Label button. The page is displayed in Split view and the insertion point is between <label> and </label> tags. Type: How often do you cook?
b. Switch to Design view and insert a line break.
c. In the Forms category in the Insert panel, click the Radio Group button. A dialog box is displayed.
   1. In the Name box, type: Cook
   2. Click the first Radio label in the list and type: Often
   3. Click the first radio value in the list and type: often
   4. Click the next Radio label in the list and type: Sometimes
   5. Click the next radio value in the list and type: sometimes
   6. Click +. Another radio button is added to the list.
   7. Click the new Radio label in the list and type: Rarely
   8. Click the new radio value in the list and type: rarely
   9. Select OK. The radio buttons and labels are added to the form.
d. Save the modified feedback.html.

Check—Your form should look similar to:

```
First Name: [      ]   Last Name: [      ]

E-mail address: [                    ]

What Bellur utensils do you own? (check all that apply)
☐ Utility Spoon
☐ Perforated Spoon
☐ Spatula
☐ None

How often do you cook?
○ Often
○ Sometimes
○ Rarely
```

③ ADD A SCROLLING LIST

a. The insertion point should be just below the radio button group. Press the Backspace key to delete the extra line break and then press Enter.
b. In the Forms category in the Insert panel, click the Label button. The page is displayed in Split view and the insertion point is between <label> and </label> tags. Type: Where do you purchase other cooking products?
c. Switch to Design view and insert a line break.
d. In the Forms category in the Insert panel, click the Select (List/Menu) button. The Input Tag Accessibility Attributes dialog box is displayed. Select Cancel. A List/Menu form object is added to the form.

e. In the Property inspector, set **Select** to: where
f. In the Property inspector, select **List**.
g. In the Property inspector, click [List Values...]. A dialog box is displayed.
  1. In the **Item Label** list, type: Grocery
  2. Click in the **Value** list and type: grocery
  3. Click [+]. Another item is added to the list.
  4. For the new item, type Catalog for the **Item Label** and catalog for the **Value**.
  5. Add another item and type Specialty Shop for the **Item Label** and shop for the **Value**.
  6. Add another item and type Internet for the **Item Label** and internet for the **Value**.
  7. Select **OK**. The dialog box is removed.
h. In the Property inspector, set **Height** to: 3
i. In the Property inspector, in the **Initially selected** list select Grocery. The scrolling list now displays three items and Grocery is selected.
j. Save the modified feedback.html.

④ ADD A DROP-DOWN MENU

a. Place the insertion point to the right of the scrolling list and press Enter.
b. In the **Forms** category in the Insert panel, click the Label button [abc]. The page is displayed in Split view and the insertion point is between <label> and </label> tags. Type: What new product would you most likely buy?
c. Switch to Design view and insert a line break.
d. In the **Forms** category in the Insert panel, click the Select (List/Menu) button. The Input Tag Accessibility Attributes dialog box is displayed. Select **Cancel**.
e. In the Property inspector, set **Select** to: newprod
f. In the Property inspector, click [List Values...]. A dialog box is displayed.
  1. Click in the **Item Label** list and type: Whisk
  2. Click in the **Value** list and type: whisk
  3. Add another item and type Pasta Fork for the **Item Label** and pasta for the **Value**.
  4. Add another item and type Ladle for the **Item Label** and ladle for the **Value**.
  5. Select **OK**. The dialog box is removed.
g. In the Property inspector, in the **Initially selected** list select Whisk. Whisk is selected in the drop-down menu.

⑤ ADD A MULTI LINE TEXT FIELD

a. Place the insertion point to the right of the drop-down menu and press Enter.
b. In the **Forms** category in the Insert panel, click the Label button [abc]. The page is displayed in Split view and the insertion point is between <label> and </label> tags. Type: Comments:
c. Switch to Design view and insert a line break.
d. In the **Forms** category in the Insert panel, click the Text Field button. The Input Tag Accessibility Attributes dialog box is displayed. Select **Cancel**.
e. In the Property inspector, set **TextField** to: comments
f. In the Property inspector, select **Multi line**.

⑥ ADD BUTTON FORM OBJECTS

a. Place the insertion point to the right of the Multi line text field and press Enter.

b. In the Forms category in the Insert panel, click the Button button. The Input Tag Accessibility Attributes dialog box is displayed. Select Cancel. A Submit button is added to the form.

c. Place the insertion point to the right of the button.

d. In the Forms category in the Insert panel, click the Button button. The Input Tag Accessibility Attributes dialog box is displayed. Select Cancel.

e. In the Property inspector, set Button name to: Clear

f. In the Property inspector, set Value to: Clear Form

g. In the Property inspector, select Reset form.

h. Save the modified feedback.html.

⑦ VALIDATE FORM OBJECTS

a. Select Window → Behaviors. The Behaviors panel is displayed.

b. In the web page document, click the Submit button to select it.

c. In the Behaviors panel, click + and select Validate Form from the displayed menu. A dialog box is displayed. Set the firstname field options to:

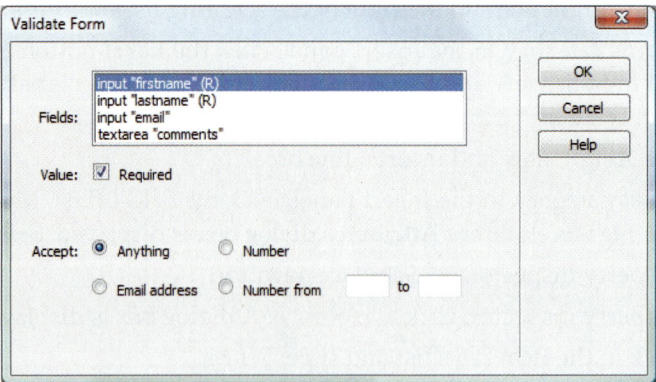

d. In the Fields list, select the lastname field and set the options to:

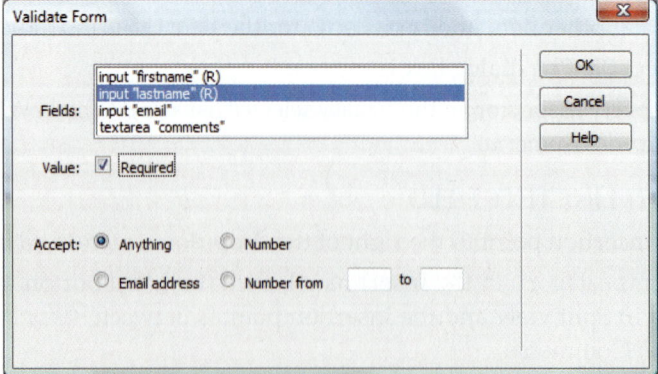

e. In the Fields list, select the email field and set the options to:

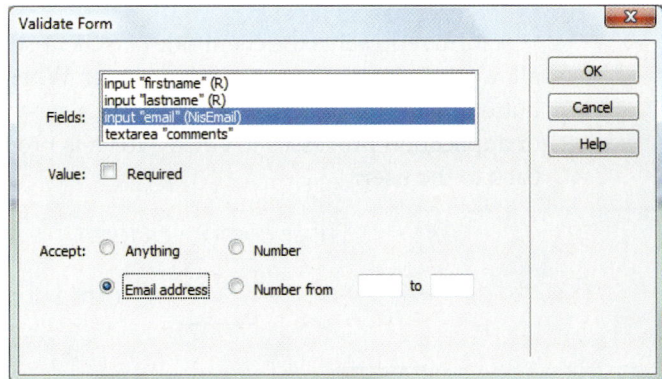

f. Select **OK**. When the form is posted to a web server, data will be required in the firstname, lastname, and email text field.

⑧ ADD A POP-UP MESSAGE
a. Select the <body> tag.
b. In the Behaviors panel, click 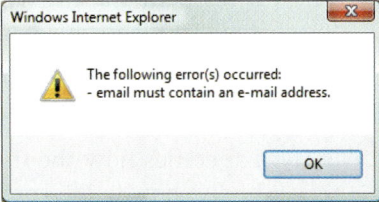, and select **Popup Message**. A dialog box is displayed.
c. In the Message box, type: Please take the time to give us your feedback.
d. Select **OK**.
e. Saved the modified feedback.html.

⑨ VIEW THE FORM IN A BROWSER
a. Press F12. The web page document is displayed in a browser window and the pop-up message is displayed.
b. Print a copy of the web page.
c. Fill out the form and click **Clear Form**. The form resets.
d. Fill out the form again, leaving the E-mail address field blank and click **Submit**. An error dialog box is displayed:

e. Test the other validated fields.
f. Close the browser window. Dreamweaver is displayed.
g. Close feedback.html.

Interactive Forms

A form represents the client side of a client-server relationship because it allows the user to interact with the server. When the user clicks the Submit button, the form information is sent to a server where a *server-side script* or application processes it. Once a form is processed, information is sent back to the user:

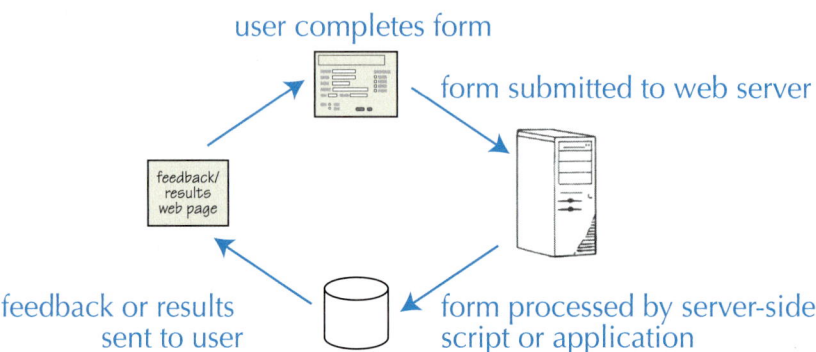

Forms can be processed by a CGI (Common Gateway Interface) script, ColdFusion page, JSP (JavaServer Page), ASP (Active Server Page) or other application. The server-side script or application used to process the form is defined in the form's **Action** property.

Select a form to display form properties in the Property inspector that allow the server-side script or application to be defined:

TIP Click the <form> tag selector to select a form.

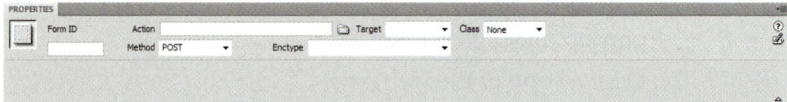

- Type a name for the form in the **Form ID** box. A form should be named because it allows the form to be referenced using a script.

- **Action** is the path and file name or script name that will process the contents of the form when the Submit button is clicked.

TIP The information for the Form properties is typically provided by the web host. web hosts are discussed in Chapter 9.

- **Method** is the method that will transmit the form data to the server. The default method is POST.

- **Enctype** specifies how the information is to be sent, so the web server knows how to interpret the information.

client-side scripts

Simple forms can use JavaScript or VBScript to create a *client-side script* which processes a form on the user's computer instead of sending the information to the web server for processing. For example, a JavaScript could be added to display one message or another when the user clicks the Submit button based on the user's choice of two radio buttons. To create a client-side JavaScript function, select the Submit button in a form and then select **Window → Behaviors** to display the Behaviors panel. In the Behaviors panel, click [+] and select **Call JavaScript**. A dialog box is displayed:

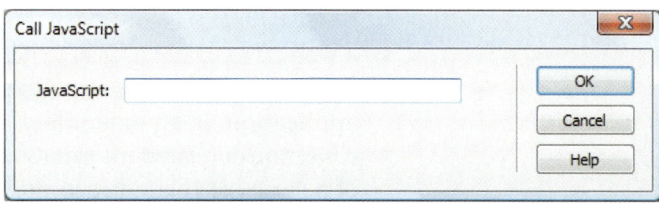

Type processForm() in the JavaScript dialog box and then add a processForm() JavaScript function to the head section of the web page document to create a client-side script. Adding a processForm() JavaScript function requires knowledge of JavaScript.

CGI (Commmon Gateway Interface) scripts are written in a programming language, such as Perl, Java, ASP or PHP. These scripts work with the web server to process form data submitted by a user. Many service providers provide a mail script for you. Alternatively, you can find free CGI scripts at sites such as www.scriptarchive.com.

Dynamic Web Pages

static web page

A *static web page* contains only text and images. A web page that contains any animation or is interactive is a *dynamic web page*. *Dynamic content* is content that changes as the source, such as a database, is updated. A website that includes dynamic content on any of the web pages is a *dynamic website*, also called a *web application*. A dynamic website employs a server technology, such as *ColdFusion*, to process input from the user and then send a web page with dynamic content to the user's browser. The information that is returned to the user is from a data source such as a database file.

TIP Adobe has a free developer edition of ColdFusion available on their website.

To create a website that uses ColdFusion technology, select Site → Manage Sites and complete a series of dialog boxes to define the site. Once the site is defined, select File → New to display a dialog box. Select Blank Page, ColdFusion, and then Create. Change the page title and then save the web page document. The extension .cfm is automatically added to a ColdFusion dynamic page.

The Databases and Bindings panels are used for the rest of the dynamic content setup. Select Window → Databases to display the Databases panel, which displays step-by-step instructions for setting up a page with dynamic content:

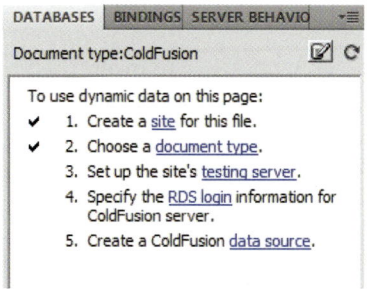

In the example above, the first two steps have been checked to indicate that they have been completed. Steps 3 and 4 require setting up a ColdFusion server. Step 5 involves creating a data source.

A *data source* is an external file that is used to display dynamic data on a web page. Databases are the most common way for websites to access dynamic content or data. *Access*, which is the Microsoft Office database application, is an example of a file-based data source. A *database* is a collection of related information organized into tables. A database consists of a series of related records. Within the records, each piece of data is referred to as a *field*. A series of records with the same fields is called a *flat-file database*. For example, an Access database that consists of one table is considered a flat-file database:

ID	Product	Price	Stock
1	Utility Spoon	$12	124
2	Perforated Spoon	$18	85
3	Spatula	$20	65

Access Table

In order to extract data from a data source into a web page, the data wanted must be specified. This specified data is called a *recordset*. The **Data** category in the Insert panel is used to create and filter recordsets.

Adding Spry Widgets

The Spry framework consists of a library of JavaScript components that you can use to create interactive web pages. The Spry widgets are found in the Spry category in the Insert panel:

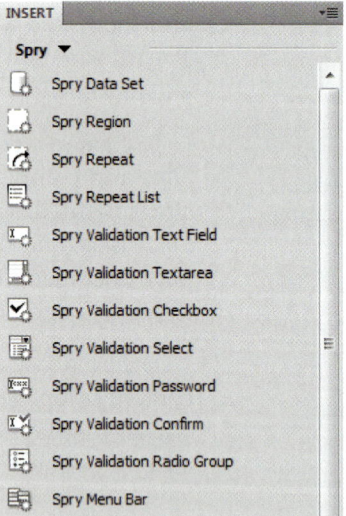

To insert the Spry menu bar, place the insertion point and then click the Spry Menu Bar button. A dialog box is displayed:

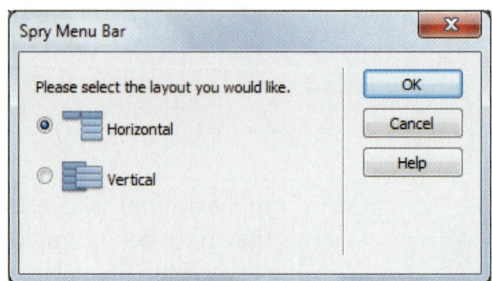

Select a layout and then click OK. The menu bar is inserted on the page.

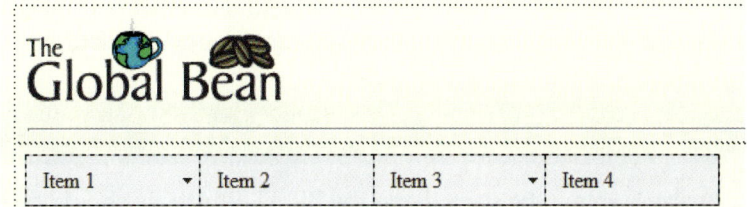

The menu can be customized using the Properties panel to enter Text and Link information:

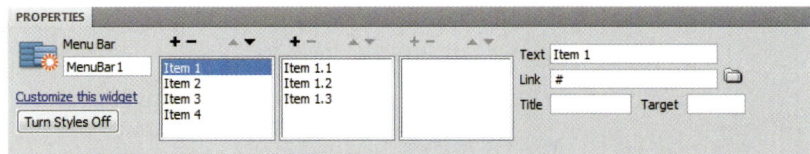

Notice that the menu contains drop-down options that are referred to as Item 1.1, 1.2, ... in the Property inspector:

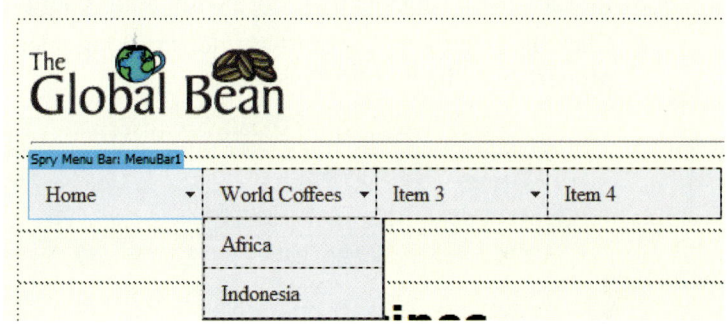

To format a Spry Menu Bar, edit the SpryMenuBarHorizontal.css rules:

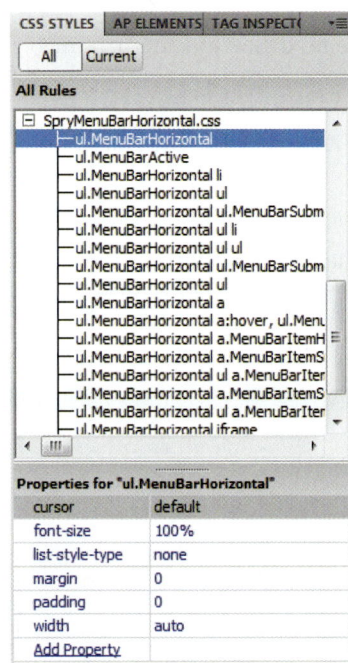

Chapter 8 Website Content, Forms, and Dynamic Web Pages

Another Spry widget you may want to use is the Tooltip. This widget is used to display additional information when the mouse moves over a page element. For example, a tooltip can be added to a form field. In the next practice, you will practice adding a Toolip.

Practice: BELLUR – part 6 of 6

Dreamweaver should be started and the BELLUR website should be the working site.

① ADD A TOOLIP

a. Open the feedback.html web page document.
b. Click the E-mail address text box.
c. In the Insert panel, click the Spry category.
d. Click **Spry Tooltip**. Tooltip trigger text is displayed:

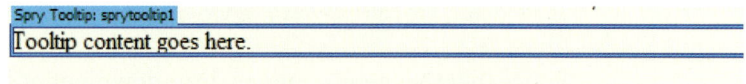

e. Replace Tooltip content goes here with: Enter your e-mail address
f. Click the <div.tooltipContent#sprytooltip1> tag selector to display Tooltip widget properties in the Property inspector:

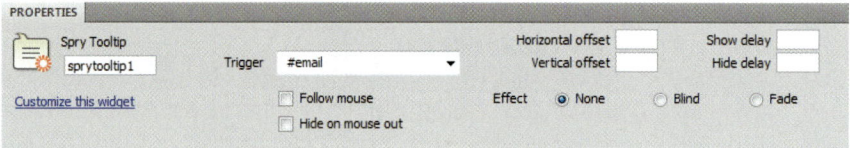

g. Click the Follow mouse check box to have the tooltip follow the mouse pointer if the pointer moves when it is over the trigger text.
h. Click the **Fade** effect option to have the tooltip fade in when it is displayed and fade out when it is removed from the page.
i. Save the modified feedback.html.

② VIEW THE FORM IN A BROWSER

a. Press F12. Note you may have to click **Allow Blocked Content** to view the Spry widget.
b. Move the mouse over the e-mail text box. The tooltip is displayed.
c. Move the moue away from the e-mail text box. Note the fade effect.
d. Close the browser window.
e. Quit Dreamweaver

Chapter Summary

An electronic portfolio stores and presents portfolio content in a digital format, such as a website. Most websites are considered to be in one of the following general categories: social media, commercial, informational, media, or portal.

A FAQ page is a page with frequently asked questions and their answers. Tables can be used for displaying tabular data, which is data that has been created in another application and is saved in a delimited text format. A site map is a navigational tool that contains links to information on other pages of the website. A jump menu contains a set of text hyperlinks and can also be used as a navigation tool.

A form allows users to communicate and interact with a web server. Form objects are used to obtain information from the user in a structured manner. Form objects include labels, text fields, check boxes, radio button groups, buttons, and List/Menu objects. Form objects can be tested in a browser window. A form will not interact with a server unless a server-side script or application has been defined. Form objects can be validated to ensure they contain the correct type of data before the form is processed.

A static web page contains only text and images. A web page that contains any animation or is interactive is a dynamic web page. A website that includes dynamic content on any of the web pages is a dynamic website, also called a web application. A dynamic website employs a server technology, such as ColdFusion. The use of dynamic data requires connecting to a data source and creating a recordset.

The Spry framework consists of a library of JavaScript components that you can use to create interactive web pages. The Spry widgets are found in the Spry category in the Insert panel.

Dreamweaver Commands and Buttons

Behaviors command Displays the Behavior panel. Found in the Window menu.

Button button Inserts a button form object at the insertion point. Found in the Forms category in the Insert panel.

Checkbox button Inserts a check box form object at the insertion point. Found in the Forms category in the Insert panel.

Databases command Displays the Databases panel. Found in the Window menu.

Form button Inserts a form at the insertion point. Found in the Forms category in the Insert panel.

Jump Menu button Displays a dialog box used to insert a jump menu at the insertion point. Found in the Forms category in the Insert panel.

Label button Inserts a label form object at the insertion point. Found in the Forms category in the Insert panel.

List/Menu button Inserts a List/Menu form object at the insertion point. Found in the Forms category in the Insert panel.

Radio Group button Displays a dialog box used to insert a radio button group form object at the insertion point. Found in the Forms category in the Insert panel.

Spry Menu Bar button Inserts a vertical or horizontal Spry Menu Bar. Found in the Spry category in the Insert panel.

Spry Tooltip button Inserts a Spry Tooltip. Found in the Spry category in the Insert panel.

Tabular Data button Displays a dialog box used to import tab-delimited data from a file into a table in a web page document. Found in the Layout category in the Insert panel.

Text Field button Inserts a text field form object at the insertion point. Found in the Forms category in the Insert panel.

Vocabulary

Access Microsoft Office database application.

Branding The technique of raising awareness about a company by making a company logo visible in many places.

Check Box form object A form object that allows the user to select an option by clicking a check box.

Client-side script A script that processes the form on the user's computer.

ColdFusion Adobe server technology.

Commercial website A type of website classification that includes corporate presence and e-commerce websites.

Corporate presence website A type of website that is created by a company or organization to present information about their products or services, but does not have online ordering capabilities.

Data source An external file used to display dynamic data on a web page.

Database A collection of information organized into tables.

Drop-down menu A form object that allows the user to select an option from a list of items that appear when the user clicks the ⌄ next to the list.

Dynamic content Content that changes based on source content changes.

Dynamic web page A web page that contains any animation or is interactive.

Dynamic website A website that includes dynamic content on any of the web pages.

E-commerce website A type of website created by businesses for the purpose of selling their products or services to consumers online.

Electronic portfolio Stores and presents portfolio content in a digital format such as a website.

FAQ A web page that contains frequently asked questions and their answers.

Field A piece of data in a record in a database.

Flat-file database A series of records in a database with the same fields.

Form Allows the user to communicate and interact with a web server.

Form object An object in a form that is used to obtain information from the user.

Informational website A type of website created for the purpose of displaying factual information about a particular topic.

Jump menu A navigation tool that contains a list of text hyperlinks.

Portfolio A collection of work that clearly illustrates effort, progress, knowledge, achievement, and skills.

Prompt The text in the first menu item of a jump menu that guides the user to select an item from the menu.

Radio Group form object A form object that allows the user to only select one radio button from each group.

Recordset Specified data from a database.

Scrolling list A form object that allows the user to select an option from a list of items by scrolling the list using a scroll bar.

Server-side script A script on a server that processes a form.

Site map A web page that contains links to information on other pages of the website.

Static web page A web page that contains only text and images.

Tab-delimited data Data where each item in each row is separated by a tab character.

Tabular data Data that has been created in another application and is saved in a delimited text format.

Web application *See* Dynamic website.

Review Questions

1. a) What is a portfolio?
    b) What is an electronic portfolio?
    c) List three reasons why electronic portfolios are preferred over traditional portfolios.
    d) List four elements that could be included in an electronic portfolio designed for admission to college.

2. a) List three general website categories.
    b) For each general website category, list a URL that would fit into that category.

3. a) What is the purpose of an informational website?
    b) List three elements or content often included on an informational website.

4. a) What is the purpose of a corporate presence website?
    b) What is branding?
    c) List three elements or content often included on a corporate presence website.

5. a) Describe the difference between a corporate presence website and an e-commerce website.
    b) List two companies that have an e-commerce website and a traditional brick-and-mortar store.

6. a) What does a FAQ page contain?
    b) What is the purpose of a FAQ page?

7. a) What is tabular data?
    b) What does tab-delimited data indicate?

8. a) What is a jump menu?
    b) Describe one advantage of using a jump menu instead of a navigation bar.

9. What are three examples of tasks that forms are used for?

10. a) What is a form object?
    b) What can be attached to a form object to help the user enter the correct data?

11. In a text field, what does the Max Chars property set?

12. a) List two objects that allow users to select from a list of predetermined choices on a form.
    b) Why is it better to have limited choices on a form?

13. Why is important to validate form content before it is submitted for processing?

14. What is the difference between a server-side and client-side script?

15. a) What type of content does a static web page contain?
    b) What is a dynamic web page?
    c) What is a dynamic website?
    d) What is ColdFusion?

16. a) What is a data source?
    b) What is a recordset?

17. Give two examples of Spry widgets not discussed in the text.

True/False

18. Determine if each of the following are true or false. If false, explain why.
    a) Electronic portfolios take up less space than a traditional portfolio.
    b) Corporate presence websites always offer online ordering.
    c) Branding is a technique used to raise awareness about a company.
    d) Tab-delimited data indicates that each item in each row is separated by a space.
    e) A site map helps users quickly find the web page they are looking for.
    f) A form is more likely to be completed by the user if they have limited choices.
    g) A dynamic web page contains only text and images.
    h) Spry widgets are used to create interactivity on a website.

Exercises

Exercise 1 ──────────────── CAKE DELIVERY

Modify the CAKE DELIVERY website by completing the following steps:

a) Open the CAKE DELIVERY website for editing, which is a website provided with the data files for this text.

b) Modify the copyright library item by replacing Name with your name. Allow Dreamweaver to update all occurrences of the library item.

c) Modify the faq.html web page document as follows:

  1. At the bottom of the list of questions and answers, place the insertion point after the period in the text from us. and press Enter.

  2. Type the following text, inserting a line break at the end of the first line:

     Q: How many calories are in each cake?
     A: One entire cake has 8,867 calories.

d) Modify the win.html web page document as follows:

   Below the text One entry per e-mail address. create a form with labels, text fields, and buttons as follows:

   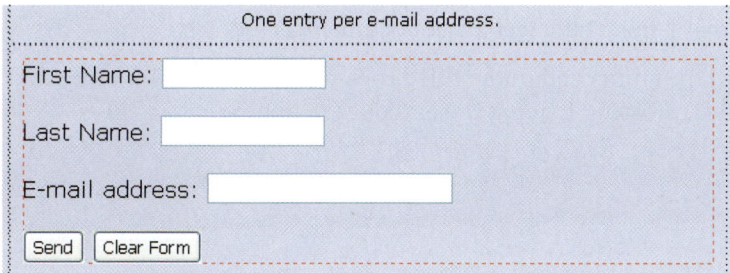

e) Modify the feedback.html web page document as follows:

  1. Below the text We'd love to hear from you! Send us your comments: create a form with labels and form objects as follows:

Chapter 8 Website Content, Forms, and Dynamic Web Pages 313

> **We'd love to hear from you! Send us your comments:**
>
> First Name: [   ] Last Name: [   ]
>
> E-mail address: [   ]
>
> Please rate your last Carter Cake delivery:
> ○ Excellent
> ○ Good
> ○ Not Quite Satisfactory
> ○ Terrible
> ○ I have never ordered.
>
> How would you like us to improve our cakes? Please check all that apply.
> ☐ More shapes
> ☐ More sizes
> ☐ More flavors
>
> Comments and suggestions:
> [   ]
>
> [Send Feedback] [Clear Form]

For each form object, include an appropriate name. Set the **Char** width for each text field to approximate the examples above.

f) Modify the sitemap.html web page document as follows:

1. In the empty cell in the third row, place the insertion point and type the following text, pressing Enter at the end of each line:

    SITE MAP
    Cakes
    FAQ
    Feedback Form
    Home
    Order a Cake
    Site Map
    Win a Cake

2. Link text to web page documents as follows:

Link the text	to the web page document
Cakes	cakes.html
FAQ	faq.html
Feedback Form	feedback.html
Home	index.html
Order a Cake	order.html
Site Map	sitemap.html
Win a Cake	win.html

g) Modify the cakes.html web page document as follows:

1. Place the insertion point after the bold text Price List and press Enter.

2. Insert tabular data, using the carterprices.txt tab-delimited file, a table width that fits the data, a cell padding of 8, no cell spacing, a border of 1, and format the top row of data as bold.

h) Add an appropriate form on the order.html page for customers that want to order a cake.

i) View each web page document in a browser window and print a copy of each web page document from the browser.

Exercise 2 ——————————————Cooking Herbs

The Cooking Herbs website was last modified in Chapter 3. Modify the Cooking Herbs website by completing the following steps:

a) In Dreamweaver, open the Cooking Herbs website for editing.

b) Modify the recipes.html web page document as follows:

1. Scroll to the bottom of the content and press the Enter key.

2. Create a form with labels, text fields, and buttons as follows:

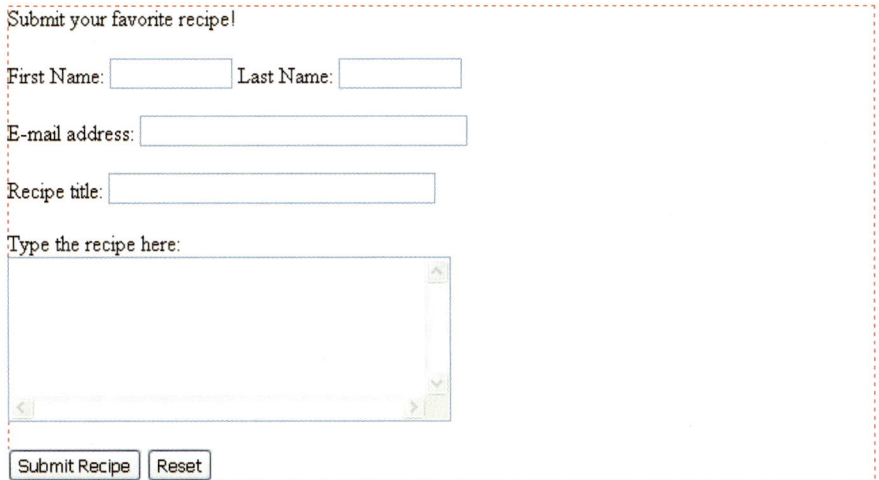

For each text field, include an appropriate TextField name. For the Multi line text field, set the Char width to 50 and Num Lines to 6. For the other text fields, set the Char width to approximate the examples above. For each button, include an appropriate Button name and set the appropriate action.

c) Add a Spry Tooltip to at least two of the form fields.

d) Modify the index.html web page document as follows:

1. Place the insertion point before the text Herbs have been used and press Enter.

2. Move the insertion point to the blank paragraph just created above the text Herbs have been used.

3. Add a form at the insertion point.

4. In the form, add a jump menu that contains the following menu items:

Menu Item Text	Go To URL
select a page	
Herbs	herbs.html
Recipes	recipes.html

   e) View each web page document in a browser window.

   f) Print a copy of each web page document from the browser.

Exercise 3 —————————————————————————— Name Portfolio

Develop an electronic portfolio website for yourself, naming it Name Portfolio, replacing Name with your name. The website should include:

- a home page with your name, contact information, a brief greeting, and a photo if possible
- a web page document that contains your detailed academic history
- a web page document that contains your detailed work history
- at least one other web page document that presents information about accomplishments or experiences
- at least one other web page document that presents work samples or contains links to samples of your work on other websites

Preview the website in a browser. When satisfied with the website, print a copy of each web page document from the browser.

Exercise 4 ————————————————————— Entrepreneur

Enhance the Entrepreneur website that was last modified in Chapter 6 by including Spry widgets. Experiment with widgets not covered in the text. When satisfied with the website, print a copy of each web page document from the browser.

Exercise 5 ————————————————————— Photographer

The Photographer website was created in Chapter 5. Modify the Photographer website to include an appropriate pop-up message. Also add form on a new page that lets visitors to the site leave their contact information if they are interested in photography services. Include a variety of form objects and apply the Validate Form Action to appropriate fields.

Chapter 9
Publishing and Promoting a Website

This chapter discusses publishing and promoting a website, and measuring its success. Maintaining a website and security issues are also discussed.

Publishing a Website

publishing a website

local sites

remote server

Publishing a website is the process of uploading a local site to a web server so that the site can be accessed on the World Wide Web. The websites developed in this text are referred to as *local sites* because the sites have been saved and edited on a local disk. A *remote server* can be a web server provided by an ISP, an intranet server, or a network server.

> **Web Server**
>
> A web server responds to requests from clients, usually a web browser, for HTML documents and any associated files or scripts.

Before a website is published, it should be checked and tested:

- each web page document should be checked for misspellings and grammatical errors
- the download time of each web page document should be checked to ensure that they are not too long
- target browsers should be determined and then each web page document should be previewed in each target browser
- the HTML should be tested for target browser compatibility
- the site should be checked for broken and missing links
- the HTML should be checked for problems such as missing Alt text, empty tags, and untitled documents

After a website is published, it still needs attention:

- the website should be constantly maintained in order to keep the content updated
- the website will need to be promoted so that users are aware that the website is available
- some measure of success should be used to ensure that the website is serving its intended purpose

Checking Spelling and Grammar

A website with spelling or grammatical errors seems less credible. Just before a site is published, all web page documents in the site should be rechecked for spelling and grammatical errors because errors are often created from last minute changes.

Each web page document in a site has to be checked for spelling errors. To check spelling, open the web page document and select Commands → Check Spelling.

Grammatical errors are found by proofreading each web page document. The web page documents should be printed from a browser because it is easier to proofread a hard copy than text on a screen. It is also a good idea to get another person to proofread the hard copy because it is often difficult to thoroughly proofread your own work.

Checking the Download Time

download time

weight of the page

Before a site is published, each web page document should be opened and the download time checked. The *download time* is the time it takes the web page document to load into a user's browser. The status bar at the bottom of a Document window displays the *weight of the page*, which is the web page document's file size and the estimated download time:

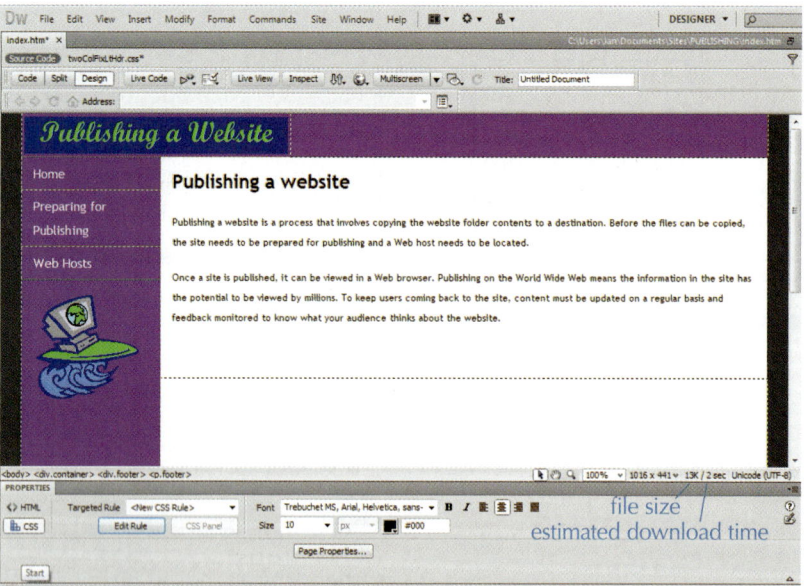

File Size

File size is typically expressed in kilobytes (K) or megabytes (M). A kilobyte is approximately 1,000 bytes and a megabyte is approximately 1,000,000 bytes.

In the example above, the file size is 13K (kilobytes) and is estimated to take 2 seconds to download the page.

The download time is calculated based on the connection speed specified in the Dreamweaver preferences. The download time for a page is important because users will only wait a few seconds for a page to load before clicking a link or the Back button in their browser. Large image file sizes or many images in one document can also affect the download time.

Practice: PUBLISHING – part 1 of 4

① OPEN THE PUBLISHING WEB SITE FOR EDITING

a. Start Dreamweaver and open the PUBLISHING website for editing, which is a website provided with the data files for this text.
b. Familiarize yourself with the files and folders for this website.
c. Open the index.html web page document and then view it in a browser.
d. Click the links to explore the two other web pages of the website.
e. Close the browser window. Dreamweaver is displayed.

② CHECK THE SPELLING

a. Open the index.html web page document if it is not already displayed.
b. Select Commands → Check Spelling. A dialog box is displayed.
   1. Select Ignore All. Another dialog box is displayed.
   2. In the Suggestions list, select Publishing.
   3. Select Change. Another dialog box is displayed.
   4. In the Suggestions list, select folder and then click Change.
   5. Select OK.
c. Save the modified index.html.
d. Check the spelling in the other two web page documents, make any changes necessary, and then save any changes.

③ CHECK THE DOWNLOAD TIMES

a. Display index.html and note the file size and download time.
b. Check the file sizes and download times for the other two web page documents.

Target Browsers

A Dreamweaver website may include elements that are not supported by all browsers, such as JavaScript. A *target browser* is a browser and version, such as Internet Explorer 9, in which the website is designed to display correctly. The websites developed in this text have been designed using Internet Explorer 9 as the target browser.

A website is going to be viewed with different browsers, monitor sizes, screen resolutions, and connection speeds. Therefore, the site should be viewed and tested in more than one target browser and resolution.

One way to determine which browsers to target is to extend the definition of the target audience for the website by asking the following questions:

1. What platforms will be used? Windows, Linux, or others?
2. What type of connections and speeds will be used? DSL or cable?
3. What browsers will be used? Internet Explorer, Firefox, or others?
4. What screen resolutions will be used? 320x480 or 1680x1050?

Browsers
Commonly used web browser applications include Internet Explorer, Opera, Firefox, Mozilla, and Safari.

TIP There are websites that track browser use and provide statistics on the most common browsers.

Previewing in a Target Browser

Once the target browsers have been determined, the **Preview in Browser** command can be used to preview the site in the target browsers. When previewing the site in a target browser, check for:

- fonts and colors displaying correctly
- page layout displays correctly when the browser window is resized
- images displaying correctly

Select File → Preview in Browser to display a submenu with a list of browsers installed on the computer. To add a browser to the Preview in Browser submenu, select File → Preview in Browser → Edit Browser List, which displays the Preferences dialog box. Select Preview in Browser in the **Category** list to display those options:

> **Downloading Browsers**
>
> In order to preview a website in a browser, the browser must be installed on the computer. Browsers are typically free of charge and can be downloaded from the browser company's website.

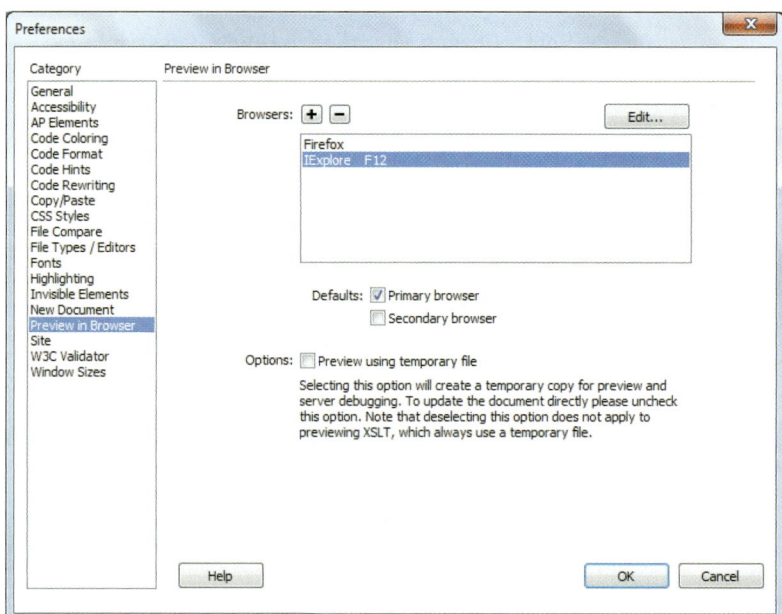

Click ⊞ to display the Add Browser dialog box:

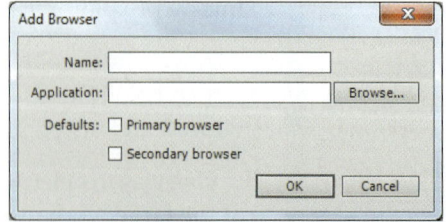

Type a name for the browser in the **Name** box and click **Browse** to navigate to the browser application file.

Adobe BrowserLab

Another way to preview a website in different browsers is to use Adobe BrowserLab. *Adobe BrowserLab* is a Preview in Browser option which lets you test any Web page in most common browsers on the Internet. Select File → Preview in Browser → Adobe BrowserLab to access this feature.

320   *Chapter 9 Publishing and Promoting a Website*

With the increased use of cell phones and other mobile devices to access the Internet, it is important to know what your site will look like in a mobile browser. In Dreamweaver, select File → Preview in Browser → Device Central to preview your site in a mobile browser:

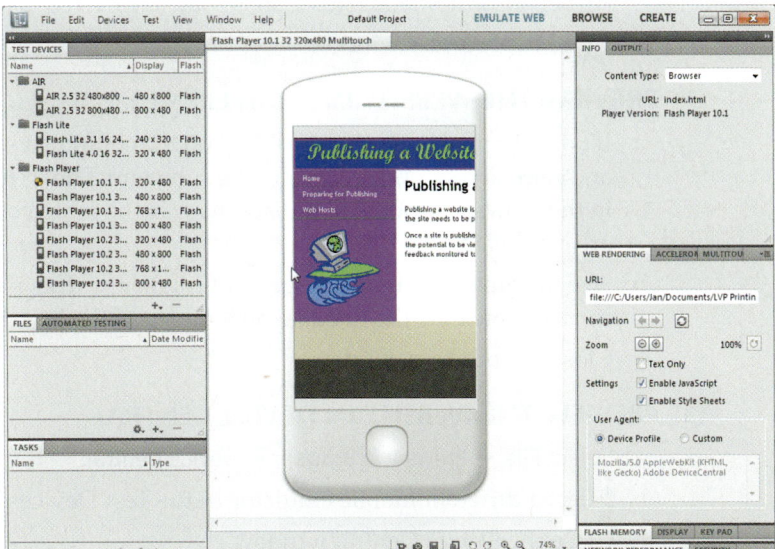

TIP Many sites create a second simplified mobile version of their site due to limited screen size, slow download times, and many mobile devices don't support Flash or JavaScript.

Click a mobile emulator in the Test Devices panel to change the preview:

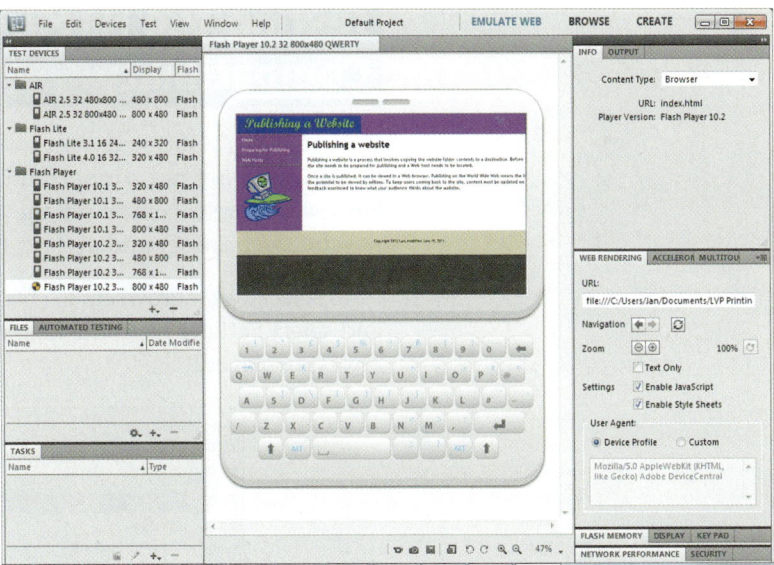

You can navigate around the website in the preview window to test links. Use the arrow keys to scroll the page.

Practice: PUBLISHING – part 2 of 4

Dreamweaver should be started and the PUBLISHING website should be the working site.

① **PREVIEW THE WEBSITE IN THE DEFAULT BROWSER**

a. Open the index.html web page document if it is not already displayed.

b. Select File → Preview in Browser and select the primary browser, which is the first browser listed in the submenu. The web page document is displayed in the browser window. Note the way the fonts, colors, alignments, and images are displayed.

c. Size the browser window larger and smaller by dragging the bottom-right window corner. Note how the fixed CSS layout stays 'fixed' as the browser is sized.

d. Close the browser window.

② **PREVIEW THE WEBSITE IN A DIFFERENT BROWSER**

a. If an additional browser is installed on the computer, select File → Preview in Browser and select the second browser in the submenu. The web page document is displayed in the browser window. Compare the way the fonts, colors, alignments, and images are displayed.

b. Size the browser window larger and smaller by dragging the bottom-right window corner. Note how the fixed layout adjusts as the browser is sized.

c. Close the browser window.

③ **PREVIEW THE WEBSITE IN DEVICE CENTRAL**

a. Select File → Preview in Browser → Device Central.

b. Select a different mobile emulator in the Test Devices panel.

c. Close the Device Central window.

Testing the HTML for Target Browser Compatibility

The HTML associated with a web page can be checked to see if any tags or attributes are not supported by selected target browsers. Unlike the Preview in Browser command, the target browser check commands do not require the browser and version to be installed on the local computer.

To select target browsers to check, click the ▭ on the Document toolbar and select Settings from the displayed menu. The Target Browsers dialog box is displayed:

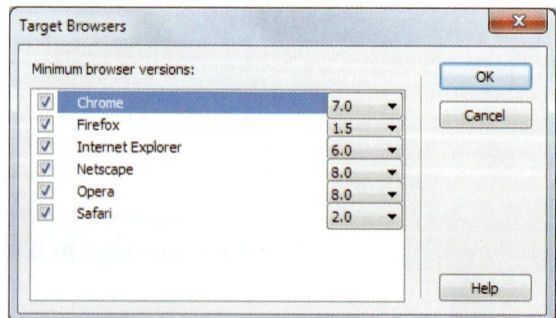

In the Minimum browser versions list, select the browsers and versions to test and then select OK. The current page can then be checked against the selected target browsers. Click ▭ → Show All Issues from the displayed menu. A report is displayed in the Browser Compatibility Check panel:

TIP Reports are temporary files, but can be saved in TXT format by selecting the Save Report button.

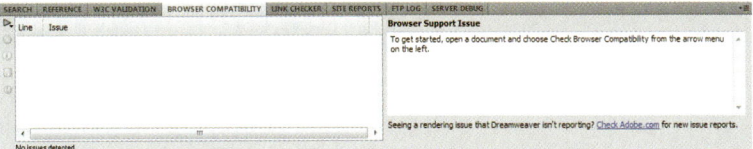

No issues detected

If issues are detected, the report will generate a list of tags and attributes that are not supported by the selected target browsers. Double-click an entry in the report to display the current web page in Split view with the unsupported element and tag selected so that it can be edited.

A web page should be designed to *fail gracefully*, which is a design technique used to ensure that a site displays appropriately even when some elements are not supported. One "fail gracefully" technique is to design similar web pages with varying elements and then check for plug-ins, such as QuickTime, Flash, or the Windows Media Player using Dreamweaver's Check Plugin action. Once plug-ins have been determined, an appropriate web page is displayed based on the level of plug-in support.

Checking an Entire Site

To check an entire site for target browser errors, select the website folder in the Files panel and then select File → Check Page → Browser Compatibility.

TIP The Check Plugin action is located in the Behaviors panel.

Testing for Broken Links and Missing Links

Document-relative links in an entire website can be checked for broken and missing links. Select the site's root folder in the Files panel and then select Site → Check Links Sitewide. A report is displayed in the Link Checker panel:

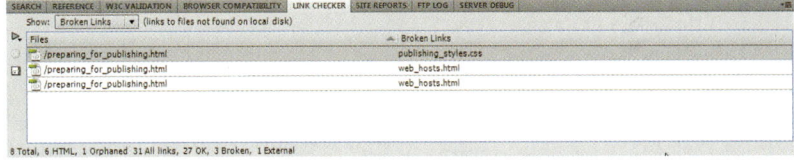

A Broken Links report is displayed by default. Any broken links need to be fixed before the site is published. Double-click a broken link entry in the Files column of the Link Checker panel to open the appropriate web page document, select the broken link, and select the path and file name in the Property inspector.

orphan files

A list of external or absolute links is displayed by selecting External Links in the Show list. External links are just listed, not checked. An *orphan file* has no links to it in the entire site. Select Orphaned Files in the Show list to display a list of orphan files, which may indicate missing links.

Chapter 9 Publishing and Promoting a Website

Checking for HTML Problems

In Dreamweaver, a report can be generated that checks external links, accessibility, missing Alt text, and untitled documents. Select Site → Reports to display the Reports dialog box. To check the entire site, select Entire Current Local Site in the Report on list:

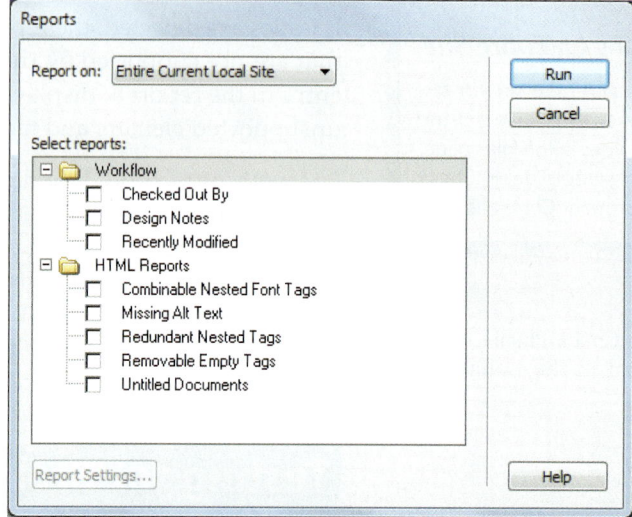

Language References
If the code needs to be checked or edited before a site is published, the Reference tab in the Results panel can be used to access information about markup languages, JavaScript, server technology, and cascading style sheets.

Accessibility
Section 508 of the Federal Rehabilitation Act stipulates that U.S. Federal agencies have to make their electronic and information technology accessible to individuals with disabilities. One requirement of this Act is that Alt (alternative) text in the form of labels or descriptors be provided for all graphics.

Select the appropriate HTML Reports and then select Run to create a report and display it in the Sites Reports panel in the Results panel group:

Double-click a file name in the File column to open the web page document so that it can be edited. Note that errors listed in the report may be able to be corrected in the open web page document by selecting Commands → Clean Up Word HTML or Clean UP XHTML.

Practice: PUBLISHING – part 3 of 4

Dreamweaver should be started and the PUBLISHING website should be the working site.

① **TEST THE HTML FOR BROWSER COMPATIBILITY**
   a. Open the index.html web page document if it is not already displayed.

b. On the Document toolbar, click ▦ → Settings. Set the options to:

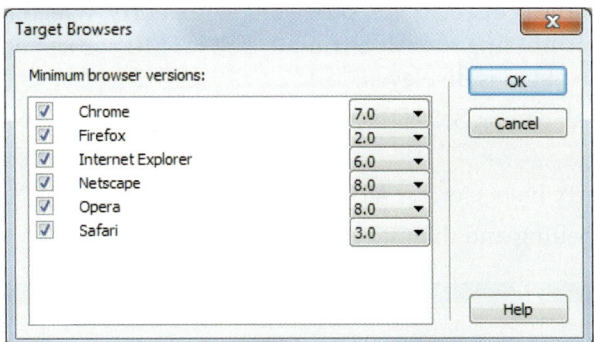

Note: your dialog box may have additional browsers listed.

c. Select OK.

d. Click ▦ → Show All Issues if it is not already selected. A report is displayed in the Results panel. Are all of the elements are supported by the selected target browsers?

② CHECK FOR BROKEN OR MISSING LINKS

a. Select Site → Check Links Sitewide. A report is displayed in the Link Checker tab of the Results panel. The Broken Links report is empty, indicating that there are no link problems.

b. In the Link Checker panel, in the Show list, select External Links. The site's external links are listed.

c. In the Link Checker panel, in the Show list, select Orphaned Files. The Orphaned Files report is empty, indicating that there are no orphaned files.

③ GENERATE A SITE REPORT

a. Select Site → Reports. A dialog box is displayed. Set the options to:

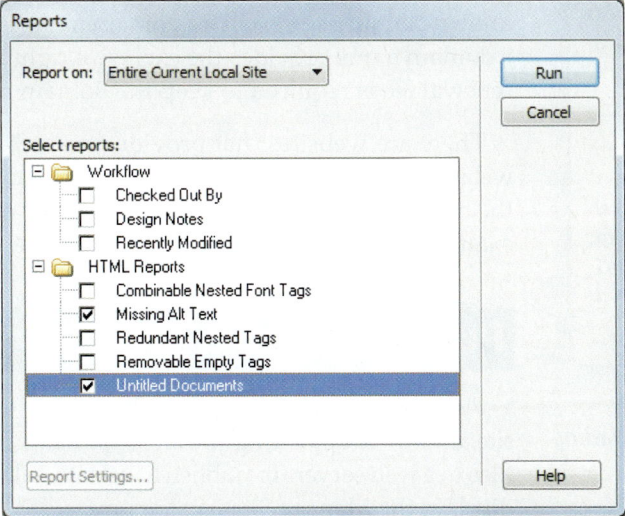

b. Select Run. A report is displayed in the Site Reports panel in the Results panel group. Note that the Site report lists two entries.

c. Double-click the index.html entry, which indicates an untitled document. The HTML associated with index.html is displayed.

d. On the Document toolbar, in the title box, replace the text Untitled Document with Publishing Home Page.

Chapter 9 Publishing and Promoting a Website

e. Check the spelling and then save the modified index.html.
f. Double-click the preparing_for_publishing.html entry, which indicates an image on the page is missing the Alt attribute. The HTML associated with preparing_for_publishing.html is displayed.
g. Switch to Design view. Select the image in the top cell of the table if it is not already selected.
h. In the Property inspector, set **Alt** to: Publishing a website.
i. Check the spelling and then save the modified preparing_for_publishing.html.

What is a Web Host?

A website on the Web has been published to a web server. A *web server* runs *TCP/IP software* (Transmission Control Protocol/Internet Protocol) in order to be connected to the Internet, and *HTTP software* (Hypertext Transfer Protocol) in order to handle the hyperlinks between web pages.

TCP/IP software
HTTP software

TIP Virtual hosts are used by companies and individuals that do not want to purchase and maintain a web server.

Web servers are often managed by *web hosting companies*, also called *virtual hosts*, which provide space on their server for a fee. Web hosts also provide services such as domain name registration and e-mail services. *Domain names*, such as www.emcp.com, are used to identify a particular web page and are made up of a sequence of parts, or subnames, separated by periods that may stand for the server, organization, or organization type.

IP Address

An IP address (Internet Protocol address) is a 32-bit binary number that identifies a computer or device connected to the Internet. An IP address is four numbers in the range of 0 to 255 separated by periods, such as 1.120.05.123.

The Domain Name System (DNS) is used because it is difficult to remember IP addresses. When a domain name is entered, it is automatically translated into an IP address.

A consideration when choosing a domain name is that users should associate it with the website, such as the business name or major topic that the site is about. It is also good if the domain name is easy to remember, and is one that users can probably guess. For example, GAP is a widely known clothing store. GAP's domain name is www.gap.com. Registering a domain name provides the exclusive right to use that name. A periodic renewal fee is required to keep the domain name.

There are websites that provide free web hosting services. However, websites posted to these sites are identified by a subdirectory name on the host's domain and the domain name is not as easy to remember. For example, www.webhostname.com/sitename.

Publishing to a Web Server

uploading

Publishing a website requires obtaining a web host, defining the remote site, and then uploading the site. *Uploading* is the process of posting the files to a web server. To publish a website, select **Site → Manage Sites**, which displays the Manage Sites dialog box:

FTP

FTP (File Transfer Protocol) is used to rapidly transfer (upload and download) files from one computer to another over the Internet.

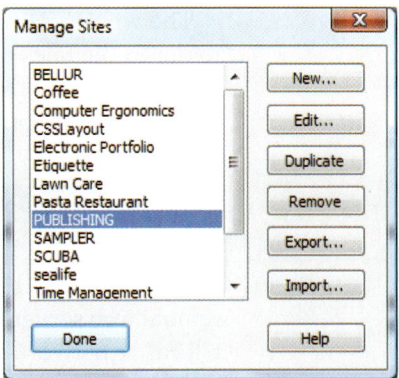

Select a site and then **Edit** to display the Site Setup dialog box. Select the Servers category to display those options:

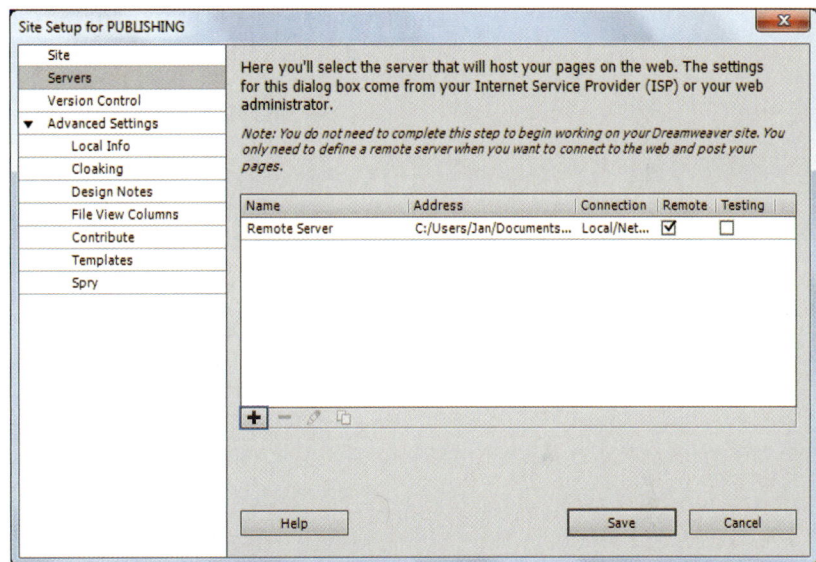

Click the Add New Server ⊞ button to display another dialog box:

TIP Security features such as a password, firewall, and SFTP protocol can be selected to protect data as it is published.

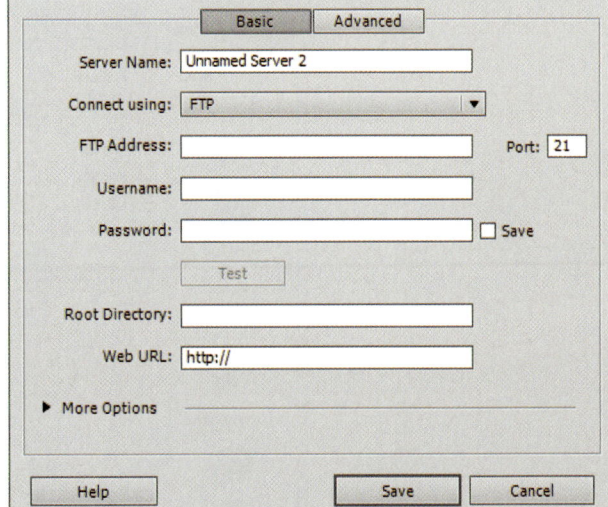

FTP Log

Dreamweaver keeps a record of all FTP activity. Select ▤ → View → Site FTP Log in the Files panel to view this activity.

Enter the server name and connection method. FTP is a common method of publishing to a web server. Select **Save** to finish setting up the remote site, and then select **Done** to remove the Manage Sites dialog box.

Chapter 9 Publishing and Promoting a Website

The website is uploaded to the remote site by selecting the site's root folder in the Files panel and then clicking the Put File(s) button. All of the site's files are uploaded to the remote server. The site should then viewed at the appropriate URL and tested.

Publishing to a Local/Network Server

A website can be published to a local or network server instead of a remote web server. Intranets are on local servers. Publishing a website to a local or network server requires obtaining server space where the site can be set up, setting up the local/network site, and then uploading the site. To define the local/network site, select Site → Manage Sites, which displays the Manage Sites dialog box. Select a site and then Edit to display the Site Setup dialog box. Select the Servers category and then click the Add New Server button. In the Connect using list, select Local/Network, which displays additional options:

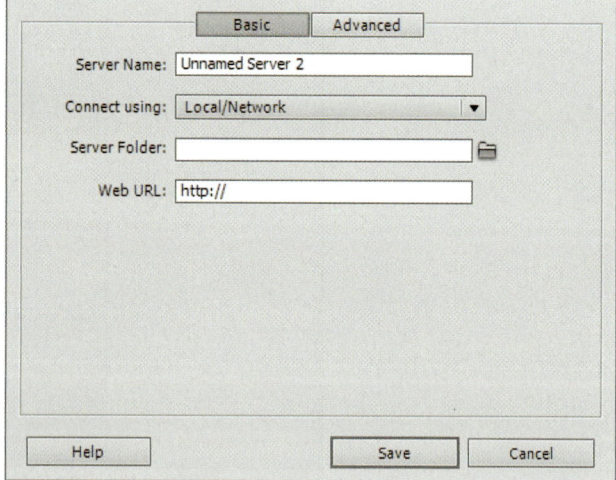

Click the folder icon to display the Choose folder dialog box:

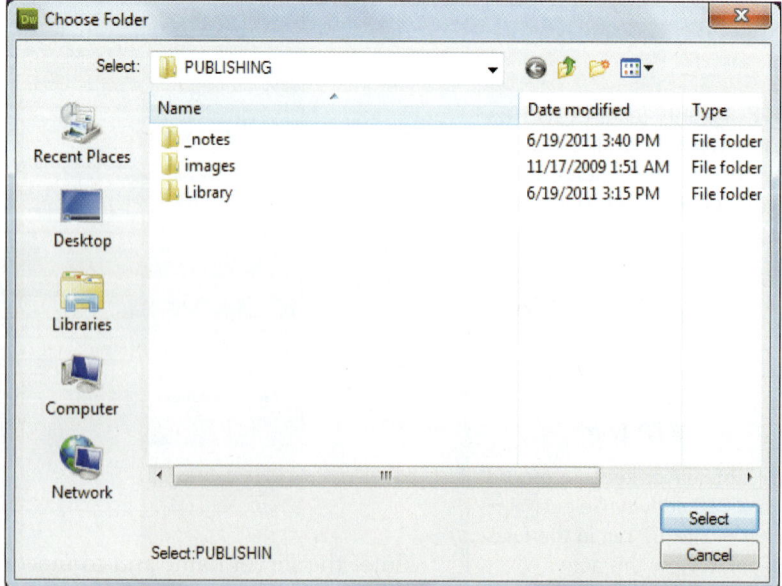

328 Chapter 9 Publishing and Promoting a Website

Navigate to the remote server folder location and click **Select**. The folder location is placed in the Remote folder box. Select **Save** to finish setting up the local/network site, and then select **Done** to remove the Manage Sites dialog box.

To upload the website to the remote site, select the site's root folder in the Files panel and then click the Put File(s) button 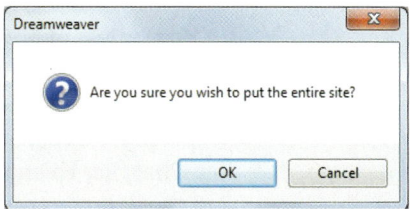. A dialog box is displayed:

Click **OK** to upload all of the site's files to the remote site. The site should then be viewed and tested.

Maintaining a Website

A website requires frequent updating in order to keep users coming back to the site. The parallel structure of the local site and the remote site makes maintaining a website simple. Both the local site and the remote site can be viewed and accessed from the Files panel.

To view the file structure of the remote site, select the Connects to remote host button and then select Remote view in the Files panel:

TIP To select multiple files for downloading, hold down the Ctrl key while selecting files.

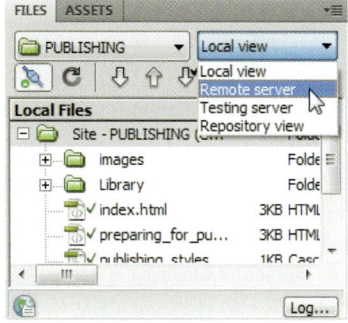

In Remote view, a file is downloaded from the remote site to the local site by selecting the file in the Files panel and then clicking the Get File(s) button.

In Local view, the local site folder is displayed in the Files panel. A web page document can be edited in the local site and uploaded to the remote site. Click the Put File(s) button to upload a selected file to the remote site. Edited pages should be viewed and tested in a browser. Note that the Put File(s) button automatically connects to the remote site if a connection is not already established.

Chapter 9 Publishing and Promoting a Website

Collaboration

Many websites are created in a *collaborative environment* where more than one person designs, develops, and maintains the same website. This approach allows for a site to be developed efficiently and take advantage of individual expertise, such as artistic abilities and technical expertise. Dreamweaver includes several collaboration features, including the Check In/Check Out feature and Design Notes.

Regardless of how website design and development responsibilities are divided, there is typically a need for team members to work on the same web pages. The Check In/Check Out feature ensures web pages are not improperly overwritten by letting team member know who is working on what file. To enable this feature, select the **Enable file check in and check out** check box in the **Advanced** tab when setting up the remote site:

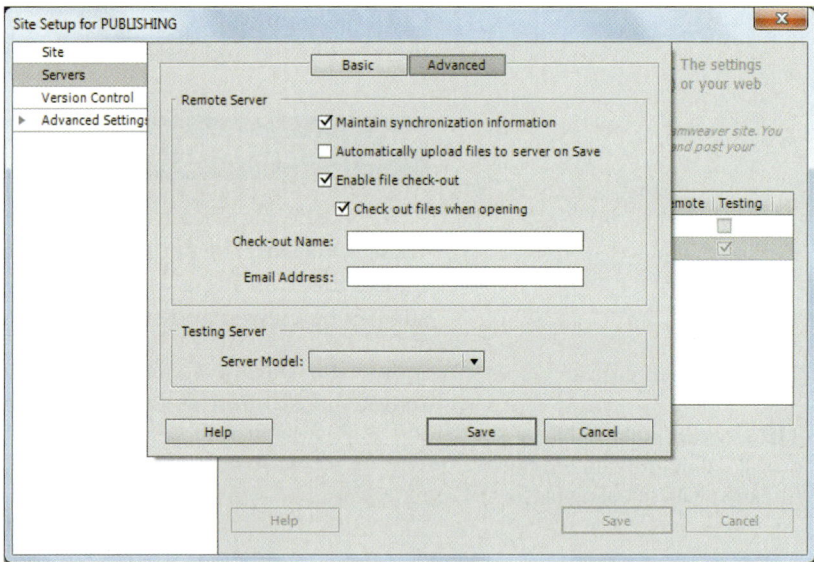

Checked out files are linked to a specified user name and e-mail address so that other team members know who has the file and how to contact them.

Once the Check In and Check Out feature is enabled, a team member can check out files from the remote site, modify the files, and check in the files when work is completed. Another person cannot work on the same file at the same time. Instead of using the Get File(s) and Put File(s) buttons, the Check Out File(s) button and the Check In button are used. In the Files panel, a green check mark indicates a checked out file that you are working on. Any associated dependent files are displayed with a padlock symbol. Dependent files are also made read-only so that they cannot be modified until the file is checked in:

TIP Click the Expand/Collapse button to view additional information about checked out files.

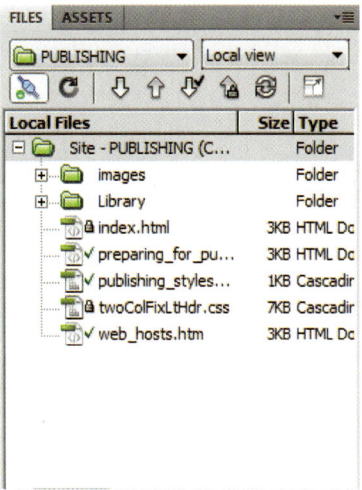

A red check mark indicates someone else is working on a checked out file.

Design Notes

A collaborative approach to website development requires a lot of organization and communication. Dreamweaver Design Notes is a feature that helps with organization and communication. A *Design Note* is a small file that can be attached to a web page.

To enable Design Notes, select Site → Manage Sites, which displays the Manage Sites dialog box. Select a site and then Edit to display the Site Definition dialog box. Expand the Advanced Settings category and then select Design Notes:

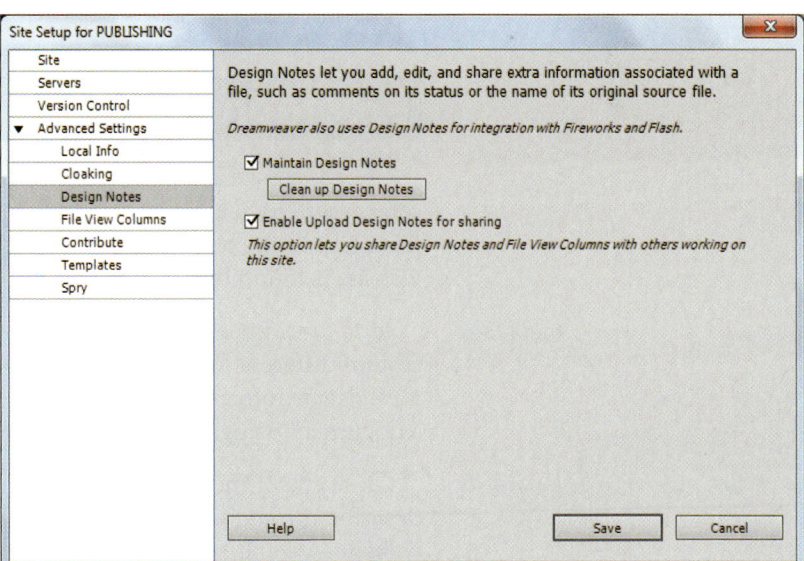

- Select the Maintain Design Notes check box to enable the Design Notes feature.
- Select the Upload Design Notes for sharing check box to transfer the design notes to the remote site for sharing with the team members.

Select OK to enable Design Notes.

Design Note Files

Design Note files are saved in an automatically created notes folder in the website root folder. Design Notes are saved with the same file name as the file they are attached to, including the file's extension, but are also designated with an .mno extension. For example, index.html.mno. The notes folder is not displayed in the Files panel.

Chapter 9 Publishing and Promoting a Website   **331**

To add a Design Note to the active file, select File → Design Notes. A dialog box is displayed:

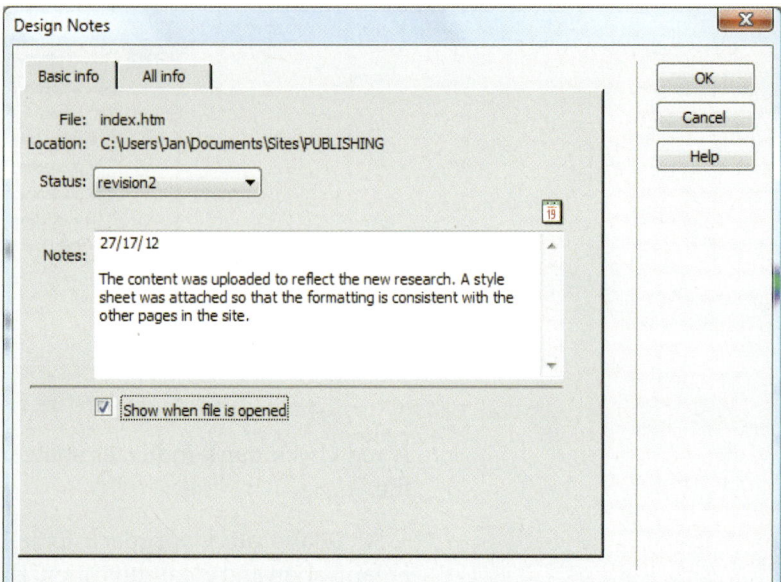

Viewing Design Notes

Design notes can also be viewed by clicking the Expand/Collapse button to expand the Files panel. In the expanded Files panel, the Notes column indicates that a Design Note exists for a particular file. If the Notes column is not displayed, select View → File View Columns and select Notes.

- Select a status for the web page from the Status list.
- Click to insert the current date in the Notes area.
- Type relevant information into the Notes area.
- Select the Show when file is opened check box to display the design note when the file is opened.

Promoting a Website

Once a website is published, there are various promotion techniques that can be used to help users find the site. One technique is to add additional meta tags to the home page of a website to increase the probability that a website is found by a search engine.

meta tags

Meta tags appear in the HTML head section of a document. There are several different meta tags that are used to add meta data to a document. *Meta data* is information about the website contents and can be added to a document using several different meta tags.

keywords

One type of meta data is *keywords*, which are words or phrases that describe the site's content. Many search engines use keywords to index websites, so the keywords should be ones that may be used as search criteria. Another type of meta data is a *description*, which search engines use to display in the search results:

description

```
1  <!DOCTYPE HTML PUBLIC "-//W3C//DTD HTML 4.01 Transitional//EN">
2  <html>
3  <head>
4  <title>Publishing a Site</title>
5  <meta http-equiv="Content-Type" content="text/html; charset=iso-8859-1">
6  <meta name="keywords" content="publishing, web host, website publishing, publishing checks">
7  <meta name="description" content="How to publish a website, including preparation checks are explained.
```

Meta tags in Code view

332　　Chapter 9 Publishing and Promoting a Website

The Content-Type meta tag is automatically added by Dreamweaver. The keywords and description meta tags can be added to the displayed web page document. To add keywords, select Insert → HTML → Head Tags → Keywords. The Keywords dialog box is displayed:

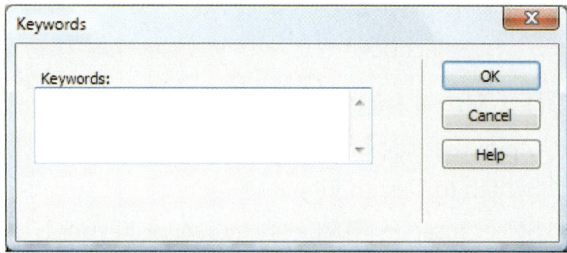

Type keywords in the Keywords box, separating each keyword or phrase with a comma. Select OK to add the meta tag. Note that the most important keywords should be listed first because some search engines limit the number of keywords that can be specified.

Select Insert → HTML → Head Tags → Description to display the Description dialog box:

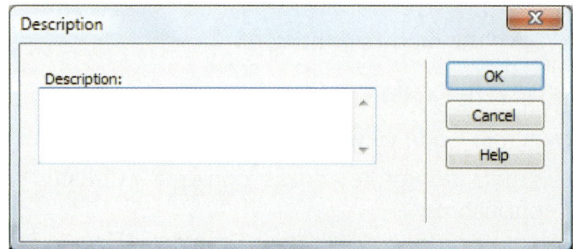

TIP In Split view, click in the meta tag code to display meta properties in the Property inspector.

Type a description of the website in the Description box and then select OK to add the meta tag.

Other techniques for promoting a website include:

- listing it with search engines and directories. Some search engines and directories charge a fee for this service.
- using *reciprocal links*, where websites with complementary information post links to each other's sites.
- advertising by e-mail or in printed media.
- adding the website address to company documents such as letterhead or business cards.

reciprocal links

Practice: PUBLISHING – part 4 of 4

Dreamweaver should be started and the PUBLISHING website should be the working site.

① **ENABLE DESIGN NOTES**

Select Site → Manage Sites. A dialog box is displayed.
1. Select PUBLISHING and then select Edit. Another dialog box is displayed.
2. Select the Advanced Settings category.
3. In the Category list, select Design Notes.

4. Select the **Maintain Design Notes** check box if it is not already selected.
5. Select the **Upload Design Notes for sharing** check box if it is not already selected.
6. Select **Save**. Design Notes are enabled and the Manage Sites dialog box is displayed.
7. Select **Done**.

② ADD A META TAG WITH KEYWORDS
a. Open the index.html web page document if it is not already displayed.
b. Switch to Design view.
c. Select **Insert → HTML → Head Tags → Keywords**. A dialog box is displayed.
   1. In the **Keywords** box, type: publishing, web hosts, preparing for publishing
   2. Select **OK**. A meta tag with keywords has been added to index.html.

③ ADD A META TAG WITH A DESCRIPTION
a. Select **Insert → HTML → Head Tags → Description**. A dialog box is displayed.
   1. In the **Description** box, type: How to publish a website, including preparing for publishing and finding a web host.
   2. Select **OK**. A meta tag with a description has been added to index.html.
b. Save the modified index.html.

④ VIEW THE CODE
Switch to Code view. Note the newly added meta tags:

<meta name="keywords" content="publishing, web hosts, preparing for publishing">
<meta name="description" content="How to publish a website, including preparing for publishing and finding a web host.">

⑤ ADD A DESIGN NOTE
a. Switch to Design view.
b. Select **File → Design Notes**. A dialog box is displayed.
   1. Select revision1 from the **Status** list.
   2. Click 📅 to add the current date.
   3. In the **Notes** area, type: Keyword and description meta data was added.
   4. Select the **Show when file is opened** check box.
   5. Select **OK**.

⑥ DISPLAY THE DESIGN NOTE
a. Save the modified index.html.
b. Close index.html.
c. Open index.html. The Design Notes dialog box is displayed.
d. Click **OK**. The Design Notes dialog box is removed.
e. Quit Dreamweaver.

Measuring Success

There are a several ways to measure the success of a website. One way is to have an online form and analyze the feedback from users to see if there are ways to improve the site.

web tracking software

Information can also be obtained from the web host if *web tracking software* is installed on the server. This software produces a report that contains information about users, such as the IP address, the URL requested, the browser, and the time spent at the site.

Negative feedback or a low amount of user traffic may require additional promoting of the site, changing site content, or changing the design of the site.

Website Security Issues

Website security is a concern for web developers, designers, hosts, and web users. For example, website content is protected by copyright, but it is difficult to monitor if users are downloading or copying the contents and using it as their own. Another concern, typically for large corporate sites, is a *denial of service attack*, which is an assault designed to disrupt website access. Antivirus and firewall software provide varying degrees of protection from this type of attack.

denial of service attack

encryption

A concern for website users is secure transactions over the Internet. Fortunately, most browsers use a level of protection for Internet transactions called *128-bit encryption*. *Encryption* translates data into a code before the data is sent over the Internet. A key or password is required to 'decrypt' the data. Banks, credit card companies, and online retailers typically use a higher level of encryption called *256-bit encryption*.

secure sites

Websites that use encryption techniques to secure data are called *secure sites*. Secure sites use a security protocol, such as Secure Sockets Layer (SSL). SSL encrypts all data that passes between a client and Internet server. SSL also requires the client to have a digital certificate. A *digital certificate* is a notice indicating that the website is legitimate. Digital certificates can be obtained from a *certificate authority*, such as VeriSign. Websites that contain SSL typically have an address that starts with https and display a padlock icon 🔒 on the status or Address bar. The padlock icon can typically be clicked to display encryption and security information:

Ethical Issues

There are many ethical issues associated with maintaining a website, such as protecting client privacy, respecting copyrights, providing secure transactions, and posting accurate and unbiased content.

Website with SSL protection

There are also security and privacy issues associated with e-mail links. E-mail is not private and should be thought of as sending a postcard. However, e-mail can be encrypted by purchasing an e-mail encryption program. E-mail can also be protected by adding a digital signature. A *digital signature* is encrypted code that is attached to an e-mail message to verify that the message is authentic.

digital signature

Chapter Summary

Publishing a website is the process of uploading a local site to a web server so that the site can be accessed on the World Wide Web. A remote server can be a web server provided by an ISP, an intranet server, or a local/network server.

Before a site is published, there are a number of checks that need to occur:

- spelling and grammatical errors
- file size and estimated download time
- view the site in more than one target browser
- compatibility problems with target browsers
- external links, accessibility, missing Alt text, and untitled documents

A web server computer runs TCP/IP software in order to be connected to the Internet, and HTTP software in order to handle the hyperlinks between web pages. Web servers are often managed by web hosting companies, also called virtual hosts, which provide space on their server for a fee.

A website can be published to a web server or to a local/network server. A website requires frequent updating in order to keep users coming back to the site. Once a website is published, promotion techniques should be used to help users find the site. To increase the probability that a website is found by a search engine, the website should contain meta tags that specify keywords and a description. The success of a website can be measured with web tracking software and user feedback.

There are many security issues associates with websites, such as copyright protection and secure transactions. There are also security and privacy issues associated with e-mail links.

Vocabulary

Adobe BrowserLab A Preview in Browser option which lets you test any Web page in most common browsers on the Internet.

Certificate authority A provider of digital certificates.

Collaborative environment Where more than one person designs, develops, and maintains the same website.

Denial of service attack An assault designed to disrupt website access.

Description A type of meta data that search engines use to display in the search results.

Design Note A small file that can be attached to a web page.

Device Central A Preview in Browser option which lets you test any Web page using a variety of mobile browser emulators.

Digital certificate A notice indicating a website is legitimate.

Digital signature An encrypted code that is attached to an e-mail message to verify that the message is authentic.

Domain name Used to identify a particular web page and is made up of a sequence of parts separated by periods that may stand for the server, organization, or organization type.

Download time The time it takes the web page document to load into a user's browser.

Encryption A process of translating data into a code. Types of encryption include 256-bit and 512-bit encryption.

Fail gracefully A design technique used to ensure a site displays appropriately when some elements are not supported.

HTTP software Software that a web server runs in order to handle the hyperlinks between web pages.

Keyword A word or phrase that describes the site's content and may be used as search criteria to locate the site.

Local sites Sites that have been saved and edited on a local disk.

Meta data Information about the website contents.

Meta tags Tags that appear in the HTML head section of document used to add meta data to a document.

Orphan file A file that has no links to it in the entire website.

Publishing a website The process of uploading a local site to a web server so that the site can be accessed on the World Wide Web.

Reciprocal links A technique used to promote a website where websites with complementary information post links to each other's sites.

Remote server A web server provided by an ISP, an intranet server, or a local/network server.

Secure site A site that uses encryption techniques to secure data.

Target browser A browser and version, such as Internet Explorer 9, in which the website is designed to display correctly.

TCP/IP software Software that a web server runs in order to be connected to the Internet.

Uploading Posting files to a web server.

Virtual host See Web hosting company.

Web hosting company A company that manages a web server and provides space on their server for a fee.

Web tracking software Software installed on a server that allows a report to be produced containing information about users to the site such as the IP address, the URL requested, the browser, and the time spent at the site.

Weight of the page A web page document's file size and the estimated download time.

Dreamweaver Commands and Buttons

Check browser compatibility button Displays a menu with target browser related commands. Found on the Document toolbar

Check In button Uploads checked-out files to a remote server and removes the checked out mark(s). Found on the Files panel toolbar.

Check Links Sitewide **command** Checks the site for broken links and displays a report in the Link Checker panel in the Results group panel. Found in the Site menu.

Check Out File(s) button Downloads file(s) from a remote server and marks them as checked out. Found on the Files panel toolbar.

Check Spelling **command** Finds misspelled words in a web page document. Found in the Commands menu.

Clean up HTML **command** Displays a dialog box used to correct HTML errors. Found in the Commands menu.

Connects to remote host button Connects to the remote server. Found on the Files panel toolbar.

Design Notes **command** Displays a dialog box used to add a Design Note to the active file. Found in the File menu.

Edit Browser List **command** Displays a dialog box used to add a browser to the Preview in Browser submenu. Found in File → Preview in Browser.

Folder icon Displays a dialog box used to select the remote root folder. Found in the Site Definition for Publishing dialog box.

Get File(s) button Downloads file(s) from a remote server to the local site. Found on the Files panel toolbar.

Manage Sites **command** Displays a dialog box used to edit sites. Found in the Site menu.

Preview in Browser **command** Displays a submenu used to select a browser to preview the web page document in. Found in the File menu.

Put File(s) button Uploads file(s) from the local site to a remote site. Found on the Files panel toolbar.

Reports **command** Displays a dialog box used to generate a report that checks external links, accessibility, missing Alt text, and untitled documents. Found in the Site menu.

Review Questions

1. a) Describe the process of publishing a website.
   b) Where are local sites saved and edited?

2. What should be checked and tested before a website is published?

3. Why should web page documents be checked for spelling and grammatical errors?

4. What does the "weight of the page" refer to?

5. What web page element may increase download time?

6. a) What is a target browser?
   b) Why should a website be viewed and tested in more than one target browser?

7. List four questions that could be asked about the target audience to help define which browsers to target when testing a website.

8. List the steps required to add a browser to the **Preview in Browser** submenu.

9. List the steps required to select two browsers and versions in the Target Browsers dialog box and then check the HTML associated with the open web page document.

10. What does "fail gracefully" mean?

11. List the steps required to check the document-relative links in a website for broken links.

12. What does the Orphaned Files report display?

13. a) What can be checked in the report that is generated by selecting Site → Reports?
    b) List the steps required to correct HTML errors if any are listed in a report that has been generated in the Site Reports panel.

14. Why does a web server run TCP/IP and HTTP software?

15. What do web hosting companies provide?

16. a) What are domain names used for?
    b) List one consideration when choosing a domain name.

17. a) What does publishing a website to a web server require?
    b) What does publishing a website to a local/network server require?

18. List the steps required to download files from the remote site to the local site.

19. What is a collaborative environment?

20. List two Dreamweaver features that help with collaboration.

21. a) Why should a meta tag be used?
    b) Give an example of three appropriate keywords for a pizza restaurant site.
    c) Give an example of appropriate description meta data for a pizza restaurant site.

22. List two ways to promote a website.

23. List two ways to measure the success of a website.

24. Describe two security issues associated with websites.

True/False

25. Determine if each of the following are true or false. If false, explain why.
    a) A website with spelling errors seems less credible.
    b) Typical users will wait about 50 seconds for a page to load.
    c) A website only needs to be previewed in one browser.
    d) Broken links affect the navigation structure of the website.
    e) Every website image should have Alt text.
    f) Companies can maintain their own web server.
    g) Uploading means to post files to a web server.
    h) Websites are always designed, developed, and maintained by one individual.
    i) Once published, a website does not need to be maintained.
    j) Meta tags increase the probability that the site will be found by a search engine.
    k) The Device Central Preview in Browser feature is used to emulate mobile browsers.

Exercises

Exercise 1

Publish a previously created website to a Local/Network site by completing the following steps:

a. Check the spelling of each of the web page documents in the website.

b. Check the file size and download time of each of the web page documents in the website.

c. Determine which target browsers the website should be tested in.

d. Preview the website in more than one browser, including a mobile browser.

e. Test the HTML in each web page document for compatibility with at least three browsers.

f. Test the website for broken and missing links.

g. Check the website for Missing Alt Text and Untitled Documents.

h. Add keyword meta data with at least two appropriate keywords.

i. Add description meta data with an appropriate description of the website.

j. Publish the website to a Local folder.

Exercise 2

Use the Internet to research the steps required to publish a website that offers free web server space. Present the research in the form of technical documentation on an informational website. Publish the website to the free web server so that the information can be shared with your classmates. Alternatively, research how you can set up your own web server.

Exercise 3

Use the Internet, newspapers, and local contacts and businesses to research the costs involved and steps required to publish a website to a virtual host. Compare at least two virtual hosts. Present the research in the form of an informational website.

Exercise 4

Use the Internet, newspapers, and local contacts and businesses to further research an ethical issue associated with websites. Present the research in the form of an informational website.

Exercise 5

Extend your knowledge on web servers and investigate the steps involved in setting up a web server by answering the following in a written report:

a) Compare two web server software applications. Include a description of the software's features, hardware requirements, and approximate price.

b) Investigate the technical needs of a web server including RAM, hard disk capacity, CPU speed, methods of connectivity.

c) Describe two electronic security methods for a web server that can be used to protect the server from unauthorized access.

d) Explain how password protection controls can be placed on individual websites to limit access to certain sites on a web server.

e) Compare two web tracking software applications that could be used to measure the success of a website. Include a description of the software's features, hardware requirements, and approximate price.

Exercise 6

Visit or research a company that hosts websites. Present your findings in an informational website. Possible interview or research questions include:

- What services do they offer?
- What security features do they use?
- What technical knowledge is needed for positions in the company?
- What hours do the employees work?
- What is the biggest challenge to this type of business?
- What modes of advertising are used to promote the company?

Exercise 7

Collaborate with two peers to develop an informational website about browser software. Plan the website design so that a separate web page is used to describe each browser. Divide the responsibilities as follows:

- One person designs the website, defines the site, creates a style sheet, and creates web pages that have navigation bars.
- A second person researches different browsers available for purchase and for free. This person adds the information to the appropriate pages.
- A third person researches browser usage by surveying peers, family, and the community. It is their responsibility to present an analysis of the survey results on the website.

Appendix A
Banner Ads and ActionScript

This appendix discusses banner ads and introduces ActionScript.

Banner Ads

It is common to find advertisements, called banner ads, on websites. A *banner ad* is an image that promotes a product or service and is usually a link to the advertiser's site. Most websites host banner ads for a fee. Banner ads are usually placed at the top, side, or bottom of a page. There are several standard banner ad sizes including 468x60 (Full Banner), 234x60 (Half Banner), and 120x240 (Vertical Banner) pixels.

rich media

Rich media banner ads are a type of banner ad that are designed to capture the user's attention by containing animated or dynamic content. They are also interactive in that they are designed to entice a user to click it, which in turn displays the advertiser's page. For example, clicking the banner ad below takes the user to the company's website:

TIP Sites that offer free hosting space typically require that banner ads be placed on the site or pop up in a new window when the site is viewed.

Many rich media banner ads on the Internet are created using the Flash application. Rich media ads can also be created using JavaScript or an animated GIF.

Creating a Banner Ad Using an Ad Template in Flash

Flash contains predefined templates that can be used to set the dimensions for a standard sized ad. To use a predefined template, select File → New and then select the Templates tab in the New Document dialog box. Select Advertising in the Category list to display a list of ad templates in the Templates list:

IAB

The IAB (Interactive Advertising Bureau) is an organization that helps online companies increase their revenue. One aspect of the organization is to set standards and guidelines for rich media ad formats. Further information can be found at their website www.iab.net.

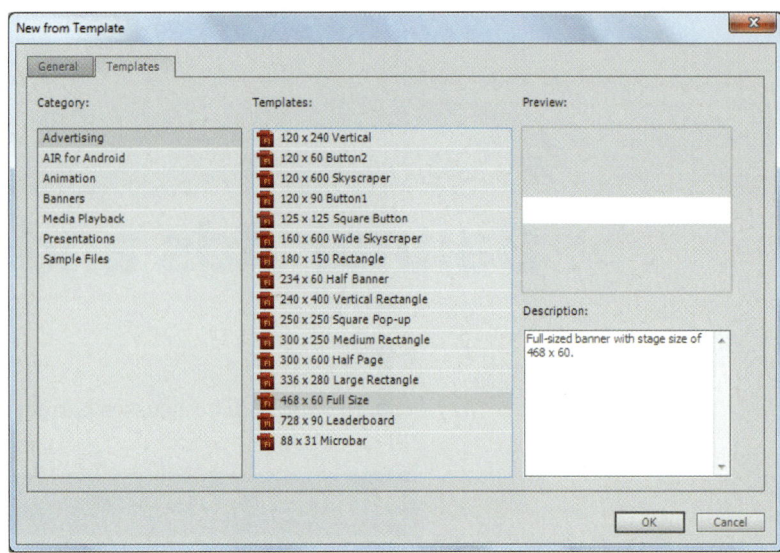

Click a template, such as **468x60 Full Size** to display a preview of the template in the **Preview** area and a description of the template in the **Description** area. Click **OK** to display the banner ad template on the Stage:

A 468x60 Banner Ad

Content can now be added to create the banner ad.

nested symbols

There are different methods of creating banner ad content. One method uses *nested symbols*, which places one symbol on top of another symbol. One symbol contains the banner ad content and is a frame-by-frame animation that has Movie Clip behavior, which allows the animation to play continuously like a banner ad. The other symbol is a button that covers the entire banner ad area and has Button behavior, which allows the banner ad to display another web page when it is clicked.

Adding Banner Ad Content

To create banner ad content, select Insert → New Symbol, which displays a dialog box. Type a descriptive name for the symbol and select Movie clip to create a movie clip symbol:

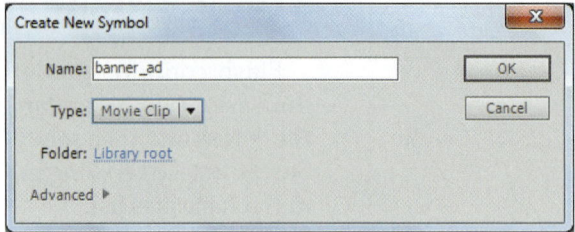

Appendix A Banner Ads and ActionScript

Click OK, which displays an empty Stage. Click the Rectangle tool and drag on the Stage to create a rectangle. In the Properties panel, set the width and height of the rectangle to the same dimensions as the banner ad. For example, to create a 468x60 banner ad, set W to 468 and set H to 60.

The image for the first frame of the banner ad can then be created by either drawing an image with the Tools panel or by importing an image. For example:

Frame-by-frame animation is then used to create an animated banner ad. Right-click a frame on the Timeline and select Insert Keyframe to add the image from the previous keyframe. The image in the new keyframe can then be modified to progress the animation. For example, the image in frame 40 could be modified to:

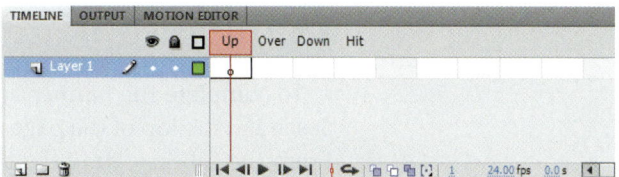

The process of inserting keyframes and modifying the image is repeated until the final frame of the application. Note that since the banner ad has Movie Clip behavior, it will therefore play continuously so static frames should be inserted after the final frame to create a pause before the banner loops back to the first frame.

Next, the button that will cover the entire area of the banner ad is created. Select Insert → New Symbol, which displays a dialog box where a descriptive name is typed and Button is selected to create a button symbol. Click OK to display an empty Stage with the button states displayed on the Timeline:

The banner ad should not change when the mouse is over or away from the banner ad so with the Playhead in the Up state, drag the banner ad from the Library panel onto the Stage. This creates an instance of the button over the entire area of the banner ad content. A button instance has to be named by typing a descriptive name, such as banner_button, in the Instance Name box in the Properties panel:

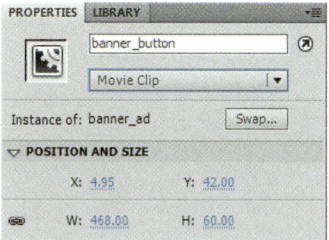

Banner Advertising Agencies

Banner advertising agencies create banner ads for a fee and find hosts for banner ads through its members, who are website publishers. Publishers hosting banner ads receive payment based on several factors:

Cost per action (CPA) The fee paid when a user clicks the ad and then completes a transaction with the advertiser.

Cost per click (CPC) The fee paid when a user clicks an ad.

Cost per thousand (CPM) The fee paid for every 1000 times an ad is viewed.

One measure of ad effectiveness is its click through rate (CTR), which is the percentage of users that click the ad. However, banner ads are often used to create product or logo awareness which cannot be measured by the CTR.

TIP An instance name cannot contain spaces.

Appendix A Banner Ads and ActionScript

Adding ActionScript

ActionScript can be added to the instance of the button to create a link to another web page when the banner ad is clicked. Press the F9 key to display the Actions panel:

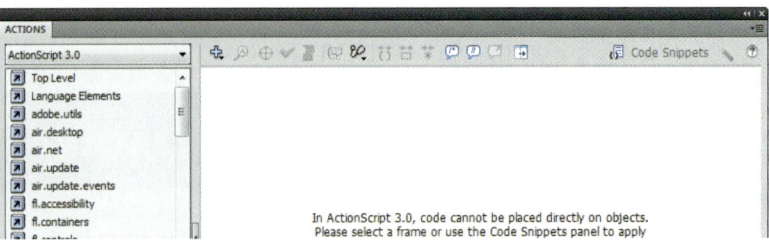

ActionScript

Scripts can be added to a Flash movie to make the movie interactive using a scripting language called ActionScript. A script is a list of commands that are automatically executed by a web browser.

Click the Code Snippets button and double-click the Click to Go to Web Page option in the Actions list:

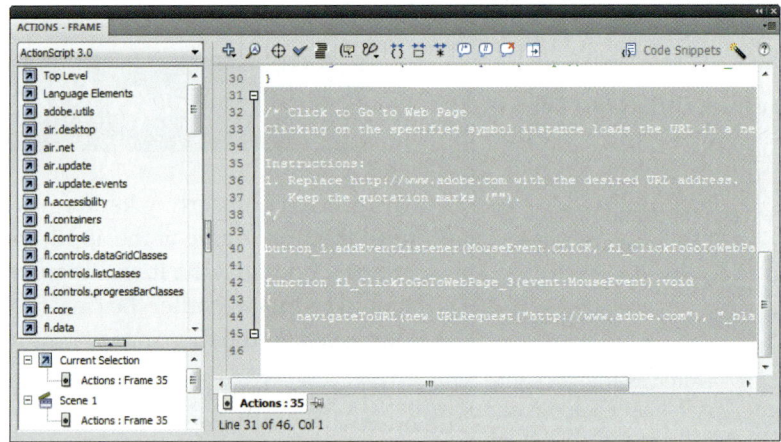

TIP The URL link may be blocked by your security settings resulting in a warning dialog box being displayed.

Replace the existing URL with the button's target URL.

Completing and Testing the Banner Ad

To complete the banner ad, close the ActionScript window and click Scene 1 at the top of the page to return to the original banner ad template. From the Library, drag the button symbol onto the Stage. Select Control → Test Movie to test and view the banner ad. The banner ad can then be exported to be used in a web page document.

Other Types of Web Ads

Other types of web ads include interstitial, SUPERSTITIAL™, and Skyscraper ads. Interstitial ads appear in a separate browser window while a web page loads. One type of interstitial ad plays in a smaller browser window:

SUPERSTITIAL™ ads appear in a separate window and can be any size on the computer screen. These ads typically contain animation, sound, and graphics, but are considered "polite" since they only play when a user stops surfing:

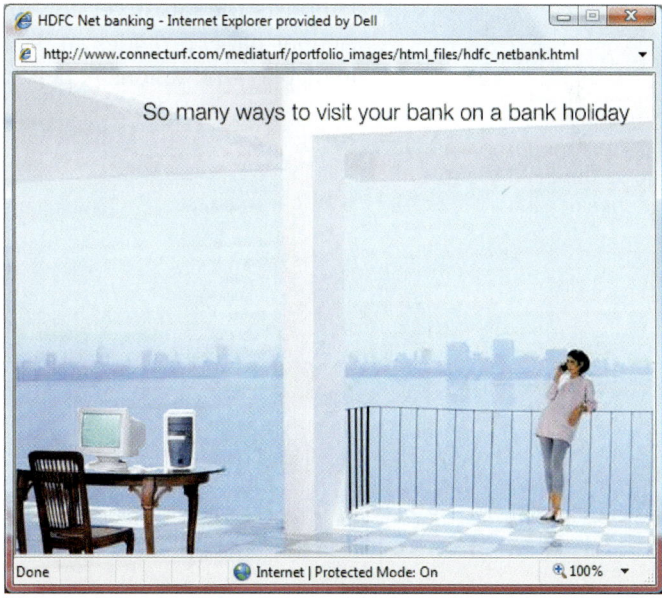

Skyscraper ads are long vertical ads that appear on either the left or the right side of a web page:

Appendix A Banner Ads and ActionScript

More on ActionScript

ActionScript allows interactivity to be added to a Flash movie. Flash supports the latest version of ActionScript called ActionScript 3. The Actions panel provides an interface to add ActionScript. Press the F9 key to display the Actions panel:

TIP ActionScript 3 is an object-oriented language that follows the ECMAScript language specifications.

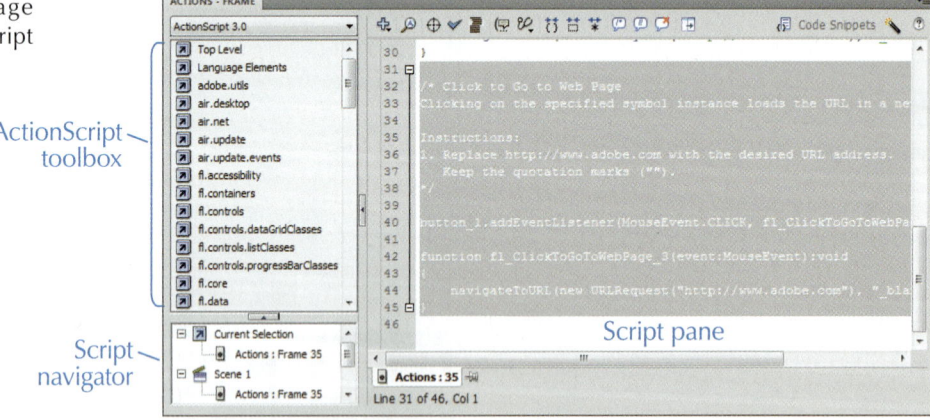

- ActionScript actions are selected from the **Code Snippets button** or **toolbox** and placed in the Script pane.
- **Script navigator** displays all scripts associated with the movie.
- **Script pane** is the area where an ActionScript is composed.

To learn more about ActionScript, refer to the Flash Help menu.

Appendix B
Digital Camera Files

Digital cameras are widely available and affordable. Even the least expensive digital cameras can produce images and video of acceptable quality for use in web pages. Digital cameras have settings that affect the image files produced by the camera. This appendix explains some aspects of digital camera image files and how to use Fireworks to change image size and resolution.

Digital Camera File Formats

When a digital camera takes a photograph, a chip in the camera collects light and converts it to data. Settings in the digital camera determine what type of file the camera creates from the data that is collected. Common file settings in digital cameras are JPEG, TIFF, and RAW. The JPEG setting produces a JPG file and the TIFF setting produces a TIF file, which can then be transferred to a computer or printer. The TIF format has better quality than a JPG, but the file size is usually larger and a TIF must be converted to a JPG for use in a web page.

The RAW setting indicates that the photograph data is not processed in the camera. The data must be transferred to a computer that has software from the camera's manufacturer installed. The RAW file can then be manipulated using the software and saved in many image file formats. Manipulating a RAW file and saving the image in a different file format can be thought of as "developing the film," because it allows adjustments to be made such as exposure and color balance. RAW files have different extensions depending on the camera, for example .mrw is a Minolta RAWS file, .crw is a Canon RAW file, and .nef is a Nikon RAW file.

Maintaining Image Quality in JPG Files

TIP Images, image file formats, and Fireworks are discussed in Chapter 5.

Setting a digital camera to process the photograph data as JPEG is a fast, convenient way to produce image files for use in a web page. However, every time a JPG image is saved it is compressed again and loses more data, because the JPG format has lossy compression.

To retain excellent image quality, the camera should set to process the photograph data as TIFF, and the TIF file can later be modified in a computer as needed and saved in JPG format. This way, the image will have much better quality than if it was a JPG that was modified and

Megapixels and Resolution

One megapixel is one million pixels. The megapixel specification for a digital camera is dependent on the number of pixels on the chip in the camera that collect light and convert it to data. For example, a camera with a chip that is 1,600 pixels wide and 1,200 pixels tall has a total of 1,920,000 pixels and is considered to be a two megapixel camera with a resolution of 1,600 x 1,200.

Resolution

The word "resolution" is used to describe the dimensions of an image in pixels and the pixels per inch of an image. Both uses are correct, but when referring to images from a digital camera, resolution is the dimensions of the image in pixels. In Fireworks, resolution refers to the pixels per inch of the image.

saved a few times. The TIF can also be saved in Fireworks as a PNG and then exported many times using different JPG settings without loss of quality.

When using a high-resolution digital camera such as a 10 or more megapixel camera, processing the photograph data as JPG is acceptable for use in a web page. In this case, the image is originally at a high resolution. After transferring the image to a computer, it can be saved at a lower, proper resolution for use on a web page, and it will still retain sufficient quality.

Digital Camera Image Resolution

Digital cameras have settings that affect the resolution of the saved images. These settings may be called "File Size" or "Quality" or something similar and have settings such as Large, Medium, and Small, which affect the resolution of the image file processed by the camera. For example, selecting Large may result in images that are 2236 x 3504 pixels, and Small may result in images that are 640 x 480 pixels.

The file size (in kilobytes) of a Large quality image will be larger than the file size of the Small quality image because it contains more data. It is better to start off with the highest-quality image possible, and then reduce the size later if needed. However, sometimes compromises may need to be made because the larger file sizes of high-quality images require more space in memory, and therefore fewer images can be stored.

Changing Image Size and Resolution in Fireworks

Fireworks can be used to change the image size and resolution of an image file. Once an image file from a digital camera is opened in Fireworks, there are two main considerations in preparing the image for use in a web page: the image size (dimensions) in pixels, and the screen resolution in pixels per inch. Although the file size (in kilobytes) is important, the file size will be small if the image size and resolution are appropriate for a web page.

Most computer monitors display at a resolution of 72 pixels per inch. An image file used in a web page should therefore have a resolution of 72 pixels per inch. Any larger number includes image data that will not be able to be displayed on a screen, and therefore just increases the file size.

To modify an image in Fireworks, click the [Image Size...] button in the Property inspector or select Modify → Canvas → Image Size, which displays a dialog box:

Appendix B Digital Camera Files

change dimensions

To change the physical dimensions of an image, make sure the Constrain proportions check box is selected and then change the Pixel dimensions of the image. Note that the Resolution does not change as this modification is made. Select OK to change the image dimensions.

change resolution

To change the resolution of an image, make sure the Resample image check box is cleared, which disables the Pixel dimensions boxes so that they cannot be changed. Change the Resolution and select OK to modify the resolution of the image.

If both the dimensions and resolution of an image need to be changed, first change the dimensions, select OK to apply the changes, and then click the [Image Size...] button again and change the resolution.

When modifications to an image are complete in Fireworks, use the Export Wizard to export the image to the images folder in a Dreamweaver website.

Smaller, not Larger

The dimensions of an image should never be increased because the software extrapolates data information to fill in the additional needed pixels, which results in poor image quality. The resolution (dpi) of an image also should not be increased, because it would reduce the quality of the image.

Appendix B Digital Camera Files   **351**

Appendix C
Templates

Website development in a collaborative environment requires different techniques to help manage and organize tasks. The use of templates is one technique that is helpful in a collaborative environment.

Templates

Many websites are created in a collaborative environment where more than one person designs, develops, and maintains the same website. For example, one person creates the website structure and page layout, and other people contribute content to the web pages. The use of templates is one technique that allows many contributors to add content to a website, yet maintain a consistent look in the site.

A *template* defines the structure, or layout, of a web page document. A designer will use a template to create the basic layout for the web pages of a website. The template "locks down" the design because web page documents created from a template are linked to the template. Other people then contribute by adding content to designated regions of the template. Layout elements, such as tables, cannot be changed without breaking the link to the template. Several templates may be needed for a site depending on the number and variety of web pages in the site.

A template can be created from an existing layout. Once the layout is created, save the page as a template by selecting File → Save as Template:

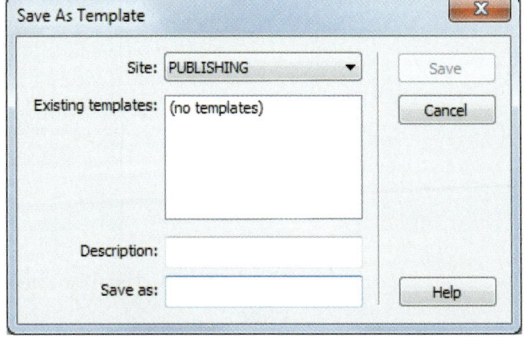

Select the correct Site and give the template a descriptive name in the **Save as** box. Click **OK**. You will be prompted to update links. Click **Yes** and the template will be saved in a **Templates** folder that is created automatically by Dreamweaver.

A template file looks similar to a web page, but displays <<Template>> in the title bar and the file extension is .dwt.

When a template is created, Dreamweaver treats all existing content as part of the master design. Pages created from the template would be duplicates and the content would be locked and uneditable. This way users will not be able to change the logo, banner, and navigation scheme. However, there will be areas of the page you will want the user to be able to edit. These areas are referred to as editable regions. An *editable region* is a placeholder for content.

The page below is a template. The content needs to be defined as an editable region. Start by clicking the <div.content> tag selector:

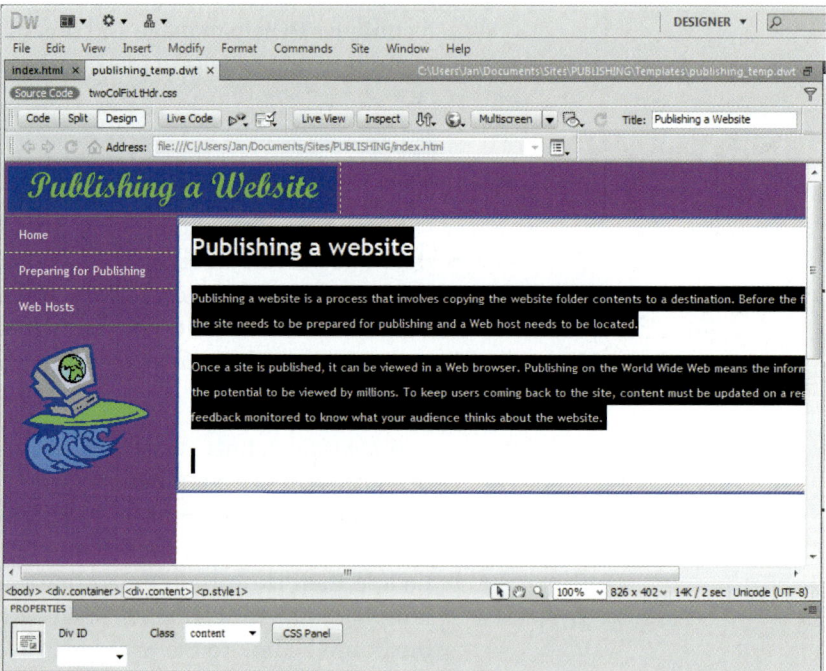

Next, select Insert → Template Objects → Editable Region. In the displayed dialog box, type a name for the editable region:

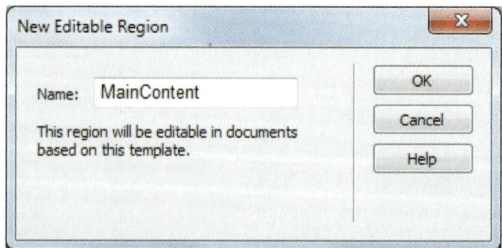

Click OK to display the editable region name in a blue tab on the web page:

354 *Appendix C Templates*

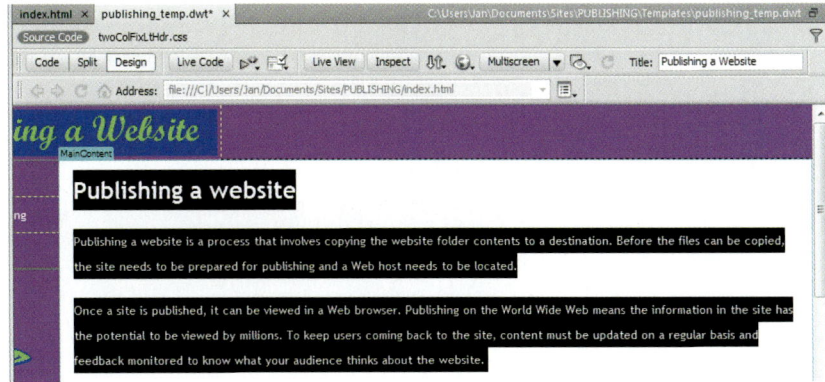

Repeat the process to define other editable regions.

Creating a Child Page

You can use the template to create a 'child' page based on the template. Select File → New and then select Page from Template:

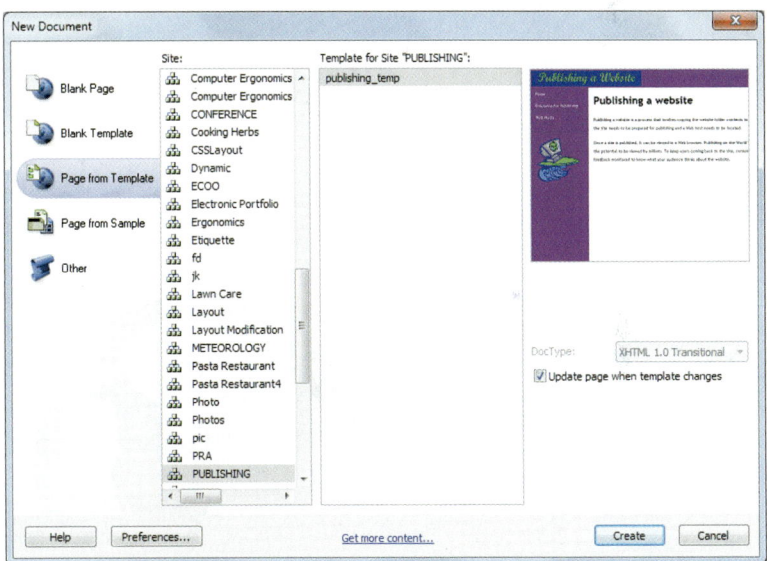

Select the template and then click Create. The editable regions can be modified to include content. The web page document is saved like any web page.

Appendix C Templates

Appendix D
HTML Tags and Attributes

Document Tags

\<html\> \</html\>
Indicates the start and end of an html document.

\<head\> \</head\>
Indicates the start and end of the head section.

\<title\> \</title\>
Used to display a title in the title bar of the browser's window.

\<body\> \</body\>
Indicates the start and end of the body section.
Attributes include:

> bgcolor="*value*"
> Sets the background color for the web page where value is a name or hexadecimal value.

Format Tags

\<!--*comment*--\>
Defines a comment.

\<p\> \</p\>
Defines the start and end of a paragraph. Attributes include:

> style="*value*"
> Indicates inline styles.

\<br\>
Inserts a line break.

\<blockquote\> \</blockquote\>
Indents text on both sides of a paragraph.

\<ul\> \</ul\>
Defines the start and end of a bulleted (unordered) list.

\<ol\> \</ol\>
Defines the start and end of a numbered list.

\<li\> \</li\>
Defines an item in a bulleted or numbered list.

\<dl\> \</dl\>
Defines the start and end of a definition list.

\<dt\>
Defines a definition term in a definition list.

\<dd\>
Defines a definition in a definition list.

\<style\> \</style\>
Defines an internal style.

Form Tags

\<form\> \</form\>
Inserts a form.

\<input type="*button*"\>
Specifies an input field where *button* can be Reset, Submit, Checkbox, or Radio.

\<select\> \</select\>
Specifies the definition of a drop-down menu field.

\<option\> \</option\>
Specifies a menu option.

Graphic Tags

\<img src="*file name*"\>
Inserts an image where *file name* is the file name of the graphic.

\<img src="*file name*" alt="*value*"\>
Specifies alternate text for the graphic where value is the alternative text.

\<hr\>
Inserts a horizontal rule (line).

\<object\>
Embeds a generic object.

Image Maps

\<map name="*value*"\> \</map\>
Inserts an image map where *value* is the name of the image map.

\<area href="*link*" shape="*shape*" coords="*w, x, y, z*"\>
Specifies an image map hotspot where *link* is a URL, *shape* is the hotspot shape default, rect, circle, or poly, and *w, x, y,* and *z* are the coordinates of the hotspot. Coordinates vary depending on the shape.

Links

`<a href="URL"> </a>`
Creates an external hyperlink where *URL* is the target URL.

`<a href="mailto:email_address"> </a>`
Creates an e-mail hyperlink where *email_address* is the target e-mail address.

`<a name="named_anchor"> </a>`
Creates a named anchor where *named_anchor* is the name of the location.

`<a href="#named_anchor"> </a>`
Creates a hyperlink to a named anchor where *named_anchor* is the target location.

`<a href="file name"> </a>`
Creates an internal hyperlink where *file name* is the file name of the target page.

Meta Tag

`<meta>`
Defines keywords used by search engines, expiration date, author, and page generation software.

Script Tags

`<script> </script>`
Inserts a script into the HTML.

`<noscript> </noscript>`
Defines the start and end of instructions for browsers that do not support scripts.

Table Tags

`<table> </table>`
Creates a table. Attributes include:

> border="*value*"
> Specifies the thickness of the cell border.
>
> cellpadding="*value*"
> Sets the amount of space between a cell's border and contents where value is a number.
>
> cellspacing="*value*"
> Specifies the amount of space between table cells where value is a number.
>
> width="*value*"
> Specifies the width of a table where value is a number in pixels or as a percentage of the document's width.

`<caption> </caption>`
Defines a table caption.

`<th> </th>`
Defines a table header, which is a normal cell with bold, centered text.

`<tr> </tr>`
Defines the start and end of a table row.

`<td> </td>`
Define the start and end of a table data cell.

`<tr valign="value">` or `<td valign="value">`
Specifies cell(s) vertical alignment where value is top, middle, or bottom.

`<td colspan="value">`
Specifies the number of columns a cell should span where value is a number.

`<td rowspan="value">`
Specifies the number of rows a cell should span where value is a number.

Text Tags

`<h1> </h1> ...<h6> </h6>`
Tag used to emphasize text. Heading 1 has the largest font size and is used to represent the most important information. Heading 6 has the smallest font size.

`<strong> </strong>`
Displays the text in bold.

`<em> </em>`
Emphasizes the text.

`<cite> </cite>`
Defines the start and end of a citation.

`<pre> </pre>`
Creates preformatted text in which all spaces and line endings are preserved.

`<abbr title="value"> </abbr>`
Displays the full version of an abbreviated word when the pointer rests on the word where value is the full version of the word.

`<acronym title="value"> </acronym>`
Displays the full version of an acronym when the pointer rests on the word where value is the full version of the word.

Color Constants and Corresponding Hexadecimal Values

Color	Hex	Color	Hex
Black	(#000000)	Olive	(#808000)
Silver	(#C0C0C0)	Yellow	(#FFFF00)
Gray	(#808080)	Navy	(#000080)
White	(#FFFFFF)	Blue	(#0000FF)
Maroon	(#800000)	Teal	(#008080)
Red	(#FF0000)	Aqua	(#00FFFF)
Purple	(#800080)	Fuchsia	(#FF00FF)
Green	(#008000)	Lime	(#00FF00)

Appendix E
Final Projects

Entrepreneur Website Project

Develop an informational website that contains factual information and tips about starting a business by completing the following steps. The target audience is potential entrepreneurs interested in starting their own business.

a) Use sources such as the Internet, magazines, and newspapers to research steps involved in starting a business.

b) Determine the web pages and then sketch the navigation structure. The site should contain at least four web pages. One of the web pages should focus on writing a business plan.

c) Determine the content and navigation links for each page. At least one page in the website should contain tabular data and there should be external hyperlinks which link the user to sites containing related information.

d) Define a new website named Entrepreneur in a folder named Entrepreneur.

e) Create web page documents, appropriately named, and add the content.

f) Apply design concepts to the web page documents.

g) Check the spelling in all the web page documents.

h) Add keyword meta data with at least two appropriate keywords.

i) Add description meta data with an appropriate description of the website.

j) Test the HTML in each web page document for compatibility with at least three browsers.

k) Test the website for broken and missing links.

l) Check the website for Missing Alt Text and Untitled Documents.

m) Publish the website to a Local folder.

n) Print a copy of each web page document from the browser.

o) Research and document in a word processor document how the site could be posted to a site that offers free web hosting.

Group Project – Electronic Yearbook Website

Develop an electronic yearbook website that showcases memories and events of the school year as a group project.

a) The website should contain at least:
- six web page documents
- an new, original school logo designed in Fireworks
- scanned or digital photographs of school events and individuals
- appropriate content
- animated Flash text
- a feedback or survey form

b) Tips for organizing the group project and developing the website include:
- appoint a group leader to organize the tasks
- assess the strengths of the group members when assigning tasks
- use Design Notes to help with group communication
- follow the development process outlined in the text

c) Following the website development process outlined in the text, create the website.

d) Run through all the pre-publishing checks and tests outlined in Chapter 9 in the text and add appropriate meta data to the home page.

e) If possible, post the site to a web server.

Group Project – School Website

Develop a school website. A school website should be a site that students, parents, and faculty access to locate information about courses, school events, faculty, and clubs. The website pages will vary, but common web pages include:

- administration
- departments or staff
- course calendar or academics
- clubs
- sports or athletics
- alumni
- calendar of events
- an interactive page which may be a survey or guest book
- student art
- school clothing
- a links page, with links to educational sites, post-secondary sites, other schools in the district, study sites, and so on

It may be helpful to get input from the administration, staff, and students before planning the website.

a) In a group:
- determine the purpose and target audience for the school website
- determine the web pages
- determine the content and links for each page
- determine the tasks that need to be completed
- divide the tasks among the group members
- appoint a project manager
- use Design Notes to help with group communication

b) Complete the web page documents in the website. The website should contain at least:
- six web page documents
- an new, original school logo designed in Fireworks
- scanned or digital photographs of school events and individuals
- appropriate content
- a Flash animation

c) Following the website development process outlined in the text, create the website.

d) Run through all the pre-publishing checks and tests outlined in Chapter 9 in the text and add appropriate meta data to the home page.

e) If possible, post the site to a web server.

Skateboard Park Website Project

Develop a website for a skateboard park by completing the following steps:

a) Define a new website named Skateboard Park in a folder named Skateboard Park.

b) Add five files to the website, naming them index.html, rules.html, events.html, location.html, and contact_us.html.

c) Each web page document should include:
- a style sheet to format the content
- a park logo created in Flash or Fireworks

d) Create content for the web page documents.

e) Modify the index.html web page document to include a banner advertisement.

f) Modify the contact_us.html web page document to include a form with check boxes, radio buttons, and a scrolling list or drop-down menu that allow the user to request prices and membership information.

g) Check the spelling in all the web page documents.

h) View the web page documents in a browser window and test the forms and hyperlinks.

i) Print a copy of each web page document from the browser.

j) If possible, post the site to a web server.

Travel Agency Website Project

Develop a website for a travel agency by completing the following steps:

a) Define a new website named Travel Agency in a folder named Travel Agency.

b) Add five files to the website, naming them index.html, flights.html, tours.html, cruises.html, and contact_us.html.

c) Each web page document should include:

- a style sheet to format the content
- a company logo created in Flash or Fireworks

d) Create content for the web page documents.

e) Modify the index.html web page document to include a Flash animation.

f) Modify the contact_us.html web page document to include a form with check boxes, radio buttons, and a scrolling list or drop-down menu that allows the user to request pricing or detailed information about flights, tours, or cruises.

g) Apply design concepts to the web page documents.

h) Use a style sheet to format the web page documents.

i) Check the spelling in each web page document.

j) View the web page documents in a browser window and test the forms and hyperlinks.

k) Print a copy of each web page document from the browser.

Index

Symbols
– 17
© 44, 127
/ 40
// 11
229
+ 17
<> 40
> 114
| 114
256-bit encryption. 335
<a> 52
<applet> 214
_blank 90
<blockquote> 45
<body> 303

 46
.cfm 305
.com 11
.css 7
<div> 228
.docx 7
.edu 11
<form> 304
.gov 11
<h1> 46, 45
<h2> 46
<h3> 46
<h4> 46
<h5> 46
<h6> 46
<head>
<hr> 47
.htm 7
<html> 43
<img> 54
.lbi 125
<li> 214
.mno 331
<object> 59
<ol> 214
<param> 60

A
About.com 17
above the fold 117
absolute hyperlink 90
academic degrees 26
Acceptable Use Policy 21
accessibility 54, 324
Access, Microsoft 306
Access Table 306
ActionScript 348
  adding 346
ActionScript 2 348
Actions panel 348
Active Server Page 304
Acts, disabilities 54
Acts, protect privacy 21
ad
  interstitial 346
  standards and guidelines 344
  SUPERSTITIAL 346
ADA Act 54
Address bar 13
address bus 2
Adobe BrowserLab 320
ads
  Skyscraper 347
advertising templates 343
AI 251
Align command 160
aligning objects 160
alignment
  change, in HTML document 56
  text 149
alignment buttons
Alt 83
Alt box 10
alternative text 284
Alt text 149
ALU 2
Amazon.com Inc.
AMD
Americans with Disabilities Act 116
anchor icon 221
anchor names 221
anchor points 247
anchor tag 52
AND 17
angle brackets (<>) 253
animated button 257
animated GIF 343
animated text 257
  steps for creating 266
animation
  defined 246
  export 250
  frame-by-frame 250, 345
  motion tweened 260
  preview 250
  shape tweened 257
  speeding up 251
  tweened 257
antialiasing 46
antivirus software 24
AOL 17
applets
  parameters 60
applications software 3
appropriateness
Arial 302
Arithmetic Logic Unit 2
ARPANET 9
Ask Jeeves 17
Attributes, reference list 357

B
backbone 5
Back button 12
background color 56, 147
  changing 219
balance 6
banner ads 343
  adding content 344
  creating 344
  rich media 343
  templates 344
  testing 346
banner advertising agencies 345
baseband
behavior 168, 175
Behaviors command 175
Behaviors panel 175
Berners-Lee, Tim 147
Bindings panel 305
bitmap graphic 247
bitmap graphics 214
Block Quote button 6
blockquotes 3
blog 10
Bluetooth 6
BMP 251

body element 56
body section 6
body tag 114
bold 45
Bookmark list 114
Boolean logic 17
bottom global navigation bar 283
bps 5
brackets, angle (<>) 167
branding 170
breadcrumb trail 317
Break Apart command 265
broadband 255
Brush tool 248
button symbol
    creating 345

C

cable 319
cable modem 10
cache 3
Call JavaScript command 304
camera, digital 349
canvas 157
    color 157
Canvas Color command 161
Canvas Size 157
Canvas Size command 161
Career
    IT 26
careers 24
carpal tunnel syndrome 22
cascading 202
cascading style sheets 7
    positioning 228
cell
    background color
Center Horizontal command 160
Center Vertical command 160
Central Processing Unit 2
certificate authority 335
CGI 304
CGI scripts 305
Change Link command 90
Characters button 79
Check Box form object 295
Check In and Check Out feature 330
Check In button 330
Check In/Check Out feature 330
Check Links Sitewide command 323
Check Out File(s) button 330
Check Spelling command 80
child page 205
Children's Online Privacy Protection Act 21
Chunking 3
circuit boards 2

class 55
    add 59
    attributes 116
Clear command 80
click through rate 345
clients 9
client-server relationship 304
client-side script 304
    create 305
Clone command 218
Close All command 88
close a web page document 84
Close button 218
Close command 84
Code view 77
ColdFusion 305
ColdFusion page 304
collaboration 330
collaborative environment 330, 353
college admission requirement
college degrees 26
color
    adding 129
    add, in HTML document 55
    analogous 127
    complementary 170
    cool 176
    hexadecimal values 358
    triads 223
    using in a website 283
    warm 180
color picker 223
color wheel 180
comments 54
commercial websites 180
computer software. *See* software
content
    from other sources 224
control bus 2
conventional modem 9
cookie 20
copy 224
    several files 223
    to website root folder 211
Copy command 80
Copy Graphic button 169
Copy HTML command 174
copyright 23
    certificate of 127
    information 127
    material 127
corporate presence websites 345
Cost per action 345
Cost per click 345
Cost per thousand 345
CPA 345
CPC 200

D

data
    encryption 21
    transmission 10
database 306
    flat-file 306
Databases command 305
Databases panel 305
data source 306
    connecting to 306
date
    inserting 126
    update automatically 126
Date button 126
Date command 126
declarations 55
defining a site 1
degrees, academic 26
Delete CSS Rule button 76
denial of service attack 335
dependent files 330
design concepts 2
    appropriateness 12
    usability 111
design considerations
    alignment 199
    fonts 201
    line height 201
    type styles 22
Design Note files 331
Design Notes 330
Design Notes command 332
design tools
    sticky notes 10
Design view 77
Desktop 156
desktop computer 57
developing a website 71
Device Central 321
device driver 4
dial-up 319
digital camera 71
digital camera file formats 349
digital certificate 335
digital signature 336
dimensions, of image 350
DirectX 268
Distribute to Layers command 266
document-relative links 323
document tags 43, 357
Document toolbar 169
Document window 147
domain name 11
domain name registration 326
domain names 326
Domain Name System 326
dots per inch 296
Down state 168
dpi 303

E

e-commerce websites 283
editable region 354
Edit Browser List command 77
Edit button 125
Edit Style Sheet button 210
education requirements 24
elapsed time 249
Electronic Communications Privacy Act 21
Electronic Freedom of Information Act 21
electronic mail 11
electronic portfolio 26
element, part of tag 21
elements 12
e-mail 11
   address 11
   etiquette 20
   hyperlink 126
   privacy 336
   protocol 23
   security 336
   software 334
e-mail encryption program 336
embedded style sheet 55
EMF 251
employee monitoring 22
empty tags
environment 3
environment, collaborative 353
ergonomics 22
Ethernet 6
ethical implications of computers 22
ethical issues 335
Excel 329
Expand/Collapse button 330
Export Wizard command 161

F

F9 348
F12 key 77
Facebook 10
fail gracefully 323
Fair Credit Reporting Act 22
fantasy font category 200
FAQ page 283, 284
FAST Search 17
Favorites list 13
Federal Rehabilitation Act 324
field 306
file 7
file formats
   sound 268
file name 7
file names 13

files 71
   copy several 122
   organizing
   selecting multiple 329
file size 7
Files panel 159, 88
Files panel group 39, 255
File Transfer Protocol 12
File View Columns command 332
Fill Color 158, 248
filtering software 21
Financial Privacy Act 23
Firefox 162
firewall 13, 335
Fireworks document
   export 161
   optimize 161
   add text 159
   align objects 160
   create a button symbol 162
   draw objects 120
   edit an Image from Dreamweaver 178
   start 156
Fit Canvas command 161
fixed fonts 201
FLA 247, 246
Flash
   ad templates 343
   Help menu 348
Flash document
   exporting 254
Flash icon 254
Flash memory card 5
Flash movie
   adding interactivity 348
Flash movie file 262
   add to web page document 255
   creating 248
   editing techniques 251
   import images 251
   placeholder 255
Flash Player 304
font
   fixed 201
   sans serif 291
   serif 254
   size 201
font category
   cursive 293
   fantasy 256
   monospace
   sans serif
   serif 296
font-family declarations 55
Font list 159
footer 293
form 292

   creating 293
   design 293
format tags 357
form tags 357

G

Get File(s) button 329
GIF 54
   compression 148
   interlaced 148
   transparency 3
gigahertz 2
global navigation bars 12
Google
grammatical errors 149
graphical user interface 3
graphic file formats 291
graphic tags 357

H

hackers 24
Hand tool 248
hard disk 7
hardware 115
header 45
heading
   formatting 54
heading tags 46
   redefining 211
head section 12
hexadecimal 55
hexadecimal shorthand 219
hexadecimal values, reference list 358
Home button 13
home page 76
   links 152
horizontal rule 47
Hotmail 152
hotspot 152
   properties 40
   testing 41
   tools 151
HTML 41
   defined 39
   edit 43
   problems in Dreamweaver 324
   reference list 357
   reports in Dreamweaver 324
   tags 50
   validating 43
HTML document 7, 43
   creating 43
   view in a browser 44
http 11
hyperlink
   colors, changing 221
   tags 358

I

IAB 11, 344
identity theft 22
IM 12
image 249
    adding 54
    align 12
    change width and height 155
    create 157
    crop 177
    edit in Fireworks 178
    export 181
    optimize 161
    placing 123
    proportionately resize 155
    quality 156, 349
    resample 155
    resize 155
    size 350
    stretch 155
    tags 357
image map 156
    tags 357
images folder 12
Images icon 123
Image Size command 274
IMAP 275
implementation stage 277
Import command 251
importing
    sound file 268
importing video 270
Import to Library command 268
Import to Stage command 270
indenting with blockquotes 22
Index transparency 163
information age 22
informational website 282
inkjet printer 2
input devices 27
Insert Frame command 251
Insert Keyframe command 250
interlaced 205
Internet Service Providers 25

J

Java 58, 305
Java applets 39, 50
JavaScript 58, 168, 304, 319, 343
JavaServer Page 304
Joint Photographic Experts Group 53
JPEG. *See* JPG
    digital camera file 349
JPG 54
    digital camera file 349
    image quality 349
    lossy compression 148
    progressive 302
JSP 304

K

Kbps 9
keyboard 2
keyframe 249
Keyframe command 250
keywords 332
kilobyte 318

L

LAN 5
language references 324
laser printer 2
layer 246, 264
    delete 265
    hide 265
    order 265
Layers list 265
LBI file 125
leading 127
Library
    in Fireworks 167
    in Flash 260
Library category 124
Library command 260
Library folder 125
Library icon 124
library item
    break a link 125
    delete 125
    edit 125
    file 125
    place 125
line break 79
Line Break command 79
line break tag 46
line height 48
line, horizontal rule 47
Line tool 48
link. *See* hyperlink
Link box 90
linked style sheets 55
links
    modifying 222
    removing 222
link tags 358
Linux 148, 3
local site 329

M

Mac 1
magnetic technology 8
mailing list server 12
malicious code 23
Manage Sites command 305, 326, 328, 331
markup language 39
marquee select 259
Maximize button
media folder 255
megabyte 318

megahertz 2
megapixel 350
memory keys 2
memory-resident 4
meta data 332
    description 332
    keywords 332
metaphors 331
meta tag 332, 358
    Content-Type 333
microphone 2
Microsoft ActiveX controls 59
Microsoft Office 306
Minimize button 200
missing links 200
Mobile computing devices 321
mobile devices 268
modem 9

N

named anchor
Named Anchor button 7
native file format 157
navigation bar 6
navigation structure 7
nested symbols 27
netiquette 6
network 4
    architecture 5
    client/server 5
    peer-to-peer 5
    wireless 6
network administrator 25
network interface card 5
network operating system 5
New command 42
New CSS Rule button 42
New Folder command 345

O

object tag 59
oblique style 205
Office, Microsoft 306
onBlur events 298
onChange events 298
onClick event 298
Onion Skin button 251
Onion Skin markers 251
onion skinning 251
online ordering 292
online profiling 20
Open command 86
opening a file 86
Opera , 319
operating systems 3
optical technology 8
optical weight
optimize 161
OR 17
ordered list 49

Ordered List button 214
orphan file 323
OS 3
Other Characters command 80
Outlook 169

P

page layout
    sketch 115
Page Properties command 23
page title 71
Paint Bucket tool 248
panel groups 59
paragraph
    tag 46
paragraph format 202
Paragraph Format command 211
parameters 60
Paste command 80
Paste HTML command 174
Paste Special command 286
PATRIOT Act 21
PC
PC card 5
Pencil tool 248
Pentium 22
Pen tool 248
peripheral devices 2
Perl 305
personal computer 23
petabyte 8
Phishing 24
photographs 147
PHP 305
PIC 251
pictures 12
piracy 23
pixel 51, 200
pixels per inch 350
pixel tags 20
placement 3, 149
planning stage 3
platform 3
platforms 319
Play command 250
Playhead 249
PNG 54
PNG source file 175
podcasting 10
Pointer button 163
Pointer Hotspot tool 151
Pointer tool 3
point of reference 3
points 200
Point to File icon 88
policy
    Acceptable Use 21
    privacy 20
polls 292
polygon 22

Polygon Hotspot tool 151
POP3 13
portfolio
    electronic 129
    traditional 109
ports
    serial 2
privacy policy 21
prompt 291
publishing
    a website 317
    checks 327
purpose 326, 327

Q

QuickTime 268
quit Dreamweaver 85

R

Radio Group form object 295
RAM 3
Random Access Memory 3
RAW file 349
Read Only Memory
real-time clock 2
reciprocal links 333
records 306
Rectangle roundness 158
Rectangle tool 247
Rectangular Hotspot tool 151
recycling 22
Refresh button 122
Refresh button, Internet Explorer 44
Refresh Site List
    command 255
Refresh Site List command 123
registration point 260
remote server
remote site 329
Remote view 329
Remove Frames command 251
Remove Link command 90
Repeat command 80
reports
    saving 323
Resample button 155
Reset icon 155
resolution 120, 350
    changing in Fireworks 350
Résumé information 54
Rewind command 250
rich media banner ads 204
ring topology 6
rule, style shet. *See also* CSS style
    sheet rules

S

Safari 39, 319
Safety and Freedom through
    Encryption Act 21
same-level pages 111
sans serif 200
sans serif fonts 201
Save All command 202
Save command 76, 247
Save in list 76
Scale tool 159
scanner 57
screen resolution 319
Script navigator 348
Script pane 348
scripts 58
script tags 358
scroll bar 13
scrolling list 296
    adding 297
    properties 297
    vs. drop-down menu 296
search criteria 17
search engine 17
search engine optimization 54
search engines 332
secondary memory 10
secure sites 335
security features 327
Selection tool 247
Select (List/Menu) button 23
selector 55
selector options 223
Select section 157
serif 10
serif fonts 40
server 5
servers 9
server-side script 295
Set magnification list 294
shapes
    selecting multiple 251
shape tweened animation
    steps for creating 257
Show Grid command 249
site definition
site map 283
    creating 43
Size box 159
Skype 13
slash (/)
slice 168
social implications of computers 22
Social media websites 75
software
    antivirus 24
    e-mail 163
    protecting 23

solid state technology 8
sound
    steps for adding 268
sound cards 2
sound effects 269
sound file
    add to an animation 268
Source command 44
source file 175
spelling checker 80
spelling errors 286
Split view 77
split view buttons 181
spreadsheet data 168
Spry widgets 256
spyware 20
SRAM 168
SSL 335
Stage 247
    change magnification 248
    change size 249
    color 249
    move 248
star topology 6
stretch 155
structure, navigation 259
styles
    duplicate 267
style sheet 55. *See also* CSS style sheet

T

T-1 carrier 10
tab-delimited data 287
table 285
table tags 51, 358
Tag Inspector panel group 175
tags 6, 43
Tag selector 109
tags, reference list 357
target audience 110
    characteristics
target browser 7, 319
    preview in 317
target browser compatibility 320
target file size 161
TCP/IP 9, 326
telecommunications 9
template
    editable region 354
    placeholder 354
templates 353
Test Movie commmand 346
text
    add 159
text, animating 265
Text category 79
text color 56
    changing 111
Text Indent button 254

Text Outdent button 202
text size 147
Text Size
    command 349
text tags 358
Text tool 159
Text tool in Flash 248
theft, identity 22
TIF, TIFF digital camera file 255
Timeline 246
Times New Roman 157
time stamp 126
Tip size 158
Tools panel in Flash 247
    Colors section 247
top global navigation bar 199
top-level domain 11
top-level page
top navigation bars 199
transmission media
    coaxial cable 5
    fiber optic cable 5

U

under construction notation 117
underlined 160
Undo command 80
Undo Crop command 178
Undo Crop Document command 178
United States Copyright Office 127
university degrees 26
Unix 2, 3
unordered list 49, 214
untitled documents 317
uploading 317, 326
Up state 168
URL 11
usability 116
    standards 114
usability standards 114
user expectations 117

V

Validate Form action 298
validation criteria 298
VBScript 304
vector graphic 157
Vector section 157
Verdana 199
VeriSign 335
video
    creating a Flash movie 272
    export 271
    import 270
    using in Dreamweaaver 271
video adapters 2
virtual hosts 326

W

W3C 40, 54, 149
WAI 149
WAN 5
WAV 268
Web 10
web accessibility
Web Accessibility Initiative 149
web ads 346
    banner 11
    button 11
    interstitial 11
    pop-up 11
    rectangle 11
    skyscraper 11
    webmercial 11
web advertising 11
web application 22, 305
web author 25
web beacons 20
web browser 10
web browser application 39
web bugs 20
WebCrawler 17
web designers 25
web developer
    ethical responsibilities 24
web developers 25
web hosting companies 326
web hosts 26
webmaster 25
web page
    author 19
    bias 19
    cite 19
    content 116
    design 109
    development 114
    elements 20
    evaluate 19
    footer 115
    header 114
    layout 10
    preview 13
    print 13
    printer-friendly version 87
    validity 19
web page document
    close 84
    create 76
    name 76
    open 86
    preview in a browser 77
    print 84
    save 76
    view 77
web server 9, 317, 326

website 129
    advertising 111
    categories 343
    commercial 282
    consistency 283
    content 109
    corporate presence 1
    design 283
    e-commerce 111
    feedback 126
    home page
    implementation 7
    informational 7
    maintaining 329
    measuring success 335
    media 333
    navigation structure 110
    open 85
    personal information
    planning 281
    portal
    promoting 332
    purpose 331
    target audience
website security 335
web tracking software 335
weight of the page 114

X
XHTML 40

Y
Yahoo! 12, 17
YouTube 10

Z
Zoom button 163
Zoom tool 248

Index

Index